CHURCH, NATION AND STATE IN RUSSIA AND UKRAINE

Church, Nation and State in Russia and Ukraine

Edited by
Geoffrey A. Hosking

Professor of Russian History
School of Slavonic and East European Studies
University of London

St. Martin's Press   New York

First published in the United States of America in 1991

Printed in Hong Kong

ISBN 0–312–06092–0

Library of Congress Cataloging-in-Publication Data
Church, nation and state in Russia and Ukraine / edited by Geoffrey A.
Hosking.
p.   cm.
Includes index.
ISBN 0–312–06092–0
1. Church and state—Soviet Union—History—Congresses. 2. Church
and state—Ukraine—History—Congresses. 3. Soviet Union—Church–
–Congresses. 4. Ukraine—Church—Congresses. I. Hosking, Geoffrey
A.
BR932.C43 1991
274.7′08—dc20   91–6751
                                                                CIP

Contents

Acknowledgements

Keston College and the School of Slavonic and East European Studies wish to record their gratitude to Gresham College, the Ford Foundation, the Economic and Social Science Research Council, the British Academy and Stichting getuigenis van Gods Liefde for financial support in the mounting of the conference which led to this publication.

Preface

The papers published here are the product of a conference organised in July 1988 by Keston College and the School of Slavonic and East European Studies of the University of London. The conference marked the millennium of Christianity in Rus', but it was not held just because of the date. Jane Ellis and I both felt that the time was ripe to try to begin correcting an imbalance which seemed to have crept into the western (and even more Soviet) writing of Russian history, that is an increasing neglect of the role of religion. This neglect derives partly from the anti-religious bias of the revolutionary movement and the Soviet state, and western scholars have often taken it on unthinkingly from their Soviet colleagues, especially as they too live in what are now largely secularised societies (though this background has not prevented historians of Britain, Germany or the USA from being sensitive to the importance of religion in the evolution of their nations).

It is not that there is a shortage of specialist books on individual aspects of religion among the East Slavonic peoples. There are a fair number of specialists around the world who have produced valuable studies. What we felt was needed was to begin the work of integrating these studies into an account of the way Tsarist Russian and Soviet society has developed. Without such integration, we are poorly equipped to understand what may be the consequences of the religious revival now taking place.

With this aim in mind, Keston College and the School of Slavonic Studies began in 1985 trying to identify those scholars in the west who would be best qualified to bring together their insights into the interaction of religion with political, social, ethnic and cultural factors. There was a ready and abundant response to our requests for papers, which seemed to confirm that our concerns were widely shared. The nature of the responses strengthened our initial inclination not to spread the collection chronologically too thinly, but to concentrate on the modern period, and primarily on the nineteenth and twentieth centuries, where the prevailing neglect of religion was most marked. Meanwhile, inside the Soviet Union itself, even as we planned the conference, the first signs of a rapprochement between state and churches made our enterprise seem more topical and urgent.

Of the various branches of Christianity, Orthodoxy is distinguished by its close identification with both the nation and the state. Over the centuries this has often been a source of strength and stability, since it has meant support both from the secular arm and from the mass of the people. Yet that same dual identification has also not infrequently generated conflict and weakness in ways which are clearly brought out in our papers. All too often the state has been peremptory and disdainful, imposing on the church functions and demanding from it tributes which accorded ill with its spiritual calling. Novgorodian church-state relations—where the Archbishop played a conciliatory role, standing above factions and symbolising national unity—were replaced, according to Mikhail Meerson, in the Grand Duchy of Moscow by a Caesaropapism initially preached by Joseph of Voloko-lamsk at the beginning of the sixteenth century. After Patriarch Nikon's abortive challenge to it, this state domination of the church then led smoothly into the secular utilitarianism of Feofan Prokopo-vich and Peter I.

Opposition to state supremacy created its own dilemmas, as Robert Crummey reveals in his study of the Old Belief. Conservatives were forced to innovate, and believers in established ritual to improvise. Nostalgic for a settled community, the Vyg Fathers had to adopt a way of life more like the desert hermits of the early Christian centuries.

A church organised, for reasons of state, on bureaucratic and hierarchical lines found difficulty in getting its own message across and in maintaining secure, healthy links with the mass of the people. Thus, despite the initial support of the Emperor himself, the rather egalitarian, evangelical Bible movement of the early nineteenth century was unable to take root, as Stephen Batalden demonstrates. The ethic of moral transformation and service to the people, inherent in the Gospel, tended gradually to be extruded from the church and to become the preserve of the secular opposition and then of the revolutionary movement: Franklin Walker describes the first stages of this process in his account of the Decembrists.

The grip of bureaucratic ecclesiastical institutions undermined the work of parish revival, necessary for contact with the people, an unrewarding enterprise, and impeded the mission of instilling tolerance in the church and of opening it to the diversity of modern secular thought. Paul Valliere recounts some revealing episodes in this unavailing struggle, while Pål Kolstø portrays in the figure of Lev Tolstoy a man whose intense and humane religious fervour was constantly at odds with the church and, lacking the discipline of give and take within a congregation, tended to dissipate into secular rationalism. Similarly, Simon Dixon indicates that, although the Orthodox Church (contrary to received wisdom) *was* concerned about the social question in the late nineteenth century, its efforts to do something effective through brotherhoods and charitable associations tended to run into the sands because of bureaucratic sclerosis: other faiths, more flexible and responsive to popular need, moved in to fill the gap.

The Orthodox Church was thus in an unstable condition at the end of the nineteenth century, its messianic pretensions undermined by a sense of haunting inner weakness and by lack of confidence in its ability to hold its own in the intellectual battles of the modern world. These contradictory currents and forebodings seem to underlie the doctrinal disagreements over relations with the Old Catholics expounded by John Basil, as well as the unrest in the seminaries described by John Morison. They also gave rise to a fervent and widely supported reform movement, which was however thwarted by the tsarist regime in its final years.

Yet worse was to come after the revolution of 1917, under a state which inscribed atheism on its banner. A ruthless and skilful Communist regime was able to exploit the tensions inside the church, and especially the idealism of the reformers, to split it from within and submit it to a humiliating and destructive tutelage. Philip Walters outlines the programmes and personalities involved in the schism of the 1920s, while Dmitry Pospielovsky evokes the martyrdom which resulted. The continuing humiliation and manipulation of the church till very recent times is vividly presented in Raymond Oppenheim's personal analysis of the Furov reports.

But the Orthodox Church has never simply been the tool and victim of the secular state. It has always had its own inner sources of strength, its own alternative tradition, even (perhaps especially) in times of secular oppression and apparent institutional aridity. Among both clergy and laity, some individuals have always derived special inspiration and spiritual fortitude from the church's doctrine, its liturgical tradition and its communal life. This latent resilience was manifested in the expansive but practical piety of men like Arkhimandrit Makary and V. I. Verbitsky, missionaries whose work is outlined by David Collins, and in the self-sacrificing, visionary devotion to duty of women ascetics and elders who created enduring monastic centres, as evoked by Brenda Meehan-Waters. Most remarkably of all, this spiritual strength is revealed in the martyrs of the Soviet period, and in the clandestine lay brotherhoods mentioned by

Pospielovsky, which kept alive a faith in danger of obliteration by militant atheism.

The national identification of the Orthodox Church with the Russian people could be exploited by the Soviet state for political and diplomatic purposes, as Peter Duncan shows. Yet that same identification could enable the spirit of the church to persist even where buildings and administrative structures had been destroyed. John Dunlop demonstrates the religious ferment discernible in literature and film under the atheist crust. His insight was confirmed in a remarkable lecture held in London at the time of our conference by Archbishop Kirill of Smolensk: at a time when the church had been unable to play its proper role in society, he said, the values of Christianity had been transmitted by Russian literature, even sometimes by writers who were not themselves believers.

The dual identification with nation and state has been especially problematic in Ukraine, where the nation has in its history been subject to various foreign political systems, all of which have affected its ecclesiastical structure. As a result conflicts and uncertainties have grown up of the kind enumerated by J. P. Himka. And in the Soviet period, Ukrainian nationalism offered a lever for the authorities to divide and dominate Orthodox believers, as Bohdan Bociurkiw shows.

Yet at its best the Ukrainian religious experience exemplifies, as Frank Sysyn suggests, a kind of 'internal ecumenism', a synthesis of lay and clerical involvement, of western and eastern culture, which differs considerably from the Russian experience and may point the way towards the future of Christianity in the Soviet Union. For the moment, however, the Ukrainian Catholic Church, which might be the bearer of such ideals, is still a church of the underground, denied normal worship and parish structure by a Communist Party which fears the revival of Ukrainian ethnic feeling.

There is a long way to go yet before the religious experience of the Eastern Slavonic peoples can bear full fruit. Yet, even as we, the conference participants, toiled in the midsummer heat, I think we all felt a breath of the *sobornost'* (spirit of community) which many Orthodox theologians see as the distinctive contribution which their tradition can make to the ecumene. We offer the papers that follow in the hope that they will do something to illuminate that tradition.

Geoffrey A. Hosking
School of Slavonic and East European Studies
University of London
May 1989

Notes on the Contributors

John D. Basil is Associate Professor of History at the University of South Carolina. Among his publications are articles on the Russian Church and the Old Catholics, and the Russian Church during the October 1917 Revolution. He has also published a book on the Mensheviks during the Revolution and is currently preparing one on the Russian Orthodox Church on the eve of the Revolution.

Stephen K. Batalden is Associate Professor of History at Arizona State University. His published work on Russian church history and Greco-Slavic relations includes *Catherine II's Greek Prelate: Eugenios Voulgaris in Russia, 1771–1806*.

Bohdan R. Bociurkiw is Professor of Political Science at Carleton University, Ottawa. He is the author of numerous studies on church-state relations in the USSR (especially Ukraine) and Eastern Europe, Soviet nationality policy and dissent, and political succession in the USSR.

David N. Collins is Lecturer in Russian History at Leeds University. He is co-editor, with John Smele, of the two-volume *Kolchak and Siberia*, has published *Colonialism and Siberian Development: the Orthodox Mission to the Altay* in a companion volume to this, and is engaged in preparing a *Bibliography of Siberia*.

Robert O. Crummey is a Professor of History and Acting Dean of the College of Letters and Science at the University of California, Davis. His publications on Russian history focus on two distinct themes— movements of religious dissent, particularly the Old Believers, and the development of the Russian aristocracy. Among them are *The Old Believers and the World of Antichrist* (1970), *Aristocrats and Servitors: The Boyar Elite in Russia, 1613–1689* (1983) and *The Formation of Muscovy, 1304–1613* (1987). Most recently, he has edited and contributed to *Reform in Russia and USSR: Past and Prospects* (1989).

Simon Dixon is a Research Fellow of Sidney Sussex College, University of Cambridge. He specialises in the history of the Russian

Orthodox Church in the imperial period, and is currently writing a textbook on eighteenth-century Russia.

Peter J. S. Duncan is Lecturer in Soviet Economic and Social Policy at the School of Slavonic and East European Studies, University of London. He wrote the chapter while working in his previous post at the Royal Institute of International Affairs. His chapters and articles on nationalism in the USSR have appeared in various journals and collective works. He is author of *The Soviet Union and India* (1989) and co-editor of *Soviet-British Relations: The Last Decade* (forthcoming).

John B. Dunlop is a Senior Fellow at the Hoover Institution, Stanford University. His publications include *The Faces of Contemporary Russian Nationalism* (1983) and *The New Russian Nationalism* (1985).

John-Paul Himka is Associate Professor of History at the University of Alberta. He is the author of *Socialism in Galicia* (1983) and *Galician Villagers and the Ukrainian National Movement in the Nineteenth Century* (1988).

Geoffrey A. Hosking is Professor of Russian History at the School of Slavonic and East European Studies, University of London. He was the BBC Reith Lecturer in 1988, and his published works include *A History of the Soviet Union* (1985) and *The Awakening of the Soviet Union* (1990).

Pål Kolstø is a Research Associate at the Institute for Defense Studies in Oslo, specialising in Soviet politics and history. From 1984–86 he held a research grant from the Norwegian Research Council for the Humanities, in order to study Russian religious thought in the last century. He is presently working on his Ph.D. on the topic of 'Leo Tolstoy and the Orthodox Faith'. Kolstø has published the books *The Russian Church and the Intelligentsia* (1982, in Norwegian) and *An Appeal to the People—Glasnost—Aims and Means* (1988).

Brenda Meehan-Waters is Professor of History and Director of the Russian Studies Program at the University of Rochester. She is the author of *Autocracy and Aristocracy: The Russian Service Elite of 1730* and numerous articles on Russian social and cultural history.

She is currently completing a book entitled *Forgotten Russia: Popular Piety and the Development of Women's Religious Communities, 1764–1917*.

Michael A. Meerson is Rector of Christ the Savior Orthodox Church in New York City, a free-lance writer for Radio Liberty and adjutant professor of Russian Church History in Hunter College (NYC) and Middlebury College Russian Summer School. His many publications in various languages include (with Boris Shragin) *The Political, Social and Religious Thought of Russian 'Samizdat', An Anthology* (1977).

John D. Morison is Senior Lecturer in Russian history at the University of Leeds. His recent publications have been on Russian and Czech educational history and Soviet education.

Raymond L. L. Oppenheim is Vicar of St Mark's, Wellington, New Zealand. From 1971 to 1975 he was Chaplain to the Embassy of the United States of America, Moscow, USSR. He is a National Chairman of Keston College, New Zealand, and Honorary Lecturer in the Department of World Religions, Victoria University of Wellington.

Dimitry V. Pospielovsky is Professor of modern European and Russian History at the University of Western Ontario. Among his publications are *A History of Soviet Atheism in Theory and Practice, and the Believer*; *Na putiakh k rabochemu pravu* (1987); *The Russian Church under the Soviet Regime: 1917–1982* (1984); *Russian Police Trade Unionism: Experiment or Provocation?* (1971). In addition many articles and essays by him have appeared in English, Russian, German, Italian and French in various journals throughout Europe. Before 1972 he worked as a research analyst and radio broadcaster transmitting to the USSR.

Frank E. Sysyn is Director of the Peter Jacyk Center for Ukrainian Historical Research, and a research associate of the Canadian Institute of Ukrainian Studies, University of Alberta. He has written numerous works on early modern and contemporary Ukrainian and East European cultural and religious history, including *Between Poland and the Ukraine: The Dilemma of Adam Kysil, 1600–1653* (1985), and is also associate editor of *Harvard Ukrainian Studies*.

Paul Valliere is Professor of Religious Studies at Butler University, Indianapolis. He is the author of a number of articles on modern Russian Orthodoxy, the article on 'Tradition' in *The Encyclopedia of Religion* and a book, *Holy War and Pentecostal Peace* (1983).

Franklin A. Walker is a Professor of History, Loyola University of Chicago. He has contributed to British and North American journals a number of essays on nineteenth-century cultural history and on Russian-British diplomatic relations. He is the author of a three-volume study of *Catholic Education and Politics in Ontario* (1955–1986).

Philip Walters is Head of Research at Keston College, the Centre for the Study of Religion in Communist Countries. He has contributed many articles and chapters to journals and symposia on Religion in Russia, the Soviet Union and Eastern Europe. He has edited two books: *Light through the Curtain* (1985) and *World Christianity: Eastern Europe* (1988).

1 The Formation of Modern Ukrainian Religious Culture: The Sixteenth and Seventeenth Centuries
Frank E. Sysyn

Few institutions lend themselves as well as the church to examination for a millennium. Religious institutions and traditions change more slowly than their secular counterparts. For example, it was only in the twentieth century that the Orthodox in the Ukraine first replaced Church Slavonic with Ukrainian in the liturgy and that Uniates (Greek or Ukrainian Catholics) introduced mandatory celibacy in some dioceses. The conservatism of the churches makes it possible to speak of millennial aspects of Ukrainian Christianity. Nevertheless, modification and change have indeed occurred at various rates in different times. The sixteenth and seventeenth centuries—the age of Reformation and Counter-Reformation, Cossack revolts and Polish, Muscovite and Ottoman intervention, the introduction of printing, and the formation of an Eastern Christian higher educational institution in Kiev—were a period of especially rapid change. The great Orthodox scholar, Georges Florovsky, labelled this age 'The Encounter with the West', and viewed it as an unstable and dangerous time, which bore only sterile progeny.[1] Other scholars have seen it as a period of great accomplishments that arose from challenges to the Ukrainian religious genius.[2]

It should suffice to list a number of 'firsts' in the early part of this period to see the beginnings of modern church life in the Metropolitanate of Kiev. In the early sixteenth century, the Belorussian printer Frantsishak Skaryna published the first liturgical books on Ruthenian territories. In the 1560s, the Peresopnytsia Gospel was translated into Ruthenian vernacular. In 1562–63, Szymon Budny published the first works for Protestant believers in Ruthenian. In 1574 Cyrillic printing began in Ukrainian territories, in Lviv, with a primer that was the first of numerous books to teach literacy. In the late 1570s, Prince Konstantyn Ostroz'kyi established the first Orthodox higher educational institution in Ostroh. In 1580–81, the Ostroh circle published the first complete Slavonic Bible. In the 1580s, the burghers of Lviv strengthened their communal life by organizing a brotherhood or fraternity centred at the newly-rebuilt Church of the Assumption. Receiving Stauropegial rights that subordinated the brotherhood directly to the patriarch of Constantinople, the brotherhood challenged the authority of the local bishop. In the 1590s, the Orthodox bishops began to meet regularly at synods to discuss reform of the church. In 1595 the bishop of Volodymyr, Ipatii Potii, and the bishop of Luts'k, Kyrylo Terlets'kyi, travelled to Rome to negotiate a church union, which was proclaimed the next year by the metropolitan and five bishops at a synod at Brest. An opposing synod attended by two bishops met in the same city and rejected the union. In 1596, Lavrentii Zizanii published the first Slavonic-Latin-Greek lexicon. In the last years of the sixteenth century, opposing sides polemicized in print in Ruthenian and Polish about the Union of Brest. Alarmed by the Orthodox counter-offensive, the Uniates began to shore up their institution, establishing a seminary in Vilnius in 1601 and creating a Basilian monastic order along western lines in 1613. In 1615, the burghers of Kiev and the inhabitants of the surrounding region formed a brotherhood and later a school. Combined with the printing press at the Caves Monastery, these institutions made Kiev the centre of religious and cultural activities. In 1618 Meletii Smotryts'kyi published a grammar of Church Slavonic that established the norms of the language. In 1632, Mohyla, as metropolitan and archimandrite of the Caves Monastery, formed a collegium in Kiev. By 1642, he had compiled a confession of the Orthodox faith, which was later accepted by other Orthodox churches.[3]

From the late sixteenth to mid-seventeenth century, the Eastern Christian believers of the Ukraine and Belorussia, with their activist hierarchs and churches, their numerous schools and monasteries, their scores of new titles of books in Slavonic, Ruthenian and Polish, their numerous innovations in institutions—brotherhoods, synods of the clergy and the laity, western-patterned religious orders—and their elaborate debates on church history, structure, and beliefs, had entered a new age. Generations of historians have examined the events and the achievements of the period. However the age is evaluated, there is agreement that from the mid-sixteenth century to the end of the seventeenth century, church life was fundamentally transformed in the Ukraine. With this transformation the foundation was laid for Ukrainian religious traditions that have endured into the modern age. More recent ecclesiastical movements find their precedents in this formative period. In acts such as establishing the Orthodox society named in honour of Peter Mohyla in Volhynia in the 1930s and as calling for the Soviet government to recognise the legality of the Uniate or Ukrainian Catholic Church, twentieth-century Ukrainian churchmen and believers have frequently used the symbols, rhetoric and institutions that evolved about four hundred years ago.[4] This paper merely aims to suggest some of the major traditions or themes that have an enduring impact on Ukrainian religious culture.

This discussion will concentrate on religious traditions among Ukrainian Eastern Christian believers. While in many respects Ukrainians shared a common 'Ruthenian' religious culture of the Kiev Metropolitanate with Belorussians, it was in the sixteenth century that Ukrainian and Belorussian political, cultural and religious history began to diverge more significantly. The Union of Lublin of 1569 divided most of the central and eastern Ukrainian territories formerly part of the Grand Duchy of Lithuania from the Belorussian territories and united them with the western Ukrainian lands in the Kingdom of Poland. The Cossack Host developed primarily in the Ukrainian lands and in time created a political and social elite lacking in Belorussia. By the same token, economic and demographic advances supported a greater vitality in cultural and religious activities in the Ukrainian territories. In religious affairs, the Ukrainian territories became relatively more important in the life of the Kiev Metropolitanate at the end of the sixteenth century, in part because elites in Belorussia were less resistant to conversion to Roman Catholicism and Protestantism. The return of the metropolitans to their titular city of Kiev in the 1590s symbolized this change. In the first half of the seventeenth century, the religious cultures of Ukraine and Belorussia diverged further because the Orthodox dominated in the Ukrainian lands, while the Uniates had more success in the Belorussian territories. Finally the formation of an Orthodox Cossack Hetmanate stimulated a development of specific Ukrainian religious traditions in Kiev and the Left-Bank Ukraine. Despite these differences, the religious culture of the seventeenth century can be viewed as a Ruthenian inheritance from which interacting Ukrainian and Belorussian variants took shape. Therefore the traditions outlined here are often also pertinent to

Belorussian religious culture, though they have evolved differently in Belorussia in the modern period.

Discussion of Ukrainian religious culture will be confined to Eastern Christians, the adherents of the traditional Rus' Church. However, the distinctiveness of Ruthenian Eastern Christian religious culture arose, in part, because of religious pluralism. Jews, Muslims, Armenian Gregorians, Latin-Rite Catholics, and Protestants all inhabited the Ukrainian and Belorussian territories alongside Orthodox, and after 1596, Uniate, Rus' Christians. These groups both interacted with the Eastern Christians and represented 'other' religious and cultural traditions. For example, the identification of Roman Catholicism as the 'Liakhs'' or Poles' faith in the Ukrainian lands made religious adherence coincide with cultural-national identification and conversion implied a change in cultural affiliation. The Protestant Reformation emerged from the Western Christian community, but made converts throughout the Ukraine, including among the Orthodox. While the Calvinists, Antitrinitarians and Lutherans did not constitute religious bodies that descended directly from the Rus' tradition, they were influenced by their Eastern Christian surroundings. The Counter-Reformation arose to meet the Protestant challenge, but it too directed its efforts to converting Eastern Christians. Latin Catholics, Protestants, and other groups challenged and stimulated the Ruthenian Eastern Christians.[5]

The major significance of the period for Ukrainian and Belorussian Eastern Christians was their division in 1596 into Orthodox and Uniate believers and churches. Before the late sixteenth century, attempts to unite Ukrainian and Belorussian believers with Rome had been episodic and had not divided the larger religious community. From 1596, Ukrainian and Belorussian believers have been permanently divided into two churches—one which rejects the Union and holds to Orthodoxy and one which accepts the Union and adheres to Catholicism. Both claim to be the true continuation of the church that was formed by the conversion of Rus' of 988.[6]

Modern Ukrainian religious culture emerged in the Kiev Metropolitanate of the sixteenth century.[7] From the conversion of 988 until the early fourteenth century, one Metropolitanate of Kiev and all Rus' had encompassed all East Slavic territories. By the twelfth century, Kiev no longer possessed the paramount political influence in Rus' and the Mongol conquest hastened the disintegration of political unity of the vast Kiev Metropolitanate. In the early fourteenth century, the Orthodox ruler of Galicia-Volhynia, Prince Iurii, convinced the Patriarchate of Constantinople temporarily to establish a Metropolitanate of Little Rus' for the eparchies of Peremyshl', Halych, Volodymyr, Luts'k, Turov and Kholm. More lasting was the migration of the Kiev metropolitans to the Suzdal lands in the early fourteenth century, where they later took up residence in Moscow. Until 1458 growing centrifugal forces made the retention of a united Kiev Metropolitanate seem difficult. The Galician or 'Little Rus'' Metropolitanate was temporarily revived in 1370 on the insistence of Kazimierz the Great, the Polish ruler who annexed Galicia to his domains. Grand princes of Lithuania, whose domains reached to Kiev by 1362, sought to have their candidates appointed metropolitan of Kiev and to have them reside in their state. When they could not do so, they strove to have separate metropolitanates established for their numerous Ruthenian subjects. In general, the patriarchs of Constantinople preferred to retain the unity of the Kiev Metropolitanate and to entrust its headquarters to the steadfastly Orthodox princes of Moscow rather than to the Catholic kings of Poland or to the pagan and, after 1386, Catholic rulers of Lithuania.[8]

The Patriarchate of Constantinople brought about the final division of the Kiev Metropolitanate by its own wavering in adherence to Orthodoxy. Muscovy refused to accept the Union of Florence of 1439 and the Greek Metropolitan of Kiev, Isidore. Consequently it rejected the authority of the patriarchs of Constantinople and declared autocephaly by electing its own metropolitan (1448). In the Ukrainian and Belorussian lands, controlled by Catholic rulers, no such rejection of Constantinople's authority or the Metropolitan Isidore occurred. Therefore, when in 1458 a new metropolitan of 'Kiev and all Rus'' was elected for the lands of the Grand Duchy of Lithuania and the Kingdom of Poland, a permanent break ensued between the two parts of the Kievan Metropolitan See. The change of the title of the metropolitan in Moscow from 'Kiev and all Rus'' to 'Moscow and all Rus'' brought titulature in line with reality. Although the Union of Florence failed to take hold in both Constantinople and in the Kingdom of Poland and the Grand Duchy of Lithuania, the division of the old Kievan Metropolitanate into Ruthenian and Muscovite churches endured.

For both metropolitanates the events of the mid-fifteenth century speeded the indigenisation, indeed, the nationalisation, of the church. In earlier centuries, metropolitans had frequently been Greeks and in the fourteenth and fifteenth centuries foreigners still figured prominently (Gregory Tsamblak and Isidore). At the same time, the cultural distinctness of Russians and Ruthenians, who differed in vernacular and administrative languages and lived under markedly different political and social systems, made a metropolitan from Muscovy or one from the Grand Duchy of Lithuania more and more alien in the other territory. From 1448 to the declaration of Moscow as a patriarchate in 1589, all metropolitans of Moscow were native Russians, while from 1458 to the subordination of Kiev to Moscow in 1686 most metropolitans of Kiev and bishops of the metropolitanate were native Ruthenians. The final division of Ruthenian and Muscovite churches and their different experiences from the fifteenth to seventeenth centuries furthered the evolution of distinct religious traditions.

For the Kiev Metropolitanate, the major problems of the fifteenth century were dealing with the consequences of the Union of Florence and finding a place for itself in Catholic states.[9] As Constantinople renounced the Union of Florence, the daughter church of Kiev reasserted its Orthodox allegiance. Nevertheless, in the first century after the fall of Constantinople, the patriarchs displayed little initiative in guiding their distant daughter church, and the church became increasingly dependent on Catholic rulers and Orthodox lay lords. Throughout the fifteenth and early sixteenth century, the Polish and Lithuanian governments enacted legislation that placed the church and its believers in a disadvantageous position in comparison to the Catholic Church. Although the Protestant Reformation weakened the privileged position of the Catholic Church, the Protestant believers and their Catholic opponents engaged in an intellectual battle in which the Orthodox Church was unprepared to take part. Western Christian political dominance and intellectual and organizational superiority combined to challenge a Kiev Metropolitanate that could not depend on Orthodox rulers, domestic or foreign, for support, and that found its Slavonic cultural inheritance deficient in answering the new challenges. Faced with the increasing defections to the Protestants and Catholics, particularly from among the Orthodox nobles, the Kiev Metropolitanate was endangered with dissolution in the sixteenth century. The response to the challenges brought about numerous innovations in religious culture. One of the responses, however, the acceptance of union with Rome by the metropolitan and most of the bishops brought about an institutional division in the Metropolitanate. After 1596, the Orthodox Church had to compete with a Uniate Kiev Metropolitanate.

From 1596 to 1620, the Orthodox Church had no metropolitan and was viewed as illegal by the Polish-Lithuanian Commonwealth. In 1620, Patriarch Theophanos of Jerusalem consecrated Metropolitan Iov Borets'kyi and Five bishops. The government viewed the election of Iov Borets'kyi and his successor, Isaia Kopyn'skyi, as illegitimate. Bowing to the pressure from the Orthodox nobility and the Zaporozhian Cossacks, the newly elected king Wladyslaw IV and the Diet recognised the Orthodox Church as legal in 1632, but assigned only half of the eparchies of the metropolitanate to the Orthodox and required the election of a new hierarchy to replace the hierarchy ordained in 1620.

From 1632 to 1647, Metropolitan Peter Mohyla strove to strengthen the Orthodox Metropolitanate's institutional structure throughout the Commonwealth, including in the eparchies assigned to the Uniates. Mohyla used his wealth and his influence with the government to carry out a far-reaching programme of development of education and printing, as well as of reform of church practices. He entertained the possibility of a union with Rome on better terms than the Union of Brest, but never made a final commitment.[10]

Mohyla's successor as Orthodox metropolitan of Kiev, Sylvester Kosov (1647–1657) led the church in more turbulent times. The Cossack revolt that developed into an Ukrainian uprising improved the position of the Orthodox Metropolitanate on a number of occasions. In 1649, the Polish King Jan Kazimierz promised to abolish the Union, and the church gained advantages even though the commitment was never carried out fully. In the territories controlled by Bohdan Khmel'nyts'kyi, Latin Catholic as well as Uniate institutions and lands were given over to the Orthodox. There were, however, negative consequences of the revolt and the establishment of the Cossack Hetmanate for the Kiev Metropolitanate. The Pereiaslav Agreement of 1654 placed the status of the metropolitanate in question. Its leadership feared correctly that ties with Muscovy would result in Russian interference in church affairs and the eventual transfer of the metropolitanate from the jurisdiction of the patriarch of Constantinople to the patriarch of Moscow.[11]

Already in Kosov's time, the Muscovites insisted that the metropolitan limit his traditional title of 'Kiev, Halych and all Rus'' to 'Kiev, Halych and all Little Rus''. In addition, victorious Muscovite armies in the Grand Duchy of Lithuania sought to detach Belorussian areas from the Kiev Metropolitanate and to annex them to the Moscow Patriarchate. Metropolitan Kosov died in April, 1657, four months before Bohdan Khmel'nyts'kyi. At this critical political moment for the Ukraine, the clergy of the Kiev Metropolitanate with the authorization of the new hetman, Ivan Vyhovs'kyi, elected Dionisii Balaban as metropolitan with the blessing of the patriarch of Constantinople. Balaban supported Vyhovs'kyi in his break with Moscow and his negotiation of the Union of Hadiach (8 September 1658), which sought to reintegrate the central Ukrainian lands into the Commonwealth as a Rus' duchy, to guarantee places in the Polish-Lithuanian Senate for the metropolitan and bishops, and to abolish the Union of Brest. The failure of Vyhovs'kyi and the Hadiach policy forced the metropolitan to abandon the city of Kiev and to take up residence in territories controlled by the Commonwealth. Until his death in 1663, Balaban could not exercise control over the Ukrainian territories on the Left-Bank of the Dnieper. The Muscovite authorities appointed Lazar Baranovych, the bishop of Chernihiv, as administrator in these territories in 1659, thereby beginning the division of the Kiev Metropolitanate along political boundaries.

Political events rapidly eroded the unity and autonomy of the Kievan Metropolitan See in the second half of the seventeenth century. In 1685–86, during the election of Metropolitan Gedeon Chetvertyns'kyi, the Russian government arranged the transfer of the Kiev Metropolitan See from the jurisdiction of the patriarch of Constantinople to that of the patriarch of Moscow through pressure and bribes. Nevertheless, the particular cultural and religious traditions of the late-sixteenth and seventeenth-century metropolitanate and the unique position of Kiev endured well into the eighteenth century. It served as a model for twentieth-century movements for the formation of autonomous and autocephalous churches in the Ukraine and Belorussia.

The Uniate heir to the Kiev Metropolitan See was not able to win a mass following in the Ukrainian lands until the late seventeenth century, but it did produce dedicated followers and important traditions. The mediocre Metropolitan Mykhailo Rahoza who acceded to the Union was followed by the energetic Ipatii Potii (1601–13) and Iosyf Ruts'kyi (1613–37) as 'metropolitans of Kiev, Halych and all Rus''. They weathered numerous setbacks. The disappointment that two bishops and a large body of the clergy and the laity would not accede to the Union was followed by the blows of the Senate's refusal to grant seats to the Uniate bishops, the Diet's concessions of benefices to the Orthodox, the government's unwillingness to move decisively against the 'illegal' Orthodox metropolitan and hierarchy consecrated in 1620 and the recognition of the Orthodox Metropolitanate as an equal competitor to the Uniate in 1632. In the first fifty years, the Uniate Church was more successful in attracting followers in the Belorussian territories of the Grand Duchy of Lithuania than it was in the Ukrainian territories of the Kingdom of Poland, except for the Kholm area. The great Cossack revolt in 1648 placed the very existence of the Uniate Church in doubt. Nevertheless, in the second half of the seventeenth century, the Uniate Kiev Metropolitanate began to take shape, assisted by support from Rome and some zealous Catholics in the Commonwealth. The retention of all Belorussia, Galicia and the Right-Bank Ukraine by the Polish-Lithuanian Commonwealth after 1667 ensured the victory of the Union in these lands by the early eighteenth century. Reaching its greatest extent in the eighteenth century, the Uniate Church took on its own stable ecclesiastical form at the Synod of Zamość in 1720. The triumph of the Russian Empire over the Commonwealth was to devastate the Uniate Church, so that it would only survive in the Galician lands annexed by the Habsburgs, the very territories that had been so anti-Uniate before 1700. Still, the Galician Metropolitan See established in 1807 continued the traditions of the Uniate Kiev Metropolitanate. Despite changes in titulature and legal rights, the Ukrainian Catholic Church asserts its direct claims to the heritage of the Metropolitanate of Kiev, Halych, and All-Rus'.[12]

The major tradition of this period, for both Orthodox and Uniates, was the emergence of new religious forms that represented an absorption and adaptation of influences from Latin Christianity, which had accompanied the control of the Ukrainian lands by Western Christian powers in the fourteenth century. At the core of Ruthenian culture was a deeply-rooted Byzantine-Slavonic tradition embodied in a church that maintained an institutional structure, permeating the thousands of settlements in the Ukrainian and Belorussian lands. As an institution of the Rus' faith, the church functioned in a conserving role for a local culture, while at the same time connecting it to a Byzantine past, a larger Orthodox community and a supranational Slavonic culture. Latin Christian political domination was accompanied by the placement of the Orthodox Church in an inferior position and with restrictions on the Orthodox and their worship. Consequently the Rus' Church in Ukraine experienced the perils that religious pluralism poses for a church in a subservient position. As Latin Christian culture evolved and flourished, the Orthodox of the Ukraine found themselves representatives of an increasingly isolated and inadequate cultural tradition.

This threat ultimately proved to be a stimulus that produced so many of the achievements outlined earlier. Although the Orthodox of the Ukraine had faced the western challenge without the protection of an Orthodox ruler or even the neutrality of a Muslim ruler, they were able to accommodate to Western practices and influences over a long period of time. Both the decision of Polish kings in the fourteenth century to tolerate Orthodoxy, and even to grant the Orthodox elite noble status, and the manifest numerical and political strength of the Orthodox Ruthenians in the Grand Duchy of Lithuania, which negated discriminatory legislation, had permitted the Orthodox Church to adjust gradually to Western Christian rule. Even in the cities, where Orthodox were subject to harsh discrimination and numerous restrictions, they were able to maintain some religious and communal institutions. By the sixteenth century, religious divisions among Western Christians and the weak powers of central administration in contrast to extensive liberties of individual nobles mitigated the pressures on the Orthodox.[13]

The process of contact with Western Christian culture has still to be studied satisfactorily. Complex cultural changes and adaptation occurred from the fifteenth century, when a Iurii of Drohobych presumably converted and became a rector of the University of Bologna to the seventeenth century, when an Orthodox university was established in Kiev. The Orthodox Church and the Byzantine-Slavonic-Ruthenian culture long seemed inert and unattuned to the challenges of the Latin West. Their eventual response demonstrated how serious the challenge was. In adapting the thought and forms of the Latin West, the Kiev Metropolitanate proved that it possessed the inner resources to reform rather than to disintegrate. Latin philosophical texts, Church Slavonic grammars, and Polish-language polemical works were components of this response. Although Latin accretions and internal inconsistencies were part of the religious culture of the period, Ukrainian or Ruthenian religious practice, both Orthodox and Uniate, represented more a synthesis of the long contact of the Kiev Metropolitanate with the West than it did a collection of disparate and contradictory religious practices. From the heights of Kievan theology to the popular Christmas carols, the Ukrainians accepted outside influences without losing their religious and cultural heritage. In the Ukraine, there were no religious schisms or divisions such as the Raskol in Russia over the introduction of new forms. Even those who objected to western influences, the polemicist Ivan Vyshens'kyi or the trans-Dnieper monks, were usually too familiar with the 'other' to be able to expurgate it from their own thought or to avoid it in totality. The division within the Ukrainian community came over a more substantive issue—union with Rome and a change of faith. Although both Orthodox and Uniate Ukrainians have undergone periodic movements to diminish Latin and Western Christian influence on their religious culture, the Westernisation of the sixteenth and seventeenth centuries is so deeply imbedded in their religious tradition that it cannot be uprooted.[14]

Most Eastern Christians have followed the models pioneered in the Ukraine. Kievan learning served as the model for the entire eighteenth-century Russian Imperial Church. Ukrainian music and art, through its importation to Russia, later spread throughout the Orthodox world. Experiments in employing the vernacular in sixteenth-century Ukraine and Belorussia were later to be repeated among other Orthodox peoples. Even when other Orthodox and Eastern Christian peoples did not directly import elements of the Ukrainian synthesis, they frequently underwent analogous processes later.[15]

The active role of the laity constitutes a second enduring tradition in Ukrainian church life. Laymen became involved in church affairs and spiritual life and new institutions emerged. The form that the Uniate Church took at the end of the seventeenth century and the remaking of the Orthodox Church in the Ukraine in the eighteenth and nineteenth centuries undermined this role of the laity and lay organisations, but new circumstances have frequently caused a revival of earlier traditions and institutions.

Laymen were essential to the administration and preservation of the Orthodox Kiev Metropolitanate. In the sixteenth century, the endangered church turned to great patrons, such as Prince Konstantyn Ostroz'kyi, to ensure its protection. Nobles, endowed with the sweeping rights of the nobiliary Commonwealth, not only served as patrons and protectors of local churches, but also spoke in the name of the church at Diets and took part in the synods of the Orthodox Church in the early seventeenth century. Burghers had organised their own reform of church and community activities, even exercising the right to dismiss their clergymen. Zaporozhian Cossacks had not only assumed protection over the new Orthodox hierarchy, but also intervened in religious councils. The urban brotherhoods or *bratstva*, enrolling burghers, as well as nobles and Cossacks, constituted the most creative response to religious and cultural problems in the Ukraine and Belorussia. They also signified how greatly Ruthenian religious culture had diverged from other Eastern Christian communities. This can be seen by the need of the Lviv burghers to explain what a brotherhood was to seventeenth-century Russians.[16]

Clergymen resented some lay interventions in religious affairs as contrary to traditional canons and as undermining the position of the clergy.[17] Some were attracted to the Union as a way of restoring full clerical control of the church. The defection of the metropolitan and five bishops increased the importance of the laity, who came to realise that they, not the hierarchs, remained steadfast in preserving the church. Twenty years of church life without a complete hierarchy (1596–1620) were followed by twelve years of governance by hierarchs who often could not take up residence in their sees and depended on the Orthodox nobles, Cossacks, and burghers to support their positions against a government that viewed them as illegal. Even after 1632, Metropolitan Mohyla, who sought to reassert clerical leadership in church affairs, had to depend on the noble laity. After 1648, the higher clergymen might find the Cossacks troublesome protectors, but they could not deny the benefits Cossack successes had brought for the church and they could not avoid adaptation to a new order in which priests and Cossack administrators not only represented dual powers, but were often members of the same families.

In the early seventeenth century, the need to compete for supporters also influenced the Uniate Church to pay heed to the laity. However, as it lost the support of the great nobles, major brotherhoods, and the Cossacks, the Uniate Church, influenced by Roman practices, reduced the role of the laity. Ultimately, it turned to laymen not its members, Latin-rite Catholic nobles, to strengthen its position.

A third element of the religious experience of the age was the 'nationalisation' of the church and the articulation of a subjective Ruthenian national consciousness based on the view of the church as properly a national institution.[18] The church had always been the Ruthenian Church, the embodiment of the conversion of the Rus' rulers and their people in the tenth century. By the sixteenth century, new conditions deepened the nation-bearing character of the church. The extinction of Rus' dynasties and polities made the church the only direct institutional link to Kievan Rus'. The assimilation of many members of the secular elite to Polish culture, accompanied by religious conversions, augmented the role of the church as a spokesman for the Ruthenian tradition. Polish penetration of the Ukraine, the development of a Polish vernacular literature and concept of nation, and the deprecation and later persecution of Orthodoxy by Polish clerical leaders and authorities combined to intensify national-religious feeling, in which the Ruthenian people and the Ruthenian church were viewed as one. The church not only embodied the national identity, it also frequently used the Ruthenian language in administration and publications, albeit without advocating the abandonment of Slavonic. All these factors heightened Ruthenian national feeling and the identification of the church as the suprastructure of 'Ruthenian nationhood'. The mix of religious and national sentiment was especially apparent in the organisation of brotherhoods among the burghers, since the Ruthenian burghers, subject to discrimination, developed an intense ethno-religious sentiment in an environment in which they competed with other ethno-religious communities, Polish Catholics, Armenians and Jews.

Even the Union of Brest, which divided the Ruthenians, worked to intensify the identification as both sides strove that all Ruthenians should be one in faith. At the same time, however, it favoured more sophisticated thinking on Ruthenian national identity since suddenly church and 'nation' were not coterminous and polemicists had to discuss the religious divide within the Ruthenian people. The essence of the debate was the historical question of which faith Volodymyr (Vladimir) had accepted. Therefore, in the Ukraine, it inspired knowledge of the Kievan Rus' past as the cradle of Ruthenian national and religious culture. Even the Protestants occasionally invoked Volodymyr and the conversion as a means of securing legitimacy. While each church could deny the other's legitimacy, it could not deny that there were Ruthenians of another religious persuasion. Orthodox might still see themselves as part of a greater Orthodox world, but they clearly viewed themselves as part of a Ruthenian (or after the mid-seventeenth century Ukrainian or Little Rus') division of that world both as an ecclesiastical and a historico-linguistic community. After 1596, they also had to integrate into their world view the adherence of fellow Ruthenians to Rome. At least the intellectuals, men like Meletii Smotryts'kyi and Adam Kysil, articulated these issues, and Smotryts'kyi argued that conversion did not mean a change of nationality since blood, not religion, defined nationality.[19] The concepts were amorphous, and the unstable political and religious situation prevented their crystallisation, but

Ukrainians had begun the discussions of religious, national and cultural issues that have continued to the present. In modern times, Ukrainians frequently invested the church with the national significance it assumed in the sixteenth and seventeenth centuries, especially when other potential national institutions were abolished or usurped.

A fourth tradition, or rather experience, of the churches in Ukraine was that of accommodation or conflict of churches with state powers. The relations of a number of political entities (the Polish-Lithuanian Commonwealth, the Cossack Hetmanate, the Ottoman Empire, the Crimean Khanate, Muscovy/the Russian Empire) with the two Ruthenian churches were diverse and frequently contradictory. In general, however, the leaders of both churches of the Kiev Metropolitanate found that their church structure and religious traditions had to be restructured to adjust to political rulers. Political power has determined much in Ukrainian religious history. Desire to obtain political influence and to find favour with the ruler to a considerable degree explains the Union of Brest. Weak central government in the Commonwealth and successful utilisation of internal (Prince Ostroz'kyi, the Zaporozhian Cossacks) and external (the Ottomans, Muscovy, the Eastern patriarchates) centres of power explain the reason for the survival of the Orthodox Church. Ultimately, however, the Orthodox Church could only ensure long-term existence by coming to terms with king and state—whether through the compromise of 1632 or the ostensible willingness to discuss a new union. In like manner, the Uniate Church survived assaults by Cossacks, nobles and burghers because it had advocates in the government of the Commonwealth, kings and senators, as well as Vatican nuncios who influenced government policy.

Changes in political structures posed great problems and opportunities for the churches of the Kiev Metropolitanate. Had Polish control of Moscow continued or Wladyslaw's candidacy to the Muscovite throne succeeded during the Time of Troubles, the Union would certainly have expanded beyond the Kiev Metropolitanate to the Patriarchate of Moscow. In contrast, the Cossack revolts and the Khmel'nyts'kyi uprising endangered the very existence of the Uniate Church. Paradoxically, the uprising posed problems for the Orthodox Church, which it actively supported. Most of the Orthodox hierarchs viewed rebellion with discomfort, particularly after the church obtained legal recognition in 1632, and were suspicious of the Cossack leaders as new political masters. They also feared that the political division of territories of the Kiev Metropolitanate would undermine its ecclesiastical unity and that the revolt would weaken the position of the church in the lands that remained in the Commonwealth. Metropolitan Kosov foresaw that Khmel'nyts'kyi's turn to Muscovy and oath of allegiance to the tsar would bring undesirable consequences for the church—above all the transfer of the Kiev Metropolitanate from the jurisdiction of the Patriarchate of Constantinople to that of Moscow.

In the second half of the seventeenth century, metropolitans and bishops strove for stability amidst an unstable political situation. Uniate hierarchs sought to avoid the consequences of political compromises, such as the Union of Hadiach, which were deleterious to the interests of their church. Ultimately, the division of Ukraine between the Polish-Lithuanian Commonwealth and Muscovy (1667, 1686) and the rise of Catholic intolerance in the Commonwealth worked to the Uniates' advantage. By the beginning of the eighteenth century the sees of Peremyshl', Lviv, and Luts'k accepted the Union and the real foundations of the Uniate Church were laid in the Ukrainian territories controlled by Poland.

The Orthodox clergymen and Metropolitanate had greater options and more diverse constituencies. Metropolitan Kosov sought to come to an accommodation with the Polish-Lithuanian authorities and to minimize the effect of the Pereiaslav Agreement, while Metropolitan Dionisii Balaban supported Vyhovs'kyi's policy of reintegrating the Ukraine into the Polish-Lithuanian Commonwealth as the Duchy of Rus'. Bishops Metodii Fylymovych and Lazar Baranovych adjusted to the influence of the Muscovite Church and state in the Ukraine, even at the price of undermining the unity of the Kiev Metropolitanate. In general, all the Orthodox churchmen found that the church must eventually accommodate to political power, though the period contained many examples of attempts to avoid this hard reality. Still the subordination of the Kiev Metropolitanate to Moscow in 1686, the loss of the western Ukrainian dioceses to the Uniates, and the church's anathema of its great patron Ivan Mazepa in 1708 revealed how political power would draw ecclesiastical boundaries and determine the role of the church.

Ultimately the failure to establish a political entity uniting the Ukrainian territories undermined the position of the local Orthodox Church. In the late sixteenth century, suggestions were made that the patriarch of Constantinople should migrate to Ukrainian territories, and in the early seventeenth century various plans envisaged Kiev as the centre of a patriarchate. Mohyla made Kiev one of the major seats of the Orthodox world, and in the seventeenth century it appeared that the Kiev metropolitans might see the prestige of their church raised by the formation of a new Orthodox state on their territory. That possibility receded rapidly after 1660.

Both Orthodox and Uniate churches were reorganised along the lines of dominance of Moscow-St Petersburg and Warsaw in the Ukraine in the eighteenth century. By the early eighteenth century, the Orthodox metropolitan residing in Kiev had lost most of his Metropolitanate's faithful controlled by Poland to the Uniates, while the diocese of Chernihiv, though part of the Hetmanate, was subordinated directly to the Moscow Patriarchate. Kiev might still be the home of great monasteries and churches, but the Kiev Metropolitanate had been dismantled and by the end of the eighteenth century even the particular practices of the Ukrainian Church were largely abolished. In the Polish-controlled territories, the Kiev Metropolitan's Uniate competitor could only use Kiev in his title but not reside in the city. His large church in the Belorussian-Ukrainian territories was to a considerable degree Latinized and Polonized. The Uniate Church not only lost the upper classes to the Latin-Rite, but also lost much of its active self-identification as a Ruthenian national church that had inspired the formulators of the Union. In the eighteenth century it became the instrument for binding Ukrainians and Belorussians to the Commonwealth that some had hoped it would be in the late sixteenth century.[20]

A fifth tradition of Ukrainian church affairs of the period was the emergence of a religious, literary, and artistic culture that was specifically Ukrainian rather than Ruthenian or Belorussian-Ukrainian. The centrality of the church, clergymen and religious themes in intellectual and cultural pursuits permeated early modern Ukrainian culture. Indeed, religious culture influenced even secular cultural expression such as administrative buildings, portraiture, or political tracts, since the clergymen and church schools controlled education. Political, economic and social changes advanced the formation of new Ukrainian cultural models in the seventeenth century. The process, associated with the nationalisation of the church as Ruthenian, had begun in the fifteenth century. By the late sixteenth century, the common Belorussian-Ukrainian religious and secular culture had come to centre more and more in the Ukrainian territories as assimilation and conversion progressed more rapidly in the Belorussian territories. The political divide of the 'Ruthenian' lands at the Union of Lublin (1569) advanced the differentiation of

Belorussian and Ukrainian cultures. In the early seventeenth century, the political border to some degree mirrored religious divisions, as the Ukrainian territories became the stronghold of Orthodoxy. More importantly, the religious institutions of Kiev and Lviv, the nobles, burghers and Cossacks of the Ukrainian lands, and the Cossack Hetmanate afforded new patrons and consumers of religious and secular culture.[21]

By the second half of the seventeenth century, a religious culture that can be called Ukrainian rather than Ruthenian Orthodox had emerged. The limitation of the Kiev metropolitan's title to 'Little Rus'' after the Pereiaslav Agreement and the Muscovite Church's claims to control Belorussia reflected the predominantly Ukrainian nature of the church. In the new political and social environment of the Ukraine, new literary and artistic forms emerged that have been called Cossack and Ukrainian Baroque. Histories such as Archimandrite Feodosii Sofonovych's *Kroinika* traced the history of the Ukraine at the same time the new Cossack elite provided patronage for art and music.[22] By the end of the century a specifically Ukrainian cultural model had matured. Centred in Kiev, the Cossack Hetmanate, and Sloboda Ukraine, this 'national' cultural style drew on the general Ruthenian tradition and continued to influence, and be influenced by, developments in the western Ukrainian and Belorussian territories. Just as the Ukrainian Church and political entities were absorbed in the Russian Church and Russian Empire, so this culture was absorbed into Imperial Russian culture by the end of the eighteenth century. However, the existence of a national Ukrainian culture closely allied with the church and religious culture provided an enduring example for relations between church and culture and for styles in Ukrainian religious art, architecture and music for subsequent generations.

A sixth tradition of the period was the formation of two churches—Orthodox and Catholic—that share the same religious culture. Both groups not only developed out of the church of St Volodymyr, but they were also formed from similar influences and conditions in the century before and after the Union of Brest. Locked in heated combat, they were always aware that they were essentially one church and one tradition, distinct not only from Western churches, but also from other Eastern churches. The Uniate Ruthenians did not easily fit into the norms and practices of the Roman Church. The Orthodox had too fully imbibed the influences of the West and the political-social conditions of the Ukraine to feel comfortable among other Orthodox churches. Institutions, men, books, practices and ideas passed from one group to the other in this formative period of modern Ukrainian religious life. Catholic coreligionists have distrusted the Uniates' Catholicism just as the Orthodox have been suspicious of the full Orthodoxy of Ukrainian believers. They have had some cause to do so since shared Ukrainian religious characteristics and consciousness have waxed and waned, but never died out. In this way they have produced a certain internal Ukrainian ecumenism despite confessional differences.

The first century after the Union of Brest, when both churches had salient national characteristics and even consciousness, was a time when that which united the two churches seemed very real. Such characteristics, so often troubling to religiously homogeneous neighbours, give an especially modern ring to many statements of the age. Consider the declaration of Adam Kysil, before an Orthodox synod composed of clergymen and laymen calling for conciliation between Orthodox and Uniates in 1629:

> Gentlemen, you are not the only ones to weep. We all weep at the sight of the rent coat and precious robe of our dear Mother the Holy Eastern Church. You, Gentlemen, bemoan, as do we all, that we are divided from our brethren, we who were in one font of the Holy Spirit six hundred years ago in the Dnieper waters of this metropolis of the Rus' Principality. It wounds you, Gentlemen, and it wounds us all. Behold! There flourish organisms of commonwealths composed of various nations, while we of one nation, of one people, of one religion, of one worship, of one rite, are not as one. We are torn asunder, and thus we decline.[23]

Throughout this period striving for the reunification of the Kievan Metropolitanate continued. Acceptance that two religious groups would arise where only one had existed came only slowly. Although subsequent divergence in religious culture and traditions has made the existence of Orthodox and Uniate believers among Ukrainians less difficult to accept, the continued instability in relations between the two groups derives in part from awareness of their common origins and shared characteristics. Consequently, each group finds the existence of the other more troubling than it finds the existence of Roman Catholics, Protestants or Greek and Russian Orthodox. Frequently, however, the two groups have found that the bind of shared religious culture and national loyalties is so strong that denominational affiliations are set aside.

A seventh tradition that arose in the period was an elevation of the Ukrainian churches to more than local significance. The Union of Brest constituted the largest lasting union of Eastern Christians with Rome and brought the Ukrainian and Belorussian territories to the attention of a wider Christian community. It served as a model for unionising efforts among the Ukrainians of Hungary and the Armenians of the Commonwealth. Clergymen active in promoting the Union, such as Metodii Terlets'kyi, used their experience in the Balkans. In discussions of how to gain acceptance of the Union, programmes for the erection of a patriarchate in Kiev only loosely affiliated with Rome were formed. Although these plans were never realised, they constituted a discussion of the structure of the Catholic church that challenged the model of post-Tridentine Catholicism. The eastern patriarchs and the Muscovite Church were vitally interested in the church in the Kiev Metropolitanate. They sought to keep it Orthodox and to draw upon its intellectual and institutional resources. The Kiev collegium made the Ukraine a major centre of religious and intellectual culture.

Although the Ukrainian churches have never again occupied as important a place in the Christian community as they did in the sixteenth and seventeenth century, the experiments and plans of this age have inspired important modern spiritual leaders and church movements. Metropolitan Ruts'kyi served as a model of a Uniate hierarch with a broad vision of the relation between Eastern and Western churches for Andrei Sheptyts'kyi. Peter Mohyla provided an example for making Kiev the centre of a reformed, reinvigorated, virtually independent local Orthodox Church for Vasyl' Lypkivs'kyi. Indeed the modern religious leaders could even draw inspiration from religious figures who did not share their confessional adherence, but who had led the Ukrainian Church at a time it played a role of international importance.

The seven traditions outlined are but one manner of assessing the significance of the sixteenth and seventeenth centuries in modern Ukrainian religious culture. All are not of equal importance, and each is but a means to analyse the rich Ukrainian religious experience of the early modern period. Other 'traditions' can surely be added. However the components of the religious culture of the age are described, the picture will remain the same. Ukrainian religious culture went through major changes in the sixteenth and seventeenth centuries that have shaped the Ukrainian religious experience throughout the remainder of its first millennium and will continue to do so well into its second.

NOTES

1. The Russian original of *Puti russkogo bogosloviia* (Paris: 1937) has been translated into English, *The Ways of Russian Theology*, ed. Richard S. Haugh, part 1, *The Collected Works of Georges Florovsky*, V (Belmont, Mass.: 1979). See my discussion of Florovsky's views on the Ukrainian church in 'Recent Western Views on Seventeenth-Century Ukrainian Culture', in *Harvard Ukrainian Studies*, VIII, 1/2 (Cambridge, Mass.: June 1984) pp. 156–87.

2. The standard positive evaluation of this period is I. Vlasovs'kyi, *Narys istoriï Ukraïns'koï pravoslavnoï tserkvy*, 4 vols in 5 books (New York: 1955–66). The first two volumes, which cover the church's history until the end of the seventeenth century, have appeared in an abridged English translation, I. Wlasowsky, *Outline History of the Ukrainian Orthodox Church*, 2 vols) (New York-South Bound Brook, NJ: 1974–79).

3. The best general treatment of the cultural achievements of this period is M. Hrushevs'kyi, *Kul'turno-natsional'nyi rukh na Ukraïni XVI–XVII st.*, 2nd ed., n.p. (1919). For the literary production of the period, see *Ukraïns'ki pys'mennyky. Bio-bibliohrafichnyi slovnyk. I Davnia ukraïns'ka literatura (XI–XVII st.)*, comp. L. Makhnovets' (Kiev: 1960).

4. For interpretations of Ukrainian religious traditions, see D. Doroshenko, *Pravoslavna tserkva v mynulomu i suchasnomu zhytti ukraïns'koho narodu* (Berlin: 1940); N. Polons'ka-Vasylenko, *Istorychni pidvalyny UAPTs* (Rome: 1964); V. Lypyns'kyi, *Relihiia i tserkva v istorii Ukraïni* (Philadelphia: 1925); *Relihiia v zhytti ukraïns'koho narodu*, Zapysky Naukovoho Tovarystva im. Shevchenka, CLXXXI (Munich-Rome-Paris: 1966).

5. The most comprehensive work on the Roman Catholic church in the Polish-Lithuanian Commonwealth is *Kościół w Polsce*, ed. J. Kłóczowski, n.p. (1969), II. The most recent study on Protestants in the Ukraine in this period is G. Williams, 'Protestants in the Ukraine in the Period of the Polish-Lithuanian Commonwealth' (*Harvard Ukrainian Studies*, II, 1 (Cambridge, Mass.: March 1978) pp. 41–72; II, 2 (June 1978) pp. 184–210). Also see M. Hrushevs'kyi, *Z istoriï relihiinoï dumky na Ukraïni* (Lviv: 1925).

6. On the Union of Brest, see the standard work by E. Likowski, *Unia Brzeska (1596)* (Poznan: 1896), available in German and Ukrainian translations. Also see O. Halecki, *From Florence to Brest (1439–1596)*, for the period before the union. J. Macha, *Ecclesiastical Unification: A*

Theoretical Framework together with Case Studies from the History of Latin-Byzantine Relations, Orientalia Christiana Annalecta, cxcviii (Rome: 1974), is an excellent discussion of church life in the sixteenth and seventeenth centuries.

7.   Fortunately there is a bibliography for the large literature on Ukrainian church history of this period, I. Patrylo, *Dzherela i bibliohrafiia istoriia Ukraïns'koi tserkvy*, Analecta OSBM, series 2, section 1, xxxiii, and the addendum *Analecta OSBM*, x (Rome: 1979) pp. 405–87. In this article only a few general works are included in the notes, as well as items not included in Patrylo's bibliography, primarily because they are too recent. The basic works on Ukrainian church history are Vlasovs'kyi, *Narys*, A. Velykyi, *Z litopysu Khrystyians'koï Ukraïny*, vols 4–6 (Rome: 1971–73); M. Harasiewicz, *Annales Ecclesiae Ruthenae* (Lviv: 1862); H. Luzhnyts'kyi, *Ukraïns'ka tserkva mizh Skhodem i Zakhodem. Narys istoriï Ukraïns'koï tserkvy* (Philadelphia: 1954), and L. Bienkowski, 'Organizacja Kosciola Wschodniego w Polsce' in *Kościół w Polsce*, pp. 733–1050. Important works in East Slavic church history are A. Ammann, *Abriss der Ostslavischen Kirchengeschichte* (Vienna: 1950), A. Kartashev, *Ocherki po istorii Russkoi tserkvi*, 2 vols (Paris: 1959); and Makarii (Bulgakov), *Istoriia Russkoi tserkvi*, 12 vols (St Petersburg: 1864–86).

8.   J. Meyendorff, *Byzantium and the Rise of Russia: A Study of Byzantino-Russian Relations in the Fourteenth Century* (Cambridge: 1981) examines ecclesiastical affairs.

9.   K. Chodynicki, *Kościół Prawosławny a Rzeczypospolita Polska 1370–1632* (Warsaw: 1934) deals with church-state relations.

10. Thanks to S. Golubev, *Kievskii Mitropolit Petr Mogila i ego spodvizhniki (Opyt tserkovno-istoricheskogo issledovaniia)*, 2 vols (Kiev: 1883–98) this is one of the best studied periods in Ukrainian church history. See also the special issue of *Harvard Ukrainian Studies* on Mohyla and the Kiev Academy, viii, 1/2 (1984) in particular I. Ševčenko, 'The Many Worlds of Peter Mohyla'. On government policy, see J. Dzięgielewski, *Polityka wyznaniowa Władysława IV* (Warsaw: 1985).

11. For Orthodox church history in the late seventeenth century, see N. Carynnyk-Sinclair, *Die Unterstellung der Kiever Metropolie unter das Moskauer Patriarchat* (Munich: 1970).

12. Although Velykyi's, *Litopys*, is a publication of radio lectures, it is derived from extensive study and editing of sources in the Basilian *Analecta*. Until a more scholarly history of the Uniate Church is written, it remains the best comprehensive account.

13. On toleration in the Polish-Lithuanian Commonwealth, see J. Tazbir, *A State without Stakes: Polish Religious Tolerance in the Sixteenth and Seventeenth Centuries* (Warsaw: 1973).

14. On the convergence of cultural traditions, see E. Winter, *Byzanz und Rom im Kampfe um die Ukraine: 955–1939* (Leipzig: 1942).

15. This question has been little explored recently, and K. Kharlampovich, *Malorossiiskoe vliianie na velikorusskuiu tserkovnuiu zhizn'* (Kazan': 1914) remains the basic study in the field.

16. On the brotherhoods, see Ia. Isaievych, *Bratstva ta ïkh rol' v rozvytku ukraïns'koï kul'tury XVI–XVII st.* (Kiev: 1966).

17. For an argument that the role of the laity in this period was a complete innovation resisted by the clergy, see V. Zaikin, *Uchastie svetskogo elementa v tserkovnom upravlenii, vybornoe nachalo i sobornost' v Kievskoi mitropolii v XVI–XVII v.* (Warsaw: 1930).

18. On national consciousness in this period, see T. Chynczewska-Hennel, *Świadomość narodowa kozaczyzny i szlachty ukraińskiej w XVII wieku* (Warsaw: 1985).

19. For Smotryts'kyi's works as well as an introduction and bibliography by D. Frick, see *The Works of Meletij Smotryc'kyi*, Harvard Library of Early Ukrainian Literature: Texts ɪ (Cambridge, Mass.: 1987). On Kysil, see F. Sysyn, *Between Poland and the Ukraine: The Dilemma of Adam Kysil 1600–1653* (Cambridge, Mass.: 1985).

20. The relations of the Orthodox and Uniate churches and the political entities that controlled the Ukraine remain poorly studied. M. Chubatyi, 'Pro pravne stanovyshche terkvy v kozats'kyi derzhavi', in *Bohosloviia*, ɪɪɪ (Lviv: 1925) pp. 156–87 remains the only general study on the Hetmanate.

21. The issue of national style has been best studied in art and architecture. See P. Bilets'kyi, *Ukraïns'kyi portretnyi zhyvopys XVII–XVIII st.: Problemy stanovlennia i rozvytku* (Kiev: 1969).

22. For a discussion of Sofonovych's work as well as cultural processes in early modern Ukraine, see F. Sysyn, 'The Cultural, Social and Political Context of Ukrainian History-Writing in the Seventeenth Century', in G. Brogi Bercoff (ed.), *Dall'Opus Oratorium alla Ricerca Documentaria: La Storiografia polacca, ucraina e russa fra il XVI e il XVIII secolo*, Europa Orientalis, ᴠ (Rome: 1986) pp. 285–310.

23. Sysyn, *Between Poland and the Ukraine*, p. 61.

2 The Spirituality of the Vyg Fathers

Robert O. Crummey

The Old Believers—those Russian Orthodox Christians who rejected the liturgical reforms of Patriarch Nikon and the authority of the government which supported and enforced them—have constituted a significant and often undervalued current within Russian religious life since the mid-seventeenth century. Founded in 1694 in a remote corner of northern Russia, the Vyg community quickly became the acknowledged centre of the 'priestless' branch of the movement.[1] Even more significantly, under the leadership of the Denisov brothers, Andrei and Semen, Vyg took the lead in the creation of an entire cultural system for the scattered Old Believer population of the Russian empire. The Denisovs and other Vyg writers and artists produced polemical, devotional and liturgical texts which drew upon the traditions of the Christian East and pre-Nikonian Russian Orthodoxy, early seventeenth-century Ukrainian apocalyptic compilations, and a growing corpus of original Old Believer compositions, beginning with the works of the earliest opponents of the Nikonian reforms, Avvakum, Deacon Fedor and others.[2]

The goal of this essay is to present a close reading of some of the most important writings of the 'Vyg fathers' of the first half of the eighteenth century in order to identify the spiritual aspirations and devotional and moral practices that, in their view, should make up the central core of the life of the true Christian believer. In other words, the investigation centres on their 'spirituality'. Many writers who use this admittedly vague concept agree on its most important dimensions. The editor of a recent collection uses 'spirituality' to refer, not to theology as an intellectualised system of belief, but to the believer's communion with God through prayer and '... the outer life which supports and flows from this devotion'. In a similar vein, G. P. Fedotov describes spirituality as '... the religious life in its innermost and deepest strata, the life with God and all spiritual experiences arising from this source. Prayer is the centre ... of spirituality.'[3]

The texts which form the foundation of this discussion include the

Pomorskie otvety, Semen Denisov's *Vinograd rossiiskii* and 'Istoriia o ottsekh i stradal'tsekh Solovetskikh', Ivan Filippov's history of the Vyg community, the vita of Elder Kornilii, a selection of the monastic 'rules' governing the life of its central monastery and convent and the outlying settlements and work camps, and some of the Denisov brothers' sermons and panegyrics, including those quoted or summarised in the articles of E. V. Barsov and P. S. Smirnov.[4] With the partial exception of the *Pomorskie otvety* which Andrei Denisov and his collaborators composed as a polemical response to spokesmen of the official Orthodox church, all of these texts served primarily to inspire the pious reflections of the faithful.[5] The historical compositions, like the historical books of the Old Testament, served, not to reconstruct events, but to reveal God's relationship with his people, the community of faith. Moreover, all were couched in an exalted diction with elaborate rhetorical devices and complex rhythmic patterns in order to inspire their readers and hearers and impress them with the seriousness of their messages.[6] The following discussion centres on the messages themselves and the probable intentions of the authors rather than the ways in which the texts were received and understood.

Before searching the writings of the Vyg fathers for comments on the spiritual life, we should examine the historical and polemical framework which they created to give meaning to the daily life and worship of the community. Russia alone, they argued, preserved the pure Orthodox Christian faith when other branches of Christendom fell into apostasy. Patriarch Nikon's reform of the Russian liturgy destroyed true faith in the last remaining Christian community, precipitated the Apocalypse, and forced the remnant of true Christians to take extreme measures to preserve the faith until the end of time. Some gave themselves up to torture and execution like the first Christian martyrs before them. Others fled to the wilderness to create havens of true faith. When confronted by the authority of the imperial Russian state—the Antichrist—the monks of the Solovetskii Monastery fought back to the death, while the advocates of self-immolation took their own lives in purifying fire rather than submit to its power.[7]

This simple historical scheme, central to the mythology of all Old Believers, revolves around a number of binary polarities. The struggle of Nikon and his followers against the defenders of the authentic Orthodox tradition and the contrast between the ancient Christian tradition (*drevletserkovnoe blagochestie*) and the newfangled liturgy and faith of the Nikonians are obvious examples.

Some of these polar opposites receive particularly elaborate treatment in the writings of the Vyg fathers and played a central part in shaping their understanding of the world and their place in it. One is the contrast between the 'world' with its temptations to sin and apostasy and the way of the *'pustyn''* (desert, hermitage). As norms to be emulated, the Denisovs repeatedly invoked the men and women of the early church who preserved the true faith by flight from the world.[8] Moreover, they were fond of recalling the image of the woman fleeing to the desert in Revelation 12:13–17 as a metaphor of their own situation.[9]

It is not difficult to understand the appeal of these images. In polemical terms, the example of the saints in the desert allowed Andrei Denisov to argue that his followers were true to the Eastern Christian tradition even though they lacked many of the external signs of a corporate religious life, a clergy, a hierarchy and most of the sacraments.[10] Moreover, the woman in flight and the desert fathers and mothers of Christianity, the exemplars of the life in the 'desert', provided an alternative ideal to the Orthodoxy of bishops, parishes and monastic communities built on the principles of this world, which Nikon had so easily and fatally corrupted.

Invoking the precedent of the desert fathers and mothers was no comforting exercise in self-congratulation. Believers in the desert, Andrei Denisov conceded, are still prey to temptation and God is more angry with their sins than those of the faithful who live in the world.[11]

A second polarity lies in a military metaphor, that of the soldiers of Christ in combat against the forces of the Antichrist. Semen Denisov's recently-discovered tale of the Tara revolt of 1722 describes how the defenders of the true faith confronted the troops of the Emperor, first with spiritual weapons, then with physical resistance which led, in the end, to the deaths of some of them by their own hand. In this, they followed the examples of the most militant defenders of the purity of Israel in the Old Testament and Apocrypha, such as Phinehas in Numbers 25:7–13 and the Maccabees. Denisov saluted the rebels with an extraordinary mixture of epithets—'. . . fiery enthusiasts for righteousness, fighters for Orthodoxy, brave warriors of Christ, true passion-sufferers, holy martyrs . . .'. Men who died in armed combat against the Antichrist were martyrs no less than those who suffered torture and execution.[12]

If a single image dominates the narrative texts of Vyg, it is that of martyrdom. The Old Believer communities derived their legitimacy from the early Christian martyrs and from their recent successors, the first victims of the struggle to defend the old faith whose memory they lovingly cherished. These men and women memorably displayed the qualities which all Christians should ideally possess—the ability to distinguish true faith from falsehood and the courage to denounce evil and, if need be, to die the most agonizing of deaths in witness to that faith.[13] So profound was the reverence for the martyrs of the past that moderate Old Believer leaders such as the Vyg fathers had to struggle to restrain some of their followers whose yearning for martyrdom led them to actions which threatened the continued existence of the entire community.[14]

As the examples of the heroes and heroines of the *Vinograd rossiiskii* illustrate, the image and rhetoric of martyrdom contain within them yet another contrast of opposites. Consistent with the language of Christian hagiography, Vyg writings repeatedly describe the martyrs for the true faith as victims, nobly accepting a fate they have not chosen. Yet, at the same time, the texts emphasise the activism of the defenders of the faith. In the histories and martyrologies of Vyg, the Old Believers take energetic measures to proselytise and defend their cause—teaching, preaching, writing and organising. Even the victims of torture and execution fought back by attempting to escape and, when there was no way out, using their interrogations and executions as a pulpit to preach resistance to the new order. In this respect, they were not so very different from those who took up arms in defence of the faith such as the Solovetskii and Tara rebels or the peasants who seized control of the Paleostrovskii Monastery.[15] In the view of the Vyg fathers, the Old Believers took the initiative in the struggle for the soul of Russia. That the reality was often the reverse—that, as I have argued elsewhere, the Russian state often acted first and the Old Believers reacted to its initiatives—does not negate the power of the myth.

Militant activism, spiritual and physical warfare, the ideals of martyrdom—these, then, are some of the central themes of the Vyg texts. Reflecting on them helps us to understand the militancy, apparent fanaticism and remarkable practical resilience of later generations of Old Believers, whose world view they helped to shape.

Within this framework, the Vyg fathers set forth their ideals of Christian spirituality. By and large, their teachings reflected the aspirations of the Eastern Orthodox tradition as a whole. Indeed, many of their admonitions to a life of prayer, self-discipline and good works would be suitable advice to Christians of any time or denomination.[16] More concretely, they drew upon many earlier Russian teachings on ecclesiastical structure and devotional practice. In their compositions, for example, one hears echoes of Nil Sorskii and Joseph of Volokolamsk and their disciples. Although the two 'schools' of Muscovite monasticism had more in common than some scholars and popular writers have recognised, their founders' writings on the spiritual life emphasise quite different things. Nil's 'rule' and pastoral letters stress the cultivation of individual spirituality within a communal setting, whereas Joseph's concern centred on the spiritual well-being of the individual through participation in an orderly Christian community. As we shall see, the Vyg fathers inclined toward the latter position. They commended the practice of the 'Jesus prayer', a pillar of Nil's devotional teachings, but did so within a vision of the spiritual life centred on the community rather than the individual believer.[17]

For priestless Old Believers, like other Eastern Orthodox Christians, the life of the believer centred around rigorous observance of the liturgy. After the Nikonian reforms, Christian commitment meant, above all, preserving the authentic, pre-Nikonian traditions at all costs. As Semen Denisov put it in his hymn of praise to the defenders of the Solovetskii Monastery: 'Holiness is . . . the guarding of uncorrupted and full faith . . . These blessed ones observed the fullness of the faith, uncorrupted piety, unharmed Orthodoxy to the end.'[18] In this context, the concepts 'faith' and 'liturgy' are virtually interchangeable.

For the priestless branch of Old Belief, however, preserving the true faith was easier said than done; for the painful admission that there were no validly consecrated Orthodox priests left in the world and no possibility of consecrating new ones left the *bezpopovtsy* with only those parts of the traditional liturgical system that could be celebrated by the laity. Perhaps the Denisovs' greatest contribution to Old Belief was their creative adaptation of the Orthodox liturgy to the constricting presuppositions within which they worked. Reasoning that the destruction of true Orthodox Christianity within the official church of Russia and the advent of the Antichrist constituted the direst emergency imaginable, they retained the sacrament of baptism and confession by making use of the canons which allowed a layperson to perform these rites *in extremis* when no priest was available.[19] In spite of their ingenuity, however, the Vyg fathers lived with the painful awareness that the central core of Christian liturgy, the Eucharist, was closed to them.

Having preserved as much of the pre-Nikonian liturgy as their circumstances permitted, the leaders of Vyg saw it as the mainstay of an orderly and strictly moral way of life and of a Godly community. The corporate worship of Vyg was complex and time-consuming. The normal cycle of services consisted of morning prayer, hours, evening prayer, compline and *molebny*. All-night vigils and other special services marked the great feasts of the church year.[20] Moreover, the leaders of the community continually admonished their followers to celebrate the liturgy correctly in an orderly and dignified manner 'according to the canons'.[21] In the tradition of earlier reformers within the Russian church, they took severe measures to guard against frivolity, disrespect and carelessness during the community's frequent and lengthy services.[22]

The admonitions of the leaders of Vyg in times of crisis underline the centrality of corporate worship and prayer in the spiritual life of the community. For example, Semen Denisov described the defenders' response at a critical moment in the government's seige of the Solovetskii Monastery—to celebrate the liturgy correctly and with tears.[23] Similarly, in Vyg's own history, in the face of a bad harvest, the arrest of a member, or a confrontation with the government or the official church, its leaders called the residents together for special prayers.[24]

As among other Eastern Orthodox, private prayer, above all the 'Jesus prayer', occupied an important place in the Christian life.[25] In Semen Denisov's account, some of the captured Solovetskii monks suffered martyrdom with the Jesus prayer on their lips.[26]

Beyond this, Vyg texts give us little sense of the content of private devotions. In one striking exception, the vita of Kornilii gives a detailed account of his spiritual exercises while living as a hermit. At the appropriate hours of the day, Kornilii chanted particular psalms, sang hymns and performed a fitting number of deep bows (*poklony*).[27] In other words, the passage describes private liturgical observances rather than spontaneous prayer or mediation. The rule of the Vyg community seems, in places, to suggest that private devotions, such as Kornilii's, were a less desirable substitute for corporate prayer. Rules for nuns who were at work away from the Leksa convent included the admonition that they pray together, not each by herself ('... *tako zhe da moliatsia vkupe, a ne sami sebe kozhdo*'). Only if a sister could not join the others for worship was she to follow a stipulated regimen of prayers and bows alone.[28]

As their writings repeatedly emphasised, the Vyg fathers believed strongly in the efficacy of prayer.[29] Again and again, when describing the founders of the community or the early martyrs for the Old Faith, the Vyg fathers used epithets such as '*velii molitvennik*' ('great in prayer').[30] Moreover, they urged their followers to maintain a prayerful attitude. One stipulation of the rule, for example, urges nuns to remain continually in prayer at meals, just as in church ('. . .*i iako v tserkvi tako sestry iadushchii prisno molitvu vo ume da derzhat*').[31]

The Vyg fathers' writings and sermons, however, rarely explore the nature and process of prayer or instruct their disciples how to pray. Andrei Denisov's homilies on prayer are elaborate rhetorical compositions, in which, through cascades of images and numerous examples from Scripture and the Fathers he exhorts his hearers. They remind his followers of the efficacy of prayer, enumerate its rewards, and warn of the dangers of neglecting to pray. While their dignified verbal music may have inspired their hearers to more intense efforts, these sermons gave them few suggestions how to pray and for what. Indeed, it is unclear whether Denisov referred to corporate or private prayer or both.[32] The rest of the writings of the Vyg fathers and the actions of the community in moments of crisis strongly suggest that he spoke of communal worship and assumed that the liturgy itself would instruct his followers in the art of prayer.

The Vyg fathers also encouraged their followers to read the Scriptures and other sacred texts. In his eulogy to his cousin, Petr Prokopiev, Andrei Denisov mentioned among his virtues the reading, copying and cataloguing of sacred writings.[33] The rule of the community enjoined literate brothers and sisters to read edifying books in times of quiet.[34] To make best use of time and to instruct illiterate brothers and sisters, the rules of the community often prescribed the reading aloud of edifying texts.[35] Which texts were read is not easy to specify. Clearly the Psalter was a favourite.[36] As scholars have long been aware, the leaders of Vyg collected a remarkably comprehensive library which they used in composing their polemical and devotional works.[37] How many of these books and manuscripts they felt suitable to be read aloud is difficult to determine: it may well be that their own devotional writings were intended, among other purposes, for oral performance. The elaborate rhetorical constructions of their major narrative and polemical works resemble the style of their sermons which evidently played a central part in the public life and worship of the community.

Consonant with the Eastern Orthodox tradition, the Vyg fathers placed heavy emphasis on the necessity of disciplining bodily urges through rigorous fasting and other forms of self-denial. Their writings frequently describe the martyrs of the faith as great 'fasters' and recommended especially rigorous fasting as an appropriate response to crises which threatened the life of the community.[38] By way of contrast, Semen Denisov listed eating apart (*'osoboiadenie'*), indulging in pastry (*'pirogoshchenie'*), drunkenness and smoking (*'tabako-pitie'*) among the vices devoutly to be avoided.[39] In praising fasting, the Vyg fathers, by implication, admonished their followers to follow rigorously the normal Eastern Orthodox rules on diet. Exceptionally severe dietary practices such as those observed earlier by the followers of Elder Kapiton elicited their admiration, but not their support. In praising the precursors of Vyg, for example, Semen Denisov admiringly described Evfimii's extraordinarily severe ascetic regimen including the refusal to eat meat, fish and dairy products at any time in the church calendar.[40] He did not recommend such extremes to his own flock.

Among their lists of Christian virtues, *'tselomudrie'* (chastity) and purity also figure prominently.[41] The need to discipline the flesh, recognised in various guises in all branches of orthodox Christendom, intersected with canonical problems. In the understanding of the Vyg fathers, most sacraments could no longer be celebrated since no validly consecrated priests existed. That meant that pious men and women could no longer enter into holy matrimony. In practice, then, chastity meant celibacy (*'devstvo'*), a condition of life which the Denisovs often praised as the ideal for all of their followers.[42] The celibate life attracted the Vyg fathers not only as a solution to immediate problems of canon law but also—and probably more profoundly—because they aspired to create a holy community which would carry on the traditions of Eastern Orthodox monasticism. Understandably some of their followers found such counsels of perfection beyond their strength—as the Denisovs' polemical opponents within Old Belief pointed out in shocked tones. As far as we know, the leaders of the community and the brothers and sisters of the central monastery and convent practised what they preached. Their attitudes are reflected in an intensely personal way in the confession of Ivan Filippov, one of the Denisovs' immediate successors as head of the community. In preparing for death, Filippov lamented among his many sins the fact that he had been married and had children before his conversion to the Old Faith. The violent language of his self-condemnation implicitly likens married life to the most sinful and disgusting of sexual practices.[43] Celibacy alone was appropriate for the true follower of Christ.

Finally, like earlier monastic writers, the Vyg fathers praised hard physical labour and sweat as signs of a pious Christian life.[44] While their emphasis on the virtue of hard work has tempted some scholars to see the Old Believers as Russian Calvinists,[45] this theme in their teaching grows from a very different root, not a doctrine of 'election', but from the ancient Christian ideal of disciplining the appetites and passions reinforced by the practical necessity of building and supporting a community of believers in a remote and hostile environment.

As though the day-to-day demands of the true Orthodox faith were not enough, each Old Believer faced the Last Judgement in an intensely personal way. Every year, before Lent, the leaders of Vyg read Andrei Denisov's sermon reminding their hearers that God would judge them for any failure to live up to the rigorous ideals of their community.[46] Even the most austere life of prayer and self-discipline, however, gave no guarantee of eternal salvation. The deathbed confessions of Ivan Filippov, Petr Prokopiev, Semen Denisov and Petr Onufriev, a resident of one of the outlying settlements of Vyg, betray a profound anxiety that all of their prayers, fasting and hard work may not have atoned sufficiently for their many grievous sins. Each felt the need to list his sins once more and ask forgiveness from his fellow believers.[47]

The narrative and prescriptive writings of the Vyg fathers give considerable attention to the role of women in the defence of the Old Faith. But did these male authors have a vision of a distinctive female spirituality? By and large, I would argue, they did not. Semen Denisov's sermon at the grave of his sister, Solomoniia, abbess of the Leksa convent, used traditional female epithets to praise her character—'mother of orphans, joy of widows, refuge of the homeless, sweet consolation of the sorrowing . . .'. Turning to her practical activity, however, he lauded her for virtues that would equally become men such as manly courage (*muzhestvo*), generosity, administrative tact, hard work and rigor in her religious observances.[48] Likewise, his praise of the female martyrs to the Old Faith contrasted their frail female bodies, subjected to unspeakable tortures, with their bravery (again muzhestvo) and militancy in confronting their interrogators and steadfastly facing a cruel death.[49] Whether the women themselves saw the world and the realm of the spirit in different concepts and images we cannot tell.

Having said this, it is only just to give the Vyg fathers credit for recognising that 'Not only men, but the weaker part, women and girls, [defended] the ancestral faith most courageously and bore the cruellest of tortures'.[50] Moreover, women such as Morozova, Urusova and, later, Solomoniia Denisova played a much more significant symbolic and practical part in the development of Old Belief than women within official Orthodoxy with its hierarchical, male-dominated authority structure. Indeed, the prominent role of women in unofficial movements of religious protest and renewal in Russia is only now receiving the scholarly attention it warrants.[51]

There is, of course, much that the Vyg texts do not tell us about the spiritual life of the community's peasant followers. Ethnographic studies have repeatedly shown that the belief system of the faithful—both Old Believers and adherents of the official church—consisted not only of observance of the liturgical practices and moral strictures of the Orthodox tradition, often with local variations, but also of a complex tapestry of folk beliefs, taboos, charms, incantations and rituals.[52]

Apart from their understandable silence on such matters, the writings of the Vyg fathers are remarkable for their failure to probe the implications of the spiritual life or develop a distinct Old Believer spirituality. The latter is perhaps not surprising since the Old Believers regarded themselves as the last true defenders of the Eastern Orthodox tradition, a role which required fidelity and vigilance, not originality. Moreover, the apparent lack of interest in the spiritual life of the individual may also reflect the attitudes and concerns of all of Russian Orthodoxy in the seventeenth and early eighteenth centuries. Jesuit curricula and 'Jesuit' architecture entered Muscovite Russia from the Ukraine; the intense self-examination and dramatic spirituality of the early Jesuits did not.[53]

Nevertheless, it is striking how rarely the Vyg texts mention devotional practices except in stock phrases or in passing. The 'rule' of the community is particularly interesting in this regard. The precise and laconic stipulations of the documents governing its day-to-day life stress the structure of the monastery and convent and the surrounding lay communities and describe the relations among them. Drawing up the 'rule' was no mean accomplishment, for, in so doing, the Vyg fathers combined traditional structures and practices of Eastern Orthodox monasticism into a unique mix, in effect creating a monastic community of a new type.[54] At the same time, the 'rule' gave little explicit attention to cultivation of the members' spiritual lives. Instead, in devotional matters, the Vyg fathers took a decidedly practical tack, issuing detailed instructions on proper behaviour during public worship and in private devotions and setting out the punishments for breaches of liturgical propriety.[55] In an equally matter-of-fact vein, many of its provisions dealt with such down-to-earth problems as how to preserve chastity by keeping the 'fire' away from the 'straw' at all times or how to keep the members of the community's work parties in a properly pious frame of mind while away from home.[56]

The strengths and limitations of the rule and of Vyg spirituality stem primarily from its leaders' primary goal—building a holy community to preserve uncorrupted Orthodoxy. The Vyg fathers put on the mantle of the saints of the desert (*pustyn'*), a claim reflected in the name which they often gave their community (the *Vygovskaia pustyn'*). The mantle fitted imperfectly, however. Like their supposed precursors, the residents of Vyg lived in a remote and inhospitable place on the fringes of organised society. Like them, they frequently suffered persecution for defending the true faith. Yet the central image of the saints of the desert is an individual one—that of a hermit choosing a life of exceptional austerity in order better to contemplate and serve God. The spiritual life of Vyg was communal, expressed above all in the liturgy. In their writings, the Vyg fathers readily praised individuals of exemplary piety, yet their most insistent message emphasised loyalty to the true Orthodox tradition and to the community, which, in defending it, worked and prayed together.[57]

NOTES

1. For the history of the Vyg community, see Robert O. Crummey, *The Old Believers and the World of Antichrist: The Vyg Community and the Russian State, 1694–1855* (Madison: 1970) and P. G. Liubomirov, *Vygovskoe obshchezhitel'stvo* (Moscow and Saratov: 1924).
2. N. N. Pokrovskii, 'Arkheograficheskie ekspeditsii i problemy izucheniia narodnogo soznaniia', *Arkheograficheskii ezhegodnik za 1968 god* (Moscow: 1987) pp. 159–63; I. V. Pozdeeva, 'Drevnerusskoe nasledie v istorii traditsionnoi knizhnoi kul'tury staroobriadchestva (pervyi period)', *Istoriia SSSR* (1988) no. 1, pp. 84–99.

3.   *The Study of Spirituality*, ed. Cheslyn Jones, Geoffrey Wainwright and Edward Yarnold SJ (London: 1986) p. xxii and G. P. Fedotov, *A Treasury of Russian Spirituality* (London: 1950) p. 1. See also Fedotov's *The Russian Religious Mind. I, Kievan Christianity. The Tenth to the Thirteenth Centuries* (Cambridge, Mass.: 1946), his *The Russian Religious Mind. II, The Middle Ages. The Thirteenth to the Fifteenth Century* (Cambridge, Mass.: 1966) and *Christian Spirituality: High Middle Ages and Reformation*, ed. Jill Riatt (New York: 1987).

4.   A. Denisov, *Pomorskie otvety* (Moscow: 1906); S. Denisov, *Vinograd rossiiskii ili opisanie postradavshikh v Rossii za drevletserkovnoe blagochestie* (Moscow: 1906); ibid., 'Istoriia o ottsekh i stradal'tsekh Solovetskikh', in G. V. Esipov, *Raskol'nich'i dela XVIII st.*, 2 vols (St Petersburg: 1861–63) 2, pp. 5–55; I. Filippov, *Istoriia Vygovskoi pustyni* (St Petersburg: 1862); D. N. Breshchinskii (ed.), 'Zhitie Korniliia Vygovskogo Pakhomievskoi redaktsii (Teksty)', *Drevnerusskaia knizhnost'. Po materialam Pushkinskogo Doma* (Leningrad: 1985) pp. 62–107; A. Denisov, 'Povest' ritoricheskaia o srete v Moskve slona persidskago', *Russkaia starina* 29 (1880) pp. 170–2; ibid., 'Slovo nadgrobnoe ottsu Petru Prokopievichu', *Russkaia starina* 26 (1879) pp. 523–37; E. V. Barsov, 'Andrei Denisov Vtorushin kak Vygoretskii propovednik', *Trudy Kievskoi Dukhovnoi Akademii* (1867) no. 2, pp. 243–62; no. 4, pp. 81–95; ibid., 'Semen Denisov Vtorushin, predvoditel' russkago raskola XVIII veka', *Trudy Kievskoi Dukhovnoi Akademii* (1866) no. 2, pp. 174–230; no. 6, pp. 168–230; no. 7, pp. 284–304; no. 12, pp. 570–88; P. S. Smirnov, 'Vygovskaia bezpopovshchinskaia pustyn' v pervoe vremia eia sushchestvovaniia', *Khristianskoe Chtenie* (1910) nos 5–6, pp. 638–74; nos 7–8, 910–34; V. I. Malyshev (ed.), 'The Confession of Ivan Filippov, 1744', *Oxford Slavonic Papers* 11 (1964) pp. 17–27; E. V. Barsov, 'Ulozhenie brat'ev Denisovykh', *Pamiatnaia knizhka Olonetskoi Gubernii za 1868 i 1869 gg.* II, pp. 85–116 and various unpublished rules ('*ustavy*') of the Vyg monastery, the Leska convent and the surrounding *skiti*.

5.   On the *Pomorskie otvety*, see P. J. Chrysostomus, *Die 'Pomorskie otvety' als Denkmal des russischen Altgläubigen gegen Ende des 1 Viertels des XVIII Jahrh. Orientalia Christiana Analecta*, vol. 148 (Rome: 1957).

6.   For an analysis of the style of the 'Vyg fathers', see N. V. Ponyrko, *Vygovskaia literaturnaia shkola v pervoi polovine XVIII stoletiia* (Leningrad: 1979), the synopsis of her candidate's dissertation. On the rhetorical tradition of the Vyg community, see her 'Uchebniki ritoriki na Vygu', *Trudy Otdela drevnerusskoi literatury* 36 (1981) pp. 154–62. As a passage from an original Vyg treatise, quoted extensively by Ponyrko (p. 162), makes clear, effective oral performance was one of the main objectives of the art of rhetoric as practised by its leaders.

7.   For examples, see *Pomorskie otvety*, pp. 2–3; Filippov, *Istoriia*, pp. 2–27, 76–95; A. I. Mal'tsev, 'Neizvestnoe sochinenie S. Denisova o tarskom "bunte" 1722 g.', *Istochniki po kul'ture i klassovoi bor'be feodal'nogo perioda* (Novosibirsk: 1982) pp. 224–41.

8.   For example, Barsov, 'Andrei Denisov', pp. 257–61; *Pomorskie otvety*, pp. 5–6.

9. Barsov, 'Andrei Denisov', pp. 87–91; ibid., 'Semen Denisov', p. 178.
10. *Pomorskie otvety*, pp. 5–6.
11. Smirnov, 'Vygovskaia bezpopovshchinskaia pustyn'', p. 643; Barsov, 'Andrei Denisov', pp. 90–1.
12. Mal'tsev, 'Neizvestnoe sochinenie', especially p. 238.
13. There are many examples in the *Vinograd rossiiskii*. A number of the short poems which conclude chapters in the work are built on the rhetoric of martyrdom. For a thorough textological analysis of the *Vinograd rossiiskii*, see E. M. Iukhimenko, '"Vinograd rossiiskii" Semena Denisova (tekstologicheskii analiz)', *Drevnerusskaia literatura. Istochnikovedenie. Sbornik nauchnykh trudov* (Leningrad: 1984) pp. 249–66. See also J. Sullivan and C. L. Drage, 'Poems in an Unpublished Manuscript of the *Vinograd rossiiskii*', *Oxford Slavonic Papers* 1 (1968) pp. 27–48.
    It should be noted that the stories of martyrdom contain little sentimentality; instead, they emphasise the steadfastness and courage of the victims.
14. See, for example, the story of Elder Markel in Filippov, *Istoriia*, pp. 330–5.
15. These themes occur repeatedly in the 'Istoriia o ottsekh i stradal'tsekh solovetskikh', the *Vinograd rossiiskii*, Filippov's history and the tale of the Tara revolt. The conviction that death in battle for the true faith is equivalent to martyrdom also forms an integral part of Islamic teaching on *jihad*.
16. For example, 'Istoriia o ottsekh i stradal'tsekh solovetskikh', pp. 40–1; Smirnov, 'Vygovskaia bezpopovshchinskaia pustyn'', pp. 922, 928, 930.
17. Nil Sorskii, *Predanie i Ustav* (ed. M. S. Borovkova-Maikova). *Pamiatniki drevnei pis'mennosti i iskusstva*, vol. 179 (St Petersburg: 1912). For an English translation, see G. P. Fedotov (ed.), *A Treasury of Russian Spirituality* (New York: 1965) pp. 90–133. Fairy von Lilienfeld published a German translation of these texts and Nil's pastoral letters in *Nil Sorskij und seine Schriften* (Berlin: 1963) pp. 195–283.
    Poslaniia Iosifa Volotskogo, ed. A. A. Zimin and Ia. S. Lur'e (Moscow-Leningrad: 1959). For the text of Joseph's 'rule', see pp. 298–319.
18. 'Istoriia o ottsekh i stradal'tsekh solovetskikh', p. 40.
19. Barsov, 'Semen Denisov', p. 175; P. S. Smirnov, *Vnutrennye voprosy v raskole v XVII veke* (St Petersburg: 1898), pp. 154–69.
20. Barsov, 'Semen Denisov', p. 173.
    An obvious point is worth emphasising. The spirituality of Vyg ultimately centred on the liturgy and was expressed primarily through participation in it. Further investigation should turn to the liturgical practices of the *bezpopovtsy* and examine the ways in which the Vyg fathers and other early Old Believers adapted and reinterpreted the system of worship of ecumenical Eastern Orthodoxy.
21. For example, A. Denisov, 'Slovo nadgrobnoe', p. 528.
22. Filippov, *Istoriia*, p. 142; Barsov, 'Andrei Denisov', pp. 90–1; ibid., 'Semen Denisov', pp. 174–6.
23. 'Istoriia o ottsekh i stradal'tsekh solovetskikh', p. 26.

24. Barsov, 'Semen Denisov', p. 181; Smirnov, 'Vygovskaia bezpopov-shchinskaia pustyn'', pp. 656, 916.

25. Barsov, 'Semen Denisov', p. 175.

26. 'Istoriia o ottsekh i stradal'tsekh solovetskikh', p. 30.

27. Breshchinskii, 'Zhitie', pp. 99–101.

28. Leningrad, Biblioteka Akademii Nauk SSSR, Rukopisnyi Otdel (hereafter BAN), Sobranie Druzhinina, no. 8, folios 220–20v.

29. For example, Smirnov, 'Vygovskaia bezpopovshchinskaia pustyn'', p. 916.

30. 'Slovo nadgrobnoe', p. 529; 'Istoriia o ottsekh i stradal'tsekh solovetskikh', p. 38; Filippov, *Istoriia*, p. 89.

31. BAN, Sobranie Druzhinina, no. 8, folio 221. Cf. *Poslaniia Iosifa Volotskogo*, p. 305.

32. BAN, Sobranie Druzhinina, no. 501, folios 10v–28; no. 122, folios 364v–375.

33. 'Slovo nadgrobnoe', pp. 528–9.

34. Leningrad, Institut Russkoi Literatury, Akademiia Nauk SSSR (Push-kinskii Dom), Rukopisnyi Otdel, Sobranie Zavoloko, no. 3, folios 109, 111, 113v. Cf. *Poslaniia Iosifa Volotskogo*, p. 310.

35. Filippov, *Istoriia*, p. 142; BAN, Sobranie Druzhinina, no. 8, folios 75v–7; Barsov, 'Semen Denisov', pp. 175–7.

36. Ibid., p. 175; Breshchinskii, 'Zhitie'.

37. See E. V. Barsov, *Opisanie rukopisei i knig, khraniashchikhsia v Vygoleksinskoi biblioteke* (St Petersburg: 1874) and I. V. Pozdeeva, 'Drevnerusskoe nasledie', *Istoriia SSSR* (1988) no. 1, pp. 84–99.

38. 'Slovo nadgrobnoe', p. 529; Smirnov, 'Vygovskaia bezpopovshchins-kaia pustyn'', p. 656.

39. 'Istoriia o ottsekh i stradal'tsekh solovetskikh', p. 38.

40. Ibid., pp. 49–50.

41. Ibid., p. 38; Filippov, *Istoriia*, p. 91.

42. Smirnov, 'Vygovskaia bezpopovshchinskaia pustyn'', pp. 646–50.

43. Malyshev, 'Confession', p. 22.

44. For example, 'Slovo nadgrobnoe', pp. 532–3.

45. James Billington, *The Icon and the Axe: An Interpretative Study of Russian Culture* (New York: 1966) p. 193.

46. Barsov, 'Andrei Denisov', pp. 82–4.

47. Malyshev, 'Confession'; BAN, Sobranie Druzhinina, no. 8, folios 205–15, 217v–18; Barsov, 'Semen Denisov', p. 584n. Even though these texts are couched in predictable verbal formulas, they seem to convey the genuine convictions and emotions of the dying, or, at the very least, to reflect the sentiments which the leaders of the community felt to be appropriate to the occasion. The Old Believer's intense sense of their own sinfulness and their uneasiness in the face of death is remarkably similar to the attitude of the New England Puritans discussed by David E. Stannard, *The Puritan Way of Death* (New York: 1977) pp. 72–95.

48. Barsov, 'Semen', p. 579–81.

49. *Vinograd rossiiskii*, pp. 47–8v, 74–6.

50. Ibid., p. 74.

51. Brenda Meehan-Waters' work on unofficial women's religious communities within official Orthodoxy is an important contribution to the study of these broad and complex issues. See, for example, her 'Popular Piety, Local Initiative, and the Founding of Women's Religious Communities in Russia, 1764–1907'. Kennan Institute for Advanced Russian studies. Occasional Paper, no. 215.

52. There is a growing literature on this subject. For two examples, see N. N. Pokrovskii, 'Ispoved' altaiskogo krest'ianina', *Pamiatniki kul'tury. Novye otkrytiia. 1978* (Leningrad: 1979) pp. 49–57 and Juha Pentikainen, *Oral Repertoire and World View: An Anthropological Study of Marina Takalo's Life History*. FF Communications, xciii (Helsinki: 1978) no. 219. Neither of the central individuals in these studies was a rigorously consistent adherent of Old Belief. See also I. V. Pozdeeva, 'Vereshchaginskoe territorial'noe knizhnoe sobranie i problemy istorii dukhovnoi kul'tury russkogo naseleniia verkhov'ev Kamy', *Russkie pis'mennye i ustnye traditsii i dukhovnaia kul'tura (Po materialam arkheograficheskikh ekspeditsii MGU 1966–1980 gg.)* (Moscow: 1982) pp. 40–71, here pp. 67–68.

53. On seventeenth-century Russian Orthodox spirituality, see G. P. Fedotov, *Sviatye drevnei Rusi* (Paris: 1931) pp. 201–4, his *Treasury*, pp. 134–6 and Georges Florovsky, *Ways of Russian Theology*, part ı (Belmont, Mass.: 1979) pp. 86–113. Both authors present a bleak picture of the intellectual and spiritual condition of Russian Orthodoxy in the period. Florovsky, however, expresses admiration for the learning and devotion of the Vyg fathers. Interestingly enough, he characterises Old Belief as a religion centred on works rather than faith (p. 101).

54. L. K. Kuandykov, 'Razvitie obshchezhitel'nogo ustava v Vygovskoi staroobriadcheskoi obshchine v pervoi treti XVIII v.', *Issledovaniia po istorii obshchestvennogo soznaniia epokhi feodalizma v Rossii* (Novosibirsk: 1984) pp. 51–63.

55. Barsov, 'Semen Denisov', pp. 174–6.

56. BAN, Sobranie Druzhinina, no. 8, folio 74–8. Semen Denisov's eulogy to Petr Onufriev praises his strict observance of the rules on prayer and fasting even while he was away from Vyg on work assignments (Barsov, 'Semen Denisov', pp. 584–5).

57. Serge Zenkovsky makes a similar point in 'The Ideological World of the Denisov Brothers', *Harvard Slavic Studies* 3 (1957) pp. 48–66. His pioneering essay, in my view, suffers from his ingenious, but ultimately misleading attempt to see in the Vyg fathers precursors of the Slavophiles. While both groups of writers emphasised the centrality in Orthodoxy of a holy community, they proceeded from radically different philosophical assumptions and drew very different conclusions from their reflections.

3 The Authority of Holiness: Women Ascetics and Spiritual Elders in Nineteenth-century Russia

Brenda Meehan-Waters

Although much has been written about the role of the *starets* (spiritual elder) in nineteenth-century Russian Orthodoxy, and Dostoevsky has made Father Zossima known to us all, the *staritsa* has remained a shrouded figure. Indeed, the existence and significance of holy women in general in pre-revolutionary Russia is seldom remarked upon in our scholarly literature. And yet popular religious and edificatory journals and hagiographic collections of the nineteenth and early twentieth century frequently noted the exemplary importance of such women. The fourteen volume *Zhizneopisaniia otechestvennykh podvizhnikov blagochestiia 18 i 19 vekov*, for example, although using the masculine *podvizhnikov* in its title, in fact included a significant number of women, with 17 per cent (104/609) of the ascetics and spiritual models included in the collection being women.[1] They are often vividly and succinctly known by the virtues and deeds they practised, such as 'Vera the Silent', 'Servant of God Tatiana', 'The Church Builder Paraskeva', 'The Ustiug Holy Fool Pelagiia Andreevna Berezina', 'The Sufferer Katen'ka Lezhanka', 'Blessed Mariia, the Belogorskaia cave digger', 'The pious staritsa Paraskeva Alekseevna Mukhanova, benefactress', 'Blessed Melaniia, the Eletskaia hermit', and 'Matrona Naumovna Popova, founder of the first hospice in the town of Zadonsk'.[2] The collection is thus a rich historical source combining the timelessness of hagiographic convention and the specificity of modern factuality.

As a hagiographic source on revered women, it invites intensive study of the kind now being done in European women's history, particularly for the medieval period. Such scholarship on European saints suggests that both the life patterns and the forms of piety of holy women differed from those of men. Male saints were more likely to undergo abrupt adolescent conversions, involving renunciation of wealth, power, marriage and sexuality, while women's lives were characterised by earlier vocations, greater continuity and less dramatic actions.[3] Caroline Bynum has argued that it is because women lacked control over their wealth and marital status that 'their life stories show fewer heroic gestures of casting aside money, property and family'; instead, women more often used their ordinary experiences, of powerlessness, of service, of nurturing and of sickness 'as symbols into which they poured ever deeper and more paradoxical meanings'.[4]

It would be instructive to learn if similar differences can be found in the lives of Orthodox saints, and if such differences apply to the modern period as well as to the medieval. These are questions I keep in mind as I read the lives of the holy men and women of nineteenth-century Russia, but the research is still at an early stage and the task ahead of me formidable.

In this article I look at the lives of two women who are held up as models in the *Zhizneopisaniia*, the hermit Anastasia Semenovna Logacheva and the Abbess Evgeniia, founder of the Boriso-Glebo-Anosino women's communal monastery, and analyse the qualities of holiness associated with each and the kind of authority derived from that holiness. As we will see, certain deeds and roles in each life are transgressive of traditional class or gender boundaries, and it is in the locus of these transgressions that holiness is most clearly articulated.

The hermit Anastasia Semenovna Logacheva (1809–75) was born of peasant parents in the village of Kudlei in the Ardatov district of Nizhegorod province.[5] Until the age of eight she was distinguished from her peers only by the gentleness of her character, but from that age on she began to show a strong yearning for prayer and a solitary life. In that year her father was drafted into the army and her mother and younger sister soon joined him, leaving Anastasia in the care of her paternal grandparents and uncle and their crowded household. Whenever Anastasia felt alone or neglected she would run to the barn and with tears in her eyes pray to the Mother of God, as her mother had urged her, for comfort. From the age of 12 she began to shun even the most innocent games with her friends, and to go instead to the woods where her grandfather kept a beehive. Not far from where he worked she found a quiet place along a ravine, and dug out for herself a cave in the hillside, where she spent as much

time as she could steal from her errands at home, in prayer and
fasting.

Hearing of the highly ascetic life of father Serafim (later Saint
Serafim) of Sarov (1759–1833) and that he never refused anyone
advice about matters of salvation, she set out at the age of 17 to seek
his blessings for her to take up the life of a hermit. At this first
encounter he told her to pray to the Queen of Heaven for blessings
upon her wishes, but that she was not yet ready for what she wanted
to do. On a second visit to him, when she again sought his approval to
undertake the life of a hermit, he advised her to go to Kiev to
venerate the holy saints and to seek blessings there for undertaking
such a difficult life; it was on this journey to Kiev that she was taught
to read by some pilgrim women.[6] On a final visit to Serafim, shortly
before his death, she again sought approval for a life of solitude in the
woods, and this time he counselled her to settle in that spot where she
could smell the fragrance of burning palms, and to wear chains for the
quieting of carnal lust. Nevertheless, between this visit, which
occurred when she was 23, and her definitive undertaking of a life of
solitude in the woods, almost 20 years elapsed probably because
Serafim had advised her not to leave her elderly parents who had
returned and were too old to work. During these years, Anastasia
supported herself and her parents with the reading of the Psalter for
the dead, with spinning and work in the fields. Upon the death of her
parents she gave whatever she had to others, and withdrew to the
woods about 12 versts from Kudlei, to a spot soon called 'Kurikha', a
spot with the scent of burning palms, where she dug herself a cave,
withdrew from the world, and began the rigorous ascetic life of a
podvizhnitsa.

But her life of solitude and prayer attracted others to her—first two
young orphan girls from nearby villages who came to visit her and to
help her (but who were frightened in the wilderness until she talked
to the bears, calmed them, and got them to respect the boundaries of
her cave and vegetable garden) and then men and women from the
neighbouring villages who came to seek her prayers and her advice.[7]
In her very withdrawal from the world, she became a magnet for the
troubled and the searching, a source of wisdom, objectivity and
certitude in an uncertain world. As one contemporary of hers
commented:

> The world doesn't love pious and good people, but sometimes it
> seeks out, marvels at the ascetic feats of, and seeks counsel from

those very people when they withdraw from the world. And so it was with Nastas'iushka: people from the local settlements began to come to her, to seek her holy prayers, to seek her counsel in the difficulties of life, and for several to seek instruction in how to be saved and how to pray.[8]

Because of the number of people who came seeking her counsel and those wanting to live near her and take up a similar life (including three women who already lived in huts near her, and a peasant man who wanted to live the same way), she decided it would be necessary to build a house, but she was advised that this required the permission of the local Crown authority since the woods she had retired to were Crown property. This led to an investigation of her request; not only was it refused but she was told she would have to leave her hermitage. After her eviction, she wandered for awhile, went on a pilgrimage to Jerusalem, and eventually settled in the new Nikolaevskii women's monastery in Tomsk province, where she was tonsured in 1863, and appointed Mother Superior in 1868.[9] At the monastery she continued to live a rigorously ascetic life and to act as a spiritual counsellor (staritsa); and she was known to have the gift of tears and the ability to foretell when something bad was about to happen. Upon her death, she was found to be wearing penitential chains under her simple garb, which were buried in the coffin with her.[10] After her death she was venerated in two ways. First, her grave at Nikolaevskii monastery became a place associated with healing, so that pilgrims and many of the sisters of the monastery believed in the curative power of dirt from her grave when mixed with water.[11] Secondly, at the initiative of peasants from the area around Kurikha, and with permission of the Tsar who ceded five *desiatiny* of land, an almshouse was opened after her death in her honour on the spot where she had lived as a hermit. In 1899, the almshouse was transformed into the Znamenskaia Kurikhinskaia women's religious community (*zhenskaia obshchina*) which in the early twentieth century had a mother superior, two nuns and 73 novices.[12]

For Anastasia, the journey from pious peasant girl to revered ascetic and staritsa was a long and disciplined one. We are struck by her long years of obedience to Serafim of Sarov, one of the most renowned startsy of modern Russia. Such obedience to a spiritual elder was a deep part of the Orthodox spiritual tradition, newly reinvigorated by the contemplative revival in Russia in the late eighteenth and nineteenth century.[13] Anastasia accepted not only the general advice to wait until she was ready before undertaking a life of ascetic solitude, but the specific admonition to fulfill her responsibility to her elderly parents before following her own spiritual inclinations. Whether such advice to fulfill family responsibilities rather than to dramatically cast them aside for the sake of a life in Christ was more commonly given to women than to men is one of the questions that I will be studying in my analysis of the lives of holy men and women described in the *Zhizneopisaniia*.[14] But one can imagine the poignance of a woman 'abandoned' by her parents at the age of eight now asked to delay her vocation for almost 20 years while caring for those parents. During these years of patient obedience and hard peasant work, Anastasia was probably viewed as a *chernichka*, a pious village spinster or quasi-nun, who commonly prepared the bodies of the dead for burial, read the Psalter for the deceased, and performed other good works in the village.[15] While the chernichka often earned the respect of her fellow villagers, the staritsa was a more revered and authoritative figure. How did Anastasia make the transition from chernichka to staritsa, and what was the basis of her later authority and veneration?

In his pioneering essay on the rise and function of the holy man in late antiquity, Peter Brown has argued that the authority of the holy man derives in part from his ascetic discipline, which both gives him a reputation for spiritual prowess and renders him capable of dispassionate judgement. By standing outside the ties of family, sexuality and economic interest, the holy man is in a free-standing position, the bearer of objectivity which makes him the ideal mediator and counsellor at first for local villagers and later, as his reputation grows, for city dwellers. The certitude and commitment of his life appeal to those troubled by anxiety and uncertainty and, through his life in the wilderness, he is frequently believed to be in communion with and have power over nature and animals.[16] In addition, the ascetic or the holy person has gained a wisdom and a knowledge that others seek—the wisdom of knowing the value of simplicity and sparingness and the joy and serenity of contemplation and inwardness.[17]

As hermit, ascetic and staritsa, we see in Anastasia many of the qualities of the holy man. Once Anastasia withdrew from the world, leaving behind family and village ties and obligations she was able to take up the life of a fully committed ascetic. As she emptied herself of bodily longings, she is described as radiant and angelic, with the 'jarring translucence' of the true ascetic, and the ability to calm bears.[18] It is from this period that her reputation for holiness and wisdom grows, and that she is sought out as mediator, model, counsellor and staritsa. The authority that she derives from this holiness transgresses traditional gender and class boundaries: men find themselves seeking the counsel of a woman, and merchant and gentry women the counsel of a peasant. The Tsar himself donates land in her honour, and the values of a hierarchical world seem turned upside down.

Of strikingly different social background, the abbess Evgeniia, founder of the Boriso-Glebo-Anosino women's monastery, was born Evdokiia Nikolaevna Tiutcheva in 1774.[19] Of her youth we know only that she was sickly and impressionable, that reading was her favourite pastime, and that she devoured the works of French thinkers with relish. At the age of 23 she married Prince Boris Ivanovich Meshcherskii, who died suddenly in an accident two months later, leaving her pregnant. The *zhitie* tells us that the early years of widowhood were extremely difficult for her, that she was overwhelmed by the care of her little daughter, Anastasiia, and that it was not in eighteenth-century French thought that she found the necessary strength and courage (muzhestvo) to carry on, but in prayer and the reading of holy books.[20] She was particularly drawn to the writings of St Dmitrii of Rostov, and years later, recalling these difficult years, she spoke of him as her healer and attributed to him 'my conversion from mad philosophizing.'[21]

In 1799, Evdokiia Nikolaevna bought in Zvenigorodskii district, Moscow province, the undeveloped estate of Anosino, where she built a cottage and spent her summers managing the property, showing particular care and concern for the orphaned children among her serfs, and educating them along with her daughter in their summer cottage. From this time she dreamed of building a church in Anosino—the closest parish church was six versts away—but she had to overcome the initial resistance of the diocesan authorities and her own lack of confidence that she had the financial resources and the spunk to undertake such a project. After overcoming these obstacles and pledging 8000 rubles for the support of a priest and clergy, the cornerstone was laid in 1810. In the summer of 1812 the church was completely ready for dedication, the five golden crosses glittering outside, the iconostasis glittering within, when Napoleon's forces invaded Russia and Evdokiia Nikolaevna and her household fled the estate. French soldiers raided Anosino three times, stripping the new church of all its gold and copper, and turning it into a shambles.[22]

This was a period of great reflection for Evdokiia Nikolaevna, whose daughter got married in early 1814. When she returned, alone, to Anosino, she prayed for guidance in how to lead her life, how to bring it closer to the path of salvation, and how to be mindful of God's will rather than her own. As she later wrote:

> From the time of Prince Boris Ivanovich's death, I had vowed in my soul to build something useful for others in his memory and for the commemoration of his soul. The church was completed and I began to contemplate something new; but various circumstances prevented me from either founding or completing that which I wanted. Eventually I came to the conclusion that in the ambitiousness of the things I had dreamed of there was very likely my own self pride, which is why God, in his goodness, had not allowed my wishes to be fulfilled. In 1820 I built at the church, not according to my original, elaborate plan, but on a much more limited one, an almshouse for twelve women, who took up their places on June 4, the birthday of the deceased Prince Boris Ivanovich.[23]

The following year Evdokiia Nikolaevna began plans to transform the almshouse into a women's religious community and pledged for its support 10 000 rubles and eight desiatiny of land. In May 1822, on the name day of Evdokiia Nikolaevna's deceased mother, Metropolitan Filaret dedicated the community, and appointed Evdokiia its guardian and Matrona Ivanovna, one of the sisters, its supervisor. The sisters were given permission to wear black clothes and caps (*kamilavki*) without veils.[24]

Now that she had fulfilled her vow, by building the church and establishing a community for 12 women, she felt that she could follow her desire, which was 'to withdraw from the world and from this place and to hide myself in some distant place to the end of my days'.[25] Feeling a strong and constant urge to retire to an isolated, distant monastery she sought advice and approval from the various hierarchs, including Metropolitan Filaret, and from starets Amfilokhii of the Rostov monastery. Their consensus was that she should enter instead the community that she had established at Anosino, which she did in 1823, at the age of 49, after settling her property and freeing those of her pupils who were her serfs.[26]

Upon entering the community she placed herself in complete obedience to the supervisor, Matrena Ivanovna, and sought her consent in everything she undertook, but her life was not to remain that of a simple novice. Before entering the community, Evdokiia

Nikolaevna had, with the advice of Metropolitan Filaret, petitioned to have the Anosino community turned into a women's monastery and had pledged her own money for the support of it and the construction of the necessary buildings. In 1823 the Synod approved this request and soon after Evdokiia Nikolaevna was tonsured, took the monastic name of Evgeniia, and was appointed abbess of the new Boriso-Glebo-Anosino women's communal monastery.[27]

Wishing to revive the spirit of the ancient monastic life, she introduced to the monastery the Rule of Saint Theodore the Studite, and she imposed upon herself all of the severity of this ancient rule. Spurning every trace of the comfort and niceties of her former life, she lived in a cell which was described not only as spare but even crude. Remembering the wise saying of the holy fathers, 'speak not with your tongue, but with your deeds', she worked tirelessly, following a regime of prayer and manual labour, and for her, the additional responsibilities of being administrator of the monastery and spiritual director of the sisters. She was a severe but loved staritsa, remembered for having taught the young women to read the scriptures and the Desert Fathers and to understand them. A model of work and of self-denial, she was admired for her patient acceptance of responsibility—when she was in her sixties, and tired and ill, she asked to be relieved of her duties as abbess, still dreaming of living the simple life of an ordinary nun, but Filaret urged her instead to take a short leave and then return to her duties at the monastery 'for the consolation of all those living there'.[28] The *zhitie* tells us that she died a peaceful death in 1837, having prepared for it with fasting.[29] Another source, Archimandrite Pimen, tells us that Evgeniia developed a reputation for wise counsel (despite a noticeable stutter), that she was renowned for the simplicity of her life, and that the community she established supported itself through agricultural work. Her granddaughter, who entered the monastery in 1844 and was the daughter of a senator, followed in her footsteps, leading a simple outdoors life, chopping wood, washing laundry, fixing food for the refectory and even, as Pimen himself witnessed, grooming horses.[30] By 1877, the monastery had 180 nuns and novices, and ran a hospital and nursing home for sisters of the community, and a wayfarers house.[31]

Upon close reading of the sources, we see that the virtues which were most frequently commented on in Evgeniia are those which are reversals for an aristocratic woman: hard work, renunciation of luxury, and a spartan life. Such virtues are also hailed in her granddaughter when Pimen comments with favour and wonder at the daughter of a senator grooming horses.

At the same time, there are certain qualities and characteristics of Evgeniia which clearly situate her within her class. The first is her administrative skill, her competency in managing an estate and supervising its development and expansion, abilities which qualified her to be an able abbess even when a persistent part of her yearned for the unburdened life of a solitary. Such administrative abilities were rare as Filaret knew all too well; he, himself, longed to give up his administrative responsibilities in Moscow and St Petersburg and retire to a contemplative life at the Gethsemane *skit* which he founded at Trinity-St Sergius lavra.[32] Instead he demanded of himself, and of others like Evgeniia, that they use their talents and abilities for the good of others rather than the fulfilment of their own wishes, believing that in such renunciation of will could the path of salvation also be found, and not just in the way of the solitary.

Evgeniia's control of property also situates her within her class and within the Russian inheritance system which rigorously protected a married woman's dowry rights.[33] And Evgeniia was not unusual in forming a women's religious community as a widow. In my analysis of the founders of women's religious communities (zhenskie obshchiny), I found that over 20 communities were formed by widows; these widows included women of all classes, although, as in the case of Evgeniia, the sources are best for aristocratic women and the resources available to them were greatest.[34]

The timing of Evgeniia's entry into the religious community she had founded fits within the long Russian tradition of entry into monastic life in mid-life, after fulfilling one's obligation to spouses and children.[35] Thus we can find women of all social classes wishing to retire in their widowhood to a contemplative life, with some of them founding religious communities to make this possible, and others entering them in search of a life of security, community and religious discipline.[36] In turn, the communities often founded shelters or almshouses for women (or grew out of them), so they became associated with the care of homeless, elderly and widowed women, 'family-less' women, as the records of the Holy Synod say again and again.[37]

We see in these communities and in the lives of Evgeniia and Anastasia a certain life-cycle aspect to the religious lives of Russian women. Evgeniia entered religious life after fulfilling her obligations to her daughter, and Anastasia took up the life of a religious hermit after fulfilling her obligations to her parents; the care of others took precedence over the desire for a life devoted to one's own salvation. Only after familial responsibilities had been fulfilled and the simple pieties of obedience and acceptance lived out, could these women turn to the more dramatic acts and virtues of radical asceticism or heroic renunciation of wealth.

Before turning to an analysis of the aspects of holiness associated with Anastasiia and Evgeniia and the authority derived from it, I would like to point out some negative comments made about each of them by contemporaries which are revealed in the texts of the *Zhizneopisaniia*; such balance will help us not only to know that we are dealing with real human beings, but also to see how the conventions of hagiography mixed with historical factuality in the nineteenth- and early twentieth-century *zhitie*. We are told that Evgeniia was a severe but loved staritsa at Anosino. Other passages of the zhitie refer to the 'murmurs' of the sisters at the severity of the religious Rule she introduced, but then attempt to soften the impact of this comment by remarking that she herself was the strictest follower of the Rule and a model to others.[38] Nevertheless, one has the impression in reading her life of a religious *stakhanovite*, and a feeling that others in the community found it difficult to live up to the standards she set for herself and expected of others. In the case of Anastasia, we see that not all the peasants at Kudlei respected her way of life or were enthusiastic about her plans to build a house for her followers on the Crown lands at Kurikha. When the local authorities questioned the peasants in connection with her request, some said that she was often out of her mind, others feared that if some of the woods went for a monastery, they would also have to give up some of the meadow and the apiary.[39] Here we have a realistic sense of the struggle over resources and a discomfort with extreme religious behaviour and standards.

But hagiography is never simply biography. Its purpose is to exhort the reader, to hold up models of Christian life, to call the reader or the audience to the task of a radical religious transformation of self in imitation of the saints who in turn have lived in imitation of Christ. Hagiography is about the intersection of the human and the divine, and in recording the lives of holy men and women, the hagiographer wishes to reveal holy presence in human life.[40]

The holiness of the women we have studied, Anastasiia and Evgeniia, is revealed first in the transformed nature of their lives, and

then in the wisdom and authority that derive from that transformation. Anastasiia, in turning to the fully-committed life of a hermit,
and Evgeniia, in renouncing wealth and society to embrace the
spartan life of work and giving, performed the radical transforma-
tions of self and the emptying of self that were believed necessary
before one could be fully open to the divine.

Asceticism and discipline were essential steps in the growth of
wisdom, that knowledge of deeper truths which made the holy man
or woman such a magnet for the searching and the troubled. As a
contemporary had said of Anastasia, people came 'to seek her holy
prayer, to seek her counsel in the difficulties of life, and for some, to
seek instruction in how to be saved and how to pray'. For this reason,
the role of the *podvizhnitsa*, the ascetic, often grew into the role of
the staritsa or spiritual elder. The authority of a podvizhnitsa/staritsa
such as Anastasiia was charismatic and individualised rather than the
result of an institutional or hierarchical position of authority. A lay
hermit in the woods, she lived the majority of her life outside the
structures of formal religious life yet her reputation for wisdom
among the local people rivalled that of hierarchs and scholars. By
contrast, Evgeniia's role as staritsa appears more institutionalised. As
abbess of her monastery, she was responsible for the instruction and
guidance of the sisters, and acutely conscious of her accountability for
them before God.[41] Either way, the staritsa was a revered teacher
and model, a teacher often of reading and literacy and Psalms and
scripture, a teacher of a lived tradition of asceticism and religious
practice, a teacher in the way of holiness.

During their lifetime, the authority of the staritsa and of the holy
woman cut across class and gender lines; men sought the counsel of
women, and the wealthy and educated the counsel of the simple and
the unworldly. Through cult and hagiography, this authority continued beyond the grave. Women like Anastasiia and Evgeniia were
held up as models of the Christian life, and part of that model was
their transgression of traditional class boundaries and conventions.
The zhitiia speak in particular wonder at the simplicity and spartan
life of an aristocratic woman, and at the authority and repute of a
humble peasant woman. They do not, however, explicitly address the
problem of a woman holding authority, and yet wonder is expressed
at their muzhestvo and their ascetic virtuosity.

If hagiography holds up to us the Christian life as a life of radical
transformation then it promises to be, almost in spite of itself, an
excellent source for women's history of gender transgressions. A

careful reading will reveal to us both the specificity of women's religious lives, such as the importance of family obligations and life-cycles, and the overcoming of gender constrictions in the radical life of the holy.

NOTES

1. *Zhizneopisaniia otechestvennykh podvizhnikov blagochestiia 18 i 19 vekov*, 12 vols (Moscow: 1906–10) and *Dopolnenie*, 2 vols (Moscow: 1912). The figure 104/609 is my calculation, based on the 12 volumes of the *Zhizneopisaniia* and the 2 volumes of the *Dopolnenie*.

2. 'Vera molchal'nitsa', *Zhizneopisaniia*, ix, pp. 201–06; 'Raba bozhiia Tatiana', ix, pp. 226–30; 'Khramozdatel'nitsa Paraskeva', x, p. 796; 'Ustiuzhskaia iurodivaia Pelagiia Andreevna Berezina', x, pp. 107–13; 'Stradalitsa Katen'ka Lezhanka', xi, pp. 697–99; 'Blazhennaia Mariia Belogorskaiapeshcherokopatel'nitsa', vi, pp. 270–80; 'Blagochestivaia staritsa Paraskeva Alekseevna Mukhanova, blagotvoritel'nitsa', x, pp. 80–6; 'Matrona Naumovna Popova, osnovatel'nitsa pervago strannopriimnago doma v gorode Zadonske', viii, pp. 346–68.

3. Caroline Walker Bynum, *Holy Feast and Holy Fast. The Religious Significance of Food to Medieval Women* (Berkeley: 1987) pp. 23–30; Donald Weinstein and Rudolph M. Bell, *Saints and Society: The Two Worlds of Western Christendom, 1000–1700* (Chicago: 1982) pp. 220–38.

4. Bynum, p. 25.

5. 'Pustynnitsa Anastasiia Semenova Logacheva, vposledstvii monakhinia Afanasiia', *Zhizneopisaniia*, ii, pp. 176–93. This *zhitie* is reprinted from *Dushepoleznoe chtenie* (1902).

6. A. Priklonskii, *Zhizn' pustynnitsy Anastasii (Semenovny Logachevoi), vposledstvii monakhinia Afanasii, i voznikovenie na meste eia podvigov zhenskoi obshchiny* (Moscow: 1902) p. 9.

7. 'Pustynnitsa Anastasiia', p. 182; Priklonskii, p. 11.

8. Priklonskii, p. 11.

9. 'Pustynnitsa Anastasiia', pp. 187–93.

10. 'Pamiati pustynnozhitel'nitsy Anastasii Semenovny Logachevoi (inokini Afanasii)', *Zhizneopisaniia. Dopolenie*, part ii, p. 256.

11. Ibid., p. 259.

12. L. I. Denisov, *Pravoslavnye monastyri rossiiskoi imperii. Polnyi spisok vsekh 1105 nyne sushchestvuiushchikh v 75 guberniakh oblastiakh Rossii i 2 inostrannykh gosudarstvakh muzhiskikh, zhenskikh monastyrei, arkhiereiskikh domov i zhenskikh obshchin* (Moscow: 1908) p. 550.

13. On the role of the startsy and on the contemplative revival, see Robert L. Nichols, 'The Orthodox Elders (*Startsy*) of Imperial Russia', in

Modern Greek Studies Yearbook, I (London: 1985) pp. 1–30.

14. Epiphanius the Wise, in his life of St Sergius of Radonezh, mentions
     that the saint, at the request of his father, delayed entry into monastic
     life in order to take care of his elderly parents. See 'St Sergius' in
     George P. Fedotov (ed.), *A Treasury of Russian Spirituality*, II
     (Belmont, Mass.: 1975) pp. 57–8.

15. L. A. Tul'tseva, 'Chernichki', in *Nauka i religiia*, XI (1970) pp. 80–2;
     M. M. Gromyko, *Traditsionnye normy povedeniia i formy obshcheniia
     ruskikh krest'ian XIX v.* (Moscow: 1986) pp. 103–05.

16. Peter Brown, 'The Rise and Function of the Holy Man in Late
     Antiquity', *Journal of Roman Studies*, LXI (London: 1971) pp. 80–101.
     In a subsequent article Brown has emphasised the bonds of love and
     esteem which bind the holy man as exemplar to his disciples and
     clients. See Peter Brown, 'The Saint as Exemplar in Late Antiquity', in
     John Stratton Hawley, ed., *Saints and Virtues* (Berkeley: University of
     California Press, 1987) pp. 3–35.

17. Rachel Hosmer and Alan Jones, *Living in the Spirit* (New York: 1979)
     p. 232.

18. For the phrase 'jarring translucence' in relation to the ascetic, see
     Sebastian P. Brock and Susan Ashbrook Harvey, *Holy Women of the
     Syrian Orient* (Berkeley: 1987) p. 12.

19. 'Igumeniia   Evgeniia,   osnovatel'nitsa   Boriso-Glebo-Anosina
     obshchezhitel'nago devich'iago monastyria', *Zhizneopisaniia*, II, pp.
     17–36.

20. Ibid., p. 18.

21. Ibid.

22. Ibid., p. 19.

23. Ibid., p. 20.

24. Ibid.

25. Ibid., p. 21.

26. Ibid., p. 22.

27. Ibid., pp. 22–3.

28. Ibid., p. 29.

29. Ibid., p. 34.

30. Pimen, 'Vospominaniia arkhimandrita Pimena, nastoiatelia Nikolaevs-
     kogo monastyria, chto na Ugreshe', in *Chteniia v Imperatorskom
     Obshchestve istorii i drevnostei rossiiskikh pri moskovskom universitete*
     (1877) kn. 1, pp. 288–9.

31. Ibid., pp. 308–09.

32. Robert L. Nichols, 'Metropolitan Filaret of Moscow and Gethsemane
     skete, 1842–4', paper presented at the American Association for the
     Advancement of Slavic Studies National Convention, New Orleans,
     1986.

33. *Svod zakonov rossiiskoi imperii*, X (1857) Part 1, arts. 109–18, 180–95,
     226, 229, 230, 256–8, 294–5, 397, part 6, 995. Brenda Meehan-Waters,
     'Women, Property and Inheritance in Eighteenth-Century Russia',
     and William Wagner, 'Women and Property and Inheritance Law in
     Russia, 1866–1914', papers presented at the American Association for
     the Advancement of Slavic Studies National Convention, Asilomar,
     1981.

34. Meehan-Waters, 'Popular Piety, Local Initiative and the Founding of Women's Religious Communities in Russia, 1764–1917', in *St Vladimir's Theological Quarterly*, xxx, 2 (Crestwood: 1986) pp. 130–5.

35. The Russian Orthodox tradition of entry into monastic life in mid-life was reinforced by the Spiritual Regulation of 1721, a pivotal Petrine reform, which made clear the state's regulation of church affairs and scepticism concerning the contemplative, monastic life. So that subjects should not flee the obligations of this world, entrance for men was strictly limited, and women were not permitted to take the veil until the age of 50. It was assumed that nuns would be widows, who had already fulfilled their obligations as wives and mothers. In the event that a young girl should 'desire to remain a young virgin with the intention of taking monastic orders', she was scrupulously supervised and made to 'remain without orders until she is sixty, or at least fifty, years old'. Alexander V. Muller (trans. and ed.), *The Spiritual Regulation of Peter the Great* (Seattle: 1972) pp. 79–80. For the Russian text, see *Polnoe sobranie zakonov rossiiskoi imperii s 1649 goda*, 1st series, 6, no. 3718. These regulations were somewhat modified in the nineteenth century: a man could be tonsured at the age of 30 or 25 if he had theological schooling; however, a woman had to wait until she was 40. (*Polnoe sobranie postanovlenii i rasporiazhenii po vedomstvu pravoslavnogo ispovedaniia. Tsarstvovanie gosudaria Imperatora Nikolaia I*) (17 June 1832) no. 430.

36. Meehan-Waters, 'Popular Piety', pp. 133–4.

37. See, for example, *Tserkovnye vedomosti* (1888) no. 42:207.

38. 'Igumeniia Evgeniia', p. 25 and p. 28.

39. 'Pustynnitsa Anastasiia', p. 188.

40. Brock and Harvey, p. 13.

41. 'Igumeniia Evgeniia', p. 31.

4 The Greek Catholic Church in Nineteenth-century Galicia
John-Paul Himka

The region of Galicia takes its name from the city of Halych (in the Old Rus' language, Galich), a medieval centre of princely and episcopal authority.[1] The principality of Galicia was located in the westernmost extension of the Kievan realm, in and near the Carpathian mountains. It grew rich from salt and from the important trade routes that crossed it. By the end of the Kievan period it had emerged, along with Vladimir-Suzdal with which it was allied, as a powerful force in Rus', overshadowing the Kievan centre. In fact, when the Mongols took Kiev, a Galician prince was in occupation of its throne. After the Mongol invasion, the capital of the Galician principality was transferred from Halych to the newly-built city of Lviv (Lvov), which has remained the political centre of the region for over 700 years. Galicia continued to flourish for some decades after the Mongol invasion, but by the mid-fourteenth century it became a mere object of the territorial claims of the expanding Polish and Hungarian kingdoms. Poland won Galicia at the end of the fourteenth century and held on to it until the first partition of Poland in 1772. At that time the Habsburg empire, basing itself on the medieval Hungarian claims, 'revindicated' Galicia. Even though the Habsburg Empress Maria Theresa took Galicia in her capacity as Queen of Hungary, the new territory was never integrated with the Hungarian part of her domains. The Austrian crownland of Galicia differed from the historical Galicia in that it was enlarged by the addition of ethnically Polish territory in the west. Galicia remained a province of Austria from 1772 until the collapse of the empire in 1918. It is this latter period of Galician history that forms the subject of this paper.[2]

Christianity was introduced in Galicia during the Kievan period, in the aftermath of the conversion of 988. Christianity of the Byzantine-Kievan type has always been dominant in the region, although Latin Christianity has existed there as well since medieval times. Our survey will only discuss the Byzantine-Kievan church. Bishops of this church are known to have existed in Halych, the capital, and in Przemyśl (Peremyshl). The bishop of Halych moved to Lviv when the political capital shifted to that city in the second half of the thirteenth century. In the fourteenth century, from 1303 to 1347, Halych was the seat of a metropolitanate. After Galicia's annexation to Poland, however, the Byzantine-Kievan church declined and for about a century there was not even an Eastern Christian bishop in Lviv. The cultural revival in the Ruthenian lands during the sixteenth century saw the restoration of an Orthodox bishop in the capital of Galician Rus' (1540). During the period of religious controversy following the Union of Brest (1596), Galicia remained a stronghold of the Orthodox faith. It did not embrace the Union with the Roman church until the turn of the eighteenth century.[3] The Galician church was named the Greek Catholic church by the Austrian Empress Maria Theresa in 1774. The new name was meant to underscore the equality of this church with the Roman Catholic church.[4]

For ease of comprehension, the history of the Greek Catholic church in Austrian Galicia may be divided into six periods:

1772–1815, ie, from the acquisition of Galicia by Austria until the end of the Napoleonic period;

1815–48, from the Congress of Vienna until the outbreak of the revolution of 1848–9;

1848–82, from the Spring of Nations until the year of the greatest internal crisis in the history of the Greek Catholic church;

1882–1900, from the crisis until the elevation of Andrei Sheptyts'kyi to the metropolitan throne;

1901–14, from Sheptyts'kyi's accession to the outbreak of the First World War; and

1914–18, from the beginning of the war until the collapse of Austria.

1772–1815

The first decades of Austrian rule, particularly the reigns of the enlightened absolutists Maria Theresa (1740–80) and Joseph II (1780–90), were distinguished by far-reaching improvements in the affairs of the Greek Catholic church. After centuries of inferior status under Polish rule, the church was elevated to legal equality with the Roman Catholic church. The eparchy of Lviv was raised to an archeparchy and Lviv also became the seat of the newly restored, after almost half a millennium's hiatus, metropolis of Halych (1808). The entire secular clergy of the Greek Catholic church, which had been largely ignorant throughout the Polish period, was given formal seminary training at institutions of higher learning in Vienna and Lviv. The income of the secular clergy was regularised and considerably increased by Emperor Joseph II. The Austrian authorities also confirmed Greek Catholic cathedral chapters (*krylosy*) in Lviv (1813) and Przemyśl (1817) and resolved a decades-long conflict between the religious and the secular clergy in the latter's favour. Apart from reforms that directly concerned it, the Greek Catholic church benefited indirectly from numerous reforms that improved the socioeconomic position of its faithful, who were overwhelmingly serfs. During this period, not surprisingly, the clergy and hierarchy of the Greek Catholic church developed a profound loyalty to the Habsburg dynasty.

The assumption of hegemony by Vienna marked not only the end of Warsaw's influence on the Galician church, but also a considerable weakening of Rome's influence. Galicia passed to Austria at the onset of the period of Josephinism, one of whose main characteristics was the subordination of the church to the government in Vienna rather than to the papal authorities in Rome. Direct contact between Austrian Catholics and the Roman dicasteries was prohibited; bishops were nominated by the emperor, sometimes against Rome's wishes; disputes between the Greek Catholic secular and religious clergy as well as disputes between Greek and Roman Catholics in Galicia were settled in Vienna rather than in Rome. This state of affairs lasted until the concordat of 1855; in fact, however, many of the Josephine arrangements lasted to the end of the empire. It was also in this early period that the practice developed of appointing as metropolitan of Halych and archbishop of Lviv only clerics who had been educated in Vienna. This practice was retained into the 1880s.

The final point to be made about this first period in the history of the Greek Catholic church in Austrian Galicia is that the sphere of East Slavic Catholicism was being constricted. The Russian state and the Russian Orthodox church, which already claimed a monopoly over the heritage of Byzantine-Kievan Christianity, began to destroy the Union in the Ukrainian and Belorussian lands acquired during the partitions of Poland. Of particular significance for the Greek Catholic church in Galicia was the forcible absorption into the Russian synodal church of the Uniates of Kamianets eparchy, which came under Russian rule in 1795. The Kamianets eparchy was a separate eparchy in name only, having long been attached to the Lviv eparchy. Bishop Petr Bilians'kyi of Lviv worked energetically to maintain the Union there, but his efforts were in vain. The forcible conversion of the Kamianets eparchy deeply disturbed both Rome and Vienna. In 1805 the Uniate metropolis of Kiev fell vacant and it soon became clear that the Russian government had no intention of allowing the seat to be filled. The absence of a Catholic metropolitan in Kiev was an important factor in the decision to re-erect the metropolis of Halych. The Union was becoming restricted to the territory of the Habsburg empire.

1815–48

During this period the most significant development was the initiation of the Ukrainian national awakening led by the Greek Catholic clergy.[5] A consequence of the education of seminarians was the rapid formation of a stratum of intelligentsia for the submerged, largely enserfed Ruthenian population of Galicia. Influenced by contacts, particularly in Vienna, with the awakeners of other non-German nationalities in Austria, by the example, particularly in Lviv, of Polish romantic and insurrectionary nationalism and also by contacts with the emerging Ukrainian movement in the Russian empire, Greek Catholic seminarians, priests and even bishops began to engage in the 'heritage-gathering'[6] work typical of the early stages of national movements. They codified their language, translated classics of world literature into it, composed poetry and literary prose, researched the history of Galician Rus' and its church and recorded the folk songs, fables and customs of the people. The work was entirely cultural without overt political import. The national identity being defined was generally referred to by the awakeners as Galician-Ruthenian and considered a branch of the Little Russian or Ukrainian nationality. The national awakening absorbed most of the intellectual energy of the Greek Catholic clergy.

Within the church there were some differences of opinion about the awakening, with Metropolitan Mykhail Levytsky (1816–58) adopting a conservative attitude towards it, while the seminarians who formed the Ruthenian Triad (Markiian Shashkevych, Iakiv Holovatsky and Ivan Vahylevych) represented the most advanced wing of the national movement. At issue were such matters as language, with conservative churchmen favouring more emphasis on Old Church Slavonic and radical youth a pure vernacular, and the degree to which liberal ideas circulating underground in the *Vormärz* were to be integrated into the national revival.

During this same period the territory of the Union was further constricted, with the eradication of the Union in Belorussia and Volhynia after Bishop Iosyf Siemashko converted to Russian Orthodoxy in 1839.[7] The defection of Siemashko caused grave apprehension in Rome. Metropolitan Levytsky issued a strong condemnation of Siemashko and declaration of loyalty to Rome. In order to strengthen the position of the Union, Rome considered elevating the metropolitan of Halych to the rank of patriarch. This far-reaching and politically complicated intention was not, in the end, executed; instead, Metropolitan Levytsky was personally honoured by being named a cardinal in 1856.[8] The last outpost of the Union remaining in the Russian empire was the Chełm (Kholm) eparchy.

According to official eparchial statistics, there were 1587 Greek Catholic parishes in Galicia in 1848 with 2 149 383 faithful.[9]

1848–82

The revolution of 1848 brought tremendous change to the Greek Catholic population of Galicia. Emancipation from serfdom set the stage for great cultural, social and political advancement over the following decades. The national movement also made the transition from a cultural to a political movement. During the revolution of 1848–9, the Ukrainians of Galicia formed the Supreme Ruthenian Council, over which Bishop Hryhorii Iakhymovych[10] presided and in whose leadership were many Greek Catholic priests. The Council demanded the division of the crownland of Galicia, which included ethnically Polish territory around Cracow in the west, into separate Polish and Ukrainian provinces. It also defended the interests of the newly emancipated peasantry. With regard to all-Austrian politics, the Council supported the emperor rather than those who rebelled against him.[11]

The political activism which the Greek Catholic clergy evinced in 1848–9 surfaced again in the 1860s when a constitution and civil liberties were introduced in Austria. Priests were elected as deputies to the Galician diet and the all-Austrian *Reichsrat*. Although the secular intelligentsia began to assume the leadership of the national movement in the 1860s, priests remained indispensable activists at the local, parish level, founding associations for adult education, economic cooperation and cultural activity as well as agitating for Ukrainian candidates during elections.[12] For many priests, this national activism became an important component of pastoral work; for some, in fact, it even became the overriding concern. The Vatican, which after the concordat of 1855 became more directly involved in Galician affairs, was not unaware of the growth of nationalism among the Greek Catholic clergy and tried to stem it. The Vatican's opposition to nationalism had many sources, including the papal opposition to Italian nationalism, but the case of Greek Catholicism in Galicia had its own peculiarities.[13]

The national movement in Galicia acquired profound confessional significance as the result of the division between those Ruthenians who identified with the Ukrainian movement in the Russian empire and those who looked instead to the tsarist Russian government. These latter, generally referred to in historical literature as Russophiles, began to argue that the Ruthenians of Galicia formed a branch of the Russian nationality. The Russophile tendency was dominant throughout the period from the defeat of the revolution in 1849 until 1882, and it grew more definedly Russian as it evolved. This is not the place to discuss all the reasons for its emergence and consolidation, but the most important was a feeling that Austria had betrayed its loyal Ruthenian population by giving control of Galicia to the Polish gentry.

The confessional implication of Russophilism was a gravitation to the Russian Orthodox church. This must be understood in perspective, however, because more was involved than simply the influence of politics on religion. Greek Catholicism shared with Russian Orthodoxy descent from the church of Grand Prince Volodymyr (Vladimir); although Catholic, it was indisputably an Eastern Christian church. However, under Polish influence, particularly but not exclusively since the acceptance of the Union at the turn of the eighteenth century, the Galician church adopted certain customs and attitudes from Latin Catholicism. There were always those in the Galician church who opposed these Latin influences as a break with religious tradition. With the awakening of national consciousness in the nineteenth century, a national consciousness, moreover, that was anti-Polish, a movement for an Easternising purification of the Greek Catholic church emerged, first in the 1830s–40s, but anew and much more vigorously in the 1860s. The political Russophiles supported the religious Easternisers and held up Russian Orthodoxy to them as an unsullied model; and the Easternisers were often drawn *volens nolens* into the Russophile camp because of a certain community of interest. The Vatican opposed Latinisation of the Greek Catholic church, but it worried about the implications of a pro-Russian purification movement, especially since Bishop Siemashko had prefaced his defection from the Union with just such a purification campaign in the much more Latinised Belorussian church. Rome's hesitations and distrust of the Russophiles only played into their hands, as they increasingly unmistakably insinuated that the Galician church could only be saved by a break from Rome.[14]

Tensions over these issues became explosive in the 1870s. For one thing, the deterioration of Austro-Russian relations because of conflicts in the Balkans meant that the Austrian state was as distrustful of the Russophiles as was the Vatican. Also, in 1875, following a period of intense ritual purification, the last Uniate eparchy in the Russian empire, the Ukrainian eparchy of Chełm, became Russian Orthodox.[15] In the suppression of the Union a leading role was played by Galician Russophiles who had been recruited by the Russian government for pastoral and pedagogical work in the Chełm eparchy; and the leading Russophile newspaper in Lviv, *Slovo*, was so sympathetic to the conversion to Orthodoxy that the Greek Catholic metropolitan forbade his faithful to read it.[16]

The tensions came to a head in 1882 when the Greek Catholic congregation of Hnylychky in Galicia requested permission to convert to the Orthodox faith. Viennese and Vatican authorities reacted in concert, swiftly and energetically. They forced Metropolitan Iosyf Sembratovych (1870–82) and his chief officials to resign; and a number of prominent Russophiles, including the priest Ivan Naumovych, were put on trial for high treason.[17]

1882–1900

The aftermath of the crisis of 1882 was marked by intense Vatican intervention in the Greek Catholic church. During this period the metropolitans appointed were no longer graduates of Viennese seminaries; they were Roman-trained. The priests promoted to higher rank were drawn from the leading lights of the journal *Russkii Sion*; founded in 1871, this journal consistently stressed loyalty to Catholicism, opposition to religious Russophilism and the subordination of national politics to religion. Men from this circle included

Sylvester Sembratovych, who was made metropolitan in 1885, and the eminent church historian Iulian Pelesh, who became the first bishop of Stanyslaviv in 1886. In 1882 the Vatican also arranged for the reform of the debilitated Basilian monastic order by the Jesuits;[18] this was a reform of great significance for the Greek Catholic church. Since its implementation, the Basilians have remained an influential factor in the church, known especially for their contributions in publishing and scholarship as well as for their absolute loyalty to Rome.

After the events of 1882 the Russophiles became both more marginalised and more extreme in their views. They had already for some time been fighting against the growing power of the national populists (*narodovtsi*), as the adherents of the Ukrainian movement proper were called, and the purge in the church and disgrace of the treason trial weakened them beyond recovery.

Although the Ukrainian national movement proper gained by the new Vatican activism in the Greek Catholic church, it nonetheless opposed it. Vatican influence was equated with Polish influence; and indeed, in the ecclesiastical interventions of the 1880s the interests of the Vatican and the local Polish gentry who controlled the Galician government did, in fact, coincide. Also, although the Ukrainian movement of the national populists was by no means anti-Catholic, it did believe in the need for the relative independence of its national church. Finally, Ukrainian leaders were generally hostile to Metropolitan Sylvester Sembratovych's efforts to promote conciliation between the Ukrainian movement and the Polish ruling class in Galicia; only for about two years (during the so-called New Era) did the metropolitan and the leaders of the national populists work hand in hand.

The end of the nineteenth century also witnessed the growth of anti-clericalism in Ukrainian Galicia, particularly among the young intelligentsia and younger, more educated peasants. These strata formed the first formal Ukrainian political party in 1890, the agrarian socialist and profoundly anti-clerical Radical party.[19]

According to official eparchial statistics, there were 1854 Greek Catholic parishes in Galicia in 1900 with 2 934 278 faithful.[20]

1901–14

The history of the Greek Catholic church in the first half of the twentieth century is dominated by the figure of Metropolitan Andrei

Sheptyts'kyi (1901–44).[21] When he was named bishop of Stanyslaviv in 1899 and not much later metropolitan of Halych, Ukrainian society suspected that he represented a continuation of the Roman, and consequently Polish, ascendancy in the Greek Catholic church that had been evident since 1882. This was because Sheptyts'kyi was by birth a member of the Polonised nobility, in fact, a count, who changed from the Latin to the Greek rite in order to enter the newly reformed Basilian order. These suspicions, although persistent, proved to be completely misplaced. Sheptyts'kyi showed himself to be a man of extraordinary vision who handled chronic problems in the Greek Catholic church in a fresh and principled manner.

One such problem was the relation to the national movement. For much of the nineteenth century the clergy had been very active in promoting this movement, often allowing national concerns to overshadow religious ones, but in the two decades prior to Sheptyts'kyi's accession relations between adherents of the national movement and the church had become very strained. The new Vatican influence on the church injected a distrust of nationalism that had previously been almost absent in Greek Catholicism and the hegemony of anticlericalism among the younger intelligentsia further exacerbated tensions. Some clerics decided that the church should withdraw from and even oppose the national movement; the outstanding representative of this tendency was the bishop of Stanyslaviv, Hryhorii Khomyshyn (1904–46). Sheptyts'kyi espoused a different and, for Galicia, new conception. In his view, the church had to remain independent of the national movement, ready to criticise and oppose it when it came into conflict with Christian principles, but equally ready to support it when it did not. Thus in 1908, for example, when a Ukrainian student assassinated the governor of Galicia and the national movement as a whole condoned the action, Sheptyts'kyi strongly condemned the murder and was exposed to many insults as a result. But in numerous other instances, Sheptyts'kyi used his exceptional influence—deriving from his personality as much as from his office and aristocratic origin—to promote Ukrainian interests in Galicia. Of many examples, one might mention his establishment of a Ukrainian National Museum in Lviv, to this day and through the most adverse times an outstanding centre for the preservation of Ukrainian cultural artifacts, and his successful mediation to win agreements to increase the proportion of Ukrainian deputies in the Galician diet and to found a Ukrainian university in Lviv. Many scholars would agree that no individual in the first half of the twentieth century contributed as much to the Ukrainian cause in Galicia as Metropolitan Andrei Sheptyts'kyi.

Another problem he approached with an original and positive vision was that of religious Russophilism. Firstly, he was very tactful in dealing with the Russophiles among his clergy, which sometimes earned him the ire of zealous adherents of the Ukrainian national movement. Secondly and much more importantly, he worked diligently to restore the Eastern traditions of his church, for example, by reviving eastern monasticism according to the Studite rule and, in the post-war period, implementing a thorough, purificatory liturgical reform. Unlike many other Easternisers, however, Sheptyts'kyi was convinced that his restoration of the Byzantine spirit could be and had to be accomplished within the parameters of what he considered the universal church, that is the Catholic church; he was also extremely distrustful of the contemporary Russian Orthodox church, which was, of course, closely associated with the tsarist regime. Not only was Sheptyts'kyi an Easterniser free from political Russophilism and gravitation to the Russian synodal church, he actually sought to expand the Union into Russian and other Orthodox territory; he himself travelled incognito into Russia before World War I to make contact with sympathisers.

In spite of Sheptyts'kyi's dynamic conception of an Easternising movement that transcended and rejected traditional Russophilism, the latter became a potent factor in Greek Catholic church life in the decade before the outbreak of world war. This had nothing to do with internal developments in the Galician church, but rather reflected the growing tensions between Austria and Russia. The Russian government qualitatively stepped up its efforts to win support among Galician Ukrainians through propaganda and outright payment. Russian efforts were most successful among Greek Catholic immigrants in the United States, many of whom entered the Russian Orthodox church during this period.

1914–18

Not long after the outbreak of World War I, in November 1914, Russia occupied Galicia. Metropolitan Sheptyts'kyi remained in Lviv and delivered a powerful sermon urging his faithful to preserve the Greek Catholic church and censuring the Russian Orthodox church as a branch of the Russian state. He was arrested and sent to the interior of Russia, where he remained imprisoned in a monastery until the February revolution. In occupied Galicia, the Russian government attempted to force the clergy and general population to convert to Russian Orthodoxy, but this attempt met with considerable resistance and proved impossible to implement. The Russians were driven out of Galicia for a year, but were able to reoccupy the territory during the Brusilov offensive in the summer of 1916; during this second occupation the Russian authorities pursued their aims, including the conversion of Galicia's Ukrainians to Russian Orthodoxy, with less brutality than during the first period of occupation. Still, the Greek Catholic church suffered great physical and moral damage during the war. By the summer of 1917 Austria reconquered Galicia and restored the Greek Catholic church. In the fall of 1918 the Austro-Hungarian empire, defeated by the Entente, collapsed; its place in Galicia was taken by the short-lived West Ukrainian People's Republic which enjoyed the full support of the Greek Catholic church.

CONCLUSION

The Greek Catholic church of Galicia traced its ancestry to the conversion of Volodymyr in 988 and preserved many features of the common Rus' heritage. Yet in spite of a shared legacy with the rest of East Slavic Christendom, there were certain features that distinguished it. These were the entry into the Union with Rome *circa* 1700 and the Austrian environment in which the church flourished from 1772 to 1918. The Roman and Austrian influences, although not unknown elsewhere in the East Slavic Christian tradition, were unusually formative of the Greek Catholic church in nineteenth-century Galicia. The Galician church was not only the object of the often competing claims of Rome and Vienna, but also the object of the claims of Moscow which sought to inherit all of Volodymyr's legacy. As a result of World War I, Vienna's claims to Galicia and its church came to an end; as a result of World War II (but during much of World War I as well) Moscow's claims were victorious.

NOTES

1. Probably the best short introduction to Galicia is *Encyclopedia of Ukraine*, ed. Volodymyr Kubijovyč (Toronto, Buffalo, London: 1984–), s.v. 'Galicia' by V. Kubijovyč, Ya. Pasternak, I. Vytanovych, A. Zhukovsky. More substantial is Paul Robert Magocsi, *Galicia: A Historical Survey and Bibliographic Guide* (Toronto, Buffalo, London: 1983).

2. For an excellent survey, see Ivan L. Rudnytsky, 'The Ukrainians in Galicia under Austrian Rule', in *Nationbuilding and the Politics of Nationalism: Essays on Austrian Galicia*, ed. Andrei S. Markovits and Frank E. Sysyn (Cambridge, Mass.: 1982) pp. 23–67.

3. In 1677 Bishop Iosyf Shumlians'kyi of Lviv privately accepted the Union, but only proclaimed it publicly in 1700. The Przemyśl eparchy, after some wavering, finally accepted the Union in 1692. The Stauropegial Brotherhood in Lviv accepted the Union in 1708.

4. The best general histories of the Greek Catholic church in Galicia are: Mykhail Harasevych, *Annales Ecclesiae Ruthenae* (Lviv: 1862); Iulian Pelesh, *Geschichte der Union der ruthenischen Kirche mit Rom von den aeltesten Zeiten bis auf die Gegenwart*, vol. 2 (Würzburg, Vienna: 1881); Anton Korczok, *Die griechisch-katholische Kirche in Galizien* (Leipzig and Berlin: 1921). A detailed bibliography may be found in Isydor I. Patrylo, *Dzherela i bibliohrafiia istorii ukrains'koi tserkvy*, Zapysky ChSVV, II, Sektsiia I: Pratsi, 33 (Rome: 1975); additions by the same author and under the same title have appeared in *Analecta OSBM*, 10 (16) (1979) pp. 406–87, and 12 (18) (1985) pp. 419–525.

5. See Jan Kozik, *The Ukrainian National Movement in Galicia: 1815–1849*, ed. Lawrence D. Orton (Edmonton: 1986).

6. The phrase is Paul R. Magocsi's.

7. Wasyl Lencyk, *The Eastern Catholic Church and Czar Nicholas I*, Editiones Catholicae Universitatis Ucrainorum S. Clementis Papae, Pratsi filosofichno-filolohichnoho fakultetu, 2 (Rome: 1966).

8. *Monumenta Ucrainae historica*, vol. XIV: *Quaestio Patriarchatus Ecclesiae Ucrainorum saeculo XIX*, ed. Alexander Baran (Rome: 1977).

9. Lviv archeparchy had 883 parishes and 1 329 091 faithful. Przemyśl eparchy had 704 parishes and 820 292 faithful. *Schematismus universi venerabilis cleri Archidioeceseos metropolitanae graeco-catholicae Leopoliensis pro anno Domini 1848* (Lviv, nd). *Catalogus universi venerabilis cleri Dioeceseos Premisliensis graeco-catholicae pro anno Domini 1848* (Przemyśl, nd).

10. There is a good scholarly biography of this bishop and later metropolitan (1860–3): Luigi Glinka, *Gregorio Jachymovyč-Metropolita di Halych ed il suo tempo (1840–1865)*, 2nd ed., Analecta OSBM, Series II, Sectio I: Opera, 30 (Rome: 1974).

11. Martha Bohachevsky-Chomiak, *The Spring of a Nation: The Ukrainians in Eastern Galicia in 1848* (Philadelphia:1967).

12. See John-Paul Himka, *Galician Villagers and the Ukrainian National Movement in the Nineteenth Century* (Edmonton, London, New York: 1988) especially pp. 105–42.

13. Very revealing is a survey of the ecclesiastical affairs of the Slavs and Romanians in the Habsburg empire prepared by the Viennese nunzio Mariano Falcinelli Antoniacci in March 1864. Archivio Segreto Vaticano (ASV), Archivio della Nunziatura di Vienna (ANV), vol. 480, pp. 27–30v.

14. For example: 'The Union was always and remains to the present time the most insidious and dangerous invention in all respects—religious, national and political. The Union was contrived by the Jesuits as a means to catholicize the Orthodox and polonize the Russians.' 'Polyty-cheskoie znacheniie relyhioznoi unii', *Slovo*, 15 (16 [28] January 1875) no. 6, p. 1.

15. Luigi Glinka, *Diocesi ucraino-cattolica di Cholm* (*Liquidazione ed incorporazione alla Chiesa russo-ortodossa*) (*Sec. XIX*), Analecta OSBM, Series II, Sectio I: Opera, 34 (Rome: 1975).

16. I. K., 'Odna duzhe vazhna sprava . . .', *Ruskii Sion*, 5 (1875) p. 301.

17. Excellent archival documentation on these issues can be found in ASV, ANV, vols 570 and 587, and in Vienna's Haus-, Hof- und Staatsarchiv, Politisches Archiv, Section 40, n. 212.

18. See Porfirio Pidručnyj, 'Relazioni dei Gesuiti sulla Riforma Basiliana di Dobromyl' (1882–1904)', *Analecta OSBM*, 12 (18) (1985) pp. 210–54.

19. On radicalism, see John-Paul Himka, *Socialism in Galicia: The Emergence of Polish Social Democracy and Ukrainian Radicalism (1860–1890)* (Cambridge, Mass.: 1983).

20. Lviv archeparchy had 751 parishes and 1 081 327 faithful. Stanyslaviv eparchy, formally erected in 1850 but without a bishop until 1886, had 433 parishes and 867 010 faithful (16 parishes were outside Galicia, in Bukovina, with 23 583 faithful). Przemyśl eparchy had 686 parishes and 1 009 524 faithful. *Shematyzm vsechesnoho klyra hr. kat. mytropolytalnoi Arkhydiietsezii Lvivskoi na rik 1900* (Lviv: 1900). *Schematyzm vseho klyra hreko-katolycheskoi Eparkhii Stanyslavivskoi na rik bozhii 1900*, XV richnyk (Stanyslaviv: 1900). *Schematismus universi venerabilis cleri dioeceseos gr.-cath. Premisliensis pro anno Domini 1900* (Przemyśl: 1900).

21. *Morality and Reality: The Life and Times of Andrei Sheptyts'kyi*, ed. Paul R. Magocsi (Edmonton: 1989). Cyrille Korolevskij, *Metropolite André Szeptyckyj 1865–1944*, Opera Theologicae Societatis Scientificae Ucrainorum, 16–17 (Rome: 1964) (an as yet unpublished English language translation of this work has been prepared by Rev. Brian [Serge] Keleher). Gregor Prokoptschuk, *Metropolit Andreas Graf Scheptyćkyj: Leben und Wirken des grossen Förderers der Kirchenunion*, 2nd ed. (Munich: 1967).

5 Printing the Bible in the Reign of Alexander I: Toward a Reinterpretation of the Imperial Russian Bible Society[1]

Stephen K. Batalden

One of the most remarkable phenomena of Alexander I's Russia was the rise and fall of the imperially chartered Russian Bible Society. Launched in Petersburg in late 1812 under the inspiration of John Paterson of the British and Foreign Bible Society (BFBS), the Imperial Russian Bible Society quickly mushroomed with the support of its President Aleksandr Golitsyn and its Tsar-protector Alexander into the most powerful and effective independent voluntary association of the first quarter of the nineteenth century. Even at their greatest strength, the Russian freemasonic societies never approached the levels of energy and support generated by the Russian Bible Society. With its local auxiliaries throughout the Empire, the Society translated, printed and distributed Holy Scripture in over 40 languages. The astronomical circulation runs of Bible Society publications knew no precedent in the previous history of Russian printing. By the time of the Society's closure in 1826, the landmark project to render the Bible in modern Russian had yielded a New Testament and Psalter in Russian translation, with circulation in several printings amounting to several hundred thousand copies. The translation into Russian of the Old Testament or Hebrew Bible had also been completed through the eighth book (Ruth).[2]

Given the extent of the Society's operation and its quite unprecedented independence of action, historians have understandably sought explanation for this remarkable rise of the Bible Society movement in Russia, as well as its rapid demise in the 1820s. Most such historical accounts have credited the Society's success to the wider world of pietism and western induced religious mysticism present in the latter half of Alexander I's reign. Building upon the pioneering work of A. N. Pypin, historians have noted the influence of such religious movements as the St Petersburg Theological Academy and in Russian society more generally. The Bible Society movement in such a context has been understood as a part of a wider post-Napoleonic European reaction to Enlightenment, one element of which was the rejection of the more sterile forms of established state churches and the parallel stress upon personal piety. Similarly, on the matter of the demise of the Russian Bible Society, historians have noted the extent to which these pietist and mystical movements in Russia began to encounter opposition both from official church circles in the Holy Synod and from leading figures in Alexandrine government and society, including War Minister Aleksei Arakcheev. Thus, the prevailing wisdom regarding the Russian Bible Society has been that it constituted at a particular moment in Russian history a powerful expression of western ideas, the fate of which was very transitory, largely limited to the decade following the Congress of Vienna.[3]

This essay, based upon the archival record left by the Bible Society in Petersburg, offers a modest corrective to such interpretations of the Russian Bible Society. For, there are two problems with the prevailing linkage of the Russian Bible Society with the momentary ascendancy of western pietist and mystical currents in Alexandrine Russia. First, such a linkage does little to explain operationally the quite phenomenal success of the Russian Bible Society. In other words, even assuming the influence of certain European-wide currents of thought, how did that translate into the unprecedented circulation of hundreds of thousands of copies of Holy Scripture? Second, it is the contention of this paper that, by focusing exclusively upon the mystical movements operating in Alexandrine Russia, the prevailing historiography has inadvertently assumed the arguments propounded in the 1820s by the Society's detractors. Why did the Society need to be closed? It needed to be closed, detractors would offer, because it had become a 'hole for Methodists and illuminationists.'[4] It is the central point of this paper that behind these ideological arguments of the 1820s there was also a fundamental *political* question posed by the success of the Russian Bible Society. The Russian Bible Society and its elaborate printing establishment posed with new technology an unprecedented western challenge to a Russian political culture that had known no such effective independence of action. It was the presence of this un-bounded energy operating outside the normal religio-political con-straints that both explained the Society's success and ultimately foredoomed it to failure.

In order to understand how this functioned—that is, how this challenge to Russian political culture developed operationally—it is necessary to revisit the unique publishing establishment of the Imperial Russian Bible Society. It is at this publishing level that technological and managerial innovations incorporated into the Russian Bible Society Press propelled the Society into an unpre-cedented challenge to the existing political culture. Thus, at least for a brief decade in the nineteenth century, technological changes in printing—particularly the early development of stereotyping—facilitated a major new publishing effort that challenged the prevail-ing political and religious culture.

In the establishment of the Russian Bible Society, the Scot John Paterson, in conjunction with the British and Foreign Bible Society (BFBS), was to play a seminal role. Arriving in Petersburg in 1812, shortly after the Napoleonic invasion of Russia, BFBS agent Paterson sought to establish a local Bible Society for the purpose of providing scripture to non-Russian nationals of the Empire. The tie that Paterson quickly established with Aleksandr Golitsyn was more than a linkage of like-minded pious faithful. That association also brought Paterson into contact with a powerful official who, among his other duties, oversaw the administration of non-Orthodox confessions in the Empire. Golitsyn's direct access to and friendship with Alexander I also would prove to be important for the Bible Society. Meeting in Golitsyn's private residence in January 1813, the newly chartered Bible Society was to include membership from among those at the highest levels of Russian officialdom and the Russian Church.

By 1816, three years after its first meeting, the Russian Bible Society had moved well beyond its initial goal of providing scripture in non-Russian languages of the Empire. Not only did it secure authority to publish and distribute copies of the Slavonic Bible, but by decree of February 1816, Alexander I granted to the Society the right to publish the New Testament in a modern Russian edition.[5] In the years that followed, an ever quickening pace of translation activity yielded a first edition of the Russian Gospels in early 1819, a complete Russian New Testament at the end of 1821, a Russian Psalter in 1822, and the non-circulating Russian Octateuch by 1825.[6] This translation into Russian of biblical texts constituted a major contribution of the Bible Society era. To accomplish the translations, a 'Translations Committee' under the leadership of St Petersburg Academy Rector and subsequent Moscow Metropolitan Filaret (Drozdov) was established to oversee the early editions through the press.

Despite the obvious long-term significance of this translation process, it was the printing establishment—the Society's own *tipografiia*—that powered the growth of the Russian Bible Society and made possible its great short-term success. The achievements of this press have been largely neglected in previous work on the subject. Under the general direction of John Paterson, the Russian Bible Society Press became the most innovative Russian printing establishment of its day. Indeed, until mid-century, no press of the empire would be able to emulate the far-reaching advances implemented at the St Petersburg Press of the Russian Bible Society.[7] It is to those advances, not to the translation process, that one must look to explain the sudden and quite remarkable impact of the Bible Society upon Russian religio-political culture.

Of all the innovations introduced by John Paterson into the Press of the Russian Bible Society, by far the most significant was that of stereotype printing. Frustrated by the inordinate expense, size, and low print runs of Slavonic Bibles published by the Holy Synod, Paterson in November 1813 submitted to the St Petersburg Society's 'Committee', its executive body, a 'Memorial on the means of procuring a sufficient supply of the Russian [ie, Slavonic] Bible and New Testaments'.[8] In his 'Memorial', Paterson introduced the question of stereotyping—that is, the creation of solid metal plates formed in gypsum moulds that, in turn, are cast from standing type. Paterson's knowledge of stereotyping antedated his arrival in the Russian Empire, even though printing from stereotype plates had only a few years earlier been developed in England.[9] The newly patented use of gypsum moulds to produce single-piece stereotype plates greatly increased potential print runs inasmuch as such plates reduced the amount of type, and thus the cost incurred for a given imprint. Moreover, the stereotype plate, unlike the traditional form of locked-up type, did not require redistribution after printing, and thus could be reused. In short, unlike the previously limited print runs normally in the range of 2000 to 5000 copies, stereotyping held out the potential for virtually unlimited circulation with reprintings from a single stereotype plate. As Paterson put it to the Committee in Petersburg, 'the only means to prevent this great loss of time [at the

Synodal Press] would be to print . . . with Stereotype'. Paterson proceeded to note that, while it 'would certainly be much preferable, and perhaps even cheaper, if there was a possibility of having them [ie, the plates] prepared here, there is reason to fear that this is at present impossible'.[10]

Nevertheless, in 1814, Paterson returned to England intent upon procuring the needed technological expertise to provide the Russian Bible Society with an efficient and independent press. Paterson did so by turning to the stereotype printing firm used by the British and Foreign Bible Society, J. Thomas Rutt of Shacklewell. Under terms worked out in cooperation with the BFBS and with Russian Bible Society funding, Rutt agreed to dispatch his son Thomas to the Petersburg Bible Society in the spring of 1815 in order to head up a stereotype printing branch office of the parent Rutt firm. Provisions were made for an up-front payment by the Russian Bible Society and an agreement that the Rutt operation in Petersburg would secure a 5% profit on sales contracted to the Russian Bible Society.[11]

The status of the arrangements that Paterson had made with printer J. Thomas Rutt were interesting. In his October 1814 report to the Russian Bible Society Committee upon return to Petersburg, Paterson indicated that the younger Rutt, his assistants, and their equipment 'ought to be encouraged . . . to establish an English printing office here to print for the Bible Society'.[12] Paterson's reference to 'an English printing office' did not entirely clarify the position of the younger Rutt. Was Thomas Rutt to be an employee of the Russian Bible Society, or was Paterson creating an independent English printing company in Petersburg? From the perspective of the elder Rutt in Shacklewell, the latter was the case. For, in his will, probated in 1821, he referred to joint ownership with his son Thomas of his own Petersburg branch:

> My dear son Thomas being already provided for by having a half share of the stereotype printing business at St Petersburg is not considered as having any share in the arrangements herein specified tho' sharing my sincere affection equally with the rest of my children.[13]

Despite the elder Rutt's understanding of his co-ownership, publications issued by the Society in Petersburg bore the sole imprint of the 'Press of the Imperial Russian Bible Society'.

In retrospect, both the Rutt claims and the integrity of the Russian Bible Society Press were to be maintained. For, the press clearly had a unique status, unprecedented in Russian history. Although it produced printed matter—namely, Bibles—it was free from both secular and spiritual censorship. Golitsyn was even able to mollify local police inspectors who questioned by what authority or formal certification Rutt and his apprentices were carrying on such a commercial venture.[14] Despite the absence of such registration, the Russian Bible Society Press included an English stereotype printer— among the earliest such establishments in the world—and, from 1818, an English bookbinder, both of whom functioned independently as subcontractors for profit within the overall operation. In the contemporary language of *perestroika*, this was a subcontracted 'joint venture'. What was so striking about this joint venture was not only that it escaped censorial review, but that it did so on such a substantive matter as that of biblical texts—an area of longstanding controversy dating from the seventeenth-century schism and earlier. For the time being, the political culture and the important official court leadership afforded the Bible Society a window of opportunity.

The young Thomas Rutt arrived in May 1815 with an assistant by the name of Astbury, with all the equipment needed for making stereotype plates, and with a new printing press.[15] A second press followed by separate ship. By the July 1815 meeting, Paterson was able to show the Russian Bible Society Committee the first specimen stereotype plate made for use in printing what would be the Society's first Slavonic New Testament (1816). Paterson remarked on the occasion:

> It is the first stereotype plate made in Russia and we may indulge the hope that the introduction of this beautiful art into the country under the auspices of the Russian Bible Society will prove a powerful means of spreading the light of Divine truth over the whole extensive Empire.[16]

Paterson's innovations were not limited to stereotyping. In order to secure proper paper at a reasonable price, he worked with the Ol'khin Petersburg paper mills, one of which (the 'Petergofskaia bumazhnaia fabrika' [Peterhof Paper Mill]) was first put into service with the encouragement of John Paterson and the Russian Bible Society. Paterson's goal was the production of lightweight, thinner English paper that would reduce the size of the Society's bound scripture.[17]

In the binding of Bible Society editions, Paterson encountered numerous delays, and at one point asked the Petersburg binder

Richter to work solely for the Society. Ultimately, Paterson again turned to England for the establishment of a professional bindery within the Russian Bible Society Press. In 1818, Ebenezer Rennie and his assistant Dixon arrived in Petersburg with their professional expertise and equipment. As in the case of the Rutt stereotyping business, Rennie and Dixon functioned as subcontractors for the Russian Bible Society Press, but with free space in the larger RBS complex.[18]

The introduction of these English artisans into the Russian Bible Society Press proved to be the easiest part of the organisational effort. To run the new machines and equipment Rutt, Astbury, Rennie and Dixon all needed an army of workers—what they commonly referred to as 'stout lads'. In his initial effort to locate such workers, Paterson turned to Aleksandr Golitsyn, who also held the post of Synodal *ober-prokuror*, with the request that able personnel from the Moscow Synodal Press be depositioned temporarily to Petersburg for assistance with the new presses.[19] Perhaps it was the precedent of turning to the Synod for assistance, but in any case, as more presses came on line and the personnel needs mushroomed, Paterson turned again to Golitsyn and the Holy Synod, this time securing approval to use the young sons of rural parish clergy for 'learners' and 'apprentices' at the St Petersburg Bible Society publishing house.

At the high point of the Bible Society's production, 1818–1820, well over 100 young sons of parish clergy, as well as recruits from the St Petersburg Foundling Home, were employed full-time by the Society's Press. The lads were brought into the press between the ages of 10 and 16, and were obliged to remain until the age of 21. The assistants were divided into two ranks—*ucheniki* and *podmastery*. Ucheniki, or learners, received their clothing, linens, room and board, and a salary of one ruble per month, with bonuses for good work. Podmastery, or apprentices, received a higher salary and their own private room. Dormitory facilities were managed within the Society's enlarged compound. Ebenezer Rennie and Thomas Rutt also started a formal school for the recruits so that the young workers would have basic literacy training. The young lads followed a rigorous schedule that involved an eleven-hour work day broken twice for lunch and dinner breaks. The work day was shorter on Saturday, and the young men were obliged to attend religious services and observe church festivals.[20]

From the perspective of the English artisans Rennie and Rutt, the basic problem was that of retaining apprentices long enough so that the skills learned on the job could be retained in the work force. In the end, the initial requirement that a young man remain at the press for five or more years frequently came to be appealed and the lengthy term was difficult, though not impossible given the wage incentives, to enforce. Responding to Rutt's chronic complaint on this score, the Bible Society secretary and aide to Golitsyn, Vasilii Popov responded in 1818:

> You know well that we have kept every one of those working boys who have petitioned for leaving the office as long as we could possibly do; some of them have also in consequence of it abandoned their project of going away; but to retain them always against their will is merely impossible, as they are free people, and cannot be disposed of by anybody.[21]

By 1819, Rutt began to recommend that 'no more lads come marching in from outside dioceses', a reflection that the supply was beginning to outstrip demand.[22]

While this unprecedented effort to replicate a modern English printing establishment in Petersburg succeeded in its major task— that of publishing large quantities of scripture at dramatically lower prices—the press was not without its problems. Paterson faced the never-ending problem of dealing with suppliers, although in the preparation of fonts, including those in Turkic languages of the Empire, the press was well served by the excellent matrices produced by Petersburg artisan Winheber.

More difficult to resolve were disciplinary problems with the young learners and apprentices. It was not unusual, particularly on pay days, for the priests' sons to become drunk. In cases where chronic drunkenness and other unspecified bad conduct interrupted the work of the press, Rutt would, as in the 1820 case of three priests' sons, Platon Smirnov, Ivan Stroganov and Aleksei Protopopov, recommend dismissal with a severance pay adequate to return them to their diocese—in this case, Moscow.[23]

In perhaps the most notable instance of worker disaffection, 19 of the assistants under the master bookbinder Rennie prepared a formal list of charges against Rennie, and filed a complaint with Aleksandr Golitsyn in late 1818. In addition to vague charges that Rennie was tyrannising the assistants and reporting them unfairly to supervisors, they charged that he was deducting from their salary when they were sick, and that, aside from clothes and food, they had yet to see their monthly salary. In March 1819, the Russian Bible Society Committee reviewed the charges, noting that each of the grievants had been interviewed. The final determination on this matter was that a core group of five lads had pressured others to sign the petition, that the charges were completely unfounded, and that the five perpetrators were routine troublemakers.[24]

Despite the occasional disciplinary problems, the best evidence for the success of the Society's mobilisation to publish scripture—all of it outside normal publishing and bureaucratic channels—were the results. Between 750 000 and 1 000 000 copies of scripture, in whole or in part, were published in Petersburg at the Press of the Russian Bible Society in the decade following 1815. Most publishing, including editions in 26 languages, occurred between 1816 and 1823. Thus, at the height of production, the Russian Bible Society was producing over 100 000 copies of scripture a year—figures that are in stark contrast to the book circulation figures of the immediately preceding century. Based upon their examination of circulation figures and readership in the eighteenth century, Gary Marker and Max Okenfuss discovered that only in the case of popular calendars and special elementary primers did circulation runs exceed much over 10 000 copies by the end of the eighteenth century—and then only because of several printings. The Russian *Psalter* alone went through multiple print runs involving over 100 000 copies.[25]

What the Russian Bible Society Press had done in a decade was to revolutionise the publication and circulation of the printed word. Part of the explanation for this rested in the ability of Paterson and his publishing operation to function outside the accepted conventions, including ownership, that governed the world of Russian book publication. In addition, the word that was being published in this case was of course a very special Word. The Bible Society was printing in stereotyped editions, and circulating, copies of Holy Scripture that heretofore were either the sole provenance of the Holy Synod, in the case of the 1751 Slavonic text, or constituted landmark first editions, as in the case of the new Russian translations.

So relatively efficient was this new publishing enterprise that, as might be expected, production effectively began to outstrip demand. Paterson complained at the end of 1823 that the auxiliary branch societies were not selling enough copies.[26] Warehouse inventories consequently began to build in the 1820s. Thomas Rutt, concerned about his profits, had earlier approached Aleksandr Golitsyn about the possiblity of using his excess stereotyping capacity to do publishing work for the government.[27] Along with some of his western friends in the capital, Paterson even went so far as to try to generate additional readership by providing copies *gratis* to prisoners and by encouraging through the establishment of Lancaster schools the wider development of literacy.[28] In short, if there was a lack of readership, then the indefatigable Paterson would explore the possibilities of forging such a readership. It was, after all, entirely consistent with their beliefs for pietist figures such as Paterson to advocate much broader access to education.

Paterson, Golitsyn, and the Bible Society Committee in Petersburg had been extraordinarily able in developing the Bible Society's publishing capacity. Yet, the new reality of the 1820s in which supply exceeded demand revealed deeper conflicts that set the Bible Society on a collision course with powerful elements in Alexandrine Russia. As the Bible Society sought an even broader readership, the Society's own increasing visibility and its broadening impact—its very success—began to alarm several prominent Orthodox prelates who became concerned over the usurpation of the Holy Synod's authority on biblical questions. The new St Petersburg Metropolitan Serafim and the tsar's own confessor, Archimandrite Fotii, were among those who began to express their dissatisfaction openly. In the highly structured religio-political culture of Orthodox Russia, the marketplace was not supposed to determine the success of religious ideas, especially in the traditionally volatile area of religious texts. Behind the new protestations directed, for example, against Bible Society Committee member Aleksandr Labzin were not just the surface issues of Labzin's journal *Sionskii Viestnik* (Messenger of Zion) and the editor's ties with religious mystics, but there was also the unspoken issue of his leadership in a Bible Society that had succeeded in reaching an ever larger audience while circumventing the conventions, sanctions and institutions normally limiting such activities.

Even more pernicious from this perspective was the Bible Society's President Aleksandr Golitsyn. Golitsyn's access to Alexander I had assured a most favourable interpretation of the activities of the Bible Society before a tsar whose benign commitment to a more Christian empire never recognised such subtleties as canon law, church tradition or textual authority. War Minister Arakcheev, who also had the ear of the tsar, loathed such unpredictable religious influences upon Alexander I. Writers such as the poet Alexander Pushkin capitalised upon the growing disaffection with Golitsyn to attack the pious tsarist advisor for his opposition to enlightenment and secular education.

On the eve of Golitsyn's forced 'resignation' in 1824, Pushkin penned the following epigram 'On Prince A. N. Golitsyn':

> . . . Here we have the soul of a slave,
> Education's chief destructor . . .
> For God's sake, put pressure on him,
> From all sides attack withal!
> From behind shall we not try him?
> That's his weakest side of all.[29]

For more narrow Russian prelates, on the other hand, the danger of Golitsyn was that he permitted those of foreign origin to circumvent the duly established arbiters of Russian religious culture—namely, themselves. There was an irony in this, for until the unprecedented success of the Bible Society's publishing operation, Orthodox prelates saw little threat in the Society and rather obsequiously rallied to its support in lockstep with tsarist patronage. Pushkin early on caught this obsequious side of the Orthodox hierarchy at a time when the Bible Society's popularity was still strong. In his untitled epigram of 1819, Pushkin wrote:

> The Bible men enjoy such bliss,
> Their asses boast such cleanliness;
> The monks just lick their sirs—
> The holy low-down curs![30]

When the tide began to turn against the Russian Bible Society and its remarkable printing operation, where could the Society turn for potential support? Paterson's instinctive appeal to a broader audience—his concern for expanded literacy, for example—revealed the central problem. Operating in a highly structured and hierarchical political and religious culture, the more egalitarian, pietist-inspired Bible movement in Russia, despite the early ecumenical support of the tsar and his favourites, lacked an independent constituency that could uphold it under fire. Bible-reading had not been a traditional form of Orthodox piety. Literacy was limited largely to an increasingly secular, urban upper class for most of whom the Society was of decidedly marginal interest.

In short, the Russian Bible Society was closed not because it provided a vehicle for religious mystics, although it may have unintentionally done that as well. Rather, the Russian Bible Society collapsed because, in extending its appeal to ever wider segments of Russian society, it circumvented those religious and bureaucratic authorities whose legitimacy rested upon maintenance of control over access to spiritual and political authority. At stake was *vlast'* (power). Given the potential power of the publishing establishment that the Bible Society had created, it was notable that even the technology of stereotyping itself fell into abeyance after the fall of the Russian Bible Society. When stereotyping resurfaced in Russian printing a quarter century later, it was no longer as an independent technology propelling change, but as a carefully managed component of a publishing industry that conformed to the dictates of official censorship.

NOTES

1. Research for this paper was made possible by grants from the International Research and Exchanges Board (USA) and the Arizona State University College of Liberal Arts and Sciences Summer Research Awards Program.

2. For circulation runs of the Russian Bible Society, see the summary article, 'Bibleiskiia obshchestva', in *Entsiklopedicheskii Slovar'* (Brokgauza-Efron) (St Petersburg: 1897) pp. 697–706. Drawing upon Bible Society statistics provided in its own *Izvestiia*, the 'Bibleiskiia obshchestva' article notes a total RBS circulation of approximately 700 000 copies by 1 January 1823. For a relatively comprehensive bibliographic listing of RBS publications, including the modern Russian editions, see under the relevant languages the entries in T. H. Darlow and H. F. Moule, compilers, *Historical Catalogue of the Printed Editions of Holy Scripture in the Library of the British and Foreign Bible Society*, vol. II (in 2 parts): 'Polyglots and Languages other than English' (London: 1911).

3. In particular, see A. N. Pypin, *Religioznyia dvizheniia pri Aleksandre I*, reprinted with an introduction and commentary by N. K. Piksanov (Petrograd: 1916). Following in the same general tradition as Pypin is the splendid dissertation of Judith Cohen Zacek, 'The Russian Bible Society, 1812–1826', Ph.D. thesis, Columbia University, 1964.

4. For the full range of epithets directed at the Russian Bible Society, see Zacek, pp. 249–309.

5. The relevant imperial decree was published as a part of the introduction to the Bible Society's first Slavonic/Russian diglot of the Gospels issued by the press of Nikolai Grech' ('K Khristoliubivym chitateliam', in *Gospoda Nashego Iisusa Khrista Sviatoe Evangelie ot Matfeia, Marka, Luki i Ioanna, na slavianskom i russkom nariechii* (St Petersburg: 1819) pp. iii–vii). Several of the subsequent Russian Bible Society editions carried the same introduction and decree.

6. For the dating and citations, see Darlow and Moule (note 2 above).

7. Regarding the activities of the Russian Bible Society Press, see the published *Izvestiia* of the Russian Bible Society through 1824. In addition, see John Paterson's *The Book for Every Land*, 2nd ed. (London: 1858). The manuscript of Paterson's published memoirs contains important information on Paterson's Russian activity that escaped publication. For these materials and accompanying papers, see 'British and Foreign Bible Society Deposited Papers: The Paterson Papers' (Memoirs [1805–1850] and Papers [1808–1847] of BFBS Agent John Paterson). These BFBS records are now located in the Cambridge University Library. For her generous help in accessing these BFBS records, I am indebted to Miss Kathleen Cann, former BFBS archivist. In addition to the documentary record in England, the archive of the Russian Bible Society remains intact in the Central State Historical Archive in Leningrad (TsGIAL), *fond* 808 (Imperial Russian Bible Society). Because of the more limited western access to the Leningrad holdings, this abbreviated essay on the press of the Russian Bible Society highlights the contents of the archival record now preserved in the Soviet Union. I am indebted to the International Research and Exchanges Board for making possible research on the Russian Bible Society in Leningrad in the spring of 1985.

8. *TsGIAL, fond* 808, *opis'* 1, *delo* 34 ('Delo ob izdanii knig Sviashchennago Pisaniia na slavianskom iazyke'), *ll*, 34–5.

9. See Paterson's discussion of stereotyping in his *Book For Every Land*. The BFBS 'Paterson Papers' also include additional records on this matter. There is an abundant secondary literature on stereotyping, but the earliest patents were secured in England only from the first decade of the nineteenth century. For the standard early guide to stereotyping, see Thomas Curson Hansard, *Typographia* (London: 1825).

10. *TsGIAL, fond* 808, *opis'* 1, *delo* 34, *l.* 35.

11. *TsGIAL, fond* 808, *opis'* 1, *delo* 10 ('Uspekhi v knigopechatnykh rabotakh i zaniiatiia komiteta dlia pechatykh del'), *ll.* 57–60. These leaves contain the only extant copy, a Russian translation, of the agreement signed by J. Thomas Rutt on 10 August 1814.

12. Ibid., *l.*, 62ob.

13. British Public Record Office, PROB 11/1645, RC/8387 ('J. Thomas Rutt'), p. 60.

14. *TsGIAL, fond* 808, *opis'* 1, *delo* 49 ('O tipografskom zavedenii pri Obshchestve i o T. Rutte'), *ll.* 15–16. These leaves contain copies of correspondence from July 1815 in which Golitsyn instructs the police not to intervene with the functioning of the press.

15. *TsGIAL, fond* 808, *opis'* 1, *delo* 10, *ll.* 95–6. These leaves contain Paterson's 'Memorial' to the Russian Bible Society Committee on 24 May 1815 announcing the arrival of Rutt.

16. Ibid., *l.* 100.

17. Ibid., *l.* 116. On the Ol'khin paper mills, see the discussion in Zoia Vasil'evna Uchastkina, *A History of Russian Hand Paper-mills and their Watermarks*, edited and adapted for English by J. S. G. Simmons (Hilversum, Holland: 1962).

18. Ibid., *ll.* 239–45. Announcement of Rennie's arrival, along with his

family and five workmen (including Dixon), was heard before the Russian Bible Society Committee on 5 June 1818.

19.   *TsGIAL*, *fond* 808, *opis'* 1, *delo* 49, *ll*. 1–2. These leaves contain copies of correspondence between Aleksandr Golitsyn and Pavel Levashev of the Moscow Synodal Press, July 1815. For the particular case of Synodal Press corrector Konstantin Nekrasov, see *fond* 808, *opis'* 1, *delo* 55.

20.   *TsGIAL*, *fond* 808, *opis'* 1, *delo* 110, *ll*. 364–467. This hefty file concerns the 'tserkovniki' who were employed at the Russian Bible Society Press. See also *delo* 104, *ll*. 3–5, regarding the establishment of the school within the press. For a complete copy in Paterson's own hand of the official 'Rules' governing the employment of priests' sons and other assistants at the Russian Bible Society Press, see *delo* 75, *ll*. 19–21. The rules were formally approved by the Holy Synod in a decree of September 1817 (*delo* 75, *ll*. 15–18).

21.   *TsGIAL*, *fond* 808, *opis'* 1, *delo* 49, *l*. 32.

22.   Ibid., *ll*. 53–4.

23.   *TsGIAL*, *fond* 808, *opis'* 1, *delo* 10, *l*. 345.

24.   *TsGIAL*, *fond* 808, *opis'* 1, *delo* 52, *ll*. 12–22.

25.   Gary Marker, *Publishing, Printing, and the Origins of Intellectual Life in Russia, 1700–1800* (Princeton: 1985) pp. 184–211. See also Max Okenfuss, *The Discovery of Childhood in Eighteenth-Century Russia: The Evidence of the Slavic Primer* (Newtonville, Mass.: 1979).

26.   *TsGIAL*, *fond* 808, *opis'* 1, *delo* 10, *ll*. 395–6.

27.   *TsGIAL*, *fond* 808, *opis'* 1, *delo* 49, *ll*. 51–2 (Rutt to Golitsyn, February 1919).

28.   See Paterson's *The Book for Every Land*, and note 26 above.

29.   Translation is that of Cyntha Whittaker, *Alexander Pushkin: Epigrams and Satirical Verse*, ed. and trans. by Cynthia Whittaker (Ann Arbor: 1986) p. 36.

30.   Ibid., p. 34.

6 Christianity, the Service Ethic and Decembrist Thought
Franklin A. Walker

At first glance it appears that the upholders of the Russian autocracy and its radical opponents in the first quarter of the nineteenth century were polarised on religious as well as on political and social questions. The Decembrist revolutionaries, in wishing to abolish serfdom, institute representative government, promote education, humanitarianism, prosperity and the rule of law, represented the Russian version of a European ferment against governments which had reacted against Enlightenment ideals. Behind Tsar Alexander I's 'Holy Alliance' was the 'throne and altar' belief that religious infidelity was a source of political subversion. The future Decembrists and their associates, on the contrary, resented increased censorship and obscurantism in domestic affairs and an anti-liberal foreign policy. But for most Decembrists Christianity in itself was not an issue. If many Decembrists thought that the authorities had oversimplified and distorted the Christian message for narrow-minded goals of political security, the revolutionaries did not set out to replace Christianity with a 'religion of reason'. They were not inchoate Saint-Simonians nor were they the last ripple of Jacobin anti-clerical Utopianism, but rather they were reformers whom Christian moral goals had profoundly influenced.

Both the Decembrists and pro-government apologists appealed to Christian sentiments and employed Christian imagery. The notion that one should sacrifice oneself for the good of others, that the objective of life was not material gain but spiritual development, that the concern of society should be the protection of the helpless, embodied a goal which Christian preachers had championed everywhere in every age. In Russia that traditional aim was combined with propaganda to motivate potential bureaucrats to serve the state with zeal and honesty. Speakers at school ceremonies asserted that educational institutions especially had the responsibility to mould future officials to become conscientious Christians,[1] but such

79

sermonising formed a large part of journal literature for the *dvoriane* (nobility) as a whole. Through serving the state, one laboured for the common good and therefore for one's fellow man. Exploitation, thievery, heartlessness and selfishness were moral and political evils. The Decembrists in repeating such pieties rejected not the Christian vision which autocracy proclaimed, but the failure to achieve that Christian ideal. Constitutional rule and serf emancipation were to be the instruments which could attain the just society which every speaker or writer advocated.

The influence of Christianity extended to members of the intelligentsia who did not utilise the Bible nor church writers, but who idealised the human spirit in a manner similar to the teachings of professed Christians. For many the term 'Christianity' was cloudy. It could have meant traditional Orthodoxy, Lutheranism, Roman Catholicism, Masonic idealism, pietistic latitudinarianism, romantic pantheism or (more often) pre-romantic melancholy.[2] But whatever differences over dogma, all accepted the obligation to strive for a Christian social order. Since the nature of that society was subject to definition, vagueness contributed to political conflict.

Earnest entreaties to the free human spirit, to the humanising work of public instruction, to the obligation of compassion and even to some kind of 'transformation' were part of pre-romanticism and of romanticism itself in Russia as in Western Europe. Religion had also been an important element in neo-classicism.[3] The large place which tendentious sentiment played in Decembrist writing reflected a common tendency in European letters. The eighteenth-century view that literature in providing entertainment should at the same time 'uplift' the soul[4] and that 'beauty' and 'virtue' were related, the great publicist and later historian N. M. Karamzin had thought in the 1790s and prominent writers such as Andrei Turgenev and Aleksei F. Merzliakov held in the first decade of the nineteenth century.[5] Ivan Rizhskii, professor of rhetoric at Kharkov University, in showing a relationship between 'rapture' and 'morality', associated the function of literature—in contributing to 'refinement of feelings, passion for the good, mildness of manners and love for justice—with the beneficent goals of Tsar Alexander I—the hero-monarch-enlightener.[6]

Promoters of knowledge and the arts saw themselves as serving the wishes of the monarch himself. Patriotic poetry pictured the emperor as under divine inspiration as he worked for the common good. There were many examples of anti-tyrannical 'freedom' jargon in the plays of the actor and poet P. A. Plavil'shchikov, but in his 'Ode to Alexander' on the occasion of the tsar's coronation, he spoke of the emperor as following the model of God in leading his people to happiness. The tsar's measures came from 'the mysteries of the holy faith'; moreover on behalf of the church the ruler exercised 'a pastoral hand'.[7] Merzliakov in 1803 similarly saw the tsar as reflecting the divine. To serve the tsar was therefore to serve one's neighbour; patriotic obligations included lofty moral conduct, the protection of the poor and support for education. Luxury and the struggle for titles and honours—a well-worn eighteenth-century theme—were to be scorned. The only 'temple' worthy of the Creator was what was useful to society and to one's neighbour.[8] The essayist Ivan M. Murav'ev-Apostol explained in 1814 that there were three ways of serving the fatherland—by 'deed', by 'thought' and by 'heart'. Soldiers, bureaucrats and 'preachers of the faith' served by deed; writers who inspired their readers to be useful citizens served by thought, while one served by heart in his private life and in his help to his neighbour.[9] State service, therefore, was linked to religion, beneficence and moral purity.

Essayists, poets and speakers frequently supported their arguments by looking to religion. Christianity was visible in society in more ways than in patriotic poetry, the liturgy or in the presence of ecclesiastics on public occasions. Advertisements in the newspapers showed the availability of edifying religious reflections for adults. Pypin incorrectly attributes to the Russian Bible Society (1813–1826) the first publication of religious tracts and the Bible.[10] From the very beginning of the century, the public could purchase Biblical readings and other religious works. Extracts of Orthodox, Roman Catholic and Protestant 'mystical' writers were provided in the Mason A. F. Labzin's *Messenger of Zion* in 1806 and 1817. Certainly the Bible Society looked to a mass audience, while the moral readings for children advertised in newspapers and journals were intended primarily for those who were educated at home, but the frequency of such notices indicates a wide interest in religious literature on the part of middle and upper class parents.[11] As to be expected, however, some 'moral readings', especially in the early part of the century, were from writers imbued more with sentimentalism than with Christian doctrine, and others came from anti-clerical Enlightenment writers, especially Voltaire, and from Rousseau.[12] The teaching of religion was part of the curriculum of all elementary and secondary schools for most of Alexander's reign, although at first such teaching was not required in the gymnasia. Boarding schools provided both religious instruction and supervised attendance at religious observances.

Future Decembrists and others at the elite Tsarskoe Selo Litsei absorbed political and social notions from their liberal teachers, and from readings as well as from conversations with classmates, but the journal of one student in 1815 shows how deeply Christian practices influenced his attitude; his diary depicts the reception of the Sacraments as a divine force which turned him away from sin and gave him peace. 'How happy is he who devotes himself to God and His Holy Church.'[13] Such an acknowledgement of Orthodox custom by no means tells the whole story of the extent of a Christian atmosphere in society when writers since the eighteenth century had equated an awareness of 'virtue' with 'an understanding of the divine'.[14] An anonymous 1804 'Stanzas to a virtuous man' demonstrates how that mood continued in the following century. A virtuous man 'loved God, honour, the law'. He looked on death with courage, seeing it as part of the natural law, for he placed his hope in God.[15] There was a long history of moral edification—compatible with Christianity and to some degree stemming from religion—behind a play which students in 1816 presented at the University of Moscow Nobles' Pansion (boarding school). The actors who denounced a 'Frenchified' education, the idleness and superficiality of 'the world', stressed honour and justice, the necessity of service and the fulfilment of obligations, were voicing puritanical and patriotic arguments reminiscent of N. I. Novikov and D. I. Fonvizin.[16] The imprecision of religious content here does not suggest a secular morality but rather an emphasis on generosity, purity of motive and self-sacrifice. Such an attitude was commonplace and may be seen especially in the Christianity of the Masons and of those persons whose views resembled those of the Masons. For some Orthodox believers the subjective pietism to be found among Masons and others deviated from dogmatic Christianity. But while some Masons were anti-clerical, others were devout observers of Orthodox ritual and many saw in Masonry a means of perfecting themselves as Christians.[17] The 'Christianity' in addresses, essays and poems in the journals for the most part lacked theological profundity or exactitude. Vague moral appeals sometimes came from writers who were Christians, as when V. A. Zhukovskii wrote that true happiness came not from wealth and renown, but rather from cleanly hearts and a virtuous family life.[18]

Minor writers in the early nineteenth century repeated the familiar eighteenth-century anti-aristocratic theme that what mattered for happiness was not rank but strength of character and love for the unfortunate.[19] Publicists sometimes drew from anti-clerical Enlightenment sources while professing a traditional Christianity. The prolific second-rate sentimentalist Prince P. A. Shalikov found consolation in Voltaire and in Rousseau, but his poetry contained 'throne and altar' expressions. We must, he counselled, dedicate our all to 'the fatherland, to the tsar, to the holy Altar'. The poet wanted to inspire a reader with 'nobility of soul' so that she would demonstrate her 'love for neighbour'.[20] In Shalikov, as in many others, it is not clear to what extent his extolling of religion represented an acceptance of Orthodox dogma, or the 'other world' aspirations of sentimentalism. However Shalikov argued that moral rules and respect for virtue depended upon a belief in the rewards and punishments of an after-life.[21] There was no greater happiness than that derived from helping others.[22] Shalikov was a late follower of Karamzin's sentimental-melancholic school,[23] whose adherents urged the comfort and creative power of religion, pointed out how the virtuous soul rose above circumstances,[24] how all things worldly would pass,[25] but faith taught us that 'a better world' awaited the virtuous.[26] He who kept the ideals of his youth would find death but a step to heaven.[27] The journals throughout the reign offered contributions from participants in the 'night and tombs' mood, as for example the poet who with many exclamation marks proclaimed the necessity of reconciliation with Providence and with death.[28] Poets who insisted against the 'sophists' that without God there would be no true friendship and that only selfishness would rule,[29] demonstrated in their protests that they feared that atheist notions remained popular. The defence of Christian benevolence was often accompanied, however, with attacks on 'the aristocratic, the powerful, the proud'.[30] This affirmed an identification between the Christian spirit and concern for the poor, as well as a compatibility between Christian teaching and the satirical motif.

If a good deal of the Christianity in literature consisted of pietistic moralising, on the other hand the reaction on the part of A. S. Shishkov and his followers against the borrowing of Western European sentimentalist and linguistic modes evoked a direct reference to Orthodox cultural values.[31] Shishkov saw the origin of the Russian literary language in Church Slavonic; the basis of traditional Russian manners was the teaching of the church; the danger to the morals of young Russians came from the frivolity and lack of faith of the

Enlightenment and revolutionary France. The 'purity of our ancestors' myth—which may be pushed back to Rousseau or even to Hesiod—encouraged a patriotic emotionalism which could be directed against either the introduction of radical Western novelties or—as in the case of the future Decembrist V. K. Kiukhel'beker's eloquent 1821 Paris address—against prevailing serfdom and autocracy.[32] The reactionary application of the myth in Shishkov, in exploiting such religious expressions as the responsibility of society 'to save the wretched from the hands of the powerful',[33] corresponded to similar utterances from writers among 'progressives' who opposed Shishkov.

The blustering character of Shishkov's attack on French influence provoked a pointed and often witty rebuttal from writers who regarded the modernisation of Russian letters in the works of Karamzin as a great advance in culture.[34] Among those who ridiculed Shishkov's obscurantism was the poet-professor A. F. Voeikov,[35] but Voeikov's frequent contributions to the journals also contained the religious theme. His hymn to God, in the majestic G. R. Derzhavin manner, made no mention of Christ or the church and may be regarded as more deistic than Christian,[36] but in another poem he spoke of Russian Christianity as a part of the 'pure faith' of Russians, who were so distinguished for their religious toleration, patriotism and love of freedom.[37] 'Love of the good, of the Creator, of our neighbour' was our obligation, he wrote.[38] He denounced those 'sophists' who 'undermined faith'—such as Helvétius, Diderot and Spinoza—to whom he opposed the 'Christians': Pascal, Leibnitz and Newton. The writer was to preach 'warm Faith' as a 'priest' of the 'higher virtues'.[39] His poem in praise of the Christian charity of the empress-mother, Maria Feodorovna, depicted faith as a counter to inhuman selfishness. In providing comfort in this world, the empress was offering a guide to the next. Christian charity sanctified mankind before God.[40]

The religious message in anti-Napoleonic propaganda resembled aspects of the literature of the later Decembrists, or those connected with the Decembrists. For one anonymous 1812 essayist, France represented falsehood, infidelity and slavery, while Russia meant truth, faith and freedom. 'Brave and honourable people take courage! It is better to die than to become slaves; it is better not to live in shame under chains. Take courage and hope in God!'[41]

This resembled the later poetry of the Decembrist Kondratii Ryleev, who similarly urged self-sacrifice to destroy 'the tyrant'.[42]

The desperate nature of the struggle against Napoleon stimulated a fiercely patriotic literature not only from simplistic chauvinists but from writers normally noted for their moderation, scepticism, criticism and wonderful sense of ridicule. Famous liberal satirists who in reaction to the French invasion wrote religious, patriotic poetry included A. Vostokov,[43] Prince P. A. Viazemskii,[44] V. L. Pushkin,[45] and Vasilii Kapnist.[46] Much of the extremism of Decembrist thought may be attributed to the heated, dualistic rhetoric of the war and immediate post-war period. The poet N. I. Gnedich was close to the Decembrists and amused his associates in the Arzamas literary club with religious parody,[47] but like others in the 'progressive camp' he used terms of loyalty and religiosity similar to those of the 'official patriots'. In 1816 he likened France to 'proud Babylon', praised the tsar who as a 'Christian hero' devoted himself to the happiness of mankind, who was 'armed not with the pride of the wisdom of this world but by the meekness of the cross of Faith'.[48] Of course writers adhered to official policy when the tsar was the source of bureaucratic posts and pensions, but Gnedich dedicated the same kind of patriotic fervour to the cause of 'enlightenment', the welfare of 'humanity' and to the independence of a writer in an 1821 address before the liberal 'Free Society of the Lovers of Russian Literature'.[49]

Ecclesiastics such as Bishop Avgustin of Dmitrov in anti-Napoleonic oratory also spoke of 'breaking the chains of a shameful slavery'.[50] The Russian victory in returning kingdoms to their rulers meant, he said, not reaction or oppression but 'freedom, peace and plenty'.[51] He promised that injustice would cease and the oppressed would be defended.[52] Lay writers also exploited the alleged arbitrariness and 'despotism' of Napoleon to idealise the Russian-Christian monarchy as the defender of the oppressed and the upholder of law and freedom. A. N. Olenin wrote in 1813 that the Orthodox church gave meaning to life on this earth and an expectation of life after death. The Russian government in adhering to Christianity ruled not by compulsion but by the natural law; love for the tsar motivated the people. The enemy, on the contrary, acted without law, without faith, without God.[53]

Mentions of virtue, justice, the oppressed, the common good, the rule of law and the welfare of the poor are to be found in sermons and religious writings which strikingly parallel phrases in Decembrist literature.[54] Religious poetry affirmed the same goals,[55] as did the pious articles in the journal *Christian Readings* which the St Petersburg Ecclesiastical Academy published.[56] Even the notoriously obscurantist instructions of the education department official M. L. Magnitskii in 1820 to the director of Kazan University observed that the purpose of government was not the good of one man or of one class, but the common good. The education department order contained phrases such as 'freedom', 'justice', and 'mutual self-sacrifice'.[57]

The government—continuing the practice of Catherine's reign—encouraged private donations for charitable (and educational) good works not only because the church no longer had the wealth to undertake such responsibilities, but because the generosity of the public had to substitute for the meagre treasury allocations for good causes. Official sponsorship in the second decade of Alexander's reign of pietistic Christianity, as seen in the encouragement of Quaker philanthropy and of the Russian Bible Society, gave a more pronounced Christian tone to propaganda for donations, but after the Napoleonic wars as before the message of preachers and publicists was the same: Christian morality implied service to one's fellow man. Service was to be realised in aiding the state, which was identified with its self-sacrificing, generous tsar, the model of Christian virtue and enlightenment.[58] Journal reports stressed the obligation of citizens to join with the tsar in the work of charity;[59] journals made appeals to help distressed individuals,[60] and accounts of donations filled many newspaper columns.[61]

The law which established the Russian Bible Society acknowledged that its activities were to meet the wishes of 'humanitarian Christians' who wanted to further the 'temporal and eternal' welfare of their neighbours.[62] The bureaucrat A. M. Bezobrazov told the Tambov section of the Bible Society in 1817 that the reading of the 'Word of God' gave one a sense of obligation, of virtue guided by reason, of justice, love of neighbour and of brotherhood.[63] An 1818 essayist in honouring the work of the Bible Society, combined religiosity with older Enlightenment anti-clericalism. The 'triumph of faith' reduced the darkness of idol worship; one could contrast, he said, the enlightened efforts of the Bible Society with the cruelty of the Spanish in the New World.[64] Many journal essays combined Enlightenment humanitarian concepts with officially approved religious-patriotic notions. Ivan Snitkin, in the liberal *Nevskii Observer* (1820), added to 'anti-tyrannical' phraseology a tribute to Christianity, which he claimed led to the 'rise of humanity' and to 'freedom', as opposed to the regressive nature of paganism and the Moslem religion. He praised the Holy Alliance, attacked the ideology of the French

Revolution and attributed Russian progress to 'the Gospel'. 'Let Russia be the means for the great purpose of Providence—the union of Faith—for which the holy Church daily prays.'[65] Prince Viazemskii, who was a friend of leading secret society members, and a hater of oppression, in his 1821 'Thoughts at Prayer' pointed out that respect for the rule of law meant a regard for the image of God in man.[66]

Some Decembrists in reacting against the political and social structure of society also opposed the official patriotic and religious cult. But other Decembrists would employ concepts from the propaganda of that cult to further what they hoped would be a more humane order. While the reactionary Magnitskii's famous 1818 address before the Simbirsk Bible Society had attacked 'human reason' as the 'idol' of anti-Christian diabolism,[67] Major-General M. F. Orlov, a prominent secret society leader, told the Kievan Bible Society in 1819 that Russian Christianity was to be identified with the 'progressive' cause against the religious and political reaction in Western Europe.[68] That Orlov used the Bible Society as a platform for his liberal arguments and that his address was filled with religious expressions shows that despite the continuation in Russia of much influence from the Enlightenment, the educated public understood and valued a Christian terminology.

The picture is too complex to reduce intellectual tensions to a conflict between Christian ideology on the one hand and the survivals of Enlightenment thought on the other. The new interest in the religious philosophy of Schelling, especially at the University of Moscow but also at St Petersburg University, influenced many of the intelligentsia, including some Decembrists.[69] The significance of Pushkin as a singer of 'freedom' is well known and his irreverent verse influenced religious attitudes. But since both Voltairean and religious sentiments are contained in his early verse, his religious position is ambiguous—his parodies of religious imagery may be seen as a reaction against official religiosity. At times he toyed with atheism and anti-clericalism, but he could be sympathetic to the church and to religious ideals.[70]

In the writings of the most prolific of the Decembrist publicists, F. N. Glinka, a Mason, there is a continual emphasis on religion. He wrote paraphrases of the psalms to place God on the side of the oppressed, who were to throw off their yoke.[71] His essays, aphorisms and poetry—often strongly patriotic—stressed 'faith' and 'hope in God'. Glinka attacked the writers of the Enlightenment for denying the freedom of the will and said that virtue rested on a belief in Revelation and the after-life.[72] Faith in God was a prerequisite for freedom.[73] The Decembrists' espousing of philanthropic Christianity, as in Glinka, must be distinguished from 'official philanthropy', however, in that the former implied an impassioned rejection of serfdom.[74]

Other prominent Decembrists were Christians. An example is the Lutheran poet V. K. Kiukhel'beker, whose writings in his imprisonment and exile did not contradict but continued an early religious interest.[75] The Catholic M. S. Lunin is another example.[76] The Soviet scholar Shchipanov lists 11 Decembrists as atheists but there were, he wrote, 'many others'. Seven fell into the vague category of 'idealists' or 'materialist-atheists', while of one hundred sent to Siberia, some 13 to 15 were 'believers', an estimate which must be only approximate since the author did not include Kiukhel'beker.[77] It is not surprising that a number of Decembrists, despite having received religious training at school or at home,[78] became attracted to French deism or even atheism through their reading,[79] when rationalism had influenced many of the 'progressive' writers since the first days of Alexander's reign,[80] and late devotees of the French Enlightenment, such as Jouy, whom the Decembrists admired, linked deism and anti-clericalism with the popular view that politics must be based on morality.[81] One Decembrist in his testimony distinguished those who after the war occupied themselves with 'mystical ideals' from those like himself who were interested in 'political studies'.[82]

Anti-religious views were common among the first organisers of secret societies in Russia.[83] The religion in A. D. Ulybyshev's Utopian 'Dream' included the immortality of the soul but omitted the liturgy and an ordained clergy.[84] But D. V. Sakharov's 1818 defence of 'enlightenment' and 'freedom' joined a conventional attack on 'medieval fanaticism and superstition' with an equally conventional attack on the 'atheism' of the French Revolution.[85] N. I. Kutuzov insisted that education had to be based on faith; a pupil was to learn his relationship 'to himself, to his neighbour and to God'.[86]

Not all the winds which blew on sensitive minds were anti-religious, as the Christianity of the Decembrist 'fellow traveller' A. S. Griboedov illustrates.[87] The diary of N. I. Turgenev shows the lasting charm which boyish religious experiences exercised over him. He disliked the 'fanaticism' of Roman Catholic monks but he could not accept Rousseau's opposition to religious training; he depicted patriotism as a 'divine force' and admired genuine Christian devotion, while he assailed 'mysticism' and Magnitskii's obscurantism.[88] Turgenev objected to the broad and vague nature of Christianity implied in the activities of the Bible Society and preferred the use of a catechism with 'positive dogmas'.[89] This was a religious position more conservative than that of some of the leading churchmen, some of whom since the late eighteenth century were under the influence of the ecumenical spirit.[90] The Constitution of the Union of Welfare proclaimed that the struggle for virtue, the service of the fatherland and efforts for the general welfare were the work of a 'true Christian', which should involve especially the clergy.[91]

French Catholic tutors and his father's 'cult of virtue', as well as a patriotic, religious emotionalism influenced Nikita Murav'ev, who remained faithful to the Christian tradition in spite of having read Voltaire's 'Henriade'.[92] Murav'ev's constitution allowed the church to keep property[93] and abolished autocratic rule and serfdom in the name of Christian principles.[94] The Lutheran P. I. Pestel' also saw serfdom as contrary to the Christian spirit; he would allow no laws which did not correspond to Christian principles. Our sense of obligation came first of all from the faith which God had placed in our hearts. His *Russkaia pravda* declared that while there would be religious toleration for cults which were not contrary to Russian laws, the Orthodox church was to be recognised as the state religion. The church was to be subordinate to the state. Religion was seen as an 'inner conviction' and therefore no inquisition was to be permitted. The government was to control the monasteries, postulants to which were to be at least 60 years of age. Gradually bishops were to come from the parish clergy, not from the monasteries. The clergy were not to form a separate caste, but were to be servants of the government. Pestel' urged the Christianisation of the native peoples of Siberia, he opposed the Uniate church and he wanted more restrictions to be placed on the Jews.[95]

Despite the protests of some Southern Society members who objected to 'fanaticism', Sergei Murav'ev-Apostol and M. P. Bestuzhev-Riumin exploited the religious motif to encourage soldiers to rise against their 'oppressors'.[96] Some time before the uprising, V. F. Raevskii in 'The Slavery of the Peasants' had included among the horrors of serfdom the forcing of peasants to work on Sundays and holy days, thereby 'weakening the force of faith, the only support and comfort for man'.[97] The anonymous 1820 proclamation to the soldiers of the Semenovskii regiment applied Christian moral principles to attack an unpopular commander. 'There is no Christian faith where people do not help one another.'[98]

Agitators who used Biblical expressions and forms of catechism to propagandise soldiers may or may not themselves have had respect for Christian doctrine. Christianity did, however, exert considerable influence on the Decembrist goal of a moral transformation of society. That objective was not only in harmony with the old Christian service ethic, but was in part an outgrowth of that ethic. Writers had always asserted the connection between Christianity and service to humanity through an honest devotion to the state. Decembrist attitudes illustrate the close connection between Christianity and revolutionary dreams. And certainly Christian ideology exercised influence on many directions of thought in the early nineteenth century.

NOTES

1. For example addresses in *Periodicheskoe sochinenie o uspekhakh narodnago prosveshcheniia* 13 (1805) pp. 107–14; 14 (1806) pp. 178–87; *Sanktpeterburgskiia Vedomosti* 5 (16 January 1816) appendix.

2. For a summary of prevailing philosophical-religious attitudes see Georges Florovsky, *Ways of Russian Theology*, Part ɪ, vol. ᴠ of *The Collected Works of Georges Florovsky*, ed. Richard S. Haugh and Paul Kachur, trans. Robert L. Nichols (Belmont, Mass.: 1979) pp. 150–3, 162–4.

3. Hans Rothe, *Religion und Kultur in den Regionen des russischen Reiches im 18. Jahrhundert* (Opladen: 1984) pp. 8–9, 95, 106.

4. Hugh Blair, *Lectures on Rhetoric and Belles Lettres*, 4th ed., 3 vols, ɪ (London: 1790) p. 16; Johann George Sulzer, *Allgemeine Theorie der Schönen Künste*, 2nd ed., 4 vols, ɪɪ (Leipzig: 1792–4) (1792) pp. 55–7. Russian professors of aesthetics in the early nineteenth century regarded Blair and Sulzer as authorities.

5. R. Iu. Danilevskii, 'Viland [Wieland] v russkoi literature', in *Ot klassitsizma k romantizmu. Iz istorii mezhdunarodnikh sviazei russkoi literatury* (Leningrad: 1970) pp. 346, 351.

6. *Periodicheskoe sochinenie o uspekhakh narodnago prosveshcheniia* (1806) no. 16, pp. 457–67, especially pp. 457, 464.

7. *Sochineniia Petra Plavil'shchikova*, 4 parts in one vol., ɪᴠ (St Petersburg: 1816) pp. 172–4.

8. 'Blagotvoriteliu Moskovskikh Muz', printed in *Vestnik Evropy* 42 (April 1812) no. 7, pp. 161–77.

9. 'Pis'ma iz Moskvy v Nizhnyi Novgorod', *Syn Otechestva* 11 (1814) no. 3, pp. 99–100.

10. A. N. Pypin, *Obshchestvennoe dvizhenie v Rossii pri Alexandre I* (Petrograd: 1916) pp. 109, 114.

11. Advertisements in *Sanktpeterburgskiia Vedomosti* 15 (19 February 1804); 18 (1 March 1804); 23 (18 March 1804); 30 (12 April 1804); 80 (4 October 1804); 8 (26 January 1806); 11 (6 February 1806); 34 (27 April 1806); 4 (11 January 1807); 85 (22 October 1807); 17 (1 March 1810); 18 (4 March 1810). Notices in *Syn Otechestva* 12 (1814) no. 10, pp. 155–6; 19 (1814) no. 3, pp. 85–92; 33 (1816) no. 39, pp. 28–9; 57 (1819) no. 45, pp. 217–18; 67 (1821) no. 5, pp. 230–1. See also N. P. Koliupanov, *Biografiia Aleksandra Ivanovicha Kosheleva* I (Moscow: 1889) pp. 167–83. Dates throughout this paper are given in the Old Style of the original publication.

12. *Sanktpeterburgskiia Vedomosti* 61 (1 August 1801); 72 (9 September 1802); 76 (23 September 1802); 1 (1 January 1804); 11 (5 February 1804); 46 (7 June 1804); 60 (26 July 1804); 97 (5 December 1805); 1 (2 January 1806); 30 (12 April 1807); 53 (3 July 1808).

13. K. Ia. Grot, *Pushkinskii litsei (1811–1817)*. Bumagi 1-go kursa (St Petersburg: 1911) pp. 10–12.

14. For example A. P. Sumarokov in *N. I. Novikov i ego sovremenniki. Izbrannye sochineniia* (Moscow: 1961) pp. 361, 364, 376.

15. *Drug prosveshcheniia* 3 (July 1804) no. 7, pp. 13–14.

16. *Vestnik Evropy* 91 (January 1817) no. 1, pp. 3–13.

17. 'Zapiski I. V. Lopukhina', *Russkii arkhiv* 52, book 1 (1914) pp. 148, 156; F. Mikhailov to A. F. Labzin, 19 August 1807, *Russkaia starina* 147 (September 1911) pp. 522–3; Count V. Musin-Pushkin-Brius to Count S. K. Viazmitinov, January 1819 in *Sbornik istoricheskikh materialov, izvlechennykh iz arkhiva sobstvennoi Ego Imperatorskago Velichestva kantselarii*, ed. N. Dubrovin, XI (St Petersburg: 1902) p. 288; T. Sokolovskaia, *Russkoe masonstvo i ego zhachenie v istorii obshchestvennago dvizheniia (XVIII i pervaia chetvert' XIX stoletiia)* (St Petersburg: [1907]) pp. 64–6, 72–6; V. I. Semevskii, 'Masony-dekabristy', *Minuvshie gody* (May-June 1908) nos 5 and 6, pp. 403–04.

18. *Vestnik Evropy* 39 (June 1808) no. 12, pp. 220–30. Also see his diary for 10 July 1805 in *Dnevnik V. A. Zhukovskago* (St Petersburg: 1903) p. 16.

19. Anon. in *Vestnik Evropy* 55 (January 1811) no. 2, pp. 93–4. For an example of eighteenth-century commonplaces about obligations to the 'orphan' and to 'neighbour' see anon., 'Oda sueta slavy mira' in *S. Peterburgskii merkurii* 3 (April 1793) pp. 81–91.

20. *Sochineniia Kniazia Shalikova*, 2 parts (Moscow: 1819) I, p. 59; II, pp. 8, 17.

21. Shalikov remarks in *Vestnik Evropy* 100 (July 1818) no. 14, p. 140.

22. Shalikov poem in ibid. 109 (January 1820) no. 2, p. 98.

23. N. M. Karamzin, 'holy, heavenly melancholy, mother of all the immortal wonders of the human soul . . .' in *Novikov i ego sovremenniki*, p. 391; also see pp. 396, 408.

24. Anna Volkova, 'Gimn sovesti', *Syn Otechestva* 29 (1816) no. 25, pp. 227–31.

25. V. Tumanskii, 'Monastyr. Elegiia', *Blagonamerennyi* 2 (May 1818) no. 5, p. 318.
26. M. V. Milonov, 'V. A. Zhukovskomu', ibid. 3 (August 1818) no. 8, pp. 129–32.
27. V. Kopylov, 'Zima', ibid., 17 (July 1819) no. 14, pp. 63–7.
28. V. N. Olin 'Upovanie', *Syn Otechestva* 77 (1822) no. 18, pp. 179–82.
29. V. Kopylov, 'Mysli', *Vestnik Evropy* 101 (20 October 1818) pp. 252–7.
30. G. Kruglikov, 'K sosedu', *Nevskii zritel'* 1 (February 1820) pp. 88–90.
31. For a recent study of Shishkov and his followers see Mark Al'tshuller, *Predtechi slavianofil'stva v russkoi literature. (Obshchestvo 'Beseda liubitelei russkogo slova')* (Ann Arbor: 1984).
32. *Literaturnoe nasledstvo* 59 (Moscow: 1954) pp. 366–73.
33. A. S. Shishkov, 'Rassuzhdenie o starom i novom sloge rossiiskogo iazyka' (1803), in *Sobranie sochinenii i perevodov Admirala Shishkova*, 17 vols (St Petersburg: 1819–1839) ii (1824) p. 86.
34. See for example V. L. Pushkin poems in *Poety-satiriki kontsa XVIII-nachala XIX v.*, ed. G. V. Ermakovoi-Bitner (Leningrad: 1959) pp. 269–71, 279ff.
35. See 'Dom sumasshedshikh' in ibid., pp. 297–308.
36. *Vestnik Evropy* 98 (April 1818) no. 7, pp. 176–8.
37. Ibid. 99 (June 1818) no. 12, pp. 265–78.
38. Ibid. 109 (January 1820) no. 1, p. 170.
39. *Novosti literatury* 7 (1824) no. 11, pp. 171–2, 174.
40. *Syn Otechestva* 75 (1822) no. 4, pp. 181–6.
41. Ibid. 1 (1812) no. 1, pp. 43–6.
42. Franklin A. Walker, 'K. F. Ryleev. A Self-Sacrifice for Revolution', *The Slavonic and East European Review* 47 (January 1969) no. 109, pp. 436–66.
43. *Syn Otechestva* 15 (1814) no. 29, pp. 118–19.
44. Ibid. 14 (1814) no. 16, pp. 280–1.
45. Ibid., pp. 282–3.
46. Ibid. 23 (1815) no. 31, p. 197.
47. M. I. Gillel'son, *Molodoi Pushkin i arzamasskoe bratstvo* (Leningrad: 1974) pp. 148–9.
48. *Syn Otechestva* 27 (1816) no. 2, pp. 51–2.
49. *Sorevnovatel'* 15 (1821) no. 8, pp. 112–47.
50. *Syn Otechestva* 11 (1814) no. 1, p. 6.
51. Ibid. 16 (1814) no. 38, pp. 211–27.
52. Ibid. 27 (1816) no. 1, p. 4.
53. Ibid. 7 (1813) no. 32, pp. 219–22.
54. Examples in *Vestnik Evropy* 79 (January 1815) no. 2, pp. 65–6; (February 1823) nos 3 and 4, pp. 317–23; (April 1824) no. 7, pp. 165–77; *Ukrainskii vestnik* 5 (January 1817) pp. 115–16; *Syn Otechestva* 79 (1822) no. 28, pp. 78–83; 91 (1824) no. 3, pp. 97–115. Just as Christian terminology influenced Enlightenment writers, so did Enlightenment phraseology influence Russian churchmen. See David M. Griffiths, 'In Search of Enlightenment; Recent Soviet Interpretation of Eighteenth-Century Russian Intellectual History', *Canadian-American Slavic Studies* 16 (Fall-Winter 1982) nos 3–4, pp. 317–56, especially pp.

355–6. Also see Robert L. Nichols, 'Orthodoxy and Russia's Enlightenment, 1762–1825' in *Russian Orthodoxy under the Old Regime*, ed. Robert L. Nichols and George Stavrou (Minneapolis: 1978) pp. 67–89.

55. As for example V. Feonov's 'Vera', *Vestnik Evropy* 113 (September 1820) no. 18, pp. 95–8.

56. *Khristianskoe chtenie* 1 (1821) pp. 9, 73, 102–03; 14 (1824) pp. 79, 81–3.

57. *Zhurnal Departamenta Narodnago Prosveshcheniia* 2 (May 1821) p. 49.

58. Judith Cohen Zacek, 'The Imperial Philanthropic Society in the Reign of Alexander I', *Canadian-American Slavic Studies* 9 (Winter 1975) no. 4, pp. 427–36; Judith Cohen Zacek, 'The Russian Bible Society and the Russian Orthodox Church', *Church History* 35 (December 1966) no. 4, pp. 411–37; Adele Lindemeyer, 'Public Poor Relief and Private Charity in Late Imperial Russia' (unpublished Ph.D. dissertation, Princeton University, 1980) pp. 107–33.

59. *Syn Otechestva* 34 (1816) no. 52, pp. 245–71; 60 (1820) no. 10, pp. 162–71.

60. For example *Vestnik Evropy* 57 (May 1811) no. 9, pp. 171–3; 85 (February 1816) no. 4, pp. 313–14; 111 (April 1820) no. 17, p. 240. Other journals contained similar appeals.

61. For example among countless such items, *Sanktpeterburgskiia Vedomosti* 77 (25 September 1808); 96 (2 December 1813); 45 (6 June 1816); 1 (4 January 1821); 62 (5 August 1821); *Severnaia pochta* 45 (5 June 1815).

62. Law 25.287 (6 December 1812). *Polnoe Sobranie Zakonov Rossiiskoi Imperii s 1649 goda* First Series xxxii (1812–15) (St Petersburg: 1830) p. 471.

63. *Syn Otechestva* 42 (1817) no. 48, pp. 87–95.

64. I. Pereslavskii in ibid. 149 (1818) no. 41, pp. 108–16.

65. *Nevskii zritel'* 1 (January 1820) p. 23; 2 (June 1820) pp. 209–11, 227. For Snitkin see V. Bazanov, *Uchenaia respublika* (Moscow-Leningrad: 1964) pp. 153–5.

66. P. A. Viazemskii, *Polnoe sobranie sochinenii*, iii (St Petersburg: 1880) p. 256.

67. A. N. Pypin, *Religioznyia dvizheniia pri Aleksandre I* (Petrograd: 1916) p. 148.

68. M. F. Orlov, *Kapituliatsiia Parizha. Politicheskie sochineniia. Pis'ma*, ed. S. Ia. Borovoi and M. I. Gillel'son (Moscow: 1963) pp. 45–52.

69. A. A. Kamenskii, *Russkaia filosofiia nachala XIX veka i Shelling* (Moscow: 1980).

70. A. S. Pushkin, *Polnoe sobranie sochinenii*, 16 vols in 20 (Moscow-Leningrad, 1937–1959) i, pp. 64, 81; ii (2) (1949) pp. 45–8, 397–403, 428; xi (1949) pp. 16–17, 271–2; xiii (1937) p. 92. See Gillel'son, *Molodoi Pushkin*, pp. 211–14. On the influence of Pushkin's irreverent poetry see memoirs of D. I. Zavalishin in *Pisateli-dekabristy v vospominaniiakh sovremennikov*, 2 vols (Moscow: 1980) ii, p. 247.

71. *Dekabristy i Russkaia kultura*, ed. B. S. Meilakh (Leningrad: 1975) p. 41.

94 Christianity, the Service Ethic and Decembrist Thought

72. *Russkii vestnik* 2, no. 9 (1818) pp. 65–82.

73. F. Glinka, *Razsuzhdenie o neobkhodimosti deiatel'noi zhizni* . . . (St Petersburg: 1818) pp. 44–5.

74. F. N. Glinka, *Pis'ma russkogo ofitsera. Proza. Publitsistika. Poeziia. Stat'i. Pis'ma*, ed. S. Serkov and Iu. Uderevskii (Moscow: 1985), especially pp. 128–9, 160, 191, 211, 215, 278, 295. See examples also in *Syn Otechestva* 29 (1816) no. 4, pp. 128–62; 38 (1817) no. 24, pp. 173–7; *Sorevnovatel'* 3 (1818) no. 8, pp. 232–39; *Severnaia pchela* 127 (22 October 1825). See incisive comment in N. Dubrovin, 'Posle otechestvennoi voiny', *Russkaia starina* (1904) pp. 514–15. Also see Franklin A. Walker, 'Reaction and Radicalism in the Russia of Tsar Alexander I: The Case of the Brothers Glinka', *Canadian Slavonic Papers* 21 (December 1979) no. 4, pp. 489–502.

75. V. K. Kiukhel'beker, *Izbrannye proizvedenia v dvukh tomakh*, ed. N. V. Koroleva, 2 vols (Moscow-Leningrad: 1967), intro., ı, p. 43. See Franklin A. Walker, 'The Ambivalent Educator: Kiukhel'beker and the Didactics of Revolution', *East/West Education* 10 (Spring 1986) no. 1, pp. 17–28.

76. G. R. Barratt, 'The Catholicism of Mikhail Sergeyevich Lunin', *The Slavonic and East European Review* 49 (April 1971) no. 115, pp. 255–71, and same author, *M. S. Lunin. Catholic Decembrist* (The Hague: 1976).

77. *Izbrannye sotsial'no-politicheskie i filosofsksie proizvedenie dekabristov*, 3 vols, ed. I. Ia. Shchipanov (Moscow: 1951), intro., ı, p. 45. Most of the exiled Decembrists in Chita were indifferent to religion, according to N. P. Sil'vanskii, 'Materialisty dvadsatykh godov', *Byloe* 7 (19) (July 1907) pp. 120–1. But on the other hand see discussion of the philosophical-religious debates among the exiles in the memoirs of A. P. Beliaev in *Pisateli-dekabristy*, ıı, pp. 236–7. For the atheist poetry (in French) of A. P. Bariatinskii see *Vosstanie dekabristov*, x (Moscow: 1953) pp. 301–04.

78. For example N. A. Kriukov testimony in *Vosstanie dekabristov*, xı (Moscow: 1954) p. 372; and P. I. Koloshin testimony in ibid., xvııı (1984) p. 164.

79. For example testimony of A. I. Saburov, ibid., xvııı, p. 68. A. S. Ganglov's testimony, ibid., p. 21, attacked the clergy as well as the landlords of White Russia. Also see S. I. Sverbeev memoirs concerning the Enlightenment views of S. M. Semenov in *Izbrannye . . . proizvedenie dekabristov*, ı, p. 655.

80. *Poety-Radishchesvtsy*, ed. P. A. Orlov (Leningrad: 1979), intro., p. 46.

81. Etienne de Jouy, *La morale appliquée à la politique, pour servir d'introduction aux observations sur les moeurs françaises aux XIXe siècle*, 2 vols in 1 (Paris: 1822), ı, pp. 13, 27, 32, 69–79, 97; ıı, p. 272.

82. *Vosstanie dekabristov*, IX (Moscow: 1950) p. 224.

83. M. V. Nechkina, 'Sviashchennaia artel'. Kruzhok A. Murav'eva i I. Burtsova 1814–1817 gg', in *Dekabristy i ikh vremia*, ed. M. P. Alekseev and B. E. Meilakh (Moscow: 1951) p. 186.

84. *Izbrannye . . . proizvedeniia dekabristov*, ı, p. 289.

85. *Sorevnovatel'* 9 (1818) no. 12, pp. 1–31.

86. *Syn Otechestva* 59 (1820) no. 1., pp. 4–5.
87. V. S. Meshcheriakov, *A. S. Griboedov. Literaturny okruzhenie i vospriatie* (Leningrad: 1983) p. 203.
88. Citations in *Izbrannye . . . proizvedenie dekabristov*, I, pp. 190, 192, 194–5, 197, 203. See also E. Tarasov, 'Detstvo i iunost' N. I. Turgeneva', *Zhurnal Ministerstva Narodnago Prosveshcheniia* new series 58 (July 1915) pp. 246–7.
89. Turgenev to P. A. Viazemskii 19 November 1819. *Ostaf'evskii Arkhiv Kniazei Viazemskikh*, 3 vols (St Petersburg: 1899), I, p. 355.
90. Robert Lewis Nichols, 'Metropolitan Filaret of Moscow and the Awakening of Orthodoxy' (unpublished Ph.D. dissertation, University of Washington, 1972) pp. 139, 146.
91. *Izbrannye . . . proizvedenie dekabristov*, I, pp. 243, 264, 266.
92. N. M. Druzhinin, *Dekabrist Nikita Murav'ev* (Moscow: 1985) pp. 53–4.
93. Ibid. p. 255.
94. *Izbrannye . . . proizvedenie dekabristov*, I, pp. 295, 301. His propaganda catechism 'Liubopytnyi razgovor' (1822) made the same points. *Vosstanie dekabristov*, IV (Moscow-Leningrad: 1927) pp. 254–6.
95. *Izbrannye proizvedeniia . . . dekabristov*, II, pp. 78–9, 157. *Vosstanie dekabristov*, VII (Moscow: 1958) pp. 114–15, 138–9, 143, 146–8, 153–6, 205–06. See Hans Lemberg, *Die nationale Gedankenwelt der Dekabristen* (Cologne: 1963) pp. 119–21. An early Soviet scholar who stressed the significance of 'free thought' among the Decembrists and held that the concessions to the church on the part of Murav'ev and Pestel' came from 'practical' considerations, acknowledged that Decembrism in essence was not anti-religious. I. P. Voronitsyn, *Dekabristy i religiia* ([Moscow], 1928) pp. 4, 22, 24, 26, 41.
96. *Izbrannye proizvedenie . . . dekabristov*, II, pp. 190–3, 221; III, pp. 44–5. See P. E. Shchegolev, *Dekabristy* (Moscow-Leningrad: 1926) pp. 231–59, especially p. 239.
97. *Izbrannye proizvedenie . . . dekabristov*, II, p. 368.
98. *Dekabristy. Otryvki iz istochnikov*, ed. Iu. G. Oksman (Moscow-Leningrad: 1926) p. 38.

7 The Role of the Orthodox Missionary in the Altai: Archimandrite Makarii and V. I. Verbitskii

David N. Collins

Archimandrite Makarii (Glukharev) (1792–1847) and Father Vasily Ivanovich Verbitskii (1827/8–1890) were both missionaries in the Altai region of Siberia. Their careers span the years 1830 to 1890, a sixty-year period during which the Mission's work flowered among the indigenous Turkic speaking inhabitants of the area and many thousands of Altaians became Christians.[1]

Historians of the Russian Empire tend to be well informed about many of the social processes which took place during the reigns of Nicholas I, Alexander II and Alexander III, but until recently there has been an ignorance of, or indifference to, developments within the Orthodox Church. This may be explained by the anti-religious, or at least secular, bias of most Russian and western researchers. We have many biographies of political activists, even relatively minor ones, but little seems to be known about major figures in Russia's nineteenth-century ecclesiastical history. Yet they formed an important part of the social fabric of the Russian Empire. A Russian history which does not include them is by definition incomplete.

Makarii and Verbitskii deserve to be better known if only because they represent some of the finer qualities of the Russian people. They manifested doggedness in the face of extreme hardships, a deep concern for the suffering and ignorance of their fellow human beings, and a preparedness to undergo personal sacrifices for a cause which they believed in profoundly. They did not write treatises from the shelter of comfortable institutions or engage in political polemic, but went out into a pioneer environment in which they had to build their own houses, travel thousands of miles on horseback through forest or swamp along rugged mountain tracks in all weathers, among a people socially and linguistically alien to them. They suffered poverty, illness, bereavement and numerous disappointments, yet working their way through these problems they were able to survive and accomplish great feats. They were active intellectually as they pioneered the academic study of the Altaians' language and ethnography. Apart from this they practised medicine, set up homes for orphans, taught the semi-nomadic Altaians a more hygienic and efficient mode of living, and showed them the rudiments of arable farming, bee keeping and domestic crafts. They set up model villages in which their converts were housed and began the process of educating them which led to the growth of a literate Altaian intelligentsia. Even those who disagree with their views, can agree that their lives were monuments to human endeavour.

For Christians their exploits are yet more significant. Between the two of them they encapsulated everything that missionaries should be. A recent book on Orthodox perspectives on mission defined the significance of missions thus:

> Through the individual members of the body of Christ, the church is unequivocally committed to communicating the *good news* and to striving towards the growth, sanctification and wellbeing of this one body . . . thus, by definition, the church can never remain static nor satisfied with a status quo. It must continually be in mission, proclaiming, announcing and teaching the good news to the oikoumene, the whole inhabited earth.[2]

The mission principles summed up in this book *Go Forth in Peace* bear a remarkable similarity to the work of Makaryii and Verbitskii. As the book suggests, they established eucharistic communities in the locality to which they were sent within the context and culture of the people concerned. Their villages provided the ground for mutual spiritual and material support and for teaching the converts. They tried to involve young people and women. They used the indigenous language for evangelism and also translated the liturgy and parts of the Bible into Altaian. Makaryii, and the other Altai missionaries after him, were keenly aware that rote mass baptisms were not effective, and stressed the need for adequate preparation and follow-up teaching. They were also opposed to any use of force; on the contrary they concentrated on drawing close to people's problems and providing for their social and health needs. Their lives were clear examples of faith, humility and love; nor did they neglect the call to proclaim justice and truth.[3] In many ways Makarii and Verbitskii have a contemporary relevance and seem to be modern figures.

Though both men received a calling to missionary work, and both served in the Altai, there were significant differences between them which will be examined at length through a biographical portrait of each in turn.

Mikhail Yakovlevich Glukharev, later to be renamed Makarii, was born into a clerical family in Vyaz'ma, Smolensk Province. Though always physically frail with poor eyesight he excelled at academic pursuits. In 1814 he was sent to the recently opened St Petersburg Spiritual Academy where he came under the influence of Filaret (Drozdov) one of the foremost churchmen of the age. German pietist concepts, popular at the time, led him to an awareness of the need for a personal rebirth of the inner man through the Holy Spirit's influence. In 1817 he was sent to teach German and history at Ekaterinoslav Seminary. He came into conflict with the diocesan authorities because he tried to investigate the loss of a sum of money which seemed to have disappeared from the seminary accounts, and because the high moral tone of his complaints upset colleagues. While he was at Ekaterinoslav he met Moldavian monks, followers of Paissy Velichkovsky, who were promoting a move towards hesychasm and under their influence decided to become a monk himself. Meeting an English and a French Quaker who were travelling in the Russian Empire to propound their views, and praying with Molokane he began to detect a true spirituality in believers who were not Orthodox. A latent desire for the contemplative life seems to have been emerging during these years, building upon the interest in contemplative literature which he had manifested in his St Petersburg period. In later years he was to translate several of these works into Russian, including St Augustine's *Confessions*, the *Ladder* of St John Climacus, the *Discourses* of St Gregory the Great, the works of St Teresa of Avila, and with the help of lay friends other spiritual classics.

In 1821 he was promoted to archimandrite and appointed rector of Kostroma Seminary and head of a local monastery. Again he fell foul of people owing to his strict sense of moral probity. In 1824 finding the strain of holding two positions too great he was released to find a suitable monastery in which he could ascertain his spiritual calling. He consulted the renowned *starets* Seraphim of Sarov, who predicted a hard road ahead for him, and eventually settled at the Glinsk *pustyn'* in Kostroma Province, where he remained until 1829 translating some of the Church fathers and parts of the Bible into Russian from the original languages.

Answering a call to mission issued by the Holy Synod in 1828 Makarii volunteered to go to Siberia. In mid-1829 he set off for Tobol'sk where he learned the 'Turkic Tatar' language and after several false trails had led nowhere decided to work among the hill people of the Altai. In August 1830 he set off towards Biisk, establishing himself at a small settlement called Maima after an unfortunate attempt to settle at the village of Ulala which led to the local population moving away from him. Initial missionary proclamation led to few results, so he turned to practical work, cleaning native houses and minding children. This created confidence between him and the local community. His 'softly-softly' approach succeeded. By 1834 he was able to move back to Ulala, which became the central point of the Mission. With time converts were gained. Before he left the Altai he had baptised 675 Altaians, but this was done only after considerable preparatory teaching. He strongly believed that baptism should not be an external act which led to no changes, but should result from a turn-around in the person's life which would initiate a process during which the person would become a Christian through and through. Consequently, he provided extensive post-baptismal instruction. Partly to protect the new converts from reprisals from their unconverted countrymen, and partly because he believed that a sedentary mode of life practising agriculture was essential for their future well-being, Makarii built five Orthodox settlements. By the time when he left the Altai he had established two churches, three schools (one for girls) and an orphanage, leaving a secure foundation for his successors such as Verbitskii to build on.

He had taken courses in medicine, agriculture and the physical sciences to prepare him for his life's work. One might be tempted to say that he was more interested in the dispensing of food, money, medicines, seeds, clothing and sewing needles than in conveying the truths of the gospel. Yet he saw no clash between preaching the gospel of a servant and serving himself. There was an essential humility, practicality and common sense about Makarii's approach to mission.

He persuaded a woman to establish a small community to care for the girls and women, particularly orphans and widows, whilst trying to attract further men to spread the work deeper into the Altai mountains.

By 1843 his chest was giving trouble, and his eyes were too weak for him to stay in the Mission. Having trained a successor, Father Stepan Vasil'evich Landyshev (18??–1883), he left and became an abbot in Orel Province where he remained until his death. There he spent time trying to teach the Russians the essence of true Christianity. Shortly before he died he published a selection of 17 religious poems set to music for singing in church entitled 'Lepta', the proceeds to go towards the Altai Mission. These plus his translations of the psalms earn him a minor, if unacknowledged, place among Russian nineteenth-century poets.[4]

The seventh poem, a Song of Thanks, reads like this:

Сердце мое
Ищет Тебя,
Благо свое
Алчно любя.

Совесть во мне
Днем и во сне
Шепчет, гласит:
"Бог тебя зрит".

Хвалит вся тварь,
Вечный мой Царь,
Славу твою,
Радость мою.

Благословлен
В вьсшних мой Бог!
Кто быть блажен
Вне тебя мог? . . .

О исцели,
Чтобы мы шли
Правой стезей
Воли Твоей.

О Егова,
Церкви Глава!
Бог – человек!
Царствуй в нас век.

Perhaps his greatest work apart from translations (the Bible, some of the fathers and European mystics into Russian; some scripture, simple catechetical texts and parts of the liturgy into a dialect of

Altaian) is his *Mysli o sposobakh k uspeshnemu rasprostraneniiu khistianskoi very*[5] composed in 1838–9 in which he set forth his ideas about preparing Russia for mission. This work contains the distillation of his thoughts and experiences.

He believed that the Russian people needed to have certain truths impressed on their soul. The Christian Bible, he held, is God's only pure and complete revelation of himself; we can come to know God and come to salvation through it alone. The Christian faith is the only way for mankind to be saved, and Jesus the only door to the Father. There is no salvation without Christ crucified. Though the Christian faith brings great benefits to people on earth, its true aim is to prepare worthy citizens of the heavenly Jerusalem. True Christians must let the Holy Spirit rule in their souls, and ought to have the compassion of Jesus for those who do not know the truth and are therefore unsaved. All peoples need a spirit of love towards God and man within them, a heavenly fire which can only be obtained through the shed blood of Christ, that same fire which first came on the apostles at Pentecost. All faiths are not equal; there is but one way. The Church in Russia has an apostolic duty to heed the great commission of Jesus to make disciples of all peoples everywhere. It is a holy task given to Russia to convert all the nations living in the realm from darkness to light.

The Russian people have not yet captured this truth. They need a complete translation of the Bible in a lively contemporary style which will equal the liveliness of the original versions. The Bible in modern Russian would witness to the truths of Christ as he promised it would. To avoid any excesses in the use of this Bible comments should be appended to show the correct Orthodox interpretations of difficult passages. The common people should be educated. Villages should have schools which run at hours fitting in with agricultural work. Since women are the first to educate children the Church should concentrate on educating them first. No priest's or deacon's wife should be illiterate. The clergy should be given a state salary for their educational work among boys, and their wives for work among girls. All settlements should have clergy attached to them, and they should spend their time in a mixture of agricultural work, education, Bible study and performing the liturgy and prayers. There is no need for elaborate church buildings: simplicity, standardisation and serviceability should be the watchword. This is an urgent task because the Russian people need to be well instructed in the things of God to be able to pass them on to the native peoples in the Empire.

Within the main task of mission there will be a diversity of ministries. All will contribute equally but in different ways to the one aim inspired by the spirit of Jesus 'to the glory of God, to the creation of the church and to the welfare of all humanity'. A missionary with a wife and family will be able to demonstrate the principles of Christian marriage and household management, as a team. Yet since there is a need for people able to give more singleminded attention to the task than a married couple can, monks, nuns and widows are required. The office of deaconess should be restored, according to the practice of the ancient church, and in conformity with Acts 2: 18 which states that the Holy Spirit will be sent upon women as well as men.

There is also a need for institutions to prepare missionaries. They would act like reservoirs used in dry times to water the ground. The establishment of a new *soslovie* of missionaries including monks, nuns and married clergy is a prime necessity. A Russian missionary society is needed also. The Missionary Society should publish Bibles in Slavonic, Russian and other languages. It should translate religious works for educational purposes. This might even include an edition of the Koran with comments exposing its disagreements with the Bible, perhaps including the Old Testament prophecies about the Messiah to demonstrate the truth to educated Moslems. Appropriate works could be prepared for activity among the Jews. Apologetic works against heresies and freethinking could be published, and also morally uplifting works including biographies of past missionaries. A periodical should be published with information about developments in the churches worldwide, including modern miracles and successes of missions in other countries.

An Institute should be established to train future missionaries, with separate sections for men and women in a monastery and convent respectively. The students should master Biblical studies, psychology, anatomy, cosmography, physical geography, natural history, historical and political geography, the laws of logic and grammar, medicine, music and art. The course would last for 12 years. The Institute would need a hospital, pharmacy and printing press as well as the usual library. The trainees should conduct evangelism in the surrounding villages, visit prisons and hospitals and preach in local churches.

A few mission centres would be established at first, then they would gradually spread through the whole Empire. Each central mission point would have small outposts scattered around it staffed by monks who would evangelise and conduct simple medical work.

The central point would have a hospital. Married clergy would live in Russian villages near the indigenous peoples, or in villages settled by converts. The deaconesses and nuns would carry out work among the women and children.

We can see from the above that Makarii was a considerable figure. An excellent linguist (he knew Latin, French, German, Hebrew and Greek) he was also endowed with considerable pastoral capabilities, as his letters show. Though he dithered before deciding what his life's work was to be, he became a most determined proponent of mission in later life. An ascetic whose meagre clothing caused smirks among the Moscow clergy, he was above all a visionary. His proposals for mission were prophetic to the extent that they are still valid today. He was in no way a politician, for when the church hierarchy told him that his Bible translation project was out of favour he persisted, causing irritability at a high level and earning himself a severe rebuke. Undeterred he proceeded, circulating parts of his translations of the Bible and fathers in *samizdat* form. He was in many ways ignorant of the harsh world outside his convictions. Asking the Tsar for a translation of the Bible just at the time when Nicholas I's ministers were closing down the Russian Bible Society, mixing with Quakers when 'mysticism' was going out of favour at St Petersburg, proposing the construction of a church with altars for Catholics, Orthodox and Lutherans at a time when ecumenical concepts were frowned upon, looking with sympathy on the Jews when late Tsarist anti-semitism was beginning to rear its ugly head, a hesychast following Paissy Velichkovsky, yet acknowledging that the German pietist Johann Arndt's 'True Christianity' was one of his favourite works when it was frowned upon in Russia, Makarii Glukharev was almost an eccentric. Yet men such as he sometimes see the way forward more clearly than their detractors who appear wiser in their contemporaries' eyes. Poet, avid letter writer, student of herbal medicines who thought that consuming raw eggs would alleviate his failing eyesight Makarii was a mixture of brilliance and quaint oddity.

A good deal has been published about the life of Makarii. Vasily Ivanovich Verbitskii is a thorough contrast to Makarii in this as in many other things. The list of works about him is extremely brief and the information in them scanty, even the date of birth being doubtful.[6] From his own voluminous writings we find out very little about his personal feelings and motivations. Hence a biographical study can only be superficial. It would be really helpful if some personal correspondence could be found.

Born into a minor ecclesiastical family, the son of a sexton of Selo Fedyakovo in Nizhnii Novgorod Province, he received his education at the Nizhnii Ecclesiastical Seminary, specialising on the science side. He graduated in 1846 aged 18 and became a teacher in a rural parish school in the village of Azrapino, being at the same time a catechist at the local church. The secular and ecclesiastical authorities seem to have been impressed by his efficiency, and he could probably have made a good career for himself within the diocese, but wanted a more challenging ministry.

In 1853 he requested a transfer to the Tomsk Diocese to work in the Altai Mission. It is possible that he was a relative of Stepan Landyshev, Makarii's successor as Head of the Mission. In June 1854 he was ordained deacon and shortly afterwards became a priest. In August 1854 he arrived in Ulala, the central Mission point, where he learned the Altaian language, taught in the school and instructed a young native boy in the faith. In the following December he was placed in charge of the Maima parish, and began to undertake varied trips on behalf of the Mission.

In 1858, aged 30, after gaining four years' experience, he was sent into the region of forest and swamp (*chern'*) in Kuznetsk District to open a new mission station on the Kondoma River. This was the first department to be opened up in Kuznetsk District, and he was to remain here for 27 of his 37 years in the Altai Mission. He was a member of the white clergy, not a monk, and was married. We learn little of his wife except for a brief note in his Journal that his long-time companion who helped teaching in the school had died in 1876. One sketch about Verbitskii mentions a son who died at some stage, but there are no other references to children.

Verbitskii's numerous and very informative published journals, which cover 19 years (1858 to 1877), tell us a good deal about the externals of missionary life. Settling at Kuzedeevo he suffered a good deal before he was able to erect a house, then a church and school. Since Russian influence was fairly high in the northern Altai he found the indigenous people relatively keen to accept the Christian faith, particularly as they came to know him well. He baptised a total of 2117 people. His journals tell us of the local topography, of the language and customs of the *Chernevye tatary*, of his medical, charitable, botanical, apiarian and evangelistic work.

In 1884 he was transferred to Ulala as Deputy Director of the Mission. He lived there until his death in his sixty-third year from a kidney problem, exacerbated by the 36 000 versts he had travelled on horseback over the virtually impassible Altaian trails.

He received various awards including orders of St Anna (third and second ranks) for evangelistic successes, the silver medal of the Imperial Russian Geographical Society for his contributions to geography and ethnography, and in 1876 was consecrated to the rank of protoierei. He was pleasant, affable, warm and wise with an attractive personality. Tactful by nature he tended to steer clear of disputes. He had the reputation of being a hard worker with a simple lifestyle, and ended his life 'a handsome old man with a silvery beard and kind eyes rather sadly gazing out at God's world'.[7]

He was a renowned beekeeper, contributed new discoveries to Annenkov's Botanical Dictionary, was a corresponding Member of the Geographical Society and a member of the Tomsk Statistical Committee. He laboured for 30 years on a massive Dictionary of two Altai dialects.[8] Though it has been discovered that the publication of a 'Short Grammar of the Altai Language' by Verbitskii is a myth, the 1869 *Grammatika Altaiskogo yazyka* contains much foundational work by him.[9] He also published a very impressive array of ethnographical materials particularly legends of the Altaians, but also items on the local Russian population.[10] Even Soviet scholars acknowledge that his works were 'valuable in the highest degree', 'a priceless source', 'a capital linguistic work'.

Verbitskii was, of course, a second generation missionary. The real spade work had been done by Makarii and his helpers from 1830 to 1853, yet we should not allow this to detract from our assessment of a remarkable man. He was predominantly a plodder with great sticking power. Thirty-seven years on the mission field is an immense achievement. The conditions which Verbitskii describes in his Journals are sometimes horrendous. During his first winter in Kuzedeevo he had no heating or proper shelter; storms and floods caused great problems for him as for other missionaries, and he lost both wife and child during his time there.

There is little indication that Verbitskii had a speculative or introspective nature. His religious, ethnographical and linguistic publications are detailed, expertly competent and efficient, as scientific works should be, but there is no spark of genius about them as there is with Makarii's prophetic concepts. Yet his *Zametki kochevogo Altaitsa*[11] sometimes rises to lyrical heights in its depiction of the wild natural beauty of the Altai scenery, as this brief excerpt will show:

От мрачного вида леса эта часть Алтая называется *черню* . . . Огромные, сплошные массы земли, одетые между дерев грубою травой, в которой скрывается человек на коне, утомляют зрение путника, шествующего зимою по глубоким сугробам снега, а летом – по всегдашней черной грязи. На за то здесь водятся белые и черные медведи, кабарги, черно-бурые лисицы, . . . и проч. Южная часть Алтайских гор, именуемая собственно Алтаем, носит характер более резкий и удивляет наблюдателя своими очертаниями. Тут виднеются и огромные зубцы, и стеновидные утесы из сплошного камня, заостренные в треугольник, и синие скалы аспидо-подобных плит с гнездами голубей и убежищем змей, живо напоминающие своим сближением 'будите мудри яко змия, и цели яко голубие'.

Verbitskii's trip to discover the remains of Noah's Ark[12] reveals another aspect of his nature—the romantic explorer, a type often met with in nineteenth-century geographical societies.

Whereas Makarii was a thinker, a grand strategist, Verbitskii was a faithful servant, precisely the type of man Makarii had in mind for his peaceful army of missionaries which would evangelise the whole of the Russian Empire.

Verbitskii was an officer in the ranks, being Deputy Head of the Altai Mission, but not a general. Makarii was the far-seeing visionary, upon whose concepts the troops' manoeuvres are based. Both types are needed for the successful running of any enterprise. Interestingly enough, in an era when scientific discoveries were leading many to renounce religious belief, both men used scientific knowledge as an adjunct to the spreading of their faith. The existence of two such able men within one of the Orthodox Church's missions in the mid-nineteenth century is clear evidence that not all of Russia's talent was to go down the revolutionary path. Their example is still of relevance today. Вечная им память.

NOTES

1. D. N. Collins, 'Colonialism and Siberian Development: A Case Study of the Orthodox Mission to the Altai, 1830–1913', in A. Wood and A. French (eds), *The Development of Siberia: People and Resources* (London: 1989), pp. 50–71.

2.   I. Bria (ed.), *Go Forth in Peace: Orthodox Perspectives on Mission* (Geneva: 1986) p. 10.
3.   C.f. Bria, *passim*.
4.   K. V. Kharlampovich, *Arkhimandrit Makarii Glukharev*. *Po povodu 75-letiia Altaiskoi missii* (St Petersburg: 1905). A full list of works by and about Makarii may be obtained on application to D. N. Collins. The poems were published as *Lepta v pol'zu Tserkovnoi altaiskoi missii* (Moscow: 1846); also in *Moskvitianin* 1846, ch. 5, no. 9–10, pp. 210–14.
5.   Parts of this had been published in *Missioner* from 1874–78. The whole text was printed in 1893–94 in *Pravoslavnyi sobesednik*, and it appeared as a separate pamphlet in Moscow in 1894.
6.   'Altaiskii missioner prot. Vasilii Ivanovich Verbitskii', *Tomskie eparkhial'nye vedomosti* (Tomsk: 1891) no. 1 otd. neoff. pp. 9–16; 'Otchet o missiakh Tomskoi eparkhii—Altaiskoi i Kirgizskoi—za 1890 god', *Tomskie eparkhial'nye vedomosti* (1891) no. 5 otd. neoff. p. 2, plus appendix which includes more information; Al. Ivanovskii 'Altaiskii missioner V. I. Verbitskii (nekrolog)' (*Etnograficheskoe obozrenie 1891 no. 8 pp. 176–9*). A full list of works by and about Verbitskii may be obtained on application to D. N. Collins.
7.   A. Makarova-Mirskaia, *Apostoly Altaia* . . . (Khar'kov: 1909) pp. 81–7.
8.   *Slovar' Altaiskogo i Aladagskogo narechiia tiurkskogo iazyka* (Kazan': 1884).
9.   F. D. Ashnin, 'Pervaia pechatnaia nauchnaia grammatika Altaiskogo iazyka (problema avtorstva)', *Tiurkologicheskii sbornik za 1975g.* (Moscow: 1978) pp. 34–61; and 'Pervaia pechatnaia nauchnaia grammatika Altaiskogo iazyka (vopros o nazvanii)', *Tiurkologicheskii sbornik za 1977g.* (Moscow: 1981) pp. 7–20.
10. Many of his ethnographical works appear in *Altaiskie inorodtsy. Sbornik etnograficheskikh statei i issledovaniia Altaiskogo missionera protoiereia V. I. Verbitskogo* (Moscow: 1893). Some of them have never been reprinted after first appearing in provincial Siberian newspapers such as *Tomskie gubernskie vedomosti*.
11. 'Zametki kochevogo Altaitsa', *Vestnik Imperatorskogo Russkogo geograficheskogo obshchestva*, 1858 tom 24, kn. 11, pp. 77–109. The quotation is from p. 78.
12. 'Kak my otyskivali Noev kovcheg', *Vostochnoe obozrenie* (1882) no. 30.

8 Theological Liberalism and Church Reform in Imperial Russia[1]

Paul Valliere

Theological liberalism and church reform in imperial Russia is a subject that belongs to the history of Russian Orthodox theology and also to the history of Russian liberalism, a tendency which by no means lacked religious and ecclesiastical connections.

By theological liberalism I mean an approach to the problems of church and society which, whatever else it involves, affirms two axioms with respect to religious life: freedom of conscience, and the relative autonomy of the secular spheres of life, such as science, politics, economics and art. As a liberal axiom freedom of conscience means not just inner, spiritual freedom, which is conscience by another name, but outward freedom as well. Liberalism demands recognition of the right of conscience to express itself in visible, public ways without fear of persecution. The granting of relative autonomy to the secular spheres makes freedom of conscience operative by freeing people to pursue their needs and interests apart from the direct tutelage of religion or a church. At the same time the concept of the autonomy of secular spheres is more than an extension of freedom of conscience. It is a way of recognising the complex nature of rationality, of affirming reason's need for critical distinctions.

In an ecclesiastical context theological liberalism is not necessarily heterodox or anti-traditional, although it may be both. Theological liberalism is even reconcilable with religious establishment, although the more thorough-going forms of liberalism have generally been antagonistic to it. But the reconciliation of theological liberalism with tradition is arduous intellectually and difficult in practice. The history of liberal theological tendencies in any church tradition is therefore bound to be a history full of conflicts.

Theological liberalism can take many forms, some more thorough-going than others. In the strict sense 'liberalism' is a term that should probably be reserved for those forms of religious thought and practice in which the liberal axioms are consciously articulated, whether in strong or weak forms. Besides liberalism in the strict sense, however, there are many types of religious thought and practice which tend in the direction of liberalism even though the liberal axioms never reach the level of consciousness and suffer qualification by contrary assumptions. This various and incohate body of theological opinions and religious practices may be called 'modernism'. Modernism prepares the ground for theological liberalism. It arises from the need to adapt the church to the changing conditions of life in the modern world. This mission requires freedom from received ways of doing things, an openness to experiment. The need for freedom orients modernism in the direction of liberalism, although few modernists follow the liberal path to the end.

Neither modernism nor liberalism in religion is an independent tendency developing strictly according to the logic of its assumptions. Both depend on tradition, if only in the sense that they are defined by their interaction with it; and usually the relationship is more complex. The interaction of liberal ideas with the forms of Russian Orthodox tradition must therefore be described.

THE TOILS OF RUSSIAN ORTHODOX MODERNISM: ARCHIMANDRITE FEODOR (ALEXANDER MATVEEVICH BUKHAREV)

The interaction between theological liberalism and Russian Orthodox tradition was shaped primarily by the tension between what may be called 'the culture of wholeness' and the critical distinctions necessary to any principled liberalism. Ideals of wholeness and related integralist practices were by no means unique to Russian Orthodoxy, but their prominence in this tradition had important consequences for the development of theological liberalism in Russia.

By 'the culture of wholeness' I mean the mentality formed by a number of related tendencies in Russian Orthodoxy: the pancosmism of Orthodox theology, the ecclesiology of *sobornost'*, the ideal of church-state *symphonia* and the ethics of consensus in traditional Russian society. These tendencies conspired to impart to Russian Orthodox culture, in its high and popular forms, an elective affinity for forms of expression that stressed synthesis and shunned analysis. The idealisation of the culture of wholeness by the Slavophiles reinforced it all the more. The axioms of liberalism, by contrast, require an act of analysis or division in the first instance. For conscience to be free in more than a purely inward sense it must enjoy a sphere of sovereignty ('rights') clearly demarcated from other spheres. The scope of this sovereignty may vary considerably from one form of liberalism to another, but some sort of division between conscience and society is necessary to liberalism. Similarly, the relative autonomy of the secular spheres of life (for example science, politics, economics, art) requires the enforcement of certain practical distinctions to keep the spheres from collapsing into each other. Thus liberalism, in religion as in other areas, divides before it unites. Such division appears threatening to a church tradition relying on the culture of wholeness. The most thorough-going liberals in the Russian Orthodox tradition, such as Chicherin and Tareev, grappled with this tension directly, if not always successfully. The modernists suffered from it without clearly understanding it, although at times their pathos was fruitful for the church.

The case of Archimandrite Feodor (Alexander Matveevich Bukharev, 1824–1871) illustrates the tensions in Russian Orthodox modernism.[2] Sensational in its day, it is a case which by now seems more ordinary: a celibate cleric, carried away by a modernist vision of the Gospel, collides with the hierarchy of his church, eventually abandons holy orders, marries and attempts to continue his ministry in a secular context without much success. The relevance of Archimandrite Feodor to the present discussion derives not so much from his biography as from the spiritual and intellectual tensions in his theology. His theological vision illustrates the antagonism between wholeness and division and the ambivalence about freedom in Russian Orthodox modernism.

The myth that forms the centre of Archimandrite Feodor's theological vision is that of Christ the Lamb of God who takes upon himself the sins of the whole world, suffers for them and by so doing opens the way to the sanctification of all things. The mission of the Orthodox Church, in Feodor's view, is to proclaim the passion of the Lamb and also to imitate it through direct engagement with all spheres of worldly life, not excepting the world's sins and confusions. What makes this vision modernist is the summons to the church to involve itself directly and freely in the life of the secular world rather than to live in holy isolation. 'Like the sun', writes Feodor, 'Orthodoxy should penetrate all spheres of civic life, all branches of our knowledge, art and politics'.[3]

The summons to the church to involve itself in the life of the world is sounded clearly in Feodor's early work, *On the Catholic Apostolic Epistles*, especially as this commentary covers material that at first glance does not appear very promising for Feodor's theme.[4] The Catholic Epistles, namely James, I and II Peter, I, II and III John and Jude, are one of the main scriptural sources of disciplinarianism in ecclesiastical tradition. Western scholars have often viewed them as directed against the Pauline doctrines of justification by faith and Christian freedom, as designed to stress works of righteousness and obedience to ecclesiastical authority. Feodor is aware of the Western scholarly view but claims that he will show that the Catholic Epistles are 'one in spirit with the Epistles of the Apostle to the Gentiles on the question of freedom and knowledge'.[5] At the same time Feodor takes a stand against the conservative use of the Catholic Epistles by his Orthodox contemporaries:

> Moreover, there are particular circumstances in contemporary Russian Orthodox life that lend special importance to the question of the Catholic Apostolic Epistles. Namely, there has crept secretly into our midst a kind of spiritually slavish and obscurantist tendency of faith and piety that holds many Orthodox in its grip, sometimes by instinct, sometimes consciously. We are told that this tendency, opposed by the epistles of Paul, supposedly can rely on the Catholic Epistles of the other apostles. See, they say, how James demolishes wisdom that is not of a purely practical sort; see how Peter (in the Second Epistle) harshly strikes down the devotees of spiritual freedom itself.[6]

By arguing for the continuity between St Paul's letters and the Catholic Epistles Feodor is claiming the entire New Testament for his message of modernism and engagement with the world.

The key to Feodor's argument is the analogy he draws between the original audience of the Catholic Epistles and the Orthodox community of his day. The original audience of most of the letters, he observes, was Diaspora Jews converted to Christianity, not Jewish Christians in the Holy Land or Gentile converts. The apostles sought to help the Jewish converts to live among pagans without the supports that traditional Judaism provided, namely the law, the Temple and political-theocratic hopes. It was not easy for these new Christians to take their stand on Christian freedom and the spiritual theocracy of the Lamb of God and at the same time to avoid anarchy and license. Feodor believes that the same problem faces his own church:

The same is the case in new Israel, among Christians, even Orthodox Christians, as regards the disclosure of the power and spirit of Orthodoxy to us in our reception through grace and appropriation through living faith of the love for the world of the Lamb of God who takes away the sins of the world: some people rebel against the principle of love for humankind in the name of the strict demands and requirements of Orthodoxy, while others scorn these demands, yielding to Christian humanitarianism and entering into its spirit of love for humankind. Both groups are equally unconcerned with perfecting themselves in true Christian virtue. The first find satisfaction in a zeal for strict Orthodoxy which dries up the spirit of love in them, the others surrender to unbridled self-will on the pretext of free spirit.[7]

By associating the adherents of a strict and exacting Orthodoxy with the Jewish legalists against whom the apostles of the early church struggled, Feodor seizes the spiritual high ground from the conservatives. At the same time, by warning against 'unbridled self-will', Feodor shows that he does not advocate freedom in isolation from other values but integrates it into the total Christian moral vision, into that which he calls 'peaceful, loving and active Christian perfection.'[8]

All this sounds quite moderate as long as one views it in purely theoretical terms. As soon as one assesses the possibilities of realising Christian moral perfection in practice, however, the exacting demands of the task come to the fore. By summoning the church to moral perfection over and against legalistic conservatism and the dangerous freedom of modernity Feodor was, in effect, calling the Orthodox flock to a new synthesis of Christianity and culture. In practice such an achievement was a far less likely outcome of the process of church reform than the splitting apart of conservatives and modernists, that is, than just the sort of breakdown that finally drove Feodor out of his clerical vocation. True, at rare moments in the history of a church or a society a moment of vision carries the whole community beyond its usual banal divisions to a new synthesis. Feodor needed such a vision. Did he have one?

In fact he did. He articulated it in his massive commentary on the Apocalypse, or Revelation to John.[9] It was a vision in which the Russian Tsar, intervening militarily to achieve the liberation of the Orthodox peoples from the Turkish yoke, would stand at the head of a renewed, worldwide Orthodox community ready to share its spiritual riches with the pagans of the West. Feodor began work on the Apocalypse commentary on the eve of the Crimean War when he came under the influence of a *starets* with historiosophic pretensions, Father Petr Tomanitskiĭ.[10] The reverses in the Crimea did not temper Feodor's devotion to this vision or halt his efforts to get the Apocalypse commentary published. The ban on the work by the ecclesiastical censor was the immediate cause of Feodor's decision to abandon holy orders. Subsequently, as a layman, Bukharev continued to press his ideas in Slavophile circles and once wrote directly to Tsar Alexander II concerning 'the great and marvellous vocation of Russian power' to bring about the scripturally prophesied victory of the Orthodox faith over its enemies.[11]

That Archimandrite Feodor nursed the hope of an extraordinary historical breakthrough of Orthodoxy was logical enough given his modernist zeal. He had an instinctive grasp of how inconsequential mere tinkering with the existing state of the church would be for the advancement of his hopes. But the form his vision took cannot fail to dismay us by its theoretical implausibility, its impracticability and, finally, its mockery of the central theme of his theology, the passion of the Lamb. As to the first flaw, suffice it to say that any interpretation of a biblical book that makes specific historical predictions pertaining to one's own time and place is bound to be implausible except to a few initiates, and it is necessarily unstable. As to practicability, Feodor scarcely stood much of a chance of exciting Alexander II about renewing Eastern adventures after defeat in the Crimean War. Arguably, Feodor evoked less sympathy from the Tsar and secular officialdom than he had from the Synod in the 1850s. Yet the greatest problem with Feodor's historiosophic ideas was that they vitiated his theology of the passion of the Lamb. It is true that military and pacifist motifs are combined in the biblical theology of holy war, but Feodor reverses the evolution. Instead of the Lion of Judah becoming the Lamb that was slain, the Lamb that was slain becomes the Lion of Judah once again; and the Lion finds a henchman in the Russian Tsar. In *On the Catholic Apostolic Epistles* Feodor celebrated the transformation of the political theocracy of old Israel into the spiritual theocracy of the Lamb.[12] In the Apocalypse commentary he revives political theocracy.

The outcome of Archimandrite Feodor's quest is an example of what may be called 'the reprise of integralism'. The phenomenon occurs often in the history of modern Russian Orthodoxy. The pattern is as follows. A modernist or liberal initiative, inspired by a vision of social and ecclesiastical renewal, inevitably produces divisions in the church and between church and society. The Orthodox sponsors of change find the divisions produced by their activism repugnant and attempt to restore the culture of wholeness by proposing new integralist projects. These, however, have the effect of restoring routinised patterns of thought and behaviour which undermine the modernist or liberal initiative.

CLERICAL LIBERALISM: THE CASE OF PARISH REFORM

Archimandrite Feodor's struggles took place in the world of specialised biblical scholarship and theological speculation, but the tensions of Orthodox modernism disclosed there can be seen also in the wider world of white-clergy activism. This 'clerical liberalism', as it has been called, was concerned with practical churchmanship at the grass roots, with issues such as material support for the clergy, the civil status of the clergy, parish revitalisation, charitable ministries and popular education.[13]

To put clerical liberalism in perspective it is necessary to distinguish between two tendencies at work in it, one essentially secular, the other religious. To be sure, no absolute distinction can be made between the secular and the religious aspects of church life. Many of the reforms sought by the clerical liberals, such as parish revitalisation, involved both. Nevertheless, it is possible to tell the difference between secular-spiritedness and theological inspiration. Some of the dearest causes of the clerical liberals in the nineteenth century, such as the drive for state salaries in place of traditional emoluments, were mainly secular in spirit. However unsatisfactory the traditional system of support may have been and however rational state salaries may have appeared in a system of church establishment, the idea of state pay-cheques for priests could scarcely be said to possess theological charisma. On the contrary, the idea could be branded as positively anti-charismatic because 'a state salary would break the patriarchal relations between pastors and their flock and give the Old Believers grounds for reproaching Orthodox priests with bureaucratism'.[14]

Parish consolidation was another reform proposal that suffered from secular-spiritedness. Again, it was a proposal that gave the appearance of rationality. Consolidation was aimed at eliminating small, poor or remote parishes and so multiplying the resources of the remaining units. Naturally, consolidation disrupted customary affiliations and so antagonised the Orthodox who did not wish to see any changes in the church. But this in itself was not an argument against the measure, since reforms of any kind were bound to disrupt custom and disturb conservatives. The real problem with parish consolidation was its hidden but basic assumption that there were too many Orthodox churches in Russia. Such an assumption was insulting to Christians called to build up the church, not close it down.[15]

The secular-spirited proposals of the clerical liberals should be seen as belonging to the history of the regulation, not the reform, of the church in Russia. The regulation of religion, usually by the state, is not necessarily a bad thing, and a certain amount of it is necessary in any society. But it is a commoner and less dynamic thing than church reform.

Parish revitalisation, on the other hand, was a genuinely theological project, whatever else it might have been. In every branch of Christianity the parish is the primary locus of the Spirit-filled community which the church is called to be. Parish revitalisation recalls the apostolic origins of Christianity. 'The idea of a parish as a completely free, independent church community is completely in agreement with the spirit of the Orthodox Church, and the organisation of such a community will represent the fully legal and desirable restoration of the order that existed in the ancient church', wrote one advocate.[16]

For Russian liberals parish revitalisation was of particular interest because it involved working out new forms of local responsibility and participation in Russian society. Genuine revitalisation, as distinct from administrative regulation, could happen only if Orthodox people, clergy and laity, took greater responsibility for the affairs of their church, including its internal governance and its ministry to the needs of society outside the church walls. A self-governing, socially engaged local church community would strike a blow against the passivity and immobilism of Russian society that dismayed liberals inside and outside the church.

In the conclusion of *Ecclesiastical-Social Questions in the Era of the Tsar-Liberator (1855–1870)*, the leading scholar of the history of the Russian Orthodox parish, A. A. Papkov, offers the following summary of the main reforms affecting parish life sought by liberal churchmen since the 1850s and also in his own day (1902):

(1) the recognition of Orthodox parishes as juridical persons,

which the Russian parishes of other confessions (Lutheran, Reformed and, in part, Roman Catholic) and even *edinovertsy* parishes already are;

(2) for this reason the granting to Orthodox parishes of the right to manage and dispose of local church monies and capital, and of the right to acquire movable and immovable property freely in the name of the parish;

(3) the construction of a better organization than the current parish trustee boards for the legal representation of the parish before the government, society and the courts, for the legal defence of parish rights and interests and also of parish property;

(4) the regularization of the ancient right of Orthodox parishes to choose their priests and ecclesiastical attendants and their right to petition the supreme diocesan authority on the naming of such candidates to parishes;

(5) the maintenance of all members of the clergy normally from the resources of a parish;

(6) the recognition of the Orthodox parish not only as the most basic ecclesiastical unit but also as the most basic territorial unit [in the Russian Empire];

(7) the granting to the Orthodox clergy of sufficiently broad family, class, professional and property rights, and provision to the clergy of an education worthy of its office, broad self-management of its own affairs and trial on a strictly canonical basis;

(8) the publication of a general code of ecclesiastical-social laws.[17]

The first three points enumerate the requirements for parish self-government: legal personhood, the right to dispose of church funds and acquire property, and a responsible parish council. These three reforms, had they been implemented, would have transformed the Russian Orthodox parish from the lowest link in a bureaucratic chain of command into a social agent in its own right. The fourth and fifth points aim at building solidarity between the local parish and its clergy, which is obviously crucial to the functioning of the parish as an independent social agent. The sixth point is problematic and will be discussed below. The seventh point calls for dismantling the clerical estate (*soslovie*) that ghettoised the Orthodox clergy in the Russian Empire. Finally, the call for codification of the laws on the church aims at institutionalising and protecting the reforms.

The language of these proposals is legalistic. But as is often the case with legalism in Russia, the substance is spiritual. Taken together the reform proposals may be seen as a way of making the abstract concept of freedom of conscience a concrete reality in the daily life of the Russian Orthodox Church. To be sure, the concept of freedom of conscience had more obvious relevance to the persecuted religious minorities and dissenters in the Russian Empire than to the Orthodox majority. Yet the many constraints imposed by the Synodal system on the life of the Orthodox Church at the grass roots amounted to no less than a means of denying Orthodox conscience its right to express itself publicly and independently, its right to proclaim the Spirit-filled community of God in its own way in Russian space and time.

The project of parish revitalisation in Russian Orthodoxy was not immune to the reprise of integralism. An example of the phe-nomenon may be seen in the sixth point of Papkov's summary of reforms: 'the recognition of the Orthodox parish not only as the most basic ecclesiastical unit but also as the most basic territorial unit [in the Russian Empire]'. Papkov advances this idea with enthusiasm.[18] He and other Orthodox reformists were of the opinion that the smallest territorial units created by the system of local government set in place by the Great Reforms, namely the *volosti*, should have been made to coincide with Orthodox parishes as much as possible. The advantages of such an arrangement in their view were that it would give the volosti a familiar and historic, as opposed to mecha-nical, character in the eyes of the peasants and, second, that it would provide a framework for eventually merging the several sosloviia into a socially unified populace. They pointed out that the Orthodox parish was the only institution in Russia that already embraced all classes on the grass roots level. Beyond these supposed advantages the coincidence of ecclesiastical and civil administrative units would have the advantage of concentrating the civic and spiritual interests of the peasants in one place. Some observers saw a similar benefit accruing to the country as a whole from parish revitalisation. Recounting the opinion of Baron M. A. Korf on the significance of parish reform Papkov observes that 'as we discuss parish organization we should by no means fail to see the role which, perhaps, the parish is destined to play as an organ of closest rapprochement [*sblizhenie*] between church and state, a rapprochement in which the church would find a sure guarantee of influence and weight among the secular public'.[19] The integralist ideal of linking church, state and society closely together is obvious here.

The motives that led some liberals, especially liberal Slavophiles, to elaborate the project of parish revitalisation along integralist lines were worthy enough. The church's transcendence of *soslovie* divisions (in theory) was an alluring feature of its existence in a country where such divisions were widely recognised to be a problem. Also, most liberal Orthodox were committed to developing more active forms of social ministry to Russian society, such as social work among the poor and sick, charitable assistance and popular education. It was natural for them to suppose that closer attunement of parochial and territorial administration in the empire might facilitate state support for their initiatives. Yet a more considered analysis of the prospects for church reform through parish revitalisation would disclose the tensions inherent in any proposed synthesis of ecclesiastical and civic affairs. On the one hand, the continued preaching of an integralist ideal tended to muffle the reformers' call for what the church probably needed most of all, which was to take responsibility for its own affairs. On the other hand, the slightest progress towards actually realising the dream of merging parochial and civic affairs would have had the effect of so overloading the mission of the revitalised parish as to explode it.

In the event, parish revitalisation failed to take hold in the Russian Orthodox Church. Except in a few experimental situations the only achievement was the authorisation of parish trustee boards (*popechitel'stva*) by the Special Commission on Orthodox Church Affairs in 1864. But far from functioning as genuine (that is responsible) parish councils, the trustee boards merely existed alongside the traditional Synodal-consistorial institutions and were denied the right to dispose of any resources save those which they themselves garnered for special projects. As institutions of ecclesiastical self-government, therefore, they were inconsequential. The traditional integralism of the Synodal system, dilapidated as it was, proved strong enough to turn back parish revitalisation along liberal lines.

To criticise Orthodox reformers for yielding to the lures of integralism is not to suggest that they would have done better not to worry about the culture of wholeness at all. It is to point out the need for priority among ideals and for matching ideals to practical possibilities. For the work of parish revitalisation what was needed in the first instance was not a new wholeness but a way to enforce some critical distinctions: between one parish and the next, between the local parish and the diocesan regime, between the Spirit-filled community of faith and the social, political and cultural communities that also commanded Russian loyalties. As for the ideal of wholeness, it could be used to criticise the pseudo-wholeness of everyday Russian Orthodox integralism. That is to say, a liberal churchman could always point to the existing Orthodox parish and ask, 'Where is the wholeness of which we speak?' He could point out, as one critic did, that:

> the elements that make up [the Orthodox parish are] broken apart and uncoordinated, and not only uncoordinated but actually hostile to each other. One segment of the parish—the parishioners—are required to play a purely passive role: to give, to sacrifice, but not to take an active part in parish and church affairs; while the other segment—the clergy, the pastors—are there to collect, to take, to manage all parish and church affairs not merely without the control of the parish but even without its knowledge. It is obvious that these parts are not organically united but sewn together arbitrarily, 'every which way', as the saying goes.[20]

But reproaching conservatives for overlooking facts that belied their ideals did not bring the liberals any closer to achieving their own synthesis of church and society. The lingering integralism of many Orthodox liberals prevented them from seeing that what they really had to offer was not a new wholeness, but some new distinctions.

THE THEOLOGICAL LIBERALISM OF BORIS NIKOLAEVICH CHICHERIN

The concepts of freedom of conscience and the autonomy of the secular spheres were of central importance to Boris Nikolaevich Chicherin (1828–1904). As a leading Russian liberal with a commitment to constructing the groundwork for a philosophy of law, Chicherin had to appropriate these two concepts in his work, and he had to be able to handle the cultural and religious tensions which they produced in the Russian context. Unlike classical liberals in the West, who often bracketed the religious and metaphysical issues connected with liberalism, Chicherin had to deal with both in order to make liberalism comprehensible in a setting where it was new and strange. Also, Chicherin was a philosophical idealist who had a positive interest in both religion and metaphysics. He was well prepared to address the problem of liberalism and the culture of wholeness.[21]

The position which Chicherin presents in his philosophy of religion, *Science and Religion* (1879), is clear and also carefully nuanced.[22] An opponent of traditional Russian integralism, Chicherin predictably takes a critical stance toward the culture of wholeness. To his credit, however, he does not make his work easier by dismissing wholeness as merely a relative, culturally determined notion fated to be swept from the historical scene by the forces of modern life. On the contrary, Chicherin sees the longing for wholeness as an inalienable part of religion. Chicherin defines religion as 'the striving for living communion with the absolute'.[23] The absolute, or God, by definition unites all dimensions of reality in itself. Religion, as the longing for communion with this reality, reflects its comprehensiveness:

> The ascent of the soul to God must encompass all sides of human nature because God is the beginning, the middle and the end of man's whole life . . . Nothing in man can be removed from this supreme relationship which embraces all the foundations of his existence. In every other sphere of human activity one or another spiritual force or capability predominates, while here the fragmented forces are united in a single supreme act through which the connection of the individual being with the absolute principle of all life is affirmed. In religion all the separate threads of human existence are tied into a single knot.[24]

The longing for wholeness, then, is characteristic of religion. But how should one construe the relation of religion to the other, more specialised spheres of human activity, such as philosophy, art and morality? This is the issue with which Chicherin begins his philosophy of religion. 'Does religion give the supreme law to the separate elements of the human spirit', he asks, 'or are they brought together in such a way that each one preserves its own independence?'[25]

The integralist defends the former position. Chicherin cites 'the writers of the theological school' in philosophy as examples:

> Philosophy, in the opinion of these writers, should borrow its principles from theology. The medieval schoolmen forthrightly termed philosophy the handmaiden of theology. And still in our own day the theological tendency, shared, incidentally, by our Slavophiles, maintains that only faith can be the source of true knowledge. In a one-sidedly logical development of thought the adherents of this school see the destruction of the wholeness of human vision.[26]

Chicherin submits this view to criticism. It has, he concedes, 'a certain measure of truth, but a still larger measure of misunderstanding of the nature of the human spirit and of the mutual relationship of its various elements'. The problem is that the integralists take as their criterion that which is in fact only the first and lowest stage of spiritual wholeness, 'the original unity that serves as a point of departure for the human spirit but at which man must not stop'.[27] In other words, the human spirit is in a state of dynamic development, and the autonomy of its separate elements cannot be suppressed. At the same time, this development is not chaotic. It points in the direction of synthesis:

> It is not a violent tearing of the branches from the common trunk, but the expression of the true nature of spirit, of the absolute principle inherent in it, by virtue of which each of its separate parts is capable of being a source of independent life and developing purely from within itself. The common link between all these aspects [of spirit] again inevitably leads them in the direction of a higher unity; but this new unity is established not through the violent subjection of [these aspects] to an authority external to them, but through their own internal development. And in this union the independence of each must be preserved. The final unity, as we have already explained, is not merely a return to the original point of departure but a higher level which combines in itself all the fullness and variety of life.[28]

Chicherin's position provides strong justification for allowing the secular spheres of life to develop freely outside the tutelage of religion and the church. Thus, in philosophy, reason and its rules, not religious faith, must direct thinking, even thinking about faith itself, which reason allows us to distinguish from superstition.[29] Likewise, the search to capture beautiful forms in art and the search for the general moral law have a logic of their own.[30] As for the concept of freedom of conscience, Chicherin does not discuss it explicitly at this point in his book (he will do so later), but it is clearly an assumption underlying what he says about the autonomy of the spheres. Conscience in this context means the responsibility that a philosopher, artist or moralist feels toward his discipline. Freedom of conscience is the right to exercise this responsibility openly and without interference.

It is important to appreciate that Chicherin does not defend the autonomy of the secular spheres as a strategy for forgetting about religion or restricting its forms of expression. A dialectical thinker, Chicherin does not eliminate the concern for synthesis as he performs the work of analysis. As the expression of the human spirit's inalienable longing for synthesis religion remains interesting to Chicherin and even indispensable to his dialectic. Without religion the tension between analysis and synthesis in human experience would be slackened; and this, for Chicherin, would diminish the dynamism of human spiritual pursuits, including philosophy, art and morality. Religion is not the lawgiver to these enterprises, but it does play the important role of challenging each to refrain from absolutising its concerns and to remain open to transcendence. In philosophy, for example, religious faith stands in judgement over one-sided positions (materialism, scepticism) and keeps abstract thinking from misconstruing concrete, living reality.[31] In morality it presses the concern for the 'moral solidarity' that comes through love and mercy, not through justice and law.[32] Chicherin's grasp of the synthesising and reconciling function of religion allows him to appreciate concrete forms of religious expression which less dialectical thinkers would not find room for, such as ritual and sacramentalism. On pages where he shows himself to be a true son of the Orthodox Church he defends veneration of the Mother of God as a form of witness to the ultimate synthesis of matter and spirit.[33]

In his chapter on the church in *Science and Religion* Chicherin vigorously advances two principles: freedom of conscience and the independence of the church. In Chicherin's view human society is composed of four distinct kinds of association: the family, based on natural love; the church, based on universal love; civil society, based on the idea of freedom and rights; and the state, based on the concept of power, by virtue of which the state plays the commanding role in secular affairs.[34] These distinctions do not drop from heaven but develop historically. In pagan times, for example, the idea of a church that was independent from other associations in society did not exist. It was Christianity that advanced the idea, although in its own history the Christian Church had to struggle to clarify the true meaning of independence, which was distorted by medieval integralism.[35]

What is the function of the church which its independence, properly understood, allows it to perform? Chicherin's reply demonstrates the categorical importance of freedom of conscience in his theory of the church:

> The moral significance of the church consists in its being the
> director of human conscience. But this supreme direction does not

exclude freedom. Morality by its very nature does not admit of blind submission. Conscience is given to a human being as an inner light which at all times should serve as his guide in life. A person may sense his inadequacy and seek higher support, but he does not have the right to extinguish this lamp within him. He is morally culpable if, to save himself from vacillation, he creates darkness in himself and gives himself blindly into the hands of others. The supreme significance of the church lies not in making this inner light superfluous, but in giving it fresh nourishment so that it flames up more brightly than before. Thus the creation of a free morality in its members is the true measure of the church's life-giving activity.[36]

Chicherin goes on to observe that the principle of freedom of conscience also helps the church regulate its internal life by guarding against the misuse of ecclesiastical power, for 'like all human institutions, the church is run by human beings, and therefore abuses are inevitable here, too'.[37]

Chicherin's theory of the church does not assign a prominent place to the specific themes of the Christian Gospel, such as the Kingdom of God, the forgiveness of sins or the transfiguration of the cosmos in Christ. It could therefore be criticised as superficial in theological terms. On the other hand, the aim of the theory is not to explicate the contents of the Gospel but simply to suggest a way of situating the communication of the Gospel as precisely as possible in the complex web of social relations and cultural pursuits that structure human life. The power of Chicherin's theory lies not in its contents, which are of a general sort, but in the rigour of its distinctions. In this respect the role assigned to the church does not lack distinctiveness. Unlike the family the church witnesses to universal love. Unlike the state it does not wield power. Unlike law, which cannot dispense with coercion (not just in practice but even in theory), the church bears its message into the world through pacific exhortation and example. Or at least this is how things would be arranged in a society embodying Chicherin's liberal philosophy of conscience. And here, perhaps, is a point of tangency between Chicherin's liberalism and the Gospel. In his way Chicherin agrees with historic Christianity that the Gospel, however one articulates it, is not a new law but a new spirit, a light shining in conscience, uncomprehended by darkness.

Chicherin takes pains to distinguish his vision of the mission of the church in modern times from negative Roman Catholic and Protestant examples. A Jesuitical church, he observes, makes common cause with the secular power to combat modern ideas and so corrupts the mission of the church through power-wielding. In liberal Protestantism, by contrast, 'the church not only comes to terms with the new principles but inculcates them in itself'; thereby it 'loses the objective foundations of its existence and sows within itself the seeds of dissolution'.[38] Chicherin sees a better way:

> The ideal situation is one in which the church, not giving battle and not trying at whatever cost to hang on to the power slipping away from it, nevertheless preserves untouched its ancient traditions and, feeding the masses with spiritual food, continues to be the refuge of all who suffer and sorrow, who grieve over their sins and thirst for spiritual relief. But in order to fulfill this mission worthily the church must have an understanding of modern needs, combining tolerance for human weakness with unshakable firmness and viewing the adherents of modern ideas not as enemies infringing on its rights but as a flock which has gone astray but must return to its bosom eventually.[39]

Chicherin does not spell out how the reform process in nineteenth-century Orthodoxy could help the church live up to this ideal, but the ideal was consistent with the Orthodox modernism of his day. In fact, it is not far removed from Archimandrite Feodor's vision of a church that continues the ministry of the Lamb of God by entering into the life of the modern world and patiently enduring the world's sins and confusions. However, there was no reprise of integralism in Chicherin's work, no pseudo-apocalypse, no new merging of church, state and society. As a philosophical idealist Chicherin could entertain a vision of wholeness, but as a Russian liberal he was dubious about proposals for putting it into practice. At the risk of making him out to be some kind of Protestant, which he most definitely was not, one might say that for Chicherin the culture of wholeness was justified by faith, not works. When it came to works Chicherin was more concerned about freedom than about wholeness. As he puts it at the end of his chapter on the church in *Science and Religion*, 'the freedom of the church and freedom of conscience ought to be fundamental laws of any educated society'.[40] This was a more than ample challenge to the Russia of Chicherin's day, as it is to Russia in our own day as well.

LATER PATHS OF THEOLOGICAL LIBERALISM:
MIKHAIL MIKHAILOVICH TAREEV

The flowering of Russian liberalism around the turn of the century intensified the critique of integralism in many areas of Russian life, including the Orthodox Church. Vladimir Soloviev's progress from the liberal Slavophilism and theocratic hopes of his earlier work to the more thorough-going liberalism of *The Justification of the Good* (1894–97) encouraged some of his younger protégés, such as Sergeĭ and Evgeniĭ Trubetskoĭ, to proceed further down the same path.[41] Prince Evgeniĭ Trubetskoĭ's critique of Soloviev, *The Worldview of V. S. Soloviev* (1913), was an important statement of the need for a break with integralist dreams by a Russian Orthodox liberal who was deeply involved in the struggle for reform in church and state.[42] The main reform current in the Orthodox Church in the first two decades of the twentieth century, the conciliar movement, embraced a wider segment of the ecclesiastical public than the liberals, but the guiding notion of the movement, the need to restore the independence of the church in society, was consistent with liberal axioms.[43] Religious toleration in the Russian Empire was granted in 1905. The autonomy of the secular spheres of life from church or state tutelage made steady progress in the late imperial period with the growing role of the liberal professions in Russia, the emergence of political liberalism with the rise of the Constitutional Democratic Party, and the critique of integralism, left and right, by the essayists of *Vekhi* (1909). But as liberalism flowered in Russia it also diversified, and this diversity sometimes obscured the implications of liberalism for the actual business of church reform.

The work of Mikhail Mikhailovich Tareev (1866–1934), professor of moral theology at Moscow Theological Academy, is an example of the complications of later Russian liberalism in the field of Orthodox theology. Tareev was perhaps the most thorough-going theological liberal of his time. He placed the concepts of freedom of conscience and the autonomy of the secular spheres at the centre of his 'system of religious thought', as he called his collected works.[44] Ironically, however, the purity of Tareev's liberalism threatened the link between theological liberalism and church reform.

Tareev began his theologising with a work on the kenosis, or self-emptying, of Christ, *The Temptations of the Godman* (1892).[45] We have already noted a modernist rendition of the kenosis in Archimandrite Feodor's theology of the Lamb of God. In Feodor's vision, however, the kenosis implies a missionary project: just as Christ, the Lamb of God, entered into all spheres of life in order to redeem the world, so, too, the Orthodox Church should engage with the world and seek its redemption. In Tareev's theology this missionary and transformationist imperative is replaced by a dualistic scheme: by emptying himself into the life of the world Christ submitted to the laws of nature and history, thus affirming their integrity and barring their disruption. It was precisely the disruption of these laws that Satan proposed to the Godman when he tempted him in the wilderness. But Christ rejected the temptations of miracle, mystery and authority and, with them, all theocratic pretensions. What was it, then, that Christ accomplished through his kenosis? He revealed the possibility of attaining 'glory in humiliation', of living the life of a son of God within the conditions and limits of human life in the world. 'Revealing Himself in outward humiliation, He bestows on man the inward worth of a son of God. He calls man to the glory which is available to him in humiliation, and to blessedness attained in sufferings instead of to happiness (Matthew 5. 3–12).'[46]

In his later work Tareev presented these ideas more systematically in a 'theory of Christian freedom'.[47] His theory of Christian freedom in fact concerns two freedoms: 'the freedom of the absolute religious spirit from the conditionality of historical forms, and the freedom of natural-historical life from the external pretensions of religious authority'.[48] The two freedoms closely parallel the central principles of theological liberalism: freedom of conscience and the autonomy of the secular spheres. In Tareev's view Christian freedom upholds both.

What makes Tareev's theological liberalism unusually thorough-going is the exclusion of any possibility of synthesising religious conscience and secular life. A provisional and purely external accommodation is the most that Tareev allows. For example, when Tareev discusses the socialist movement of his day he concedes the worth (from a Christian point of view) of the socialist ideals of justice and equality, but he points out that the motives of Christians and socialists are very different: 'the desire of one group to get and receive and the desire of the others to share and sacrifice, while coinciding in their outward, proximate results, diverge radically in their inner essence'. Most people, failing to observe this difference, fall into erroneous positions. They reject economic justice in the name of Christianity or Christianity in the name of economic justice, or they invent Christian socialism, a compromise that satisfies neither side.

But one has only to admit the heterogeneity of these spheres, the personal-religious and the social-conditional, in order to eliminate the essential necessity of a conflict between them and to bring them to full harmony: the sphere of the personal, religious-absolute relationship to the world and the sphere of the material construction of earthly life are heteronomous spheres proceeding from completely different inward sources but coinciding in their proximate, outward results.[49]

Tareev's theory of Christian freedom is cast in such a way as to rule out not only the reprise of integralism but the very notion of wholeness as a theological or ecclesiastical ideal. The implications of Tareev's liberalism for the institutional forms of Russian Orthodoxy in his day were thus considerably more negative than those of Chicherin's liberalism, even though Tareev occupied a professional position within the Orthodox Church. Tareev's dualism also had negative implications for the 'new religious consciousness' of his time. Critical as they were of traditional integralism, most of the expositors of the new consciousness still sought a synthesis of religion and culture. Thus it is not surprising to find Berdiaev faulting Tareev along with Evgenii Trubetskoi for making too sharp a distinction between the realm of religious conscience and the secular spheres of life.[50]

Whether or not Berdiaev is right in some absolute sense, it is difficult to see how any struggle for church reform can do without the hope of a new cultural synthesis, however modestly envisioned. To put the matter theologically, it is difficult to see how any struggle for church reform can do without the hope of sanctification, without the expectation that the secular world will be transfigured in some way by the Spirit. There is no prospect of sanctification, no room for it really, in Tareev's liberalism. Tareev meant it when he wrote, 'In the whole Gospel the word "hope" does not appear'.[51] May one infer from Tareev's case that fuzzy-minded but visionary modernists dreaming of sanctifying the world through the *aggiornamento* of their church are more likely to accomplish the work of church reform than rigorous liberals?

The inference may not be justified. There were, after all, different ways of imagining what a reformed Russian Orthodox Church would look like. Evgenii Trubetskoi, like Tareev a dualist liberal, found inspiration in the picture offered as a prophecy by Vladimir Soloviev in the latter's work, *Three Conversations* (1899). The picture is far removed from the visions that stirred most traditionalists and many modernists before the Revolution, yet it is haunting for being close to what may be the best picture that has any likelihood of realisation in today's Soviet Union:

> Russian Orthodoxy, after political events had altered the official position of the church and although it had lost many millions of its sham, nominal adherents, nevertheless experienced the joy of uniting with the best part of the Old Believers and even with many sectarians of a positive religious orientation. This renewed church, while not growing in numbers, began to grow in strength of spirit.[52]

The vision is a modest one, and modesty is certainly a liberal virtue. Whether it is also an evangelical virtue is an issue to be debated elsewhere.

NOTES

1. Paper presented at the Millenium Conference on Christianity in the Eastern Slav Lands, School of Slavonic and East European Studies, University of London, July 11–15, 1988.
2. For an overview of the case of Archimandrite Feodor with extensive bibliography see Gregory L. Freeze, 'Die Laisierung des Archimandriten Feodor (Bucharev) und ihre kirchenpolitischen Hintergründe', *Kirche im Osten* 28 (1985) pp. 26–52.
3. Archimandrite Feodor, *O pravoslavii v otnoshenii k sovremennosti* (St Petersburg: 1860) p. 316, quoted by Freeze, 'Die Laisierung des Archimandriten Feodor' (see note 2 above) p. 31.
4. A. M. Bukharev, *O sobornykh apostol'skikh poslaniiakh, Bogoslovskie trudy* 9 (1972) pp. 149–225. The work is undated but probably belongs to the period when Archimandrite Feodor was lecturer in biblical theology at Moscow Theological Academy, 1846–53. It treats only the first four Catholic Epistles: James, I and II Peter and I John.
5. Ibid., p. 149.
6. Ibid.
7. Ibid., p. 152.
8. Ibid.
9. A. M. Bukharev (Arkhimandrite Feodor), *Issledovaniia Apokalipsisa* (Sergiev Posad: 1916).
10. For a detailed account of Archimandrite Feodor's relationship with Father Petr see A. M. Belorukov, 'Vnutrennii perelom v zhizni A. M. Bukhareva', *Bogoslovskii vestnik* (1915), iii (Oct–Dec) pp. 785–867.

11. See Freeze, 'Die Laisierung des Archimandriten Feodor' (see note 2 above) pp. 48–9.
12. See Bukharev, *O sobornykh apostol'skikh poslaniiakh* (see note 4 above) p. 181.
13. See 'The Emergence of Clerical Liberalism' in Gregory L. Freeze, *The Parish Clergy in Nineteenth-Century Russia: Crisis, Reform, Counter-Reform* (Princeton: 1983) pp. 389–97.
14. A. A. Papkov, *Tserkovno-obshchestvennye voprosy v epokhu Tsaria-osvoboditelia (1855–1870)* (St Petersburg: 1902; reprinted with introduction by Dr G. Florovsky, Gregg International, 1972) p. 17. Papkov attributes the view to A. N. Murav'ev, an influential Orthodox publicist and former Synodal official.
15. For examples of negative reaction to parish consolidation see Freeze, *The Parish Clergy in Nineteenth-Century Russia* (see note 13 above) pp. 363–9.
16. Papkov (see note 14 above) p. 160. Papkov is summarising the view of the author of 'Vopros o tserkovno-prikhodskikh popechitel'stvakh', an article that appeared in *Beseda* in 1872.
17. Papkov (see note 14 above) p. 182. Most of these proposals remain reform agenda for the Russian Orthodox Church in the USSR today.
18. See ibid., pp. 66–73.
19. Ibid., p. 129.
20. Ibid., p. 159. Papkov is relaying the opinion of a publicist writing in *Beseda* in 1872 (see note 16 above).
21. For a discussion of Chicherin's philosophy of law see Andrzej Walicki, *Legal Philosophies of Russian Liberalism* (Oxford: 1987) chap. 2, 'Boris Chicherin: The "Old Liberal" Philosophy of Law', pp. 105–64.
22. B. Chicherin, *Nauka i religiia*, 2nd ed., rev. (Moscow: 1901). The first edition appeared in 1879.
23. Ibid., p. 174.
24. Ibid., p. 177.
25. Ibid., p. 186.
26. Ibid., p. 188.
27. Ibid., pp. 188–9.
28. Ibid., p. 189.
29. Ibid., pp. 189–91.
30. Ibid., pp. 194–215.
31. Ibid., p. 191.
32. Ibid., pp. 206–08.
33. Ibid., pp. 213–15.
34. Ibid., p. 216.
35. Ibid., pp. 228–9.
36. Ibid., pp. 218–19.
37. Ibid., p. 219.
38. Ibid., p. 220.
39. Ibid.
40. Ibid., pp. 231–2.
41. For a discussion of Soloviev's place in the history of Russian liberalism see Walicki (see note 21 above) chap. 3: 'Vladimir Soloviev: Religious

Philosophy and the Emergence of the "New Liberalism"', pp. 165–212.

42.   Prince Evgeniĭ Trubetskoĭ, *Mirosozertsanie V. S. Solov'eva*, 2 vols (Moscow: 1913).

43.   For an account of the conciliar movement see James W. Cunningham, *A Vanquished Hope: The Movement for Church Renewal in Russia, 1905–1906* (Crestwood, New York: 1981).

44.   M. M. Tareev, *Osnovy khristianstva: sistema religioznoĭ mysli*, 4 vols (Sergiev Posad: 1908). A supplementary fifth volume, *Religioznaia zhizn'*, appeared in 1910.

45.   M. M. Tareev, *Iskusheniia Bogocheloveka, kak edinyĭ iskupiteľnyĭ podvig vseĭ zemnoĭ zhizni Khrista, v sviazi s istorieiu dokhristianskikh religiĭ i khristianskoĭ tserkvi* (Moscow: 1892). A shortened version of the work appears in *Osnovy khristianstva* (see note 44 above) iii, pp. 157–318.

46.   Tareev, *Osnovy khristianstva* (see note 44 above) iii, p. 269.

47.   See especially Tareev, *Osnovy khristianstva* (see note 44 above) iv, *Khristianskaia svoboda*.

48.   M. M. Tareev, 'Kratkoe izlozhenie sistemy moego bogoslovstvovaniia. Stranitsa iz nedavneĭ istorii bogoslovskoĭ nauki (Reviziia akademiĭ v 1908 g.)', *Bogoslovskiĭ vestnik* (June–Dec. 1917) ii, p. 391.

49.   Tareev, *Osnovy khristianstva* (see note 44 above) iv, p. 386.

50.   Nikolai Berdiaev, *Smysl tvorchestva: opyt opravdaniia cheloveka* (Moscow: 1916) p. 341, note 1.

51.   Tareev, *Osnovy khristianstva* (see note 44 above) ii, p. 253.

52.   Quoted by Trubetskoĭ, *Mirosozertsanie Vl. S. Solov'eva* (see note 42 above) ii, p. 32.

9 Alexander Kireev and Theological Controversy in the Russian Orthodox Church, 1890–1910

John D. Basil

In 1888 a pamphlet was published in Europe whose authors declared that the Russian Church was facing a doctrinal crisis. Perhaps an effort of the Society of Jesus, the work concluded that the scholarly exchanges of the early 1870s between the German Old Catholics and some Orthodox theologians inspired a questioning among Russian participants about important Orthodox dogmatic teachings. The central issue concerned the dogma of the procession of the Holy Spirit (*filioque*). The crisis was induced by an inability of the Russians to accept all their former traditions in the light of the superior logic and historical understanding of western theologians.[1] The publication was denounced in St Petersburg as a falsity typical of the Jesuits. The Orthodox faithful were assured that traditional Eastern instructions on the Trinity were intact, and that the Old Catholics had presented nothing that required change.[2] By 1890, however, it was quite clear that the Russians were quarrelling over the *filioque* and also over other dogmatic and ecclesiastical matters. They denied, of course, that a crisis had broken out. In his memoirs, Georges Florovsky referred to the debate as merely a vigorous controversy, and N. N. Glubokovskii insisted that it was only a sympathetic discussion, in spite of some signs of extreme intransigency.[3]

One of the leading figures to take part in this controversy was Alexander Alekseevich Kireev, a lay theologian in the Russian Orthodox Church and a prolific polemicist. He was born in 1833 into a well-placed Muscovite family that had faithfully served Russia, its tsars and emperors, since the seventeenth century. His forefathers had been military officers and bureaucrats of very high rank and often the personal friends of members of the royal family itself. The dynasty and the empire were not merely employers or overseers to the Kireevs, they were commanding themes in a tradition both loved and protected. Olga Novikov, Alexander's younger sister became a well-known figure on the European diplomatic scene about whom Stephan Graham wrote: 'She stood for Russia, she was Russia'.[4] A younger brother, Nicholas, was killed in the Balkans in 1875, a volunteer military officer, fighting in what he regarded as a Russian cause. Young Alexander was enrolled in the Imperial Corps of Pages at the age of 16 and was well-prepared for a career in the army or the diplomatic corps; he conversed fluently and read easily in five languages. During his young manhood he served as a cavalry officer, and in 1864 was appointed as an adjutant to the Grand Prince Constantine Nikolaevich who was ruling in Poland.[5] To the very end of his long life, he considered himself a loyal servant of the Romanov family and a defender of the finest Russian traditions. He died in 1910 at the age of 78.

Kireev was known among his contemporaries as a Slavophile, and, indeed, he called himself a Slavophile. At home during his youth, he met Alexis Khomiakov and Ivan Kireevsky. He also knew Iury Samarin and enjoyed friendship with both Ivan Aksakov and Fyodor Tiutchev. He shared many of their views on both the special place of Orthodoxy in Russian history and the decrepit state of the religious spirit in Western Europe. He studied European history and the history of Christianity at the University of Moscow and the University of St Petersburg, but his writings gave favourable citations only to those professors, like M. I. Koialovich, A. M. Ivantsov-Platonov and A. A. Lebedev, who leaned toward the defence of Orthodoxy against Roman Catholicism and who promoted the Slavophile ideology. His first literary effort was an attack against nihilism, which he considered to be a corrosive agent carried into Russia from Western Europe by revolutionaries. This work was followed by over 100 letters and essays written on Orthodoxy in its relations with Catholicism, the internal development of the Roman papacy, which he saw as a corrupt tyranny, and the place of the Slavs in world affairs.[6]

Throughout his career as a publicist, Kireev worked energetically to advance the cause of the Old Catholics both in Western Europe and Russia. This religious group attracted his attention when it first formed as an independent sect in Germany in 1871; its members rejected the Vatican's celebrated definition of papal infallibility and separated from the main body of the Roman Catholic faithful. Kireev was one of the first Orthodox thinkers to draw attention to the newly formed organisation, and he quickly became a champion of close relations between the separatists and the Russian Church. He saw in the future of this small collection of dissidents a base for Orthodoxy of a Western Christian character. In his opinion, the Old Catholics stood firmly with every important tradition and dogma held in the Christian East. It was aggressively anti-papal, it looked for dogmatic guidance only in the Ecumenical councils of early Christian history, it rejected the strong individualism of Protestantism and it expressed a sympathetic interest in the life of Eastern Christianity. As a bonus, according to Kireev, it had the potential value of luring Catholic Slavs away from Rome and toward greater political conformity with the leaders of the Russian empire.[7] For Alexander Kireev, the good fortune of Old Catholics was a missionary cause which he espoused among the Russian clergy and Russian political leaders. He tried to persuade the indomitable Constantine Pobedonostsev to give material support to the sect in its European environment and to encourage the circulation of its ideas in the western sections of the Russian empire.[8] He spoke to the Emperor himself on behalf of an Orthodox union with the Old Catholic leaders, and he gave material support to the *Revue Internationale de Théologie*, one of the best known of the Old Catholic journals.[9] To his great satisfaction, Russian officialdom expressed an interest in the Old Catholics. In 1872, Kireev himself was appointed by Alexander II to a quasi-official position and charged with the responsibility of opening a channel of communication between the Old Catholic leadership in Munich and in Bonn and the church hierarchy in St Petersburg. He saw this appointment as a way to forge formal and firm links binding the Russian Orthodox Church to the Old Catholics, a task that initially appeared manageable. As events unfolded, however, the road soon became bumpy and eventually impassable.

In the early 1870s, little criticism against the Old Catholics could be detected in the Russian ecclesiastical press and none whatsoever in official political circles. After 1890, however, Old Catholicism became a fashionable cause among some West European religious intellectuals, seeking a fresh spiritual base for modern European life. The renewal of interest in Europe brought about a closer review of the sect in the East. The result was criticism and polemical exchanges among Russians and Greeks, and between East and West. The debates revealed divisions in the ranks of Eastern theologians about how to respond to both the Old Catholics and to Kireev's enthusiastic pleading for their cause. And on a deeper level, they revealed serious differences within Russian Orthodoxy over what constituted its own dogmatic and traditional foundations and how Orthodox teachings should be defended in the world outside the empire. In these circumstances, the argument over custom proved to be one of the most important and one of the most difficult to resolve.

Perhaps the most candid defence of Orthodox custom and spirituality was put forth as an attack against the Old Catholics. It came from E. K. Smirnov, at one time the Orthodox chaplain in London and later a professor at the St Petersburg Theological Academy. Writing in *Tserkovnyi vestnik*, the weekly newspaper publication of the Academy, Smirnov made no effort to use scripture or dogmatic teaching to defend the Russian religious way of life. He stated directly that Old Catholicism was basically a Protestant movement whose leaders held little respect for the Russian Orthodox Church. Its appeal was not aimed at Eastern Christians nor did its leaders have any hope or indeed any intention of bringing West Europeans back to the truths of ancient Christianity. Its meagre energies were drawn from the superficial excitement generated by a fad that was currently favouring ecclesiastical unity and sweeping the Protestant world, and on a sheer hatred of the papacy of Pius IX and Leo XIII. Furthermore, he continued in *Vera i razum*, the journal of the Kharkov Theological Seminary, the core of its teaching relied heavily on the Declaration of Utrecht (1888), a snobbish and rationalist-inspired document that made the rejection of all dogma an essential feature of a proposed union of all Christians. In this scheme, Orthodoxy was expected to play a subsidiary role, supplying material support but remaining silent on matters that Russians clearly considered heretical. He went on to criticise the Old Catholic Congress at Lucerne held in 1892 as a sort of church picnic devoted to light entertainment and relaxation. He wondered how seriously the ancient fathers would greet the Old Catholics who would be likely to appear before them holding a cigar in one hand and a glass of beer in the other. Under no circumstances, he demanded, should the Russian Orthodox Church meet as an equal in any kind of union with the Old Catholics. Such an act would inhibit Orthodox autonomy and soil the purity of its traditions.[10]

Kireev was quick to respond to the polemic, pointing out that Smirnov's facts about the Lucerne Congress and the Old Catholics were fantastic. In articles written for *Svet*, a St Petersburg journal devoted to general social topics, and *Bogoslovskii vestnik*, the journal of the Moscow Theological Academy, he accused Smirnov of gleaning information from unreliable sources, wrenching statements out of context and misrepresenting Old Catholicism by discussing it only in connection with some of the more eccentric trends that were to be found in contemporary Protestantism. He was particularly upset by the charge that the Old Catholics had no roots whatsoever in the teachings of the early church fathers and no genuine commitment to the creeds of the ancient Ecumenical councils.[11] He was joined in this exchange by his close colleague, I. L. Ianyshev, the rector of the St Petersburg Theological Academy and a strong supporter of close relations between Old Catholics and Russian Orthodoxy. Ianyshev dismissed Smirnov's assertion that the Protestant influence on the Old Catholics was strong and saw nothing wrong in serving beer to clergymen. It was, after all, the national drink among Germans and Swiss. Both he and Kireev stressed the idea that Orthodox societies in the modern world were obliged to recognise that many customs unfamiliar to their style of religious devotion might be quite legitimate when practised by Christians in Western Europe or North America.[12]

The exchange between Kireev and Ianyshev on the one hand and E. K. Smirnov on the other was crucial. On the surface, of course, it is easy to conclude that Smirnov was careless in collecting factual material and hasty in condemning the Russian friends of the Old Catholic movement, but there was a deeper meaning to the controversy. Kireev himself sensed it when he confessed that scientific theology, logic and the correction of factual errors would have little influence on Smirnov and those others who took his side. Rational debate on questions of fact could not resolve this problem. Smirnov identified true Christianity as being inseparable with the ecclesiastical institutions and customs of the East, in this particular case with the Russian, and he saw any union with Western Christians as a dangerous tie to an alien and weak spirit. The only true equality between Orthodox Christianity and Old Catholics could come about with the conversion of Old Catholics to one of the Eastern national churches and their acceptance of the whole tradition as it had unfolded to the present day. He revealed this sentiment when he urged the Old Catholics to learn Russian, to visit and even to take up residence in Eastern monasteries. In one exchange, he compared an Orthodox union with the Old Catholic leadership to a betrayal against 'our faith and the testament of our Fathers'.[13] Smirnov's position was conservative and provincial. It was a powerful and emotional call to retain Orthodoxy without changes and as it appeared in the social and political fabric of the Christian East.

Kireev and Ianyshev were not trying to change Smirnov's vision, at least not immediately, but they did want to supplement it with a modern belief. They wanted to fashion an exportable Orthodoxy, unencumbered by many of those local customs, canonical regulations and pious practices, which were surely unacceptable to Western Christians. It was for this reason that Kireev stressed most energetically the Old Catholic reliance on the teachings of both the Ecumenical councils and the ancient fathers. In these writings of the past, he believed, a living formula for Christian life could be found to direct all peoples of different cultures toward redemption, while, at the same time, it left them with local autonomy. It was not the adulteration of Orthodoxy that concerned him, as it concerned Smirnov. Kireev wanted to help in the foundation of a Western (European) Christian Orthodoxy, grounded in the ancient teachings, fully recognised by the Russian Church and, hopefully, useful to Russian political causes.

Smirnov soon faded from the circle of argument, but his convictions were shared by many influential Russians. A. P. Maltsev, in a less ironic style, made a similar point in 1898 and again in 1902: 'We must have agreement not between the Old Catholics and the Church of the first eight centuries, but between the Old Catholics and the contemporary Eastern Church'.[14] Pobedonostsev made a similar argument in a rationalised form in 1897. In an article entitled 'The Church', the powerful Oberprocurator of the Holy Synod made a statement that was clearly an attack against the cause of Old Catholicism in Russia: 'Faith is interwoven and interconnected with the roots and psychological characteristics of each different society. Union beyond this tribal realm, with some other church, would be impossible or totally false'.[15]

Perhaps the most forceful presentation of this conservative position was expressed in 1902 by Sergei, Bishop of Iamburg and later the Patriarch of Moscow. The church, according to Sergei, began in the collective worship of the sacred mysteries by the immediate disciples of Christ. It then grew as a community of believers who celebrated their devotion within a visible and functioning organisation. This institution was the only one true church that had been rejected by Nestorians, Arians, Monophysites and then by Western Christians (misguided by papal leadership). It was, in fact, the Eastern Orthodox Church. The Old Catholics failed to understand that they were not a church on an equal footing with it, even if they had somehow acquired the necessary skills to distinguish between false and true dogma. They were still members of a fallen away group who must now rejoin the real church.[16]

Kireev and his associates responded to Sergei with the same irrelevant argument used in the polemic against Smirnov. They again stressed point by point the principles and outward symbols that Orthodoxy supposedly shared with the Old Catholics and again declared that ecclesiastical organisation by itself should be of secondary importance when seeking an agreement with the Old Catholics.[17] Kireev placed Sergei's argument in the category of opinion, but seemed not to notice that Sergei's so-called opinion was shared by enough educated Russians to place a union with the Old Catholics out of reach for the General and his friends. Ianyshev did not openly contest Sergei's argument, but emphatically stated; 'Neither East nor West can claim the title of being the undivided, fully complete Church of Christ. The churches are now divided and errors have crept into all its parts.'[18]

While reviewing this religious debate in Russia, there is a certain irony when one recalls the prediction of Julian Joseph Overbeck, the German former Roman Catholic and then Protestant who eventually converted to Orthodoxy. Overbeck himself had tried unsuccessfully to establish a Western Orthodox church with the help of the St Petersburg hierarchy, and at one time he was a strong supporter of the Old Catholic movement. As early as 1875, however, he concluded that union between the Old Catholics and the Russian Orthodox Church would be achieved only when the Old Catholics converted and were accepted into the Orthodox Church.[19]

Another line of argument developed in Russia against Kireev and his colleagues who wanted to prepare a modern Orthodox package suitable to Christians living outside the East Slavic world. This criticism came from academic circles where the chief focus of interest was neither custom nor traditional practice, nor the idea of the church, but dogmatic differences, those intelligently derived and written formulas that distinguished Eastern from Western Christianity. Kireev and his friends tried first to set a framework favourable to themselves by announcing that no dogmatic problems separated Orthodoxy from the Old Catholic leadership, but there was little likelihood that such a declaration would be taken for granted. The so-called dogmatists would let nothing pass without a thorough investigation, particularly since General Kireev espoused a theology that appeared to many of his opponents in Russia as an effort to reduce to a minimum the number of obligations required for salvation. A controversy unfolded that became serious in Russian theological circles during the late nineteenth and early twentieth centuries, and it will come as no surprise to church historians that the dogma of the procession of the Holy Spirit rested at the centre of debate.

To a secular-minded and future-oriented Europe of the late twentieth century, it seems incomprehensible that a few words written in a document in AD 381, which was then supplemented in the sixth century, could inspire heated argument almost 1600 years later, but this was exactly what happened. Explaining their understanding of the unity and the separation of the Trinity, the churchmen at the second Ecumenical council wrote that the Holy Spirit, the so-called third person of the Trinity, proceeded from the Father (*éx toû patrós*). In AD 589, this dogma was interpolated unilaterally by the church in Spain, which changed the creed to read: the Holy Spirit proceeded from the Father and from the Son (*filioque*).[20] The measure was probably taken to weaken the strength of Arians on the Iberian peninsula, but the act aroused indignation among many Christians, particularly in the East where the change was largely rejected. Most Byzantine theologians argued that the *filioque* addition encouraged the heretical belief in two separate origins of the Holy Spirit, and, of course, they denied emphatically that any local church held the right to add to the sacred creed without ecumenical approval. As a defensive measure, and in clear contradiction to its own position, some Eastern versions of the creed now appeared with an added new word: only. The new Eastern creeds instructed that the Holy Spirit came: 'from the Father only (*mónon*)'. It was a strong expression of opposition against the *filioque*.[21] The issue grew as a serious source of contention in the Middle Ages and in the early modern periods of history. As relations between the churches deteriorated, the rejection or acceptance of the *filioque* became quite useful, like a litmus paper test, in distinguishing Eastern from Western Christians.

It was not considered unusual, therefore, that the Old Catholics were expected to reject the *filioque* in order to gain a favourable acceptance in Russia. There already had been discussion of the topic in the early years of Russian-Old Catholic relations, and a possibility that the first breakdown in negotiations between the German sect and St Petersburg in 1876 occurred over this very matter.[22] Furthermore, some theologians in the Orthodox world approached the *filioque* question looking for more than just conformity. They were also in search of gravity. In 1872 Ignaz Dollinger, the best known of the Old Catholic intellectuals, was heard to refer to the entire *filioque* theology as logomachy. As discussion intensified at the end of the century, this casual treatment of the issue would also prove to be a stumbling block.

In 1893, the Holy Synod published a formal report moderately criticising how the *filioque* was being explained in many of the Old Catholic liturgical books and catechisms.[23] The report was inspired by the revival of interest in the Old Catholic cause which followed the 1892 Lucerne Congress. The Old Catholics, the Synod concluded, correctly rejected the illegal introduction of the term into the creed, but failed to condemn completely the theological arguments that defended the concept. This position fell short of a fully truthful exposition of the teaching. Throughout the report, moreover, the language used by the Synod implied that the Old Catholics were not taking the dogma as a serious matter.

Alexander Kireev challenged this criticism in a series of letters and articles that were written and published in the period between 1897 and his death in 1910. His initial argument took the form of a defence of the *Theses* of V. V. Bolotov, a professor of Eastern Church History at the St Petersburg Theological Academy. The *Theses* suggested that the *filioque* theology be reduced in importance from the realm of dogma to the less serious level of theologumen (rational or speculative theology).[24] The professor was a supporter of the Old Catholic cause in Russia and he hoped to remove the contentious issue from its sensitive place in the debate. Bolotov's recommendation was rejected by the Synod,[25] but forcefully supported by Kireev. In 1897, he wrote that Bolotov's opponents put forth a primitive understanding of the *filioque* question, which would not help to resolve the issue as it now appeared in theological controversy. The ancient fathers, he pointed out, did not always agree among themselves on the *filioque*, so it would be wise to follow Bolotov's tactics and confine the problem to a harmless zone of speculative discussion. Kireev stopped far short of accepting any Western version of the creed as valid church teaching (it was certainly not his wish to create new dogma), but he did propose that the ability to send the Holy Spirit was probably 'eternally inherent' in the character of the Son.[26] Ianyshev, Kireev's strongest ally in the discussion, also took a stand against the Synod, but he was cautious and avoided giving praise for the rejected *Theses*.[27]

The Holy Synod and the anti-*filioque* party were not persuaded by

Kireev, Bolotov and Ianyshev, nor by the arguments of Pavel Svetlov, professor of Theology at St Vladimir's University, who joined the controversy as an important participant in 1904. In their view, the General and his friends were making ready to reduce the number of dogmatic truths necessary for Orthodox belief, just as they had been prepared to strip away many of its beloved customs. One of their strongest proponents was Alexander Gusev, professor of philosophy at the Kazan Theological Academy, who wrote a conservative criticism of Kireev in *Khristianskoe chtenie*, the monthly journal of the St Petersburg Theological Academy, in 1897.[28] Gusev rejected what might have been called the moderate interpretation of the *filioque* theology, which accepted the procession of the Holy Spirit from the Father but proposed that its passage into the world may have come through (*diá*) the Son. This was a compromise gesture, according to Gusev, aimed at satisfying disputants at the expense of the truth. It was newly-invented, erroneous and equally as dangerous as the *filioque* itself. It encouraged the heretical belief that the Son was a dual source with the Father as the origin of the Holy Spirit. He also attacked Bolotov for suggesting that the *filioque* be treated merely as a matter of speculative opinion rather than dogma.[29] Such a step would undermine belief in the sacred and unchangeable character of church teaching and encourage the spread of the subjective Protestant practice of self-interpretation.[30] Gusev's argument unfolded in its fullest form in two articles written for *Vera i razum* in 1898 and 1900. In these frontal attacks against Bolotov and Kireev he defended the most extreme anti-*filioque* position known in Eastern theology. He emphasised the validity and the importance of amending the ancient creed to assure the rejection of any hint that the Son might be a participant with the Father in the generation of the Holy Spirit; this change called for using the Greek word *mónon* (only), following Father, to describe the procession of the third person of the Trinity.[31] Throughout his analyses, Gusev also defended his use of bishop's letters, synodal decrees and catechetical writings that had appeared in the East between the eighth century AD and the present days. These writings were valid evidence in theological debate. To Gusev, Orthodoxy had not remained frozen in form since the close of the seventh Ecumenical council. It was a divinely guided church whose recent acts were as important for the instruction of the faithful as the deeds of its ancient days.

The *filioque* debate continued into the twentieth century. Kireev replied to Gusev in a series of articles written for *Khristianskoi chtenia*, where he renounced any effort to amend the ancient creed. It was precisely this kind of action that had caused the controversy in the first place, he declared. As usual, he insisted that his opponent represented only one opinion among many others and that it should not be understood as an official teaching of the Christian Church. It was an opinion, moreover, that tied the future of Orthodoxy to a 'dying formalism'.[32] But he reserved his strongest statements for a criticism of Vladimir Kerensky, professor of Western church history at Kazan Theological Academy and a former supporter of the Old Catholic cause in Russia.[33] In this exchange Kireev referred to the dogma of the *filioque* and the theological arguments surrounding its history as *impedimentum dirimens*. This phrase came dangerously close to logomachy, the word used by Dollinger to describe the controversy. Kerensky pointed out that even Bolotov had not made such a statement. Kerensky himself then took the offensive by defending his ally, Gusev. He did not go quite as far as Gusev and support supplementary wording in the creed to distinguish between opponents in the *filioque* argument, but he believed that an intelligent argument could be advanced to justify the inclusion of *mónon* into the creed.[34] It was obvious throughout these debates that the editors of *Pravoslavnyia sobesednik* and *Vera i razum* joined in support of the anti-*filioque* camp and that Kireev could not muster sufficient support to persuade the Holy Synod to revise its criticism of Old Catholicism.[35]

Kireev's efforts to soften the edge of Eastern Christian dogma in order to pave the way to closer Orthodox Old Catholic relations did not stop with the *filioque* question. It went on to include exchanges over the definition of the eucharist as well as disagreements about the validity of Old Catholic orders. In each of these cases, many of the same people were engaged in the debate. Kireev found himself fighting against both theologians and an interpretation of dogma that seemed immune to change. Both issues were very important for the Old Catholic cause in Russia, especially the question of orders, because an invalid priest was not able to administer the sacraments nor could an invalid bishop ordain men to the priesthood. It was the question of the dogma of the eucharist, however, that caused the greater disturbance within Orthodoxy itself, particularly once it was agreed that the question of orders was more juridical than dogmatic.[36]

How bread and wine becomes the body and blood of Christ in the eucharist is a Christian mystery that is beyond rational comprehension, but that fact has not stopped theologians from trying to capture in words what is too elusive for the mind of man. At the Council of Trent, the Roman Catholic assembly made just such an effort when the word transubstantiation was employed to summarise a theory that explained how the outer form of bread and wine remained the same while its inner substance changed. The fathers of the Reformation generally rejected this effort as unsatisfactory, and belief in the mystery itself began to wane in Western Europe in the eighteenth and nineteenth centuries. In the East, however, the church held fast to its belief, and in the seventeenth century some of its theologians began to use the word transubstantiation (*presushchestvlenie*) to describe the change.

Like the issue of the *filioque*, it was scepticism of the Old Catholics that led Russians to quarrel among themselves. Gusev remained the most prolific spokesman for the dogmatists. Old Catholic relations with the Anglican church, he stated, revealed their gross indifference to the sacrament of the eucharist. In addition, several Old Catholic writings, especially those of Joseph Langen, described the change in bread and wine in a way that was incompatible with Orthodox dogma. In order to assure harmony in thought and practice, Gusev recommended that the Holy Synod demand the acceptance of the word transubstantiation as a test of good faith.[37] He was joined by others, including Ianyshev, his old adversary, who also harboured suspicions about the Old Catholic belief in this mystery.

General Kireev quickly came to the defence of the Old Catholics by striking at the use of the term transubstantiation. The word was papal terminology, first introduced into Christian literature by the obscure and controversial ninth century Flemish monk Paschasius Radbertus. It was not church dogma. It was employed by the Ecumenical patriarch only briefly in the eighteenth century solely to defend the faith against the symbolic interpretation of the eucharistic mystery by the Calvinists. It could not be found in Russian liturgical services nor in the authoritative instructions of Filaret. Moreover, Kireev concluded, its use in contemporary theological debate threatened to substitute an obscure and materialistic philosophy (Aristotle) for the true teachings of the church. Men in Russia who were accustomed to see truth locked in formulas, he said, were clinging only to what appeared to be a higher truth. He wanted to abandon the use of transubstantiation in favour of the simple word transposition (*prelozhenie*) to describe the mystery.[38]

Gusev's replies to these arguments were designed to increase suspicion of the Old Catholics and to show that the use of the word transubstantiation was an important strand in the fabric of Eastern Christianity. It had been used by Filaret, he contradicted Kireev, as well as by Makarii.[39] It came into usage in the fifteenth century and not in the eighteenth as Kireev suggested. Furthermore, the use of the word *prelozhenie* was inadequate to deal with the issue, because it was too vague to describe the wide distance that separated Orthodoxy and the Old Catholic teaching about the body of Christ. Orthodoxy was threatened by false arguments from the West and also by so-called progressive Russian theologians at home. The use of transubstantiation was the perfect defence.

The discussion on the eucharist resembled in many of its aspects the controversy on the *filioque*, although it was of a short duration and seemed to arouse few emotions. The dogmatists concluded that the teachings of Orthodoxy as they had developed between the eighth and the twentieth centuries were correct and absolute. Gusev and Kerensky resisted efforts to weaken or abandon dogma that had accumulated in the modern centuries of Eastern history. On the other hand, Kireev and his colleagues presented a fresh approach. They wanted to use only the writings of the distant past as a standard for Orthodoxy, and then only those writings that had enjoyed universal approval in the church of the first eight centuries. They wanted to free Orthodox belief from what they called a dying formalism that had grown on the corpus of faith since the ancient days. Kireev, in particular, wanted to rely only on expressions about dogma that were shrouded in the mystery of the distant past and unlikely to present obstacles to an Orthodoxy he hoped to expand into Western Europe.

The fact that these debates in Russia came to focus in excruciating detail on subtleties in philosophy and theology does not mean that they were insignificant or outside the currents of modern religious thought. Just beneath the surface of so-called scholastic argument one can detect the tension created by contending groups of Russians determined to settle the problem of how to meet the influence of the West. Furthermore, when debate goes on among public figures for a period of 15 years and it is accompanied by personal animosity, the winner's stakes are imagined to be very high, so historians should be sensitive to the issues being discussed. One might also add that a long tradition of government censorship often denied to educated Russians the freedom to discuss many so-called dangerous opinions. As a result, learned people became accustomed to concentrate their creative energy in those few breathing areas that could sustain honest intellectual life. The analytic study of Christian dogma was just one of those areas, particularly because it could be skilfully used to support or criticise the West. It is for these reasons that the debates over culture, the *filioque*, and transubstantiation are important. They were serious issues to Russians and they also served as a way to criticise the status-quo without fear of punishment.

Were the Jesuits correct in detecting a crisis of dogma in the Russian Church, and was the Italian Slavist Aurelio Palmieri correct when he called Kireev a modernist in the Russian Orthodox Church?[40] If one makes careful qualifications, the answer to both questions is yes. Certainly, teachings familiar to the East on the *filioque* and transubstantiation were being challenged and the assault commanded a great deal of attention in Russia; it also is clear that the questioning began as a result of Western theological pressure, which at that time was moving to reduce the importance of dogma in the lives of the Christian faithful. Finally, the unresolved aspects of the exchanges in Russia leave one to suspect that the Holy Synod lacked some confidence on these issues. Judgement was suspended and the official statements that both sides of the quarrel hoped to see never appeared.

In regard to Kireev, one can conclude that his adversaries in Russia considered him to be a modernist or a reformer who represented Western fads or practices threatening to Orthodoxy: Smirnov on the question of custom, Maltsev on tradition, Bishop Sergei on the concept of the church, Pobedonostsev on religion and society, Gusev on dogma and Kerensky on the sacraments. Moreover, Kireev was fond of talking about his opposition to 'crusted formalism', the unacceptable fusion of custom and tradition with the true faith, and the use of theology and philosophy as defensive weapons against change. It should also be added that he often seemed to believe that historical science, not revelation, would produce the evidence needed to support the formula of true faith. Finally, the General himself felt comfortable in the company of Western theologians and Russian theologians who enjoyed close contact with the West and not in the monastic atmosphere that dominated the moods of Leontev or amidst the liturgical beauty that appealed to Pobedonostsev. At least in these respects, Kireev was a reformer and the controversy that grew around him was partly inspired by a desire to curtail his ambitions.

NOTES

1. Vasilii Livanskii, *Protopresviter Ianyshev i novyi doktrinal'nyi krizis v russkoi tserkvi: otvet g. Bogorodskomu* (Freiburg: 1888) pp. iv–vi, 19.
2. A. Gusev, 'Iezuitskiia apologii filiokvisticheskago ucheniia', in *Vera i tserkov*, IV (April 1900) pp. 523–5.
3. Georges Florovsky, 'The Orthodox Churches and the Ecumenical Movement Prior to 1910', in *Christianity and Culture*, in *Collected Works of Georges Florovsky*, II (Belmont, Massachusetts: 1974) p. 221, and N. N. Glubokovskii, *Russkaia bogoslovskaiia nauka v eia istoricheskom razvitia; i noveishem sostoianii* (Warsaw: 1928) p. 12.
4. Olga Novikoff, *Russian Memoirs* (London: 1917) p. 1.
5. 'Kireev', in *Pravoslavnaia bogoslovskaia entsiklopediia*, ed. N. N. Glubokovskii and A. P. Lopukhin, x (St Petersburg: 1909) pp. 479–82. 'Kireev, Aleksandr Alekseevich', in *Entsiklopedicheskii Slovar*, xv (St Petersburg, Leipzig: 1895) 29, pp. 153–4.
6. A. A. Kireev, *Sochineniia*, ed. D. N. Iakshich, 2 vols (St Petersburg: 1912); (hereafter Kireev, *Soch*). The *Sochineniia* is a two volume collection of Kireev's articles and letters. It was edited by D. Iakshich, a priest of the Russian Orthodox Church at the Dresden consulate, with the assistance of Kireev's sister, Olga Novikov. It was published by Suvorin. Unfortunately, the editor did not always list the names of the newspapers and journals where his material first appeared. Nor does the collection include all of Kireev's published work.
7. John D. Basil, 'Russian Orthodox Response to the Old Catholics, 1870–1905', in Dennis J. Dunn (ed.), *Religion and Nationalism in Eastern Europe and the Soviet Union* (Boulder: 1987) p. 68.
8. *K. P. Pobedonostsev i ego korrespondenty: pis'ma i zapiskii*, ed. M. N. Pokrovsky, I (Moscow: 1923) p. 180.
9. V. A. Sokolov, 'Pamiati A. A. Kireeva', in *Bogoslovskii vestnik*, xx (Sergiev Posad: September 1911) 3, p. 179.
10. E. K. Smirnova, *K starokatolicheskomu voprosu: pravoslaven li inter-communion, predlagaemyi nam starokatolikami?* (Kharkov: 1894) (hereafter Smirnov, *Voprosu*), pp. 14, 65, 75–7, 84, 100–13.
11. A. Kireev, 'Po povodu knigi o. protoiereia E. K. Smirnova: "K staro-katolicheskomu voprosu". Pravoslaven li Intercommunion, pre-dlagaemyi nam Staro-katolikami?', in *Bogoslovskii vestnik*, III (Sergiev Posad: May 1894) pp. 330–4, 338, 341.
12. I. L. Ianyshev, 'Pravda li, chto starokatoliki predlagaiut nam pravos-lavynm intercommunion (vzaimoprichashchenie) i s nim— protestantizm?', in *Tserkovnyi vestnik*, XI and XII (St Petersburg: March 1894) pp. 164–5, 179.
13. Smirnov, *Voprosu*, p. 112–14.
14. A. P. Mal'tsev, 'Starokatolitsizm i pravoslavie', *Vera i tserkov*, IV (May 1902) 5, p. 701. Additional comments by Mal'tsev appeared in 'Altkatholicismus und Orthodoxie', *Germania*, CLXXX (Berlin: 10 August 1898). A later Russian translation appeared in 'Starokato-lichestvo i pravoslavie', in *Pribavleniia k tserkovnym vedomostiam*, XLII (1898) p. 1565.

15. K. P. Pobedonostsev, 'Tserkov i gosudarstvo' and 'Tserkov' in *Moskovskii sbornik* (Moscow: 1897) pp. 4–5, and especially 207–08.

16. Episkop Sergii, 'Chto nas razdeliaet so starokatolikami?', *Tserkovnyi vestnik*, ILIV, and ILV (St Petersburg: October, November 1902) pp. 1379, 1409–15).

17. A. Kirejew, 'Ein Versuch zur Verständigung Antwort an Bischof Sergius', in *Revue Internationale de Théologie*, XLVI (Berne: April–June 1904) pp. 191–3.

18. [I. L. Ianyshev], 'Eshche raz—k raz"iasneniiu', in *Tserkovnyi vestnik*, XXXIII (St Petersburg: August 1902) pp. 1025–7.

19. Wilhelm Kahle, *Westliche Orthodoxie: Leben und Ziele Julian Joseph Overbecks* (Leiden: 1968) p. 141.

20. Richard Haugh, *Photius and the Carolingians, the Trinitarian Controversy* (Belmont, Mass.: 1975) pp. 25–9.

21. Some scholars have denied that the word *mónon* was introduced into Eastern versions of the creed, but the evidence in support of the opposite conclusion is substantial. Dollinger wrote in 'Von der Unions-Conferenz', *Deutscher Merkur*, XXXIV (Cologne and Munich: 21 August 1875) p. 295: 'die Confessio orthodoxa hat ihrerseits willkurlich den zusatz *mónon* ins Glaubenskenntnitz gebracht, wie die Abendländer das *Filioque*'. One can also examine Martino Jugie, *De Processione Spiritus Sancti: ex Fontibus Revelations et Secundum Orientales Dissidentes* (Rome: 1936) pp. 378–9, as well as the Greeks themselves in *Grigoriou tou palama: Suggrammata*, ed. B. Bobrinsky, P. Papaeuaggelou, I. Meyendorff and P. Khristou (Thessalonika: 1962) p. 23. The Russian Bishop Sergei was cautious, but said much the same thing: 'Chtoby otstoiat etu istinu protiv latinstva, greki gotovy pribavit k simbolu slova "ot odnogo" (Ottsa) . . .'. Episkop Sergii, 'Chto nas razdeliaet so starokatolikami?', in *Tserkovnyi vestnik*, XLXXX (St Petersburg: October 1902) p. 1347.

22. Smirnov, *Voprosu*, p. 19, and Arkhimandrit Sil'vestr, *Otvet pravoslavnago na predlozhennuiu starokatolikami skhemu o sviatom dukhe* (Kiev: 1875) pp. 1–19.

23. 'Donesenie S. Peterburgskoi Kommissii Sv. Sinodu', in *Tserkovnyi vestnik*, XXXVIII (St Petersburg: September 1896) pp. 1220, 1221.

24. 'Thesen über das "Filioque"; von einem russischen Theologen', in *Revue Internationale de Théologie*, VI (Berne: October–December 1898) pp. 681–712.

25. A. L. Katansky, 'Ob iskhozhdenii Sv. Dukha (po povodu starokatolicheskago voprosa)', in *Khristianskoe chtenie*, LXXIII (St Petersburg: May–June 1893) pp. 401–25.

26. A. Kireev, 'K starokatolicheskomu voprosu', in *Bogoslovskii vestnik*, VI (Sergiev Posad: February 1897) p. 325, and 'K starokatolicheskomu voprosu: otvet professoru Gusevu' in *Soch*, II, pp. 269–70.

27. [I. L. Ianyshev], 'Eshche raz—k raz"iasneniiu', in *Tserkovnyi vestnik*, XXXII, XXXIII, XXXIV (St Petersburg: August 1902).

28. A. Gusev, 'K starokatolicheskomu voprosu: pis'mo A. A. Kireevu', in *Khristianskoe chtenie*, LXXVII (St Petersburg: May 1897) pp. 733–71.

29. A. Gusev, 'Tezisy po voprosu o *Filioque* i presushchestvlenii', in

Pravoslavnyi sobesednik (Kazan: January 1901) pp. 3–39. Gusev continued his attack in 1903 in response to an Old Catholic rebuttal of his article of 1901: A. Gusev, 'Starokatolicheskii otvet na nashi tezisy po voprosu o *Filioque* i presushchestvlenii', in *Pravoslavnyia sobesednik* (Kazan: January–May 1903) pp. 75–130, 177–232, 319–38, 435–84 and 637–48.

30. A. Gusev, 'Fal'shiviashchee upriamstvo v otstaivanii *Filioque* i v otverzhenii presushchestvleniia', in *Vera i razum*, Kharkov, ix (May 1900) pp. 504–5.

31. A. Gusev, 'Fal'shiviashchee upriamstvo v otstaivannii *Filioque* i v otverzhenii presushchestvleniia', in *Vera i razum*, Kharkov, xi (June 1900) pp. 666–70.

32. A. Kireev, 'Moi poslednii otvet professoru A. Th. Gusevu po starokatolicheskomu voprosu', in *Soch*, ii, pp. 299–301.

33. A. Kireev, 'Otvet professoru V. A. Kerenskomu', in *Soch*, ii, pp. 361–3.

34. V. A. Kerensky, 'K starokatolicheskomu voprosu', in *Khristianskoe chtenie*, lxxxiv (St Petersburg: July, September 1904) pp. 112–28, 387–409.

35. A. Brilliantov, 'Trudy prof. V. V. Bolotóva po voprosu o *Filioque* i polemika o ego "Tezisakh o Filioque" v russkoi literature', in *Khristianskoe chtenie*, xcii (St Petersburg: April 1913) p. 445.

36. V. K. Sokolov, 'Mozhno-li priznat zakonnost ierarkhiu starokatolikov', in *Bogoslovskii vestnik*, ii (Sergiev Posad: April 1893) pp. 111, 116.

37. A. Gusev, 'Otvet A. A. Kireevu po starokatolicheskomu voprosu o "Filioque" i "Presushchestvlenii"', in *Vera i razum*, xv (Kharkov: August 1897) p. 203.

38. A. Kireev, 'Vtoroi otvet A. Th. Gusevu po povodu starokatolicheskago voprosa' in *Soch*, ii, pp. 277–83.

39. A. Gusev, 'Otvet starokatolicheskomu zhurnalu: Nemetskii merkurii', in *Vera i razum*, xiii (Kharkov: July 1897) p. 39, and A. Gusev, 'Fal'shiviashchee upriamstvo v otstaivanii Filioque i v otverzhenii presushchestvleniia', in *Vera i razum*, xiii (Kharkov: July 1900) p. 45.

40. P. A. Palmieri, 'Le teorie del Generale Alessandro Kireev sul'unione delle Chiese', in *Bessarione*, ix (Rome: 1912) 3, p. 200.

10 Leo Tolstoy, a Church Critic Influenced by Orthodox Thought
Pål Kolstø

The Russian intelligentsia in the nineteenth century was, by and large, vehemently opposed to organised Christianity in general and to the Russian Orthodox Church in particular. The main reason for this was, in my view, the intimate relationship between religious and secular authority in the tsarist state. The intelligentsia dedicated their lives to the overthrow of the existing political order, and not without reason perceived the church as an integral part of this order.

For an alternative *Weltanschauung* the *intelligenty* turned to Europe. Here they found in due order socialism, materialism, positivism and Marxism. Their religious and anti-religious ideas were also largely imported from abroad.[1] As Berdiaev has pointed out, however, when transplanted to Russian soil European systems of thought acquired new traits, reflecting the peculiar socio-political conditions in Russian society and the country's unique cultural traditions. Foreign ideas were never slavishly copied, but transformed and adapted to suit the indigenous situation.[2]

This general statement holds true also for the intelligentsia's treatment of religion. It is my contention that any criticism of the Christian faith inevitably must be directed against and influenced by the church with which the critic is familiar. Religion *per se* does not exist, only specific, historical religions. In a similar way there can be no timeless, unconditional criticism of religion. Different churches leave their imprint on their adversaries in different ways: their critics hold a number of presuppositions which they share with the church against which they rebel; on the other hand their revolt is often triggered by a reaction against dogmas or forms of spirituality which are especially salient in this particular church. As Eastern Christian tradition in many ways differs from Western tradition, Russian religious criticism cannot be a mere repetition of Western positions.

To elucidate this thesis I will analyse the relationship of Leo Tolstoy to the Orthodox Church. The case of Tolstoy is in some ways

148

special. In contrast to most members of the contemporary Russian intelligentsia he retained a religious world view and indeed constructed his own religious faith, commonly known as Tolstoyanism. However, he shared with the intelligentsia at large a number of important attitudes and sentiments, such as its anti-authoritarianism and above all its animosity toward the Russian state church. In *What I Believe* from 1884 Tolstoy characterised church Christianity as 'the darkness Jesus fought against and told his disciples to fight against'.[3] But if most of the intelligentsia dismissed Orthodoxy out of hand, without bothering to look into its inner life in any detail, Tolstoy made a thorough theoretical and practical study of this church. Towards the end of the 1870s he underwent a deep personal crisis, the outcome of which was a temporary return to the Orthodox faith he had abandoned in his adolescence. For about a year and a half he went to church regularly, said the Orthodox prayers morning and evening and adhered strictly to the dietary restrictions on fast days.[4] Gradually, however, he grew restive and dissatisfied with the church as he encountered more and more dogmas that he could not reconcile with his reason or moral sense. In the end he plunged into an all-encompassing study of Orthodox theology, and closely examined most of the catechisms and textbooks of systematic theology in current use at the time.[5] As a result of his studies he wrote the voluminous book *Investigation of Dogmatic Theology*,[6] in which he stated his reasons for breaking with Orthodoxy anew.

Thus, while most members of the intelligentsia left few writings on religion and none devoted exclusively to the Orthodox faith, Tolstoy provides us with an abundance of material for the study of his relationship to the Russian church. This material has, however, been almost totally neglected. When *Investigation* appeared, it was ignored by clergy and laity alike. In striking contrast to the rest of Tolstoy's religious writings, almost all of which created an immediate uproar and elicited numerous commentaries and rebuttals, this book fell dead straight from the printing press. With the singular exception of the Archimandrite (later Metropolitan) Antonii Khrapovitskii[7] no one even bothered to engage in polemics against it. There are several explanations for this reticence. Most churchmen felt that the accusations launched against the church in this book were so absurd that they did not warrant counter-attack. In the opening chapter, for instance, Tolstoy claimed that the compendiums in dogmatics that were studied at the theological seminaries, had been written by non-believers with the deliberate intention of deluding the students.[8]

They consisted of 'pure fantasies', 'blasphemous ravings', and 'pitiful, dishonest distortions'. These charges were so grotesque that one was free to overlook them. On the other hand, some of the Russian Christians who did take Tolstoy's criticism to heart, felt that the rather arid dogmatics taught at the seminaries did not adequately express the faith they lived by. *Even if* Tolstoy should succeed in undermining the authority of certain textbooks it would in no way shake their religious foundations.[9]

Furthermore, *Investigation* was not published until 10 years after it was written, in 1891. At that time the Russian public had already been exposed to Tolstoy's *Confession* and *What I Believe*, two works that expounded his religious teaching in a much more direct and succinct way. Finally, *secular* Russian readers took even less interest in Tolstoy's high-pitched assaults against Orthodoxy than did the devotees of the Church. They regarded this book as part of a private joust between Tolstoy and the divines which need not concern them.

It is thus relatively easy to explain why *Investigation* did not enjoy any degree of popularity in Tolstoy's time, but it is harder to explain the almost total lack of interest in this book among contemporary scholars. Most recent studies of Tolstoy's religion either make no reference to this work at all, or acknowledge its existence in a footnote only.[10] Even if one agrees that this work is devoid of any literary merit, it is nevertheless an important source for the understanding of Tolstoy's religious ideas. It can, moreover, be proven that Tolstoy himself attached great importance to this work. It was one of the first books that he wrote after his 'second birth' (as he called his conversion to Tolstoyanism), the first to be completed after the masterpiece *Confession*. These two works are intimately connected. *Confession* describes Tolstoy's long and desperate quest for existential meaning, and his consecutive disenchantment with nineteenth-century cultural optimism, Schopenhauerian pessimism and Orthodox Christianity. For him none of these 'understandings of life' solved the riddle of human existence. *Confession*, however, does not end with a total rejection of Orthodoxy as is often assumed. On the contrary, in this work Tolstoy ventures the opinion that Orthodoxy contains a mixture of lies and truths, 'interwoven with the finest threads'.[11] The concluding phrase of the first edition of *Confession* runs as follows:

> That this doctrine contains truth is to me unquestionable, but just as unquestionably it also contains falsehood. I had to find both the

truths and the lies and separate them. This I set out to do. What I found of falsehood and truth in this teaching, and the conclusions I drew, constitute the succeeding sections of this work.[12]

'The succeeding sections' are nothing other than *Investigation*. In the manuscript the first lines of *Investigation* immediately follow the concluding lines of *Confession*,[13] which properly speaking is only a preface to the main work. Indeed, in the first printed edition *Confession* had a subtitle: *Introduction to an Unpublished Work*.[14]

It is thus legitimate to consider the conclusion of *Confession* as a methodological starting point for the study of *Investigation of Dogmatic Theology*, that is, one should be consciously on the lookout for the rays of light that Tolstoy detected in Orthodox darkness. The further he dug himself into dogmatic theology the more his indignation grew, and when he finished writing the book, he was markedly more anti-Orthodox than when he started out. Still, even in the final version of *Investigation* it is possible to find positive evaluations of certain elements of Orthodoxy side by side with invectives and denunciations, in accordance with the formula 'truths interwoven with lies'. More often than not, however, these positive evaluations are not explicit, but must be deduced from Tolstoy's method of reasoning and the general structure of his arguments.

Even though Tolstoy pretends to undercut the entire corpus of Orthodox theology, his work is on the face of it a refutation of only one theologian, namely metropolitan Makarii of Moscow (1816–82). This erudite bishop was the author of several standard textbooks on theology. The most important of these was *Orthodox Dogmatic Theology*, a bulky 1200 page compendium. Tolstoy decided to focus on this work for several reasons. It was the most recent and comprehensive of all the theological works he had read, and it contained numerous references to the church fathers and theologians of earlier centuries. Tolstoy felt that Makarii's work summarised the entire Orthodox tradition and represented, as it were, the pinnacle of Orthodox wisdom.[15] *Orthodox Dogmatic Theology* had moreover been recommended to him by an Orthodox priest in his home town, Tula.[16] Tolstoy had also visited the Most Reverend Makarii in Moscow the year before and discussed religious questions with him.[17] Tolstoy thus had ample reason to concentrate on this work. Still, the choice was unfortunate. Makarii's book has not survived its age and is now largely forgotten. Even in Tolstoy's time the book was deplored by Russian believers as basically flawed. The lay theologian Aleksei

Khomiakov, for one, ridiculed it as 'charmingly silly'.[18] Metropolitan Filaret (Gumilevskii) claimed that *Orthodox Dogmatic Theology* was 'an absurd confusion', 'lacking logical order and containing unconvincing proofs'.[19] These characteristics were strikingly similar to some of Tolstoy's judgements. He maintained that *Orthodox Dogmatic Theology* was 'self-contradictory' and 'with no inner connection between the parts'.[20]

The French scholar Nicolas Weisbein has suggested that if Tolstoy had made a study of Thomas Aquinas instead of the mediocre Makarii, he might have ended up with a much greater appreciation of Christian dogmatics.[21] This observation, I think, misses the point. As a Russian, Tolstoy had been grafted into the Orthodox branch of Christianity as a child, and it was naturally this church he had to come to grips with.

Weisbein is one of the few modern scholars who have attempted to penetrate *Investigation of Dogmatic Theology*. He reaches the conclusion that the book is soaked in rationalistic criticism.[22] According to Weisbein Tolstoy turned Anselm's celebrated formula upside down: instead of *credo ut intelligam* he lived by *intelligo ut credam*.[23] Admittedly, some sentences in *Investigation* make this interpretation plausible. At one point, for instance, Tolstoy insists that 'we can only believe what we can understand'.[24] Yet at the same time as he wrote *Investigation* he made other, contradictory statements. To his confidante Alexandra Tolstaia, Tolstoy wrote that 'we can only believe that which we cannot understand, but which at the same time we cannot reject'.[25] Between these two statements there exists an obvious tension which runs through the entire texture of Tolstoy's religious thinking. Thus, Weisbein's claim that, for Tolstoy, 'le seul critère valable, c'est la raison',[26] is misleading in its one-sidedness. This is expecially evident in Tolstoy's treatment of the dogma of God.

The discussion of the nature of God and of man's possibility of acquiring knowledge of Him, is crucial to the thinking of both Makarii and Tolstoy. Makarii is strongly theocentric in his dogmatic approach. No matter what topic he intends to treat, he takes the dogma of God as his point of departure, and the first 350 pages of his book are devoted exclusively to the theme of 'God in himself' (*v samom sebe*). Similarly, Tolstoy grappled all his life with the problem of the divinity which he approached from many different angles, never feeling that he had solved it satisfactorily (as indeed no serious theologian would claim to have done). A number of Tolstoy's remarks on the topic of God were collected by his close collaborator

Vladimir Chertkov, and published under the title *Thoughts on God*. Many of the sayings in this booklet bear a strong resemblance to the treatment of the question of God in Orthodox theology. In some cases the similarities are so great that one is tempted to think that they were 'lifted' from Makarii's work.

Makarii starts with a discussion of epistemology: is God at all accessible to human understanding? His preliminary answer is a flat denial: God is 'incomprehensible' to man. This is explained in different ways: God is unlimited, while the spirit of man is limited; furthermore man is a corporeal being while God is pure Spirit; finally, human understanding is obscured by sin.[27]

With this introduction to the topic of the Godhead one might think that Makarii's vessel of theology had foundered before it was properly launched. An utterly incomprehensible God can hardly be made the subject of a textbook study. But soon Makarii qualifies his initial statement: God's incomprehensibility is not absolute, in as much as God has decided to reveal himself to mankind, through creation and in the scripture. Thus, the bishop claims, it is possible to reach a 'partial' knowledge of God.[28] This contention is immediately attacked by Tolstoy: if God is truly incomprehensible, then even a partial knowledge of him is out of the question.[29]

The inconspicuous word 'partial' serves in Makarii's book as a springboard to the substance of his theology. He ventures to list a number of characteristics that may be attributed to God. It turns out that there are quite a few: God is self sufficient, autonomous, ubiquitous, eternal, immutable, almighty and omniscient. He possesses plenitude of wisdom, freedom, holiness, benevolence, faithfulness and justice. To each of these characteristics Tolstoy stubbornly raises the same standard objection: Makarii has forgotten the incomprehensibility of God.

The notion of God's incomprehensibility is not a peripheral theme in Orthodox theology. On the contrary it is one of its cornerstones. Ultimately it reaches back to the Old Testament prohibition against graven images of God. Even Moses, who met Him in the burning bush, was not allowed to see His face—all he saw was God's back as He passed by (Exodus: 33.23). In the New Testament strict Jewish transcendentalism was modified as God became flesh and took up His abode among men, but even here God the Father is understood as principally incomprehensible and inaccessible. St Paul teaches that God 'dwells in unapproachable light'. No man has ever seen Him or will see Him (I Timothy: 6.16).

This insight is preserved by all Christian denominations in one form or another. Luther, for instance, developed a doctrine of the hidden God, *Deus absconditus*, and his teaching was accompanied by a warning: the faithful should not try to penetrate the hidden reaches of the Godhead, but rather concentrate on God in his revelation.[30] God's incomprehensibility is thus strictly speaking not a topic of Lutheran theology. In the Eastern Christian tradition, however, this mystery has engaged the shrewdest theological minds. An elaborate theological tradition has been spun around it. Known as the 'negative' or 'apothatic' theology, this theory may be found in embryonic form as early as the fourth century in the writings of the Cappadocian fathers. It is, however, principally associated with *Corpus Areopagiticum*,[31] a collection of theological treatises that have been attributed to Dionysius the Areopagite who, according to Acts 17.34, became a Christian under the influence of St Paul's teaching in Athens. Modern scholars, however, have shown that the treatises originated in Syria in the sixth century. Partly due to their purported origin, but also thanks to their own unquestionable merits, these writings have made a tremendous impact on the subsequent history of theology.

In one of these treatises, *On Mystical Theology*, the author distinguishes between two fundamentally different approaches to knowledge of God, the cataphatic and the apophatic.[32] By means of the cataphatic method men try to determine the nature of God by attributing certain characteristics to Him: He is benevolent, almighty, all knowing. This method has been made possible by God's own historical acts: in a series of theophanies, of which the incarnation is the greatest, He has made himself known to man. The cataphatic method relies heavily on the principle of analogy: we understand God as analogous with the world as we know it. Therefore, however indispensable, this approach is only of limited value.

A higher form of theology is the apophatic way. To say that it is higher does not mean that it gives more precise knowledge of God. In fact, it gives no positive knowledge at all. It approaches God by means of negation and limits itself to statements about what God is *not*. As the sculptor chisels off chips of rock to form a portrait, so the negative theologian removes all man-made definitions and perceptions of God that do not properly belong to Him. Pseudo-Dionysius reminds us that God has no form or shape, and adds that He is neither soul nor intellect. God may not be described as small or big, He is neither in time, nor in eternity, neither truth nor falsehood, neither light, nor non-light. Confronted with God not only words, but even thoughts must be abandoned. God shows Himself as unutterable and incomprehensible. Whereas Makarii attributed the incomprehensibility of God to man's limited capacity for understanding, pseudo-Dionysius sees this phenomenon as an essential and inalienable trait of God himself.

Cataphaticism and apophaticism are opposite, but not mutually exclusive approaches. While the former is deduced from God's immanence, the latter safeguards His transcendence. The apophatic negations lead to 'the darkness of unknowing', but not to emptiness or absence. Rather they lead the faithful toward a presence, toward an encounter with the living God. Apophaticism is not abstract speculation, but a way of purification. The believer empties himself of all concepts in order to be filled by God. Not knowledge of God, but *union* with Him is the ultimate goal.

In Tolstoy's diaries and published writings several passages reveal a strikingly apophatic way of expression. A few examples will have to suffice. In his diary for 1904 Tolstoy described God as:

> *Deus absconditus*, incomprehensible . . . He is unknown to me, but I know that my destination is in Him, and my participation in Him constitutes the unshakeable foundation of my life.[33]

Another note 10 years earlier elaborates the point:

> The more seriously and honestly I think about myself, about life and the origin of life, the less I feel a need to form a concept of God, the more destructive such concepts become. The closer I approach God, the less I see Him. Not because He does not exist, but because it becomes frightening to talk about Him, to mention Him, not to speak of defining Him.[34]

In *Thoughts on God* Tolstoy gives a similar description of the apophatic way:

> My life consists in movement toward Him, but this movement in no way enhances my knowledge of Him. . . . Any attempt to formulate a concept about Him (for instance that He is creator or that He is benevolent) removes me from Him.[35]

In his spiritual life Tolstoy had the same experience as pseudo-Dionysius. The similarity of expression, however, is due not only to their sharing a common psychological background, but to their participation in a common tradition. Tolstoy had immediate knowledge of the apophatic tradition of the Eastern church, and accuses Makarii explicitly of distorting 'the profound and sincere utterances of the apostles and the church fathers who demonstrate the incomprehensibility of God'.[36] Anchored in this tradition Tolstoy blames Makarii for being *insufficiently* Orthodox in his thinking.

Attempts have been made to attribute Tolstoy's theory of God to influences from other sources than Orthodoxy. It is known that Tolstoy made a thorough study of the German philosopher Immanuel Kant. Kant goes to great lengths to prove that it is impossible to reach any positive knowledge of God.[37] There is, however, a major distinction between the thinking of the church fathers and that of the German idealist. Whereas the Orthodox theologians take God's existence for granted, and only deny the possibility of defining His essence, in *Critique of Pure Reason* (the only Kantian *critique* Tolstoy had read by the time he wrote *Investigation*) Kant is an agnostic also concerning the existence of God. In this dispute Tolstoy sides with the fathers:

> If we talk about God as the fountainhead of all things, then clearly we recognize, comprehend, His existence. But if we talk about the very essence of God, we obviously cannot comprehend Him.[38]

Tolstoy may have learnt about Orthodox apophaticism in several places. He probably did not read any of the Areopagitic writings, but that tradition was kept alive by many later church fathers whom Tolstoy knew well. A classical statement of apophaticism is, for example, given in *On the Orthodox Faith* by John of Damascus,[39] one of the theological books Tolstoy studied while he worked on *Investigation*. Strong apophatic statements have also made their way into Orthodox liturgy. In the standard prayer book (*Trebnik*) God is addressed as 'eternal Tsar, without beginning, invisible, unexplorable, incomprehensible and unutterable'. These and many other apophatic sources are quoted by Makarii,[40] who is, ironically, the main supplier of the ammunition Tolstoy uses against him.

Tolstoy, however, like the Orthodox theologians before him, does not stop with the notion of God's incomprehensibility. He recognises the need to supplement negative theology with positive statements. He is perfectly willing to state that God is one, and that He may be described in terms of Love, Will and Reason. Makarii makes the same points in *Orthodox Dogmatic Theology*.

The demonstration of the oneness of God is the first and most fundamental stage of Makarii's cataphatic deduction. He emphasises, however, that this term is not to be understood in a strictly mathematical sense. God is not 'one' in the sense that He may be designated by the figure 1, but in the sense that He is complete in Himself (*vsetselyi*).[41] Tolstoy sees this statement as an opportunity to vent his sarcasm: this is tantamount to saying that the foliage is green, but not coloured, he jeers. 'The words "one" and "singular" denote figures, and therefore cannot be applied to the God we believe in.'[42] Here, however, Tolstoy lets his polemical bent get the better of him; in fact he is in complete agreement with Makarii on this point. In *Thoughts on God* he states that: 'About God we can only say what Moses and Muhammed said: that he is one'. What is more, he immediately goes on to qualify this statement in the same way that Makarii did. He repeats the bishop's phrase almost verbatim: 'God . . . is not "one" in the sense of the figure 1, but only in the sense that He is one-centred (*odnotsentren*)'.[43] Tolstoy was obviously quite unaware of the fact that in this sentence he to some extent rehabilitated the Orthodox theologian upon whom he had heaped so much scorn.

A central point at which Tolstoy seems to depart from Orthodox theological thinking is on the question of God's personality. Tolstoy repeatedly denies that it is possible to ascribe personality to God. As the notion of a personal God is absolutely essential to all Christian theology, many commentators have concluded that this disagreement constitutes an unbridgeable gulf between Tolstoy's thinking and the Christian tradition. Tolstoy's concept of God has frequently been classified as pantheistic.[44] It is worth noting, however, that Tolstoy explicitly dissociates himself from pantheism. According to him, God is:

not a concept, but a being, what the Orthodox call 'the living God', in contrast to a pantheistic God. That is, He is the highest, spiritual being who lives in everything.[45]

Tolstoy's rejection of God's personality may possibly be explained as a semantic misunderstanding. The term 'personal' in the Russian language, *lichnyi*, also means 'individual'. To claim that God is individual is not a Christian idea, some might say that it is a meaningless statement. When Tolstoy argues against the 'personality' of God he usually does so by saying that *lichnyi* implies 'limited'.[46] It seems to me that this argument refutes the individuality rather than the personality of God.[47]

What is meant in Christian theology by saying that God is personal is usually that He is endowed with mind and will and takes a genuine interest in the well-being of His creatures. Indeed, He has a plan for the life of every single one of us. This is a basic tenet of Tolstoy's theology as well. He emphasised time and again that God has a will, not just a general will *à la* Schopenhauer, but a specialised will for each individual human being. It is our task in life to realise this will and carry it out.[48] The Orthodox writer Vladislav Maevskii, who has devoted a whole book to Tolstoy's religion, sees this idea as irrefutable proof that Tolstoy's God, in the last resort, must be transcendental. His God is in possession of a personal will and a personal reason. In short, He is identical with the God of the Church, Maevskii claims.[49]

Personally I cannot subscribe to this conclusion. Even though Tolstoy, as I have attempted to demonstrate, is heavily indebted to Orthodox thinking on a number of important issues, on other just as important points he places himself well beyond the pale of historical Christianity. It should suffice to mention his emphatic rejection of the Trinity, which he could not 'understand', and his one-sided Christology. Christ was in his view not the son of God, but simply an extremely enlightened human who understood God's will better than anyone before or after him. He rejects the central Christian dogmas of redemption and grace on the grounds that they remove the burden of moral responsibility from our shoulders. Finally, ecclesiology and sacraments have no place in Tolstoyan theology. There is therefore no reason to believe that Tolstoy would have reached a different opinion of Christian dogmatics by reading *Summa theologiae*.

The purpose of this presentation has not been to 'christianize' Tolstoy and enroll him among the members of the Orthodox church against his will. Rather I have attempted to show how some important Orthodox ideas live on in the thinking of this active and articulate opponent of the Russian church. This heritage is largely taken over unconsciously, and has been so transformed and blended with ideas taken from other sources that it can be isolated and identified only through a careful analysis.

Most commentators have taken for granted that Tolstoy could not be influenced by a Church which he denounced so indignantly. To identify his spiritual ancestors they have therefore concentrated on the sources on which Tolstoy himself lavished most praise—for example, Rousseau, Kant, Schopenhauer and Confucius.[50] Most of these have unquestionably left their imprint on Tolstoy's thinking, but not to the exclusion of sources closer to home.

The first Western scholar to make the Orthodox faith his frame of reference for a study of Tolstoy's writings is Richard F. Gustafson. His method is structural—that is, he seeks out similarities between Tolstoy's turn of thought and that of 'the Orthodox mind'. Nowhere does he enter into a discussion of *how* Tolstoy has been exposed to Orthodox influence. Indeed, at the outset he dismisses the Orthodox theology of the day as 'slightly dressed-up versions of Western systems of thought, Catholic and Protestant'.[51] It is never explained to the reader how Tolstoy was able to peel off these layers of foreign influence to reach the genuinely Orthodox core of Russian Christianity.

Nevertheless, Gustafson's intuition has served him well. His close reading of Tolstoy's writings brings him to the conclusion that: 'Tolstoy may not be an Orthodox thinker, but certainly he is an Eastern Christian artist and theologian within the culture of Russian Orthodoxy'.[52] While I personally would have chosen a somewhat more cautious wording and dropped the epithet 'Christian', I basically think this is a sound conclusion. My own research may be understood as an attempt to support Gustafson's hypothesis by giving it a more solid empirical basis.

Finally it should be noted that dogmatic theology was not the only Orthodox source of which Tolstoy availed himself. Just as important was his exposure to the mystical-ascetical tradition in the Russian Church. This tradition had been driven underground after the defeat of 'Trans-Volga elders' in the conflict with the Josephites in the sixteenth century. It was revived by Paisii Velichkovskii two centuries later and brought back to Russia by his disciples. Paisii had visited the Holy Mountain Athos in northern Greece, that flourishing greenhouse of Orthodox spirituality to which the Russian church owes so much.[53] Here the learned monk Nicodemus had just finished his compilation and translation of ancient and medieval monastic texts which were published under the title *Philokalia*, 'Love of Beauty'. This collection reached the Russian church, first in Paisii's Church Slavonic translation, later in Bishop Feofan's enlarged Russian version, and did more than any other book in the last century to bring about a spiritual rebirth of Russian Orthodoxy.

Tolstoy read Philokalia in Paisii's translation and received important impulses.[54] There is convincing evidence to suggest that the strong ascetical element in Tolstoy's ethics may best be understood in the context of Eastern Christian monasticism and not primarily as a distant echo of Buddhism or Stoicism.[55] Tolstoy's ideal of indifference to scorn, pain and desire seems to have been moulded on the Orthodox idea of passionlessness, *apatheia* (Church Slavonic: *bezstrastie*).[56] Both the Greek fathers and the Russian novelist insisted that true love can spring forth from our heart only insofar as we have managed to quench our lusts and passions.[57]

Among the ancient traditions reintroduced in Russia by Paisii's disciples was the institution of elders, *starchestvo*. A starets is an experienced (not necessarily old) monk that guides novices and laymen on the thorny path to holiness. Starchestvo is a charismatic ministry, that is, the authority of the starets rests exclusively on his special gift for guidance. He is not necessarily an ordained priest, and his ministry is not a part of the established hierarchical structure of the monastery.[58]

The most famous centre of starchestvo in nineteenth-century Russia was the Optina Pustyn' monastery in the province of Kaluga. The Optina startsy were sought by throngs of pilgrims, uncouth peasants as well as representatives of the intelligentsia—Ivan Kireevskii, Nikolai Gogol', Fyodor Dostoevskii and Vladimir Solov'ev, to mention some of the more prominent visitors.[59] Tolstoy visited Optina no less than four times, in 1877, 1881, 1890 and 1910. In 1890 he went on foot, dressed in a simple peasant garb and bast shoes, intent on experiencing starchestvo in the same way as common, humble pilgrims. Apparently, he did not come primarily to receive spiritual guidance—his travel notes reveal a surprisingly low opinion of the startsy's teaching.[60] It is more likely that his mission was to study the very institution of starchestvo which he soon more or less consciously imitated in his own ministry from Iasnaia Poliana.[61] Like the startsy he did not criss-cross the country to spread his teaching, but received the seekers of truth in his own home. As mentioned, the institution of starchestvo was loosely attached to the monasteries. It could fairly easily be even further removed from its monastical setting and transplanted to more secular surroundings. As with all the impulses Tolstoy received from Orthodoxy, he did not copy mechanically what he found at Optina. His authority was for instance not based on miraculous works or prophetic gifts like those ascribed to the Orthodox startsy, nor did he, like them, demand unquestioning obedience of the faithful.

Tolstoy apparently never called himself a starets, but this honorary title was frequently bestowed upon him by others—Orthodox and non-Orthodox alike.[62] The *fin de siècle* novelist Leonid Andreev, for example, visited Iasnaia Poliana in 1910, the year that Tolstoy died.

A year later Andreev described his meeting with the deceased in almost hagiographical terms and asked the rhetorical question: 'Where in the world is it possible to find a better starets?'[63] This designation was so commonly given to Tolstoy that the Orthodox bishop Nikon accused the enemies of the Church of having purloined a title from the sacred Christian language to adorn the memory of a heretic and blasphemer.[64]

The enlightened classes in Russia in the last century were predominantly anti-clerical and even atheistic. Only a few marginal groups, such as the Slavophiles and the *pochvenniki* group around Fyodor Dostoevskii, professed the Orthodox faith. This is not to say that all the others were immune to Orthodox influence. In the writings of many of the intelligentsia a residue of Christian thinking is discernible. E. T. Weiant has demonstrated how Belinskii and even the militant anti-theist Bakunin passed through a period of intense religious devotion. Weiant claims that their attack on Christianity was not occasioned by the religion itself, but by a distorted interpretation of Christianity as the religion of power and a supporter of the autocratic state.[65]

Berdiaev points out that the intelligentsia leader Nikolai Chernyshevskii in his influential novel *What to do?* preaches stark asceticism: the hero sleeps on nails to harden himself.[66] In this connection it is worth remembering that Chernyshevskii, as well as his friend Dobroliubov, was the son of a priest and himself a seminary drop-out. The German Jesuit scholar Bernhard Schultze suggests that the entire tradition of Russian atheism must be understood in the light of Orthodox apophaticism: when apophaticism is cultivated in isolation from cataphatic theology, it is but a short step from denying the attributes of God to denying God himself.[67]

In most cases the spiritual debt of the intelligentsia to Orthodoxy can be established by means of structural analogies alone. In the case of Tolstoy the situation is different. He not only produced a whole library of religious tracts, but also confronted the Orthodox theological and spiritual tradition in a direct way. This makes it possible to establish beyond reasonable doubt a genealogical connection between some of his ideas and their Orthodox counterparts. Even in his most anti-Orthodox diatribe, *Investigation*, Tolstoy, in spite of himself, reveals a high degree of indebtedness to Orthodoxy.

It is a testimony to the strength of Orthodox spiritual tradition that in a century when it did not command the adherence, or even the respect, of the best and the brightest in Russian society, it nevertheless left an indelible mark on the thinking of many of them.

SUMMARY

The Russian intelligentsia of the last century was, generally speaking, strongly opposed to the Orthodox church. This was primarily due to the intimate connection between this church and the tsarist state which the intelligentsia endeavoured to overthrow. In as much as Orthodoxy was viewed as the epitome of organised Christianity, this led to a rejection of the Christian faith in general. This did not, however, prevent a substantial influx of Christian ideas into the world view of many *intelligenty*. More or less unconsciously they took over a number of Orthodox tenets and tacit presuppositions, which were transformed to fit into their own teaching.

No member of the radical intelligentsia wrote as much on Church and religion as Leo Tolstoy. Indeed, shortly after his conversion to 'Tolstoyanism' he wrote a voluminous *Investigation of Dogmatic Theology*, in which he stated his reasons for breaking with the church in which he had been baptised. This book makes it especially easy to trace the relationship between his thinking and the Orthodox faith, in order to find possible areas of overlapping. This source has, however, been little utilised. For several reasons *Investigation* has been almost completely overlooked, at Tolstoy's time as well as by modern scholars.

An analysis of this book shows that Tolstoy's refutation of the Orthodox doctrine of God is based to a large extent on the negative or 'apophatic' theology of pseudo-Dionysius the Areopagite. It can be demonstrated that Tolstoy was well versed in the apophatic tradition and had a high opinion of it. This apophatic approach is later taken up by Tolstoy when he develops his own positive teaching of God, for instance in *Thoughts on God*.

Dogmatic theology was, furthermore, only one of several points of contact between Tolstoy and Orthodoxy. He was well acquainted with Eastern spiritual writings of the monastic tradition and took over their teaching of passionlessness as a prerequisite of true love. His ministry from his estate Iasnaya Polyana also bore some resemblance to the ministry of the Orthodox startsy of Optina Pustyn, whom he visited several times.

This is not to say that Tolstoy was an Orthodox Christian in spite of himself. His rejection of such central Christian dogmas as the Trinity and the redemption makes any such claim extravagant. The elements of Orthodox thinking which he takes over are removed from their original context and in the process take on a distinct 'Tolstoyan' hue. This is obviously the reason why they have until recently been almost totally overlooked.

NOTES

1. A valuable account of this import can be found in George L. Kline, *Religious and Anti-religious Thought in Russia*, Weil Institute Lectures, Chicago, 1968.
2. Nikolai Berdiaev, *Istoki i smysl russkogo kommunizma* (Paris: 1955).
3. Lev Tolstoy, *Polnoe sobranie sochinenii v 90-i tomach*, vol. 23 (Moscow: 1930–72) p. 437. Unless otherwise stated, all subsequent quotations of Tolstoy are taken from this standard critical edition.
4. See for example his *Answer to the Synod's Decision*, vol. 34, p. 247.
5. The books Tolstoy studied were: John of Damascus (675–749), *Tochnoe izlozhenie pravoslavnoi very* (De fide orthodoxa); *Poslanie patriarkhov vostochno-kafolicheskiia tserkvi* (1723); Petr Mogila of Kiev, *Pravoslavnoe ispovedanie* (original title, Confessio fidei, 1640); Metropolitan Plato (Levshin) of Moscow, *Pravoslavnoe uchenie* (1757); Metropolitan Filaret (Drozdov) of Moscow, *Prostrannyi khristianskii katekhizis* (1827); and Metropolitan Makarii (Bulgakov) of Moscow (1816–82), *Pravoslavno-dogmaticheskoe bogoslovie*. See Tolstoi, vol. 23, p. 61.
6. In the West this book has traditionally been referred to as *Critique of Orthodox Theology*. This was the title given by Tolstoy's European publishers, obviously in an attempt to give it a Kantian colouring. Tolstoy's original title was resuscitated by the editors of the critical 90 volumes edition, and has been retained here.
7. Antonii Khrapovitskii (1864–1936), 'Vozmozhna li nravstvennaia zhizn' bez khristianskoi religii'? Po povodu 'Kritiki dogmatiches-kogo bogosloviia' L. N. Tolstogo', in *Pravoslavnyi sobesednik* (April 1897). Reprinted in *Zhizneopisanie ... i tvoreniia ... Antoniia*, vol. xiv (New York: 1967) pp. 174–201. N. N. Gusev's claim that the *Investigation* 'did not receive a single response in church literature' is thus an exaggeration. N. N. Gusev, *Lev Nikolaevich Tolstoi, materialy k biografii s 1870 po 1881 god* (Moscow: 1963) p. 625.
8. Tolstoy, vol. 23, p. 63.
9. Antonii Khrapovitskii, op. cit., p. 176; M. A. Novoselov, 'Otkrytoe pis'mo grafu L. N. Tolstomu' in *Po povodu otpadeniia ot pravoslavnoi tserkvi grafa L'va Nikolaevicha Tolstogo* (St Petersburg: 1905) p. 116.

10.   These works include: E. B. Greenwood, *Tolstoy: The Comprehensive Vision* (London: 1975); Aylmer Maude, *Tolstoy and his Problems* (London: 1905); G. W. Spence, *Tolstoy, the Ascetic* (London: 1967); Richard F. Gustafson, *Leo Tolstoy: Resident and Stranger* (Princeton: 1986). Ernest J. Simmons claims that the *Investigation* is perhaps the least read of Tolstoy's religious works and 'undeservedly so, for it is an unusually fervent and compellingly logical attack on revealed religion and especially on the Russian Orthodox Church'. E. J. Simmons, *Introduction to Tolstoy's Writings* (Chicago: 1968) p. 99.

11.   Tolstoy, vol. 23, p. 53.

12.   Ibid. p. 57.

13.   N. N. Gusev, op. cit., p. 618.

14.   Tolstoy, vol. 23, p. 522.

15.   Ibid. p. 61.

16.   Aleksandr Ivanov, 'Pis'mo k gr. L. N. Tolstomu' in *Tul'skie eparkhial'nye vedomosti* (1901/7–8) p. 264.

17.   Tolstoy, vol. 62, p. 499.

18.   A. S. Khomiakov, *Polnoe sobranie sochinenii*, vol. viii (Moscow: 1900–14) p. 189.

19.   G. Florovskii, *Puti russkogo bogosloviia* (Paris: 1981) p. 222.

20.   Tolstoy, vol. 23, p. 61f.

21.   Nicolas Weisbein, *L'évolution religieuse de Tolstoï* (Paris: 1960) p. 177.

22.   This is the conclusion reached by most scholars: 'In the name of reason, he rejects all that is beyond his understanding'. Henri Troyat, *Tolstoy* (Harmondsworth: 1980) p. 549; 'Reason has done its job: Of the Scripture not a trace is left'. Lev Shestov, 'Iasnaia Poliana i Astapovo' in *Umozrenie i otkrovenie* (Paris: 1964). While this may be true in some instances, at other times Tolstoy accused the church of being too rationalistic, as in its treatment of the fall. Here, he maintains, the church has forgotten that the struggle between good and evil in man is 'mysterious, unfathomable', vol. 23, p. 143.

23.   Weisbein, op. cit., p. 155. This idea is taken up by Simmons, op. cit., p. 99.

24.   Tolstoy, vol. 23, p. 106.

25.   Ibid. vol. 63, p. 6.

26.   Weisbein, op. cit., p. 156.

27.   Makarii (Bulgakov), *Pravoslavno-dogmaticheskoe bogoslovie*, vol. 1 (St Petersburg: 1895) 5th ed., p. 69.

28.   Ibid. p. 66.

29.   Tolstoy, vol. 23, p. 70.

30.   This doctrine is expounded in *De servo arbitrio*.

31.   Vladimir Lossky, *The Mystical Theology of the Eastern Church* (London: 1973) p. 33f. This is one of the best expositions of Orthodox apophaticism available, and my own presentation is heavily indebted to it.

32.   A modern English translation of *The Mystical Theology* can be found in F. C. Happold, *Mysticism—A Study and an Anthology* (Harmondsworth: 1967) pp. 190–6.

33.   Tolstoy, vol. 55, p. 51.

34. Ibid. vol. 52, p. 144.
35. Tolstoy, 'Mysli o boge', in *Polnoe sobranie sochinenii*, vol. 15 (Moscow: 1912–14) p. 59.
36. Tolstoy, critical edition, vol. 23, p. 71.
37. Tolstoy read *Kritik der reinen Vernunft* as early as in 1869 and was greatly impressed. (*Kritik der praktischen Vernunft* he read only in 1887.) R. Quiskamp claims that 'Der Dichter ist, was seine Gotteslehre angeht, ein überzeügter Schüler Kants', *Der Gottesbegriff bei Tolstoy* (Emsdettenü: 1937) p. 60. In another book written seven years earlier, however, Quiskamp explicitly excludes the epistemology of God from the topics in which Tolstoy may be influenced by Kant. See *Die Beziehungen L. N. Tolstojs zu den Philosophen des deutschen Idealismus* (Emsdetten: 1930) p. 59.
38. Tolstoy, vol. 23, p. 69.
39. 'God is infinite and incomprehensible, and all that is comprehensible about Him is His infinity and incomprehensibility. . . . God does not belong to the class of existing things: not that he has no existence, but that He is above all existing things, nay even above existence itself', *De fide orthodoxa*, part 1, chap. 4.
40. Makarii, op. cit., vol. 1, p. 69f.
41. Ibid. p. 77, quotation from Rufinus.
42. Tolstoy, vol. 23, p. 79.
43. Tolstoy, *Mysli o Boge*, op. cit., p. 68.
44. This is the standard objection of a long number of Orthodox authors. See for example, A. F. Gusev, *O sushchnosti religiozno-nravstvennogo ucheniia L. Tolstogo* (Kazan' 1902), pp. 80ff. Gusev's book is one of the most thorough analyses of Tolstoy's teaching ever written by an Orthodox theologian (619 pages) and his opinions were very influential in the Russian church before the revolution.
45. *Mysli o Boge*, op. cit., p. 68.
46. Ibid.
47. Robert Quiskamp has pointed out that 'an eine Persönlichkeit Gottes hat Tolstoj nicht glauben wollen, was er immer wieder betont. Hier ist aber sein Persönlichkeitsbegriff zu beachten, den er stets mit der leiblichen Individualität verbindet'. Quiskamp, *Der Gottesbegriff bei Tolstoy* (Emsdetten: 1937) p. 118.
48. See, for example, letter to V. K. Zavolokin, 1900, '*Man did not come to this world by his own will, therefore he ought not to live by his own will, but by His will, Who sent him to this world*'. Tolstoy, vol. 72, p. 527. Italics in the original.
49. Vladimir Maevskii, *Tragediia bogoiskatel'stva L'va Tolstogo* (Buenos Aires: 1952) p. 76.
50. Milan Markovitch, *J.-J. Rousseau et Tolstoi* (Paris: 1928); Franz-Heinrich Philipp, *Tolstoj und der Protestantismus* (Giessen: 1959); Derk Bodd, *Tolstoy and China* (Princeton: 1950).
51. Richard F. Gustafson, *Leo Tolstoy. Resident and Stranger* (Princeton: 1986) p. xi.
52. Ibid. p. 457.
53. Fr. Sergii Chetverikov, *Starets Paisii Velichkovskii* (Belmont: 1980).

54. *Biblioteka L'va Nikolaevicha Tolstogo v Iasnoi Poliane* (Moscow: 1972) book 1, part 1, p. 265.
55. In his diary, 22 September 1900, Tolstoy explicitly compares Stoic and Buddhist asceticism with Christian teaching and makes it clear that he prefers the latter. Tolstoy, vol. 54, pp. 43–4.
56. Tolstoy never used the words *apatheia* or *besstrastie* in his writings. Instead he developed his own terminology, and used the word *ravnodushie*, 'indifference' in a way clearly reminiscent of the ancient ideal of apatheia. See for example Tolstoy, vol. 36, p. 261 and vol. 55, p. 262.
57. Callistus and Ignatius in *Philokalia* write that love and 'apatheia' are identical entities, only the appelations differ. See *Dobrotoliubie* (Moscow: 1902), book 1, part 2, p. 113 on the reverse side. This idea clearly anticipates the central message of *The Kreutzer Sonata*: 'If the goal of mankind is, as is written in the Prophets, that all men shall be united in love, that they shall beat their spears into scythes, etc., what prevents us from reaching this goal? It is the passions. . . . If the passions were done away with, the prophesy would thus be fulfilled.' Tolstoy, vol. 27, p. 30.
58. Good presentations of *starchestvo* are given in Igor Smolitsch, *Leben und Lehre der Starzen* (Wien: 1936); and 'Pustynnozhitel'', 'Starchestvo' in *Dushepoleznoe chtenie* (Moscow: 1906) nos 2, 3, 5, 6 and 7.
59. Sergius Bolshakoff, *Russian Mystics* (London: 1977) pp. 184ff.
60. Starets Amvrosii is described as 'pitiable'. Tolstoy, vol. 51, p. 23. The story that Tolstoy after his meeting with Amvrosii should have characterised him as 'an absolutely holy man' (for example, *Dushepoleznoe chtenie*, 1911, no. 1, p. 23) appears to be apocryphal.
61. 'He was the lay equivalent of starets Ambrose, the sage of Optina-Pustyn' claims Henri Troyat, *Tolstoy* (Harmondsworth: 1980) p. 652.
62. In the obituaries collected in *Pamiati Tolstogo, Otkliki stolichnoi pechati* (St Petersburg: 1911) Tolstoy is frequently referred to as 'the Great Starets'. Also Tolstoy's own bishop in Tula, Parfenii, used this epithet about him. See B. Meilach: *Uchod i smert' L'va Tolstogo* (Moscow: 1979) p. 112.
63. *Solntse Rossii* (1911) no. 53.
64. *Missionerskoe obozrenie* (1911) no. 11, p. 687.
65. E. T. Weiant, *Sources of Modern Mass Atheism in Russia* (Mount Vernon: 1953) p. 120.
66. Nikolai Berdiaev, *Istoki i smysl russkogo kommunizma* (Paris: 1955) p. 43.
67. Bernhard Schultze, *Das Gottesproblem in der Osttheologie* (Münster: 1967).

11 The Church's Social Role in St Petersburg, 1880–1914

Simon Dixon

Historians customarily denigrate the social and pastoral work of the Russian Orthodox Church. Even Orthodox themselves recognise its limitations. Florovsky declared that 'there was no important movement of social Christianity in modern Russia', and Meyendorff has rightly noted that 'if the Christian East has any established reputation, it consists in its purported detachment from historical realities, its concern with "mysticism", its one-sided dedication to liturgical contemplation of eternal truths, and its forgetfulness of the concrete needs of human society'.[1] It is not my purpose to refute these judgements entirely, and to claim that a long lost, coherent Orthodox conception of social Christianity existed in late nineteenth-century Russia. However, it is possible to show that a significant group of Russian churchmen—those educated in the four ecclesiastical academies—were led by the challenge they perceived from other faiths to reconsider their attitudes to pastoral work in this period and furthermore that this reconsideration had tangible practical consequences in those parts of the country where academy graduates became parish priests and attempted to put their ideas into practice. By examining some aspects of both the theory and practice of this reorientation in Russian Orthodoxy—essentially a renewed emphasis on the church's teaching role (*uchitel'stvo*)—it is possible to throw light not only on the church itself, but also on its relationship with society.

The renewed interest in the efficacy of pastoral practice was a direct result of a growing feeling within the church that even in the heartland of Russia, Orthodoxy was under pressure from the challenges of other faiths. The demise of the Russian Bible Society in 1824 had released a powerful current of nationalist particularism within the church, which, whilst always present, had been submerged in the previous century beneath the supranationalist religious policy of the state (whose expansion into non-Russian and non-Orthodox lands had increased the potential problems for the church should an element of rivalry recur in religious affairs) and the derivative nature of Orthodox scholarship. From a position in which it had had to be content with being first among equals in Russia, during the reign of Nicholas I the Orthodox Church set about restoring its dominant status in relation to the other faiths allowed to practise in Russia— faiths which had taken advantage of a long period of relative quiescence to grow in number and in confidence. Initially, it seemed that with state support the campaign to acquire converts would be successful. During the course of the 1830s, foreign missions were closed down, schismatic communities forcibly dispersed and their chapels closed, and the Uniate Church was 'reunited' with Orthodoxy. In the following decade, Orthodox turned their attention to Lutherans in the Baltic, to Muslims in the south (whose affairs were to be the concern of the newly created ecclesiastical academy at Kazan') and intensified their efforts to convert Jews.

But, despite this confident beginning, in the long term the conversion campaigns were a failure. Alarmed at the prospect of civil unrest, the state authorities withdrew their support for Orthodox aggression, and were increasingly inclined instead to surrender qualified religious privileges to some of the Orthodox Church's rivals in return for supposed political loyalty. The key decade was the 1860s. It was then that Orthodox discovered beyond all doubt that, deprived of political force, their conversions had little effect. Like other missionaries before them, they had been guilty of arrogance in assuming that ignorance was the only barrier to the triumph of Orthodoxy. In the event, Protestantism, Catholicism, Shamanism, Judaism, Islam and numerous other sectarian beliefs were shown to be capable of inspiring a greater loyalty among their followers than the Orthodox Church could achieve amongst its own. Now, at least in the minds of Orthodox churchmen, the tables were turned. Their confidence had ebbed to the point where their fear of apostasy was greater than their hope for conversion. Long standing fears that the church had lost its grip on the intelligentsia now assumed greater proportions as they were joined by the spectre of a growing proletariat. As a result, the emphasis of their thought and practice, initially concentrated on conversion of their rivals, now turned to preventing the apostasy of Russian Orthodox themselves.

The natural means of doing so was the transfer of evangelical techniques which had been employed in the mission field to use in everyday pastoral practice among Russians. The term used to describe the new tendency, 'internal mission' (*vnutrenniaia missiia*), is a striking indication of the Orthodox debt to other faiths in developing these techniques. Whilst I know of no explicit reference to Wichern's *Innere Mission* in a Russian source, there can be no doubt that Orthodox owed much to the radical German Protestants who, during the course of the 1860s and beyond, shifted their attention from dogmatics to ethics, and to the conception of Christianity as a moral community devoted to living according to Christ's example. Ritschl, Wuttke and Rothe lay only just below the surface of much Orthodox argument in this period. There is nothing surprising in this. Flowing with the intellectual tide, Orthodox had devoted much of their efforts since the 1820s to distinguishing what was truly Orthodox (and purely Russian) in their faith in order to show the rectitude of their claim to unique apostolic authority. Ironically, the poverty of Orthodox scholarship had forced them to rely on foreigners, and especially on the Germans, both Protestant and Catholic. Orthodox justified this reliance by claiming that Protestantism and Catholicism were sick and incomplete parts of the healthy, organic whole which was Orthodoxy. It was therefore thought legitimate to take from the west that which rightly belonged to Orthodoxy, and to separate it from inauthentic accretions to apostolic Christianity. Orthodox pursued this line not only in their theological and theoretical work, but also in their pastoral work. What we shall be examining in this paper is essentially the Orthodox attempt to come to terms with the pastoral strengths of their rivals, the assimilation of foreign forms and the effort to infuse them with an authentically Orthodox content.

Of course, there were obstacles in the way of these new pastoral initiatives. The state, whilst anxious after the Crimean War to devolve responsibility (and especially financial burdens) to the local level, had no wish to surrender political control. The church's pastoral work had therefore to be done in a society where, despite increasing pressure for reform, the parish—which might have been expected to be the focus of the whole scheme—was not legally recognised, and could therefore neither buy nor sell property, nor take effective independent action. Bishops, too, were sometimes suspicious of rank and file clerical activism, fearing a menace to their authority. The parish system itself was weak: the provision of worship corresponded geographically very badly with the areas of greatest need; new church building, although declared a priority, was frustrated by red tape; priests had only the most formal relationships with their parishioners, hampered by difficulties which arose over their principal functions at baptisms, weddings and funerals, by the popular perception of them as policemen rather than pastors, and by the fact that the very rhythm of Orthodox liturgical practice allowed little personal contact between priest and parishioner. As a result, much of the pastoral work we shall be discussing was focused not on the parish, but on societies and brotherhoods sometimes nominally attached to it, sometimes quite separate and in many cases responsible to the Ministry of Internal Affairs rather than the Holy Synod.[2]

The focus of the paper is on St Petersburg for two reasons. In the first place, the diocese, with its major contrast between the rural and urban areas, represents a unique religious microcosm of the empire as a whole. The anonymity of a growing metropolis and the wastes of the surrounding countryside presented the ideal opportunity for every sect and rival to Orthodoxy to set down roots. Foreign faiths served the capital's foreign communities, and the surrounding areas harboured large numbers of indigent Protestants. (The whole of Finland formed part of the diocese of St Petersburg until 1892.) Here, more than anywhere else in the empire, Orthodoxy's rivals were arraigned in concentration against her. Yet here, too, Orthodoxy's own ranks were more powerful than elsewhere. In contrast to the dim-witted provincial priests who populate the historiography of the nineteenth-century Russian church, the capital was staffed by a clergy who had been conditioned and prepared by their sophisticated education in the ecclesiastical academy (even some of St Petersburg's psalmists were academy graduates) to take part in precisely the struggle of faiths I have outlined above. In St Petersburg, then, not only were the lines of battle drawn with particular clarity, but we can go so far as to say that if the Orthodox effort were unsuccessful there, then it is difficult to see how it could have succeeded anywhere, so great were the odds stacked against it by the inadequacy of its own provincial proponents.

I begin in 1880 because it was then that the first coherent, tangible consequences of the Orthodox pastoral impulse emerged. 1914 is a proper date to end because during World War I, the nature of Orthodox pastoral work was radically changed as monasteries and churches were adapted to tend the war wounded.[3]

I have space in this paper to deal with only three aspects of the renewed Orthodox pastoral impulse: evangelical preaching, charity and temperance. Education and the workers' movement, important issues which properly fall within the scope of this paper and which ought to be seen precisely in this context, are the subject of other papers.

Orthodox recognised that if they were to increase their influence on society they must first improve their communication with society. They knew that both the educated classes and the illiterate, however religious they might be, lived their lives outside the sphere of influence of the church. Orthodox hoped that an intensification of preaching activity would help them to bring society closer to the church. Preaching was not traditionally strong in Orthodoxy. The liturgy itself was held to embody the edificatory material which other confessions, notably the Lutherans, delivered separately in the form of the sermon.[4] Until the 1860s, homiletics formed an insignificant part of both a priest's education and his pastoral practice. The very design of churches symbolised the lowly status of the sermon: in the 1840s only two Moscow churches had pulpits, and no Orthodox church had seating to support a congregation through the rigorous course of a lengthy sermon.[5] But the turn towards *uchitel'stvo* signified a change. After the 1867–9 educational reforms, homiletics was a key part of the curriculum for those who specialised in the 'practical' subjects at the academies.[6] The approach to the subject, exemplified by Professor Pevnitskii at Kiev and at Kazan' by Antonii (Vadkovskii), the future metropolitan of St Petersburg, was characteristically historical. Concentrating on patristic and early medieval Russian sermons, scholars aimed to prove that there could be sermons with a legitimately Orthodox and distinctively Russian pedigree. Whilst establishing this intellectual pedigree for their subject, they did not lose sight of the essentially practical concern of the sermon. Sermons with a scholastically expounded dogmatic content were to be replaced by more vivid sermons on biblical texts; pulpits, though never pews, were installed in many newly built churches.[7]

The impetus for this activity came from outside the Russian church. If Orthodox needed to be convinced of the efficacy of a good sermon, they had only to look at the success of their rivals. In 1859 the Dominican father Soyard, the first foreign preacher in St Petersburg since the expulsion of the Jesuits, made a huge impression on the capital's educated population, who flocked to hear his sermons, preached in French. Reactionaries reacted predictably. Askochenskii denounced Soyard's performance as trickery and charlatanism. But there was also a less predictable and more intelligent reaction from

Orthodox. A professor at the St Petersburg Ecclesiastical Academy proposed to respond on Soyard's own terms: he wanted to set up a series of public lectures in which the Orthodox view might be stated. The attempt came to nothing—Filaret (Drozdov) would not allow anything that appeared merely to imitate Catholicism.[8] But in the 1880s, with Filaret long dead, and the challenge in the shape of Russian evangelical sectarians (especially the Pashkovtsy) now much stronger since they appealed to a wide range of social classes, Orthodox responded in kind.

The importance of the Orthodox attempt to revive their preaching did not lie wholly in sermons within the church service. Even some of preaching's most vocal advocates remained suspicious of overt imitation of the Lutherans and stressed the need for adaptation.[9] Furthermore, there is abundant nationwide evidence to show that the criticism of the general standard of preaching in 1905 was depressingly similar to that which characterised the 1870s: sermons, if they were delivered at all, were all too often merely read out in an inaudible mumble from one of the many almanacs of noted sermons that were published in an attempt to encourage the parish priest to develop his own homiletic skills. Preaching rotas, initially introduced with the aim of ensuring general participation without too great a workload for any one individual, were resented as an imposition on priests' already over-used time.[10] It proved impossible to infect the majority of Russian priests with the enthusiasm and energy necessary to be successful preachers, and the attempt to do so merely exposed some of the willing but inadequate men to the ridicule of the secular press. Indeed, it seemed at first as though this effort to improve the church's communication with society might backfire. That it did not do so was a result of the fact that from the beginning of the 1880s, the edificatory sermon was increasingly used outside the church service in halls, factories and other workplaces in a flexible way which allowed the argument to be tailored to the needs of the audience to a greater extent than was usually feasible in church, and also allowed the church to deploy zealous laymen, notably the students of the St Petersburg Ecclesiastical Academy, in the pastoral cause.

The first tentative steps in this direction were taken in the early 1870s. Readings, *narodnye chteniia*, took place in factories in St Petersburg from 1873. But only priests were allowed to conduct them and they were held within strict limits, not being allowed to depart from a prepared text. Attendances, initially over 400, dropped markedly to under 50 in the course of the year.[11] The real breakthrough came only later, in the early 1880s, when Father Mikhail Sokolov, who had been involved in these early initiatives, founded the Society for the Spread of Religious and Moral Enlightenment in the Spirit of the Orthodox Church (1881), which Rozanov later lampooned as the Society with the Very Long Name.[12] The impulse behind the creation of the society was the clear success of the Pashkovtsy in the capital.[13] From modest beginnings in those areas of the capital infected by this sect, notably the dockland, the society grew and strengthened under Father Filosof Ornatskii, Sokolov's successor as president, until by 1905 its power and autonomy of action were such as to alarm some members of the hierarchy that the authority of the diocesan consistory was being bypassed.[14] Despite these suspicions, the society not only survived but prospered, probably thanks to the protection of Metropolitan Antonii (Vadkovskii) (1898–1912), who, like his predecessor Palladii (Raev) (1892–98), had encouraged the embryonic efforts of the society and supported its work by encouraging his students at the academy, where he was rector in the late 1880s, to participate from 1887.

The essence of the society's work was to provide teams of preachers to evangelise the city's workers and peasants—to expose the false teachings of Orthodoxy's rivals, and to expound the true faith in those parts of the city where there were few churches, or where parochial life was impotent. The society had its base in its own churches (of the three, the principal one is still a landmark on the Obvodnyi canal next to the Warsaw station) but the major part of its work was to communicate by a direct mission to the factories and halls of the capital. Naturally, its activities provoked intense discussion of the value and efficacy of different types of preaching: relatively abstract debates on charismatic preaching and the theoretical analysis of sermons (which were also conducted by the Amateur Society of the Art of Oratory formed in the early twentieth century) were held both at the academy and at the pastoral assemblies of the capital's priests which became a distinctive feature of the society's activities and which were later to provide a forum for the expression of radical reformist opinion.[15] But the indisputable emphasis of the society's work was practical. Its members, and especially its officers, acquired a reputation as men who could get things done. Ornatskii was the clerical representative on the city Duma, and steered through the transfer of municipal land not only for his own society's church but for others. At least two church building committees employed him as their adviser.[16] The society pioneered the method of using a temporary wooden church whilst funds were raised for a permanent stone structure. Once this was built, the wooden church was dismantled for use elsewhere. As it expanded, the society organised sermons and meetings in all the major factories and many other schools, doss-houses, and halls in St Petersburg, and although there were difficulties in financing a permanent presence in all of them simultaneously, and Orthodox suspected sabotage by foreign Protestant factory owners and managers, this was an impressive enterprise by any standards. By 1908, the society was in a position to consecrate its third church, built since 1904 at a total cost of 450 000 rubles.[17]

In content, the *besedy* conducted by the society were frequently a mixture of bible stories, saints' lives, and singing (choirs formed a very important part of the Orthodox Church's attempt to regain its hold on the community) though in specific instances they could be frankly polemical or denunciatory. Once the besedy were established at a particular venue there seems to have been a tendency to set up thematic series, typically dealing with Christ's life on earth, though this approach evidently posed problems of continuity of personnel. Nevertheless, some preachers, especially the academy students, survived their initial nerves in a daunting situation, and developed a touching rapport with their regular audiences.[18] Significantly, there is also evidence that these audiences proved most receptive to stories of the saints' lives, and least receptive to those preachers who concerned themselves with matters of everyday life.[19]

The Society for the Spread of Religious and Moral Enlightenment in the Spirit of the Orthodox Church grew into an active, vital organisation under whose auspices—at least partially free from the dead hand of consistorial control—much of the most significant pastoral work of the diocese was done. Following the Pauline text, 'If you put these instructions before the brethren, you will be a good minister of Christ Jesus, nourished on the words of faith and of the good doctrine you have followed' (I Timothy, 4:6), it inspired a dedicated group of priests in the capital to pursue the church's mission in a more intensive way than imperial Russia had ever known, and in a way which involved them in much more than preaching the word of God. In turning to the moral content of their sermons, we shall be particularly concerned with the linked enterprises of charitable and temperance work.[20]

In the Orthodox attempt to re-establish the church's links with the community it proved much less difficult to establish a legitimate

Orthodox tradition of charitable activity than of preaching. But the monastic almsgiving which had formed the core of medieval social Christianity could not cope, even where it survived, with the needs of a growing population.[21] Furthermore, Orthodox increasingly came to think that the practice of individual almsgiving might be counter-productive—it was 'too idealistic for the contemporary conditions of social life and has left us with an inheritance of a severe plague in our social organism: begging, with all the signs of social malignance'— and that what was needed was a co-ordinated system of social charity.[22]

In coming to these conclusions, Orthodox were heavily influenced by foreign examples. They looked with some envy at the combination of charitable and evangelical work which seemed to offer Protestants especially an efficient means of recruiting society to the Church's cause. From the 1860s, articles in the ecclesiastical press drew attention to the existence of orphanages, workhouses and mutual-aid societies, and stressed the initiative taken by the clergy in their foundation and operation. Later, envious eyes turned towards the success of the SPCK and the Salvation Army in cementing links between church and society. In 1885 it was pointed out that in London alone there were more than 200 charitable societies, and that the Doctor Barnardo homes were particularly effective, all being operated on 'an independent and commercial basis'.[23] Nearer home, the schismatics and sectarians of Russia, who had been obliged to establish their own mutual aid networks in order to ensure their very survival, offered another pertinent example of what might be done. They knew how to look after their own. Some, notably the Tol-stoyans, made mutual sociability (*vzaimoobshchitel'nost'*) a corner-stone of their ideology.[24] New evangelical sects, such as the Pash-kovtsy, made urban soup-kitchens and tea-shops the focus of their campaigns. No matter how much Orthodox publicists complained about their rivals 'bribing' apostates away from Orthodoxy, they could no longer afford to sneer at the Old Believer hospitals and almshouses and claim that although they looked 'outwardly' splen-did, the faithful should not be blind to their 'internal' rottenness.[25] Instead, they decided quite explicitly that they must compete on their rivals' own terms, adopting the outward form of action which had proved so successful to their competitors, whilst attempting to infuse it with a pure, Orthodox content.

Those Orthodox who made this attempt hoped to convince their contemporaries of its legitimacy by reviving the institution of the brotherhoods (*bratstva*), initially formed as unions of clergy and laymen for the defence of Orthodoxy in the face of Latin proselytism in the late fifteenth and especially sixteenth centuries in Lithuania, Little Russia and White Russia. Orthodox affiliated to the Slavophiles began scholarly investigations designed to show that these institutions, which provided in their combination of a charitable and evangelical function the ideal foil to Orthodoxy's rivals, had survived even the turbulent history of the western provinces, and were ripe for reinvigoration.[26] The state, anxious to encourage local financial initiative, sanctioned the formation of the new brotherhoods and the newly instituted parish trusteeships which the church hoped would act as the vanguard of their new efforts to reassert community interest in ecclesiastical and spiritual affairs.[27]

But not everyone in the church was convinced that the new pastoral impulse was justified. Throughout the 1870s and beyond, ecclesiastical scholars and publicists debated in the press the relative merits of 'active' and 'passive' Christianity, of individual alms-giving and institutionalised social charity, of material and spiritual gifts.[28] They were, of course, concerned not only with the material well-being of the recipient of charity, but the spiritual well-being of the donor, for in acting charitably man approached the sacrifice of Christ himself:

> The whole strength of Christianity consists in the death of the God-Man on the cross through which the love of god was revealed to us, and according to the thought of the Lord's beloved disciple the pious deed of charity is linked with the pious deed of the cross precisely because in both one and the other is revealed that true love which in the field of human relations, attempts to demonstrate itself visibly and tangibly . . . Our pious deed of charity determines in one way or another our preparedness to participate in the pious deed of the cross.[29]

But they could never fully agree on the way in which this 'visible and tangible' demonstration of God's love should be made. Some arch-conservatives feared that if any material donation were to be made to the needy, Orthodox were in danger of imitating Old Testament (and therefore Jewish) practice. Far better to show the superiority of the New Testament's advocacy of spiritual succour. Fortunately, there were also men who argued that the value of the Christian teaching lay in the combination, rather than the separation, of material and spiritual aid: 'If I give away all I have, and if I deliver my body to be burned, but have not love, I gain nothing' (1 Corinthians, 13:3).[30] In particular, there were those who drew on Wuttke and Rothe, and the Danish bishop, Martensen, to construct a framework of charitable activity in the spirit of God's love, in which both donor and recipient took part in a moral act—an ideological framework which created a close ecclesiastical parallel to the secular, paternalist relationship between donor and recipient, a characteristic of Russian practice in this period just as it was in the west. For men who argued in this way—and their arguments are represented in classic short form by the Petersburg priest Ioann Labutin—there could be no question of reaching 'by artificial means the unequal property qualifications of members of human society'. 'General equality', Labutin went on, 'so much desired by adherents of the Commune, is as unrealisable as it is contrary to the Holy Scriptures: "The rich and the poor meet together; the Lord is the maker of them all"' (Proverbs, 22:2).[31] And yet there were also men in the church who were prepared to go much further, and to make the radical admission that 'poverty in its totality and progressive development originates from the imperfect construction of the social and economic relations of society, and from the inequitable distribution of wealth between its members in such a way that to one too much is given, whilst to another not enough'.[32] It was on the basis of such radical ideas as these that churchmen in St Petersburg would involve themselves in the problems of the workers' movement in the early twentieth century.

For although historians have been rightly sceptical of the achievements of parish trusteeships in Russia, many of which were concerned more with the welfare of the clergy and the upkeep of the church itself than the welfare of the parishioners, in St Petersburg the position was different.[33] From the first charitable society founded by Father Aleksandr Gumilevskii in the area '*na peskakh*' in the 1860s, the scale and scope of charitable work in the capital expanded rapidly, at least until 1905, by which time almost every parish church and chapel organised some form of charity.[34] It is difficult to make an accurate statement of the number and activities of the capital's ecclesiastical charitable societies and brotherhoods. Despite protests from the church, they remained responsible to the Minister of Internal Affairs and not to the Holy Synod and therefore leave little trace in ecclesiastical archives. The most useful source we have is for the period to 1900—a compendium by S. G. Runkevich based on materials submitted to the secular authorities and on the voluminous published reports of the societies.[35] As Runkevich notes, it was impossible even for him to provide a complete record, since some societies were reluctant to provide details of their activities. Some, as Metropolitan Filaret (Drozdov) had mordantly predicted, found it difficult to prosper after the initial enthusiasm had evaporated.[36] Nevertheless, some generalisations are possible. First, the charity offered was notably material: virtually all the societies which became firmly established gave money not only in single donations but in monthly instalments (up to an annual limit of around five rubles) in especially deserving cases. In addition to money, the societies doled out food and clothing, and most strove to build their own permanent accommodation for the homeless—an effort which threatened to exhaust the slender resources of some of the smaller societies which made a vain effort to keep up with their more splendid rivals. Secondly, the recipients of the charity were overwhelmingly female (usually girls and widows), the classic case being the workhouse established in the name of the eighteenth-century saint Kseniia, at the Smolensk cemetery, where a dozen or so well-fed women, each given her own room, set to work to make military uniforms.[37] Thirdly, it is clear that great efforts were made to distinguish the idle from the deserving poor. A typical parish would be divided into a number of sectors, each under the control of a priest who was responsible for ascertaining the specific causes of poverty there and for apportioning the benefit distributed. Ironically, it was this, no doubt overrational, system which eventually marked the failure of the church's charitable network. Although it was motivated partly by the need to involve the community in ecclesiastical affairs and by the need to rechristianise all levels of society, and to this end charged each member of a charitable society a small annual fee, the handful of rubles collected in this way were never enough to sustain even the most meagre charitable work. In practice, if not in the ideal, these societies all relied on the support of a few rich patrons, each of whom vied with his friends to establish a larger and more splendid society. The evidence seems, perhaps not surprisingly, to point towards their withdrawal after 1905, disillusioned by the revolutionary inclinations of those on whom they had lavished their wealth, and whose trust and loyalty they no doubt thought they had bought.[38]

Finally, we examine in detail one aspect of the work of many charitable societies: temperance, an enterprise which seemed to many to offer the ideal combination of spiritual and material aid, and moral improvement to both the individual and society as a whole. It is common knowledge that the temperance movement in Russia was even more clearly based on foreign models than the charity movement. It spread to Finland and Russia from Britain and Germany, 'bringing with it a perspective which stressed the moral responsibility of individuals', characteristic of a Protestantism whose Lutheran representatives in St Petersburg set an example which Orthodox looked on with some envy.[39] However, even though no legitimate Orthodox tradition of temperance work existed (and none was invented—perhaps an indication of the degree to which the need for pastoral action was increasingly implicitly accepted in most church circles) the issue of temperance, like the issue of charity, was not swallowed whole in its western form: it was discussed, among churchmen no less than among their secular contemporaries, in a specifically Russian context.

Notoriously, drink has always posed problems for Russian authorities anxious to profit from its revenues but to escape the social consequences. The late nineteenth century was no exception. As even a British diplomat managed to notice in 1881, the Russians had a distinctive, accommodating attitude to alcohol. 'What . . . is wanted is a change in public opinion. The sight of a drunken man causes no feeling of disgust . . . Not only among the peasantry, but among the educated classes a more healthy and manly tone of feeling is required.'[40] This was not an initiative that might have been expected from the clergy. As those churchmen who became interested in the temperance movement guiltily acknowledged, the history of clerical involvement with drink was far from glorious. With the possible exception of a hiccough of anti-alcoholic activity in 1859–60, not only had churchmen in the past failed to warn their flock of the dangers of alcohol, but they had themselves succumbed to its temptations.[41] Indeed, as many apostates testified, the personal misconduct of Orthodox clergy in this respect remained, even in the early twentieth century, a significant reason why men chose to abandon Orthodoxy for other faiths whose clergy lived their lives more closely in accord with the precepts they preached.[42] This was a problem of which the clergy were themselves acutely conscious: the more alert amongst them constantly warned of the need for sobriety, especially during the service. The scale of the problem was serious. An assembly of rural priests called to discuss the potential for pastoral unity in the face of drunkenness in 1911 even found it necessary to remind themselves to:

(i) refrain from loud, inappropriate conversations at the altar; (ii) refrain from making loud comments to the psalmist; (iii) refrain from interrupting the service by making a remark whatever disturbance might break out among the congregation; (iv) appoint selected parishioners to remove trouble makers from the church.[43]

Not for nothing did Orthodox preachers need to be reminded of the scriptural text: 'Take heed to yourself and your teaching; hold to that for by so doing you will save both yourself and your hearers' (I Timothy, 4:16). But for all that, the Russian church's involvement in the temperance question spread far beyond the clergy.

The concern with the problem of drink dates from the late 1880s. As Pobedonostsev's report to the Tsar for 1888–9 recognised, drunkenness, especially among the lower classes, was a vice with a pernicious influence on the religiosity and morality of the population.[44] It was from 1889 onwards, after a Synod edict of 5–11 July had invited diocesan bishops to submit their comments on the means by which the people might be led away from drunkenness, and at the same time to encourage priests to struggle against it, that the Orthodox Church intensified its interest in the temperance question.[45] The response was not universally vigorous. Undoubtedly some clergy were resentful of the implication that they were themselves to some degree responsible for popular immorality. The authorities, it seemed to them, took a Utopian view of what changes in the popular mentality it was possible for the parish priest to effect.[46] No doubt there was some justice in this scepticism. But this did not prevent the development of temperance activity in St Petersburg on quite a considerable scale, though, as we shall see, proper co-ordination proved beyond the grasp of those involved and their ultimate success was limited.

Initially, the characteristic Russian concern remained with drunkenness rather than with alcoholism. Many churchmen long retained the view—supported by select biblical texts—that drink in itself was not only not harmful but positively good for the health: it was man's immoderate consumption, rather than the natural properties of alcohol, which did the damage. Preaching in 1881, Father Vasilii Sinaiskii recalled both the Pauline text, 'No longer drink only water, but use a little wine for the sake of your stomach and your frequent ailments' (I Timothy, 5:23) and Psalm 104's approval of 'wine to gladden the heart of man'. The same text haunted the two pastoral assemblies of the capital's priests, convened under the auspices of the Society for the Spread of Religious and Moral Enlightenment to discuss the question of drink in 1898. But by then there was support not only for the principle of *umerennost'* but also for complete abstinence, and the discussion became so animated that those present were unable to summarize their conclusions or arrive at resolutions. The principle of total abstinence never achieved complete acceptance, although there are grounds for suggesting that it may have become more popular in later years, when the concept of signing the pledge seems to have become more widespread.[47]

Just as there was no agreement about the degree to which drink was an evil in itself, so there was no inbuilt clerical consensus on the best way to counter whatever evil it represented. Initially, the emphasis was on the confession and the sermon. But it was soon realised that a more concerted effort would be needed if any real impression on the problem were to be made. Consequently, churchmen began to seek a more institutionalised response. The option seemed to be either to participate in the secular temperance trusteeships which were currently being set up, or to create parallel organisations of their own. At first, the result was a mixture of both. For example, there was a clear clerical involvement in the nascent St Petersburg Municipal Trusteeship for Popular Temperance. Ioann, bishop of Narva, organised its first besedy in 1898, employing clergy and students from the ecclesiastical academy. From 1900, there were services, followed by illustrated talks, in the trusteeship's refectories every Saturday and on the eve of festival-days.[48] However, by then independent church societies were already flourishing at a number of the capital's churches, at factories, and under the auspices of the Society for the Spread of Religious and Moral Enlightenment: it was these specifically ecclesiastical institutions which came to form the basis of the church's involvement in temperance.

There were two principal attractions for the church in operating independently. In the first place, independent operation offered a rare chance to escape secular control. In 1894 it was reported that the Deputy Minister of Internal Affairs had written to Pobedonostsev to ensure that newly opened clerical societies obtained permission from the provincial authorities. Pobedonostsev replied that only those establishments with a wide programme of activities—soup-kitchens, tea-rooms and so on—needed such permission. Those connected purely with the parish, with the sole aim of preventing the use of strong drink within the parish, should stay within the sole control of the ecclesiastical authorities.[49] Secondly, and more importantly, independent operation allowed the church to escape the formalist activities and abstract debates of the secular societies and tailor its temperance drive to its own needs: in particular, to use it as a spearhead of its own campaign to rechristianise the population. It was no coincidence that the principal figures in the church's temperance drive in St Petersburg were either members of the evangelical Society for the Spread of Religious and Moral Enlightenment or actively involved in diocesan missionary work, and that all three campaigns— evangelical, missionary and anti-alcoholic— were so closely linked as to be practically inseparable.

From the start, the church saw in the temperance movement a means of drawing men back into its own fold, and designed its work to increase popular contact with the church. Father Sergii Slepian's Temperance Brotherhood of St Boniface, which had more than 400 members (mostly craftsmen and petty-tradesmen) by 1893, its third year, led huge icon processions to holy places within reach of St Petersburg, notably to Kolpino and Sergiev Pustyn. He even claimed to have converted 163 people to Orthodoxy, most of them Jews.[50] The same techniques persisted. Father Akimov's society in Bolshaia Kolomna organised a temperance pledge in 1909. The pledge was taken in front of an icon of the Virgin, and followed by a special service. Those who took it then attended religious-moral homilies conducted on Sundays by Father D. G. Liubimov in the parish school at 104 Sadovaia. There were several icon processions each year: at Easter to the Lavra, and in the summer to Sergiev Pustyn'.[51] The largest ecclesiastical temperance society, from which many of the smaller ones drew their inspiration and techniques, the Alexander Nevsky Society, also organised pilgrimages to the Valaam Monastery. During the voyage, there were sermons and edificatory readings. On one such pilgrimage, in 1904, the preacher was Ieromonakh Mikhail (Semenov) from the ecclesiastical academy—later famous for his apostasy when the reform movement he advocated failed— whose sermon provides clear evidence of the church's motivation in participating in the temperance movement:

> We are not travelling to Valaam to admire the beauty of the surroundings, however beautiful they may be; at least that is not our primary aim. We are going to study the strict, monastic life, to learn exploits [*podvigi*] of faith and piety, and to pray to Valaam's saints. My conception of a temperance society is as an institution all of whose members take their own sort of monastic oath to help each other in temperance, not only in the sense of abstinence from alcohol but in the sense of leading a sober life in general.[52]

Although the concern with hygiene and public health (so characteristic of the secular, and particularly medical, zealots for temperance) was not wholly absent from the clerical discussion of the issue, there can be no doubt that it was specifically ecclesiastical, ethical and increasingly evangelical concerns which lay at the heart of Orthodox involvement in it.

The size of the movement is difficult to quantify. The Alexander Nevsky Society claimed 75 889 members by 1905–6, and even if this figure includes some of the same people more than once, it clearly operated on a large scale. Its nine divisions in the capital deployed preachers from the clergy and the academy to give illustrated talks to huge audiences, it produced a journal (*Otdykh khristianina*) and published thousands of pamphlets—most of them on the workers' question. It ran its own school accommodating 30 girls and 27 boys: influence at the earliest age was recognised as vital.[53] It also encouraged, though much less intensively, temperance work in the rural areas. At least one of these, that at Staraia Ladoga between 1906 and 1910, boasted a mutual-credit society, since, as Father Dobrovol'skii stated, it conceived the task of a temperance society in the broadest terms—'first of all to reawaken the popular will from the apathy which envelops it, and then to direct these reawakened energies to the creation and construction of life, and amongst other things to the foundation of its economic well-being'.[54] When the society's founder and guiding spirit, Father Rozhdestvenskii, died in 1905, hundreds of workers and their families flocked to his funeral, where the eulogy was fittingly said by Father Ornatskii.[55] But 1905 did not mark the end of expansion: Rozhdestvenskii's successor, Father Mirtov, continued his work, and was much in demand as a lecturer in other parts of the empire keen to follow the capital's initiative.[56] By 1912, the year of the first All Russian Congress of Practical Activists in the Struggle against Alcoholism—organised by Mirtov, held in Moscow and attended almost solely by clergy and those associated with the church—the St Petersburg diocesan journal counted 84 temperance organisations in the diocese, though nothing in detail was known about 31 of them.[57]

The success of the venture is still more difficult to estimate: statistics are hard to find and impossible to verify. But some indication may be derived from the knowledge that of those who took the pledge at the Alexander Nevsky Brotherhood in 1905, 1602 did so for three months, 113 for six months, 36 for nine months, 253 for a year, and only one for two years. The suspicion that taking the pledge was a temporary commitment is strengthened by the detailed report made by Father Akimov to the Moscow conference on the experience of his own society in St Petersburg. Seventy-six point one per cent of his members were aged between 20 and 40. By estate, the huge majority of his members were peasants (92.6 per cent), and an even greater proportion were men: the society had only 25 women members, although many men were brought to the church by their wives. By occupation, the largest categories were construction workers (34.41 per cent), craftsmen (17.33 per cent) and other unskilled workers (10.41 per cent). As Akimov realised, most of these men were temporary residents in the capital. His prime recruiting time was when they first arrived—April, May and June—when men would take the pledge for the duration of their time in the capital. Another common occurrence was for men to take the pledge 'until Easter', 'until Christmas' or 'until' some other festival day—the clear implication being that the period of temperance would be followed by a huge drinking spree. Thus it seems likely that all the careful schemes devised by the temperance societies for supervising their charges (Akimov himself employed the not uncommon, but nevertheless controversial, method of elected delegates from different streets in the parish, each with a brief to observe the men in his area) were wrecked, like so many of the church's pastoral initiatives, by the fluctuating, transient population of St Petersburg, which rendered almost any attempt at pastoral co-ordination impossible. Neither temperance nor a consistent ecclesiastical hold on Orthodox parishioners was achieved.[58]

If, in concluding, we try to draw together the threads of this evident Orthodox attempt to increase and strengthen its social role, to examine the extent to which it changed and developed over the period under discussion and cast a brief glance at some of its implications, what do we see?

Undoubtedly the initial motivation for the new pastoral impulse was the success in these very enterprises of the rivals of Orthodoxy. Why is it, Orthodox asked themselves in language no more subtle than mine, that they, who are heretics, are successful in their pastoral work, whereas we, for all our superiority and unique spiritual authority, fail so dismally? They were still asking themselves the same question in 1914. If anything, their concern with countering the sectarian and schismatic challenge was intensified by the tidal wave of apostates from Orthodoxy released by the Toleration Act of 17 April

1905. From a covert, illegal status before that date, Orthodoxy's rivals had come out triumphantly into the open. It was still necessary to petition the consistory to transfer to another faith. But by 1910, the transaction was simply effected by a rubber stamp.[59] Little wonder that the diocesan reports from the St Petersburg consistory to the Holy Synod—formulaic, dry documents for the most part—come uniquely alive in the sections (and they were always by far the longest and most detailed sections) devoted to the struggle with other faiths. Little wonder that pastoral work should retain a vital connection with the missionary activity from which it was originally derived.

But it would be wrong to imagine that nothing had changed. What had begun as a spiritual mission to rechristianise society in the spirit of Orthodoxy—a movement which drew on the revival of the monastic spirit in the academy during the 1880s—and was still so conceived by many, had been transformed by force of circumstance into a more political statement. What had started, in the hands of older men like Father Mikhail Sokolov, as a purely ecclesiastical movement which could earn the approval of at least some elements of the tsarist administration under Alexander III became, in the hands of younger men like Father Grigorii Petrov, a potentially subversive movement which could only cause alarm. Churchmen had been led ineluctably from a concern with the languishing moral state of Russian society to become advocates of social reform and to engage in agonised discussion of the workers' question.

The classic case is that of Father Georgii Gapon. Like Petrov a product of the St Petersburg Ecclesiastical Academy, his education had led him to an understanding of the need for a revival of parochial pastoral work—his undergraduate dissertation compared the virility of Slavonic parochial life with the torpor of its Russian variant—and equipped him with experience of the nascent preaching circles co-ordinated by the Society for the Spread of Religious and Moral Enlightenment in the Spirit of the Orthodox Church. The debacle of January 1905 not only exposed his own political activities but also called into question the social role of the church in the way in which it had been conceived and developed over the past 25 years.[60]

Ironically, therefore, it was in the reactionary years after 1905, when the church's developing pastoral techniques should in principle have been of greatest value to the state, that they came under greatest suspicion. The doubt cast on them from above in turn opened up the internal contradictions which had always lain not far below the surface—Orthodox dependence on foreign forms (in this case a notable inclination to Protestant evangelism); tensions between the diocesan authorities and semi-autonomous clerical organisations; the precarious reliance of such organisations on the financial support of a few individuals. All of these led to increasingly bitter and factionalist debate within the church in St Petersburg, a debate which had a debilitating effect on the practical work being done. By 1914, one has the distinct impression that the pastoral impetus which had seemed to hold out so much promise in the years before 1905 was almost exhausted: the same incantations were made; the same *pia desideria* outlined in the press and in private; the same societies continued their work. But few now believed the Orthodox revival could happen: whereas initially the expansion of the pastoral work and publishing activity of the various preaching, charitable and temperance societies had seemed to presage progress, now it seemed only to indicate the magnitude of the task ahead. The men who had done so much to promote the church's social role were either dead or running out of steam.[61] Antonii (Vadkovskii), the symbol and inspiration if not the initiator of much of what this paper has discussed, died in 1912.[62] The appointment as his successor of Vladimir, formerly metropolitan of Moscow, signalled a change of heart in the church in St Petersburg. Reaction triumphed over reform when reform was most needed. But that is not to say that reform, as it was conceived in these years, would have succeeded if it had been left to run its course: its social and geographical base, and its intellectual foundations, were too precarious for that.

NOTES

1.   G. Florovsky, 'The Social Problem in the Eastern Orthodox Church', in *Christianity and Culture*, Collected Works, vol. 2 (Belmont, Mass.: 1974) p. 136. J. Meyendorff, 'The Christian Gospel and Social Responsibility: the Eastern Orthodox Tradition in History', in F. F. Church and T. George (eds), *Continuity and Discontinuity in Church History*, Studies in the History of Christian Thought, vol. xix (Leiden: 1979) p. 118.

2.   This introductory section draws on arguments defended in detail in my forthcoming dissertation for the University of London: 'Church, State and Society in Late Imperial Russia: The Diocese of St Petersburg, 1880–1914'. Here we note only the explicit comparison with missionary work drawn by Innokentii, bishop of Narva, at a 1902 prayer meeting

in the St Petersburg police cells conducted by the Society for the Spread of Religious and Moral Enlightenment in the Spirit of the Orthodox Church, one of the prime instruments of the new pastoral drive in the capital. 'Whereas missionary work is external, ours is internal—in the one instance, priests bring [men] to Christ's truth from the gloom of heathenism, in the other they try to infuse faith in Christ and a feeling of repentance in hearts which have sometimes hardened to stone'. See Tsentral'nyi gosudarstvennyi istoricheskii arkhiv SSSR, Leningrad (hereafter *TsGIA*) f. 796, op. 442, d. 1966 (1902g.), l. 63 ob.

3. This is a topic worthy of investigation in itself, although any such attempt would be frustrated by archival disarray. See the outline in S. G. Runkevich, *Velikaia otechestvennaia voina i tserkovnaia zhizn'*. *Kn. 1: Rasporiazheniia i deistviia sviateishago sinoda v 1914–1915gg.* (Petrograd: 1916). The fate of some of the priests mentioned here, especially of those who survived into the troubled 1920s, is an important topic which lies beyond the scope of this paper.

4. A letter of P. S. Kazanskii's (19 February 1868) gives a classic statement. See 'Perepiska professora moskovskoi dukhovnoi akademii Petra Simonovich Kazanskogo s Aleksandroi Nikolaevnoi Bakhmetevoi', ed. A. A. Beliaev in *U troitsy v akademii, 1814–1914gg.: iubileinyi sbornik* (Sergiev Posad: 1914) p. 529.

5. N. P. Giliarov-Platonov, *Iz perezhitago*, 2 vols (Moscow: 1886) ii, pp. 196–207.

6. On these reforms see Gregory L. Freeze, *The Parish Clergy in Nineteenth-Century Russia: Crisis, Reform and Counter-Reform* (Princeton: 1983) pp. 326–9. Academy students henceforth specialised in the historical, the theological or the practical subjects.

7. *Russkoe propovednichestvo, istoricheskii ego obzor i vzgliad na sovremennoe napravlenie* (St Petersburg: 1871) is a useful early review. N. S. Grossu, 'Professor V. F. Pevnitskii kak gomilet', *Trudy Kievskoi dukhovnoi akademii* (hereafter *TKDA*) (September 1911) pp. 207–30 surveys his work. Antonii's lectures, some of which survive in draft (Otdel rukopisei, Gosudarstvennaia Publichnaia Biblioteka imeni Saltykova Shchedrina, Leningrad, f.26) were later published as a collection: *K istorii khristianskoi propovedi: ocherki i issledovaniia*, 2nd edn (St Petersburg: 1895). The archival drafts are now published: 'Iz bogoslovskogo naslediia mitropolita S Peterburgskogo i Ladozhskogo Antoniia', ed. V. Sorokin, in *Bogoslovskie Trudy: Sbornik posviashchennyi 175-letiiu Leningradskoi dukhovnoi akademii* (Moscow: 1986) pp. 295–350. The principal figure in St Petersburg was N. I. Barsov. See his *Istoriia pervobytnoi khristianskoi propovedi* (St Petersburg: 1885).

8. *Domashniaia beseda* (1859) no. 12, pp. 102–4; *Dukhovnaia beseda*, (1859), no. 2, pp. 57–60; *Sobranie mnenii i otzyvov Filareta, mitropolita moskovskago i kolomenskago po uchebnym i tserkovno-gosudarstvennym voprosam*, 6 vols (Moscow: 1885–8) vol. iv, pp. 383–5, 501–3.

9. See, for example, N. P. Giliarov-Platonov, *Voprosy very i tserkvi: sbornik statei 1868–1887gg.*, 2 vols (Moscow: 1906) vol. ii, pp. 396–8,

and V. Rozanov, *Religiia i kul'tura: sbornik statei* (St Petersburg: 1899) pp. 239–46.

10. For evidence from 1905 see Erwin Immekus, *Die Russisch-Orthodoxe Landpfarrei zu Beginn des XX Jahrhunderts nach den Gutachten der Diözesanbischöfe* (Würzburg: 1978) pp. 56ff. Preaching rotas were introduced in diocesan capitals in 1866, see *Polnoe sobranie zakonov Rossiiskoi imperii* (St Petersburg) 2nd series, no. 43495, 20 July 1866. They were meticulously kept in the capital first in manuscript, then in published form. Under Antonii (Vadkovskii) a special commission was created, 1906–10, to draw up the rota, in which leading lights of the Society for the Spread of Religious and Moral Enlightenment played a large part. See Leningradskii gosudarstvennyi istoricheskii arkhiv, Leningrad, hereafter LGIA, f. 19, op.' 97, d. 11 and ibid., op. 102, d. 21.

11. See V. F. Shishkin, *Tak skladyvalas' revoliutsionnaia moral': istoricheskii ocherk* (Moscow: 1967) p. 217.

12. V. V. Rozanov, *Okolo tserkovnykh sten*, 2 vols (St Petersburg: 1906) vol. ɪ, pp. 323. My account of the society draws on its published annual reports, on its summary reports detailed in the diocesan consistory's annual reports to the Holy Synod, (*TsGIA*, f.796, op. 442), on its own publications, and on information published in the press. I found little direct information in the archives, but it would appear from Shishkin's useful work (see n.11) that some relevant material survives in an archive I was not able to consult in the Soviet Union, Gosudarstvennyi istoricheskii arkhiv Leningradskoi oblasti, Leningrad, f. 2215.

13. It is remarkable that *throughout* the period under review, this comparatively small sect was firmly identified as the greatest thorn in the side of Orthodoxy in St Petersburg.

14. See the complaint of suffragan bishop Kirill of Gdov, LGIA f. 19, op. 97, d. 7, 11. 60–1. Ornatskii was a graduate of both St Petersburg seminary and academy where he specialised in the practical subjects from 1881–85. See N. A. Skrobotov, *Pamiatnaia knizhka okonchivshikh kurs S. Peterburgskoi seminarii s 1811g po 1895g.* (St Petersburg: 1896) p. 221, *TsGIA* f. 796, op. 163, (1882g.) d. 1189, l. 63ob., and for his full service record to 1915, LGIA f. 1016, op. 2, d. 10, ll. 41ob–48.

15. Preaching was the theme of special city-wide assemblies in October 1897, see *Sankt-Peterburgskii dukhovnyi vestnik*, hereafter *SPbDV* (1897) no. 43, 24 October, pp. 854–6, but was also discussed at the society's own regular preaching assemblies.

16. *Izvestiia Sankt-Peterburgskoi gorodskoi (obshchei) dumy*, vol. 102 (April 1891) no. 17, pp. 310–17, for church on Gutuevskii ostrov; ibid. vol. 114 (May 1894) no. 8, pp. 439–46, for the society's own church on the obvodnyi canal. LGIA f. 19, op. 92, d. 3, ll. 1–50 for the church at Lesnaia; ibid. op. 91, d. 15, ll. 1–62 for a similar case at Novosivkovskaia ulitsa.

17. *TsGIA*, op. 442, d. 2290, p. 93.

18. S. G. R. (unkevich), *Studenty propovedniki: ocherki peterburgskoi religiozno-prosvetitel'noi blagotvoritel'nosti* (St Petersburg: 1892) is an evocative early memoir. In 1895 the student N. K. Chukov was given

an icon on completing four years of *besedy* to a regular audience of 50 or so at the Vargunin factory. See *SPbDV* (1895) no. 11, 17 March, pp. 249–50.

19. See *Tserkovnyi vestnik* (hereafter *TsV*) (1886) no. 1, 4 January, pp. 6–7.

20. It is important to notice in passing that militant Pauline precepts permeate Orthodox argument on all these issues.

21. There is evidence that monasteries—worthy of separate investigation—were lax in their social responsibilities in both St Petersburg and Moscow. See *TsGIA* f. 834, op. 4, d. 1201, ll. 1–3, and LGIA f. 19, op. 102, d. 41 ll. 37–40.

22. G. P. Smirnov-Platonov, the major Muscovite advocate of systematic charity, in his journal *Detskaia pomoshch'* (1885) no. 1, cols. 48–54. For a good example from St Petersburg, see *Strannik* (1878) no. 12, pp. 358–68, Sviasch. N. Vishnaikov's sermon in St Isaac's cathedral on 9 May 1878.

23. For example, *Missionerskoe obozrenie* (October 1899) pp. 416–17; *Detskaia pomoshch'* (1885) no. 1, cols. 27–37.

24. See Professor A. M. Ivantsov-Platonov's attempt to offer an Orthodox counter to Tolstoyan charity in *Za tret'e desiatiletie sviashchenstva 1883–1893gg.: slova rechi i nekotoryia stat'i*, pp. 127–61. Guide to the literature on Ivantsov-Platonov, in I. Smolitsch, *Geschichte der Russischen Kirche, 1700–1917* (Leiden: 1964) pp. 513–14.

25. *SPbDV* (1900) no. 34, 25 August, p. 41. A visit to the Malaia Okhta prompted the anonymous author to reflect that although schismatic charity was 'not true charity, not in the Christian spirit', nevertheless 'by their sacrifices the schismatics win over Orthodox, who often, so I hear, speak of the schismatics and their widespread almsgiving in flattering terms'.

26. See the debate which was begun by the publication of Sviashch. I. Flerov, *O pravoslavnykh bratstvakh, protivoborstvovavshykh Unii v iugozapadnoi Rossii v XVI, XVII, i XVIII stoletiiakh* (St Petersburg: 1857) and continued largely by Professor Koialovich in the pages of Aksakov's *Den'* in the 1860s.

27. The resultant edicts date from 1864: *Pravila o pravoslavnykh tserkovnykh bratstvakh i polozhenie o prikhodskikh popechitel'stvakh pri pravoslavnykh tserkvakh* (St Petersburg: 1881).

28. There is no comprehensive treatment of these debates. Useful material on the early years may be found in Smolitsch, *Geschichte*, pp. 507–26, and in the rather narrow account by Julia Oswalt, *Kirchliche Gemeinde und Bauernbefreiung* (Gottingen: 1975). Most helpful of all is Ross Chambers' treatment of one of the debates in *Pravoslavnoe Obozrenie*, 'Orthodoxy and Reform in the reign of Alexander II', in *Journal of Religious History*, XII (Sydney: 1983) no. 3, pp. 233–49.

29. N. A. Nikol'skii, 'Ob obshchestvennoi blagotvoritel'nosti i eia organakh—prikhodskikh popechitel'stvakh', in *Pravoslavnoe Obozrenie* (May 1876) pp. 81–127, quoted at p. 83.

30. See Glagolev, 'Drevneevreiskaia blagtvoritel'nost'', *TKDA*, (January 1903) pp. 1–83.

31.   Sviashch. I. Labutin, *Kharakter khristianskoi blagotvoritel'nosti* (St Petersburg: 1900) p. 30.

32.   N. A. Nikol'skii, 'Ob obshchestvennoi blagotvoritel'nosti', p. 82, a very early (1876) statement of an attitude later echoed by those priests in St Petersburg, such as Mikhail Galkin (Gorev), who advocated ecclesiastical participation in setting up labour exchanges, and the advocacy of workers' rights. See *Izvestiia Sankt-Peterburgskoi eparkhii*, hereafter *ISPbE* (1911) no. 3.

33.   Adele Lindenmeyr, 'Public poor relief and private charity in late imperial Russia', unpublished Ph.D. dissertation, Princeton University, 1980, is rather dismissive of ecclesiastical charity, and is not concerned with its motives. See also P. N. Zyrianov, *Pravoslavnaia tserkov' v bor'be s revoliutsiei 1905–1907gg.* (Moscow: 1984) p. 23. In the rural areas of the diocese of St Petersburg, there were parish trusteeships and charitable societies whose interests conformed to the national pattern, reaching no further than the upkeep of the church and its clergy. See, for example, LGIA f. 19, op. 87, d. 1, ll. 26–8, on Gdov *uezd*.

34.   See N. A. Skrobotov, *Prikhodskii sviashchennik A. V. Gumilevskii* (St Petersburg: 1871). For doubts about Gumilevskii's claims to be the initiator of charitable work in the capital see *Khristianskoe Chtenie*, (September 1872) pp. 162–4.

35.   S. G. Runkevich, *Prikhodskaia blagotvoritel'nost' v Peterburge: istoricheskie ocherki* (St Petersburg: 1900). p. vii stresses his debt to the published accounts.

36.   Filaret, *Sobranie mnenii i otzyvov*, vol. IV, pp. 285–7. Letter to Over-Procurator A. P. Tolstoy, 4 November 1857.

37.   Established in 1900, 18 000 rubles of an initial outlay of 19 000 rubles, and the subsequent running costs were provided by the cemetery church, probably one of the richest in the capital. TsGIA, f. 796, op. 442, d. 2046 (1904g.), ll. 39ob–43ob. The cult of St Kseniia survives in Leningrad, and she appears in contemporary poems, by Bobyshev and Ivask, which imitate eighteenth-century models. See G. S. Smith, 'Eighteenth-Century Russian Topics in Recent Russian Unofficial Literature', in *Study Group on Eighteenth-Century Russia Newsletter*, 16 (1988) pp. 7–10. J. Bradley, 'The Moscow Workhouse and Urban Welfare in Russia', in *Russian Review*, 41 (1982) no. 4, pp. 427–44, is a useful piece on contemporary secular practice which notes, pp. 436–7, the influence of Lutherans and the emphasis on character regeneration.

38.   The following accounts of individual societies are particularly informative: Prot. I. D-n, *Prikhodskaia zhizn' pri Blagoveshchenskoi Vasil'eostrovskoi tserkvi 1862–1912 so storony tserkovno-obshchestvennoi blagotvoritel'nosti* (St Petersburg: 1912); D. E. Bogoliubov, *Tserkov' sviatyia zhivonachal'nyia troitsy v galernoi gavane v S Peterburge* (St Petersburg: 1892) pp. 77–102; P. M. Dmitriev, *Obshchestvo vspomozheniia bednym prikhoda tserkvi pokrova Presviatyia Bogoroditsy chto v Bol'shoi Kolomne v gorode S Peterburge, 1871–1911* (St Petersburg: 1912).

39. J. Hutchinson, 'Medicine, Morality and Social Policy in Imperial Russia: the early years of the Alcohol Commission', in *Histoire Sociale/Social History*, 7 (November 1974) pp. 202–26, quoted at p. 203. See also Hutchinson, 'Science, Politics and the Alcohol Problem in post 1905 Russia', in *Slavonic and East European Review*, 58 (London: April 1980) pp. 232–54.

40. *G. B. Foreign Office, Confidential Print*, ed. D. C. B. Lieven, part I, series A, vol. 2, doc. 12, p. 10. Stanley to Granville, 1 August 1881, Odessa.

41. N. P. Rozanov, *Deiatel'nost' dukhovenstva v bor'be s narodnym p'ianstvom: istoricheskii ocherk* (Moscow: 1912).

42. See, among many, *TsGIA* f. 796, op. 442, d. 2407, pp. 246–8.

43. *ISPbE* (1911) no. 22, 30 November, pp. 7–9, report of pastoral assembly in the fourth division of Luga *uezd*.

44. *Vsepoddanneishii Otchet za 1888–9gg.*, pp. 77–9.

45. See Sviashch. D. G. Bulgakovskii, *Rol' pravoslavnago dukhovenstva v bor'be s narodnym p'ianstvom* (St Petersburg: 1900) and Sviashch. A. V. Rozhdestvenskii, *Chto sdelalo pravoslavnoe dukhovenstvo dlia bor'by s narodnym p'ianstvom* (St Petersburg: 1900). The relevant archival file is no longer kept in its proper chronological place. Of course, there had been individuals concerned with the problem of drink in earlier years, but Leskov was right in more than a strictly bibliographical sense to describe a pamphlet in his collection, *Slovo o p'ianstve, govorennoe sel'skim sviashchennikom v odnom iz blizlezhashchikh k Sankt Peterburgu selenii* (St Petersburg: 1838), as 'very rare'. See L. N. Afonina, 'Knigi iz biblioteki Leskova v gosudarstvennom muzee I. S. Turgeneva', in *Literaturnoe nasledstvo*, 87 (1977) p. 154.

46. See, for example, *TsV* (1893) no. 7, pp. 101–02 and no. 31, pp. 485–7.

47. Sviashch V. Sinaiskii, *Lepta v sokrovishchnitsu tserkovnoi propovedi, 1881–3* (St Petersburg: 1884) pp. 264–76. *SPbDV* (1898) no. 13, pp. 254–5, and no. 17, pp. 327–30.

48. *Kratkii ocherk deiatel'nosti S Peterburgskago gorodskago popechitel'stva o narodnoi trezvosti, 1898–1912* (St Petersburg: 1913) pp. 14–15.

49. *TsV* (1894) no. 9, p. 41.

50. *TsV* (1893) no. 3, p. 46, no. 15, pp. 238–9, and no. 26, p. 414. For further material on Slepian, see M. S. Agursky, 'Die Judenchristen in der Russisch-Orthodoxen Kirche', in *Ostkirchliche Studien*, 23 (Würzburg: 1974) no. 4, especially pp. 281–96. I am grateful to Professor Agursky for sending me a copy of his article.

51. I. Turenskii, *Tserkov' Pokrova Presviatye Bogoroditsy chto v Bol'shoi Kolomne v S Peterburge: eia istoriia i opisanie* (St Petersburg: 1912) pp. 152–3. For further details see the statistical results compiled by the priest's son in *Narodnoe obrazovanie* (August 1912) and below.

52. Quoted in M. Gorev, *Kak trezvenniki ezdili na Valaam*, 2nd edn (St Petersburg: 1909) pp. 9–10.

53. *Otchet o deiatel'nosti Aleksandro-Nevskago obshchestva trezvosti za 1905 i 1906gg.* (St Petersburg: 1907). Digests of the Society's reports

appeared in the diocese's annual report to the Synod.

54.   Sviasch. G. Dobrovol'skii, *Znachenie kreditnykh tovarishchestv v dele otrezvleniia naroda i uchastie v nem dukhovenstva* (St Petersburg: 1910) pp. 3–4. By 1910 it had a total of 1152 subscribers, and had made 2093 loans in 1909 for the purchase of horses, cattle food, seed and building projects.

55.   *Moskovskiia Vedomosti*, 25 July 1905, p. 3; 20 August 1905, p. 3.

56.   For example, he was expressly invited to Simferopol by the bishop of the Tauride in 1913. See *TsGIA*, f. 796, op. 196, otd. 1, 1 st., d. 424, l. 3.

57.   *ISPbE* (1912) no. 17–18, 15 September, pp. 21–3.

58.   *Otchet . . . Aleksandro–Nevskago obshchestva za 1905 i 1906 gg.*; *Trudy vserossiisskago s″ezda prakticheskikh deiatelei po bor'be s alkogolizmom*, 3 vols (Petrograd: 1914–16) vol. II, pp. 17–22.

59.   The regulations for transferring from one faith to another were ambiguously phrased. See *TsGIA*, f. 797, op. 75, II otd., 3 stol, d. 402, ll. 1–4. The numerous, slim files (nothing more than rubber-stamped forms) surviving in LGIA, f. 19, op. 102 (1910) contrast sharply with the weighty dossiers cataloguing the church's attempts to prevent apostasy before 1905. On this issue in general see Peter Waldron, 'Religious Reform after 1905: Old Believers and the Orthodox Church', *Oxford Slavonic Papers*, 20 (Oxford: 1987) pp. 110–39. I am grateful to Dr Waldron for sending me a copy of this article.

60.   I was not permitted to see much archival material on Gapon. Walter Sablinsky, *The Road to Bloody Sunday: Father Gapon and the St Petersburg Massacre of 1905* (Princeton: 1976) remains a good synthesis of the printed sources.

61.   Ornatskii himself was reputedly murdered by revolutionaries in 1917. His attendance at the municipal duma in latter years dropped significantly from 21.4 per cent in early 1913 to only 6.4 per cent in 1915, though this may have been a result of wartime preoccupations. See *Petrogradskaia gorodskaia duma v 1913–1915gg: deiatel'nost' gruppy obnovleniia* (Petrograd: 1915) p. 250. There was no connection between this group of 'renovationists' and the clerical group of the same name. Ornatskii was not a renovationist, though other leading lights in his society certainly were, notably Mirtov and Lakhostskii. Ornatskii joined the Octobrist party, whereas a number of renovationists, including the diocesan missionary, Chel'tsov, were Kadets.

62.   Gerhard Simon, *Church, State and Opposition in the USSR* (London: 1974) pp. 41–63, is an excellent introduction to Antonii's life. Mikhail Agursky considers his political position in 'Caught in a Cross Fire: The Russian Church between Holy Synod and Radical Right (1905–1908)', in *Orientalia Christiana Periodica*, 50 (Rome: 1984) fasc. 1, pp. 163–96.

12 The Church Schools and Seminaries in the Russian Revolution of 1905–06

John D. Morison

The Russian Orthodox Church faced the revolutionary events of 1905 and 1906 in a weak and divided condition, but also in a spirit of optimism. It remained financially more than ever dependent on the state. It was still subjected to lay control and to detailed bureaucratic supervision. It was still reliant on state protection against the inroads in its popular support made by Old Believers, other sectarians, Uniates and Catholics, and Muslims. Internally, the white clergy deeply resented the domination of the church hierarchy by the black clergy, and even within the hierarchy there were widely divergent views and bitter disputes. Like other interest groups in society, the church hoped to take advantage of the revolutionary disturbances to persuade the state, or, to be more precise, the Tsar, to make significant concessions in favour of its own vested interests. In particular, it wished to regain independent, self-governing status under a Patriarch, without necessarily sacrificing the material advantages and protection which it derived from its peculiar relationship with the state.[1]

By the beginning of the twentieth century, the church had become a major provider of education to the population at large, as well as to the children of its own servitors. Its educational establishments were seriously affected by the revolutionary disturbances of 1905–07, but in a distinctive manner that reflected the particular position which it occupied in Russian society.

Pobedonostsev's forceful encouragement coupled with the enormous financial subventions which he had extracted from the treasury had led to a vast expansion in the number of parish primary schools in the two decades preceding the revolution. By 1906, there were 41 233 of these, with a total of 1 998 529 pupils, which represented a dramatic increase from the 4213 in existence in 1884.[2] They significantly outnumbered the *zemstvo* and other secular elementary schools. The church's parish schools had limited aims and a restricted curriculum. Their basic task was to develop in their pupils 'religious feelings, and a clear consciousness of their duties, based on the principle of humaneness and justice'. Each academic day should begin with morning prayers conducted by the duty senior pupil, in the presence of a teacher. Each lesson should begin and end with a prayer, as should lunch. All pupils should be compelled to attend church services, and some of them should serve at the altar.[3] These religious acts could, however, easily degenerate into a meaningless and formal routine. Academically, these schools imparted little beyond basic literacy, numeracy and religious instruction. The village priests were expected, as a matter of duty, if often reluctantly, to be involved in the teaching of religion. Additionally, 49 173 classroom teachers were employed in 1905, of whom all bar 5416 were lay persons. 19 885 were women. These teachers were lowly in social status and very poorly paid. Their annual average salary in 1906 was 120 rubles, with 4862 of them being paid 60 rubles or less. By comparison, the mass of village school teachers in secular employment received 180 to 240 rubles, which was still considered to be a miserly and wholly inadequate sum.[4] The general educational level of the parish schoolteachers was low. If 11 405 had secondary or even higher education and 6098 were qualified as elementary school teachers, 8444 were simply classed as competent to teach in parish schools, 5934 were classified solely as teachers of literacy and 11 876 had no qualifications at all, except presumably very basic literacy. Their conditions were extremely poor, and they were beset by supervision and interference from priests and bureaucrats alike. Peasant parents also kept a wary eye on them, and tended to be suspicious if they did not frequently hear the sound of church singing emanating from their village schoolroom. They wanted their children to learn to live a godly life from the school.[5]

Thus, the parish schoolteachers were in an even worse plight than their colleagues in zemstvo schools, and might reasonably have been expected to behave in a similar manner. Zemstvo school teachers were fully caught up in the general movement of protest in 1905. A small minority of them openly strove to incite disorders among the peasantry and to lead them in a political struggle to overthrow the government. For instance, by interpreting newspapers to the villagers they helped to educate them politically.[6] The behaviour of the church school teachers seems to have been different. Reports from diocese after diocese preserved in the archives of the Holy Synod maintain that their parish schools remained calm in the revolutionary year, even if there were disorders in the village and Sunday schools and public readings of enlightening texts to the masses often had to be suspended. A report from Iaroslavl' is typical, in reporting that the established routine of school life remained unaltered, with classes, services and prayers conducted as always with enthusiasm.[7] The Orthodox Church has been known to cover up events that it would rather keep concealed. However, there is no reason to doubt the authenticity of these reports on this occasion. The archives contain detailed reports on the widespread troubles in the seminaries. Moreover, they do note the occasional lapse in the parish schools. In Penza, there was exceptionally some trouble in the Mikhailov boys' school when the pupils held a meeting in November, an anonymous letter was sent to the director, and school property was damaged.[8] In Mozhaisk in December some teachers took part in meetings, demonstrated with red flags and were promptly sacked, even though in the province everything in general went on as calmly as normal.[9]

There is evidence of a small minority of priests becoming actively involved in oppositional or even revolutionary activities. The handful of priests elected to the Duma who adhered to the Trudovik group are well known, The police detected one village priest and teacher of religion from the Novgorod province who was a Socialist Revolutionary.[10] One priest from Perm' signed a petition demanding the exclusion of religious teaching from the schools.[11] Other isolated cases can be found. However, it is difficult to find the evidence to support and make convincing the belief of John Geekie that many, and possibly the majority, of the white clergy were hostile to the autocratic order, or the assertion by Gregory Freeze that outside Petersburg and Moscow most priests 'silently supported the liberation movement or openly approved the kind of liberal reform espoused by the Kadets'.[12]

So far as the lay teachers in church parish schools were concerned, a small minority certainly threw in their lot with the opposition to the regime. A certain number of church school teachers joined the radical All-Russian Union of Teachers, and a small group of them moved a resolution at the Union's Third Congress condemning these schools for 'destroying the personality, sowing hopelessness and despair', turning children away from their studies and maiming their moral nature. They demanded radical reforms, based on the principles of democratisation and freedom.[13] Three church school teachers were caught inciting the peasants against the authorities in Ekaterinoslav province.[14] It would not be surprising if the teachers were behind an isolated petition from parish school pupils in the Stavropol district in the province of Samara which demanded a secularisation of the curriculum, free tuition, the right to enter secondary schools without an examination, and urgent repairs to the school building.[15] However, such cases were the exception rather than the rule. The Journal of the All-Russian Union of Teachers noted ruefully in December 1905 that little progress had been made in organising the church parish schools. 'According to all the facts, there are still too few organised elements in them for it to be decided to enter into open struggle with the clergy.'[16]

Any explanation of the relative passivity of the parish school teachers has to be speculative. Their poverty made it difficult for them to risk their livelihood and threaten the survival of their families by engaging in open opposition, and thereby courting dismissal or worse. They were closely supervised not only by the police but even more so by their local priests. The duties of the priest included passing over details of politically disloyal individuals to the authorities, and many performed their role as informers with relish. Perhaps more important was the openly hostile and bitterly critical attitude of their colleagues in the zemstvo and other secular schools towards the church establishments. This led the All-Russian Union of Teachers to include as two of the main planks in its programme the banning of religious instruction in the schools, and the transformation of the church parish schools into free, self-governing and completely secular schools that were planned as the bottom rung of a democratic system of education.[17] Thus, if teachers in the church parish schools were to join in the general movement of elementary school teachers they would effectively have to renounce religion and to vote for the abolition of the schools in which they earned their living. They would be well aware that this would be a programme that would not find favour with the religious majority of the villages. Moreover, it is not unreasonable to suppose that the large majority of parish school teachers were religious by conviction, given the fundamentally religious bias of these schools and their curriculum. Those with more secular leanings would tend to seek employment in zemstvo or other lay establishments. Only one in eight of village schoolteachers joined a Union and thereby committed themselves to active struggle in 1905–06.[18] The remainder lay low and hoped to survive by avoiding trouble. It is not surprising if an even higher percentage of parish school teachers also decided to adopt the lowest possible of profiles, whether out of self-interest, fear or conviction.

In the elementary schools of the Empire, the initiative in trouble-making had naturally been taken by the teachers, sometimes acting in collusion with the parents, rather than by the pupils. In the secondary schools the situation was reversed. The teachers, mostly state employees, relatively well paid and secure in their positions, generally adopted a moderate line, seeking to exploit the situation to secure academic and professional goals, such as academic freedom and curricular reform. The pupils, by contrast, took the lead in open acts of defiance of the regime and engaged in the conflict as activists on the side of the opposition. Initially, they were caught up in the general ferment that swept Russian society following Bloody Sunday, and demonstrated in search of remedies for the deficiencies which they identified in the life of their schools and in support of the commonly heard demands for basic civil liberties. The fierce government reaction to these moderate requests which resulted in a terrible massacre of secondary school pupils by the police and troops in Kursk on 12 February 1905, and a series of other only slightly less horrible incidents, led to a popular reaction which reverberated through the Empire.[19] Politicised and given solidarity by these events, many secondary school pupils eagerly joined in the political struggles of 1905–06. The pupils at the church's seminaries formed a part of this general pupils' movement, but their actions had their own time schedule, their own characteristics and specific objectives, and were notable for their violence.

In 1905, there were 57 seminaries in the Empire, with a total staff of 1192, and 19 348 pupils of whom 15 339 were the offspring of priests.[20] Their condition was far from satisfactory, as was revealed for all to see by the explosion of discontent in 1905. In the years before the reform of 1867, when the clergy had been a closed caste, their function had been to train the sons of priests to become priests. The measures of 1867 attempted in some measure to dismantle the caste structure of the clerical estate. As a consequence, priests' sons now had the opportunity to find other careers, whilst the seminaries were opened to outsiders, a step which contributed to their radicalisation. In 1884, as part of the counter-reforms, the clock was put back somewhat when a quota of 10 per cent was imposed on those who were not clerical offspring. Even if the better-off clergy tended to send their children to the lay secondary schools, the imposition of heavy fees at these establishments in the 1880s, as part of a deliberate policy of excluding the poor and other undesirables, had effectively denied access to the children of the mass of the impoverished white clergy. The seminaries, by contrast, were very cheap for the sons of clergy. No fees were charged, hostels were subsidised and many scholarships were available. As a consequence, the seminaries were flooded with the sons of priests who very often had no intention themselves of becoming priests, knowing as they did from personal experience the difficulties of the profession. Inevitably, there was a large exodus from these schools at the end of the fourth year when the disaffected were allowed to depart to seek access to other schools or to employment. At the same time, the imposition of the 10 per cent quota made it difficult for those with a genuine vocation to enter the very schools designed to train them to become priests. As a result, the church was left with a serious shortage of priests and the seminaries, intended to be strictly vocational, were inundated with pupils who required from them a general education as preparation for access to further education. The seminaries were faced with an impossible task. It was not possible both to train priests and simultaneously to provide a broad and non-vocational education for the sons of priests. The mass of their pupils were intensely frustrated. They were denied access to the large majority of higher educational establishments. Since 1879, they had effectively been denied entry to universities. In 1888, they were allowed to enrol at Tomsk University if they passed a special exam, a concession designed to attract an inflow of students to the depths of Siberia and thereby to solve an otherwise intractable recruitment problem. Later, again as a solution to student shortages, they were also allowed into the Eastern languages faculty of St Petersburg University, into the Demidov Lycee in Iaroslavl', and into some faculties in Warsaw and Iur'ev universities to reinforce the Russian element in those troublesome non-Russian areas. But even these limited concessions raised serious problems for the seminarists. The nature of the seminary curriculum made it very difficult for them to satisfy the general educational requirements even of those universities which were allowed to accept them. They had particular problems with mathematics, physics, cosmography and modern languages.[21] The extent of their frustration can be judged by the effect of a rumour in 1906 that Kazan' University would accept seminarists from the fifth class. Immediately, 1235 desperate seminarists appeared from all over Russia.[22]

Whereas the 1867 reform had tried to bring the seminary curriculum for the first four classes closer to that of the general educational classical schools, the 1884 decree had again widened the gap. The fifth and sixth classes, preparing people for the theological academies and the priesthood, were inevitably dominated by religious studies, but so too now were the lower classes. Thirteen hours a week of biblical studies were supplemented by bible and church history, study of the liturgy and the theory of preaching, church singing and basic theology. Church Slavonic had also to be mastered. This of necessity severely restricted the hours available for general educational subjects, although nine hours a week were devoted to mathematics in the first three years. Russian literature was halted after the first three years, only one hour of physics was possible, and history suffered to the extent that eighteen-year-old seminarists finished in a state of total ignorance even of the achievements of Peter the Great and Alexander II. Greek and Latin had become less important. Modern languages were available only as voluntary extras, in out-of-school hours. To make matters worse, even the general educational subjects were supposed to be imbued with religious content. The majority of seminary pupils who had no vocation to be priests had therefore to suffer what seemed to them to be a largely irrelevant curriculum, and to spend their free time working hard on maths, physics and classics in the hope of transfer to a gymnasium or of passing the entrance hurdles to universities. Others reluctantly suffered the vocational religious content of the fifth and sixth years of the seminary course in the expectation that upward mobility into the universities would thereby be made easier. Teaching methods were leaden and rote learning was the norm.[23]

Added to all this, the discipline enforced by the inspectors was harsh and often brutal. Living conditions were bad and grossly overcrowded, with the hostels resembling military barracks. Restrictions on free time activities were oppressive, banning theatre and concert visits, dances and the like. Notwithstanding this, a hostile observer alleged that drunkenness and thieving were rife, and that 50 per cent of seminarists left their course suffering from venereal diseases. As religion was brought into disrepute, some became atheists. To make matters worse, there was a wide range of ages subjected to this regime, from fourteen-year-olds to young adults of 22 and 25.[24]

It was consequently not surprising that there was a long and well-established tradition of disorders in the demoralised seminaries. The seminarists were thus, at least in this respect, well ahead of the pupils in other secondary schools, even before 1903 when 20 seminaries were devastated and their pupils sent home, many of them never to return. In 1905, the seminarists struck early, from the start of the year, with a renewed burst of activity following the October Manifesto. By November, as many as 43 seminaries had been closed. The announcement by the Holy Synod that it would consider reforms did little to calm the situation, and the disturbances continued throughout 1906 and even into 1907. Many of these were extremely violent. On 28 February in Kharkov, the seminarists produced a 'chemical obstruction', broke into the rector's flat and demanded the immediate release of their colleagues. When this was refused, acid was thrown in the rector's face, leaving it scarred although the eyes were undamaged. The porters were then also attacked with acid, and furniture, mirrors and the telephone destroyed. In Minsk, the seminary, its classrooms and the administration's files were set on fire. The rector's flat was completely devastated, down even to the household utensils, in an orgy of destruction. In Nizhnii Novgorod, there was an explosion on 12 May in the seminary, and two more bombs were found there. Bombs were also found in Kostroma and bombs exploded in Moscow and in Tomsk. In a vicious circle, violent outrages bred violent repressions by troops, Cossacks and police, which in turn bred more violent outbursts. In that way, the authorities played into the hands of the desperate minority of extremists who succeeded thereby in inflaming the passions of their more moderate fellow pupils. Even in the majority of seminaries where disorders were milder and confined to meetings and protests, the news of police outrages elsewhere had a knock-on effect, provoking further trouble. There is clear evidence of the infiltration of seminaries by Social Democrats and, more dangerously, by Socialist Revolutionaries wedded to the use of terror as an instrument of revolution. Police reports in the archives specifically mention Social Democratic circles and publications in seminaries in Kostroma, Pskov, Nizhnii Novgorod, Tambov, Iaroslavl' and Vologda, with a Socialist Revolutionary presence in all these seminaries except Kostroma and Nizhnii Novgorod, and additionally in Vladimir. This list is certainly far from complete.[25] The role of the Tiflis seminary as a breeding ground for revolutionaries is, for instance, well known.

Nevertheless, it would be unwise to conclude that even the activists were dominated by the revolutionary parties. A notable feature of the seminarists' movement was the formation of the 'All-Russian General-Seminary Union', which the police tracked down in 50 towns, even if in five of these the Union's Central Committee had no contact address. The police first noticed this organisation in the spring of 1907. It apparently arose from the establishment of a circle 'for material aid to political exiles and prisoners' in the seminary in Viatka in October 1906. This enjoyed success and was emulated in other towns. Moves for unification followed, and the 'Central Committee of the General-Seminary Union' was formed in Viatka on 31 January 1907. It issued a circular letter to seminaries, giving a short history of the rise of the Viatka circle and recommending the establishment of similar circles elsewhere, linked to the Central Committee. By January 1907, the Union had held three congresses of representatives of local groups and had drawn up a programme, the central point of which was the slogan common to all opposition movements in 1905–06 of 'a free school in a free state'. They saw a particular role for seminarists in 'the political and cultural liberation of the people' by means of lectures, propaganda and publicist activities. They succeeded in publishing their own journals, 'Svetoch' in St Petersburg and 'Rozsvit' in Poltava. Secret libraries were established. They also focused attention on one of their own main grievances in demanding the admission of the seminarists to the universities. They planned to organise a boycott of examinations, but this tactic did not succeed as a result of widespread opposition among seminarists. The results of a meeting in Pskov on 6 May 1907, when 30 voted in favour of a boycott but over 60 against, was not untypical. Nevertheless, pupils in nine seminaries 'demonstratively' refused to take their examinations. Some infiltration of the Union by revolutionary elements was shown at the congress in Moscow on 26–27 December 1906, when delegates from 16 seminaries resolved, alongside their professional academic tasks and the 'general emancipation struggle', to work hand in hand with the parties of the extreme left and to 'collaborate with them in all ways' in their work within the walls of the seminaries 'in organising circles, libraries, lectures, meetings, the distribution of literature, etc'. By spring 1907, the seminary authorities had got wind of the existence of the Union and had alerted the police. The proposed fourth congress of the Union, to be organised by the Vladimir branch after Easter in 1907, never took place as only six delegates turned up, to be greeted by the police who promptly arrested them. The Union had perished by the summer of 1907, a victim of the general police repression.[26]

The fact that seminarists found it necessary to found their own union rather than to join the general union of secondary school pupils showed that they were very conscious of the individual character of the seminaries and of the distinctiveness of their own problems. The refusal of the majority of the seminarists to support the move to boycott examinations, and the need felt by the Union to include academic and professional issues in its programme showed that the majority of the seminarists were not extremists. They recognised the urgent need for reform of the seminaries, and for remedies to their specific grievances, but were wary of involvement in the general revolutionary struggle, even if they were at times caught up in the general excitement. They did participate in general meetings and even peaceful street demonstrations, and were ready to sign petitions. However, it generally took provocative acts of violence by the extremist minority followed by harsh repressive acts by the authorities to provoke the majority into action. Even then, there were often many who were concerned, despite everything, to keep classes going and to stay out of trouble. Far from all of the demonstrations were violent, sometimes being limited to barracking unpopular teachers, organising dance evenings on the premises or lectures of a socio-political character and the like. For all its inadequacies, the seminary was the only avenue open to its pupils for upward mobility, and they were reluctant to jeopardise their chances of a leaving certificate or to run the risk of being branded for life as an unreliable element and troublemaker. To give some examples, on 8 March 1906, the sixth class at the Don seminary refused to join in a memorial service for the Sevastopol' mutineer, Lieutenant Shmidt. One hundred and six stayed in their classes in Perm' in February 1906, despite considerable pressure from their colleagues to join them in a walk-out. The sixth class in Riazan' was taught by the rector whilst their colleagues paraded outside singing the Marseillaise. Some pupils in Stavropol' petitioned their bishop to allow them to resume their studies in December 1905. A Iaroslavl' teacher reported in January 1906 that between the minority wishing to study and the minority who were revolutionaries there was a large group of idlers who simply enjoyed mischief and liberation from the classroom. In Kharkov in January 1906, the numbers returning to class grew to the majority as soldiers were called in to protect them from the strikers.[27]

Large numbers of petitions were presented to the authorities by seminarists from all corners of Russia. An analysis of a sample of these (seven from Samara, Riazan', Voronezh, Saratov, Novgorod, Ekaterinburg and Orenburg) supports the conclusion that seminarists in general were interested above all else in matters concerning their schools and their own lives, and were prepared to respond *en masse* to the general political ferment when provoked in the heat of the moment by brutal police or Cossack action or in so far as they acknowledged the validity of the proposition that the radical school reforms which they demanded depended for their realisation on fundamental changes in the political order. These petitions are individually phrased and vary in content, an indication that they originate from the individual seminaries and not from some central source. They were adopted at general meetings of the seminarists and may be presumed to represent their feelings, or rather the basic demands to which all could subscribe. There is no reason not to believe them to be representative of the seminarists' movement as a whole.

Only one of these, from Orenburg, included the general demands of the secondary school movement for a unified system of lower, secondary and higher education, each rung leading naturally to the other without artificial barriers, and for a free and democratic school system emancipated from government interference. The remainder concentrated exclusively on the problems of the seminaries. Most considered that the district school (*dukhovnoe uchilishche*) should be combined with the seminary to form a seamless eight-class secondary school, with an additional optional two extra years of theological instruction for those going on into the priesthood. Entry should be open to all without restrictions on estate (*soslovie*) or racial origin. This secondary school should be accorded the same rights as the gymnasium, and its graduates from the eighth class should be allowed unobstructed access to all universities and higher educational establishments. Those completing the extra two years of theological instruction should be given a similar right to pass freely into the theological academies. There should be exams only at the end of the course, and not yearly tests forming a hurdle to be jumped before gaining entry into the next year. They were united in demanding significant changes to the curriculum. More time should be devoted to mathematics, physics, natural science and cosmography. Two modern languages, French and German, should be studied, one of them on a compulsory basis. Pre-Petrine literature should be replaced by modern works. More Russian and general history should be taught, using less tendentious textbooks. To make room for all this, the classical languages should be made, at best, optional, and less time devoted to many of the vocational subjects such as biblical history, preaching and church history. However, it is notable that they wanted basic theology to be included in their course, thus indicating that they wished to some extent to retain the distinctive character of the seminaries. All the petitions laid stress on disciplinary issues, demonstrating the deep resentment which the present brutal regime aroused. The removal of some inspectors was demanded. They and their staff should treat pupils with respect, and degrading punishments should be abolished. The punishment cell and the 'hungry table' in particular should go. Bad marks for conduct should be awarded only on the basis of undisputed facts, and should not be carried over from previous terms or even schools. Searches and the censoring of pupils' letters should end. Pupils should have the right to live in flats of their own choice, freely to visit the town in out-of-school hours, to go to theatres, concerts and the like, and to use public libraries and reading rooms. The seminary libraries should be run by the pupils who should have the right to acquire any book allowed by the censor and to subscribe to journals and newspapers of their own choice for the reading room. Pupils should be allowed to establish mutual aid funds. Some demands were made for comrades' courts. Parents and pupils should have some rights of attendance at pedagogical councils, particularly when proposals to expel students were being considered. Orenburg, the most radical, demanded that seminaries should be made independent of the bishops and that power should pass to the teachers' council, which should elect the rector and the inspector from its own ranks. Riazan' agreed with the latter point, specifically stating that it was undesirable to have a monk as a rector.[28]

In the Poltava seminary, Ukrainian nationalism, with demands for Ukrainian schools teaching in the Ukrainian language, was a significant additional factor. From May 1899 a circle called 'Gurtka' had worked intensively in the seminary. It hectographed full and uncensored versions of the works of Shevchenko, which it distributed in large numbers to the Poltava cadet corps and the girls' gymnasium. When some of the circle's members were expelled, all the seminary windows were broken and further incidents followed. The circle revived in 1900, and published Shevchenko's *Kobzar* in 350 copies. Its activity culminated in the autumn of 1906 with the publication of a journal, *Rozsvit*. This foundered in 1907 after its seminarist editors and production staff had been expelled, and the circle itself was also suppressed by the authorities.[29]

There is little evidence that the seminary teachers were actively involved in the events of 1905–07. All the indications are that they were demoralised. On the one hand, they were in constant fear of offending in the eyes of the church authorities by showing any sympathy for their pupils' actions and demands, and thereby threatening their livelihood. As state servants they faced immediate dismissal for any anti-governmental activity.[30] On the other hand, they were frightened of showing themselves to be too clearly on the side of the authorities, a posture which could lead to their being victimised by their pupils and branded as members of the Black Hundreds. Most teachers therefore left it to the administration to lead the struggle to restore order.[31] Nevertheless, shortly after the publication of the October Manifesto in 1905, V. Kolosov, a history teacher in the Tver' seminary, organised some of his colleagues into a 'Union of Teachers in Church Educational Establishments'. This Union aimed to unite all working in such schools for mutual aid and material support, and to help in the renewal of the church schools. Its main aim was outlined in article 3 of its statutes, 'The Union will follow no political aims and under no circumstances will join any general or local strike'. It alleged that its purpose was to collaborate with the authorities in the reform process which was then under active discussion. Similar organisations were reported to the Holy Synod from Samara and Zhitomir. Notwithstanding their moderation, their meetings were banned and their members pressurised by the rectors and higher authorities into ceasing their activities.[32]

Consequently, the seminary teachers were far behind their colleagues in the state secondary schools who at least managed to get their own relatively moderate union off the ground. Local priests on occasions seem to have been bolder in supporting the pupils' demands. In Samara, some of the younger priests were reported to have warmly supported the seminarists' petition. In Iaroslavl', some of the town's priests, and especially the younger ones, took part in a meeting in the seminary on 24 November and in subsequent meetings in the hostel to work out a petition to the authorities. When reprimanded by the bishop, one of the priests replied that if they had not been present the seminary would have been ransacked and the rector killed.[33]

At the summit of the church's educational system were the four prestigious theological academies in St Petersburg, Moscow, Kiev and Kazan'. Designed to be on a par with universities and to educate the future spiritual and administrative leaders of the church, they deliberately restricted their entry and never contained more than a total of 700 students. Entrants had to have excellent academic records and unblemished political and character references. By the eve of 1905, an increasing percentage was not of clerical origin. Throughout the four-year course of intensive study they were closely supervised in an attempt to isolate them from the general students' movement. Nevertheless, academy students were affected by the revolutionary atmosphere. A general meeting in the Moscow Academy on 11 February 1905 resolved to stop their studies, and 154 went on strike. Those who decided to ignore this call met such disapproval from some professors that they went over to the side of the protesting majority. The Temporary Regulations of February 1906, an ill-judged concession, made the academies autonomous and allowed the reformers among the staff and students their head. Some students went so far as to hold requiems for revolutionaries and to preach that Christ himself had been a revolutionary. Students from the Kazan' Theological Academy sent a telegram to the governor-general of Tambov on 16 March 1906, protesting against the death sentence which had been passed on the socialist revolutionary Maria Spiridonova. With the reaction of 1908, a purge of the staff of the academies was carried out, and the repressive disciplinary order for the students was restored. It was not surprising that significant numbers of staff and students should have become caught up in the liberation movement, given the vigorous debate then going on in the church between the liberal and conservative wings on the proposed reforms in the church and the liberals' wish to undermine the powers of the bishops.[34]

In 1905–06 there was a widespread movement in Russian society for basic civil rights, a much more restricted movement for political emancipation and an advanced constitutional or even socialist regime, and a general tendency amongst interest groups to attempt to use the situation to obtain remedies for their specific grievances. Elementary school teachers formed a union and struck out for radical improvements in their material and working conditions, and in the schools in which they worked. For a period, at the height of the revolutionary excitement, the Union also espoused political aims, which were renounced after exhaustive debate at their Third Congress. Relatively few teachers from the church primary schools joined actively in this struggle. Although they had grievances enough, the anti-religious and anti-church bias of the Union was for the large majority an insuperable obstacle.

The lead in all the secondary schools of the Empire was taken by the pupils. The seminaries were no exception to this. They had a long tradition of disorders, and were quick to respond, often in a violent manner, to events such as Bloody Sunday. A new peak came after the publication of the October Manifesto, in the heady days of press freedom but also of often vicious counter-revolutionary demonstrations. There is no clear evidence of separate organisation before the ill-fated attempt to set up a Seminarists' Union in 1906. In general, the movement seems to have been relatively spontaneous, with news of disorders in one seminary provoking trouble in another, although the small revolutionary minority certainly tried by violent acts to provoke the police and troops into brutal repression as a means of activating their colleagues. However, it is clear that the main cause of the disturbances in the seminaries was the incongruity of being expected to provide a vocational education for future priests to pupils who mostly wanted a general education to prepare them for higher education and secular employment. The seminarists inevitably responded excitedly to the events of 1905–06, with the first-formers being notably volatile in efforts to show how grown-up they were. From late 1904, political leaflets were flying around the seminaries and extravagant demands for freedom, universal suffrage and a Constituent Assembly were being made. However, the majority of the pupils would respond only to demands which were relevant to their particular situation, and to grievances which were specific to seminarists. Even at the height of the troubles, a minority resolutely affirmed that it wished to continue to study. This minority soon became a majority as the revolution's tide ebbed in 1906, and as it seemed as though their demands for school reform were being taken seriously, although the extremist minority continued to cause problems until 1907. Secondary school teachers, better off than their colleagues in elementary schools and enjoying the status of being state servants, were restrained in their actions and easily kept under control by the authorities. There is, however, clear evidence of younger priests in a number of towns giving support to the seminarists as they drew up petitions, although whether they acted as a restraining factor or as initiators of confrontation is not clear. This indicates that there may well have been a divide in attitudes towards the events of 1905 and 1906 between the urban and rural white clergy. Even the small and select theological academies were dragged into the revolutionary turmoil, thereby reflecting the aspirations of the reform party within the church for its democratisation and spiritual revival, but also mirroring the general students' movement in being dragged in the heat of the moment into support of revolutionaries.

The troubles in the church's educational establishments reflected the problems and aspirations of society at large, but to a much greater extent mirrored the particular problems of the church and its schools.

NOTES

1. For a discussion of the debates within the church see James W. Cunningham, *A Vanquished Hope. The Movement for Church Revival in Russia, 1905–1906* (Crestwood, New York: 1981).
2. *Vsepoddaneishii otchet ober-prokurora sviateishago sinoda po vedomstva pravoslavnago ispovedaniia za 1905–1906 gody* (St Petersburg: 1910) p. 223; A. G. Rashin, 'Gramotnost' i narodnoe obrazovanie v XIX i nachale XX v.', in *Istoricheskie zapiski*, vol. 37 (1951) pp. 37–9. Some of these schools were very short-lived, so the figures have to be treated with some caution.
3. 'Otchet o sostoianii tserkovnykh shkol za 1905–1906 gg. Samarskago eparkhial'nago uchilishchnago soveta', Tsentral'nyi Gosudarstvennyi Istoricheskii Arkhiv SSSR (hereafter *TsGIA*), fond 803, op. 10, d. 1032.
4. John D. Morison, 'Les Instituteurs de Village dans la Revolution de 1905 en Russie', *Revue des Etudes Slaves*, vol. LVIII/2 (1986) p. 207.
5. N. Bunakov, *Sel'skaia shkola i narodnaya zhizn'* (St Petersburg: 1906) p. 9.
6. Morison (see note 4 above) pp. 212–16.
7. *TsGIA*, fond 803, op. 10, ed. khr. 1498, l. 18.
8. *TsGIA*, fond 803, op. 10, d. 880, l. 15.
9. *TsGIA*, fond 803, op. 10, d. 711, ll. 3–4.
10. Tsentral'nyi Gosudarstvennyi Arkhiv Oktiabr'skoi Revoliutsii (hereafter TsGAOR), fond DO, ed. khr. 1800, ch. 38 (1905) l. 16.
11. TsGAOR, fond 102, op. 0oo, ed. khr. 999, ch. 1, t. 3 (1905) l. 62.
12. John Geekie, *The Church and Politics in Russia, 1905–1917*, unpublished PhD dissertation, University of East Anglia, 1976, p. i; Gregory L. Freeze, *The Parish Clergy in Nineteenth-Century Russia* (Princeton, New Jersey: 1983) p. 470.
13. *Vestnik vospitaniia* (October 1906) no. 7, Khronika, p. 143.
14. TsGAOR, fond 102, ed. khr. no. 999, ch. 1, t. 4 (1905) l. 244.
15. Ia. I. Mal'tsev, 'O tserkovno-prikhodskoi shkole i eia uchitel'', in *Vestnik uchitelei* (7 May 1906) no. 2, pp. 70–1.
16. *Vestnik vserossiiskago soiuza uchitelei i deiatelei po narodnomu obrazovaniiu*, (December 1905) no. 3, p. 3.
17. *Vestnik vserossiiskago soiuza uchitelei i deiatelei po narodnomu obrazovaniiu* (December 1905) no. 2; *Proiekt ustava vserossiiskago soiuza uchitelei*, TsGAOR, fond 518, op. 1, d. 75, l. 7.
18. Morison (see note 4 above), pp. 218–19.

19. For an account of the Kursk incident, see G. Rokov, 'Shkol'nyia volneniia 1905 goda', *Vestnik vospitaniia* (December 1905) no. 9, pp. 121–4.

20. *Vsepoddaneishii otchet ober-prokurora sviateishago sinoda ... za 1905–1906 gody* (see note 2 above) p. 155.

21. *Vestnik vospitaniia* (1905) no. 6, Khronika, pp. 117–20; P., 'Dukhovnaia shkola i eia budushchee', *Vestnik vospitaniia* (1905) no. 9, pp. 150–9.

22. S. Bel'deninov, 'Sibirskaia molodezh' v kazanskom universitete', *Sibirskie voprosy* (1907) no. 2, pp. 64–5.

23. P., *Dukhovnaia shkola* (see note 21 above), pp. 159–64; *Otchet o sostoianii obriadtsovoi odnoklassnoi tserkovno-prikhodskoi shkoly pri Simbirskoi dukhovnoi seminarii*, TsGIA, fond 803, op. 11, d. 1873, ll. 1–11.

24. P., *Dukhovnaia shkola* (see note 21 above), pp. 165–70; A. Amitrov, 'Temnoe tsarstvo (k voprosu o reforme dukhovnykh seminarii)', *Golos sredne-uchebnych zavedenii* (22 January 1906) no. 2, pp. 3–9.

25. *Vestnik vospitaniia* (1905) no. 9, Khronika, pp. 116–17; *Vestnik vospitaniia* (March 1906) no. 3, Khronika, pp. 96–7; Rokov (see note 19 above) pp. 138–42; TsGAOR, fond 102, op. 8, ed. khr. 89, t. 2/1907, ll. 192, 213; *TsGIA*, fond 802, op. 10, ed. khr. 21, l. 35; *TsGIA*, fond 802, op. 10, ed. khr. 109, l. 15; TsGAOR, fond 102, op. 8, ed. khr. 89, t. 2/1907, ll. 128–9, 179, 190–2.

26. TsGAOR, fond 102, op. 8, ed. khr. 89, t. 2/1907, ll. 6–457; *TsGIA*, fond 802, op. 10, ed. khr. 43, ll. 56–70.

27. *TsGIA*, fond 802, op. 10, ed. khr. 115, ll. 2–7; *TsGIA*, fond 802, op. 10, ed. khr. 30, ll. 5, 14; *TsGIA*, fond 802, op. 10, d. 80 (1905) ll. 20, 39–40, 70; *TsGIA*, fond 802, op. 10, ed. khr. 84, ll. 2–9.

28. *Samarskaia gazeta* (26 January 1906) no. 18, p. 3; TsGAOR, fond 102, op. 5, ed. khr. 0oo, 3, ch. 104/1905, ll. 3–4; *TsGIA*, fond 802, op. 10, ed. khr. 68, ll. 5–6; *TsGIA*, fond 802, op. 10, d. 12, l. 13; *TsGIA*, fond 802, op. 10, d. 80 (1905), ll. 2–3, 18, 98–100.

29. TsGAOR, fond 102, op. 8, ed. khr. 89, t. 2/1907, ll. 366–7.

30. *TsGIA*, fond 802, op. 10, d. 121, ll. 112–13.

31. *TsGIA*, fond 802, op. 10, ed. khr. 109, ll. 41–2.

32. *TsGIA*, fond 802, op. 10, ed. khr. 85, ll. 1–3, 22, 25.

33. *Samarskaia gazeta* (26 January 1906) no. 18, p. 3; *TsGIA*, fond 802, op. 10, d. 80 (1905), ll. 36, 39–41.

34. Cunningham (see note 1 above), pp. 45–7, 319–21; TsGAOR, fond 102, (DO), ed. khr. 3, ch. 120/1905, l. 19; TsGAOR, fond 102, op. 5, ed. khr. 0oo, 3, ch. 48/1905, l. 7.

13 The Political Philosophy of the Russian Orthodox Episcopate in the Soviet Period

Michael A. Meerson

The political philosophy of the Russian Orthodox Church[1] in modern times would be unreconstructable without taking into consideration the heritage of the past. The Revolution of 1917 ended a period of history which lasted for more than 15 centuries. It has been called the era of Constantine the Great, who established the Orthodox theocracy, according to which the secular kingdom was sacred and the state was considered the earthly reflection of the heavenly kingdom. One monarch on earth was the reflection of the one God's sovereignty in heaven. The church was incorporated into the imperial structure, and this incorporation assumed institutionalised forms. The Synod of Bishops complemented the Senate, thus providing Byzantium, and later on the Russian Empire, with the symbolism of the double-headed eagle. The Senate codified the political decrees of the emperor and was responsible for their orderly applications, while the Synod of Bishops legislated theologically for both the church and the Empire—for, if approved by the emperor, its decrees were recognised as laws.

Thus the church leaders, who before Constantine had enjoyed purely moral authority, saw themselves transformed into imperial officials with the power of coercion. Few could resist the temptation to resort to force, even the best and the holiest of them. Even St Athanasius, himself persecuted by the state for his fearless defence of Orthodoxy from the Arians, asked the Emperor to direct state persecution against his opponents.

One who suffered much at the hand of the state, Avvakum, the leader of the Old Believers in seventeenth-century Russia, had similar expectations of state protection and support. From his exile he beseeched Tsar Alexei Mikhailovich to take his side in the religious controversy of the time and to give him the authority to do away with his religious opponents, the Nikonians, who enjoyed the full support of the state.

Under very different circumstances, the leaders of the 'Living Church' appealed to the Soviet government in 1922 with the requests for the arrest of all those bishops who had refused to recognise the authority of the Living Church's leadership.[2]

The theory of *symphonia*, that is, a concord or harmony, between the church and the state, introduced by Emperor Justinian in the sixth century, put a roof over the new structure of the Eastern Orthodox political philosophy. Two distinct elements, the priesthood (*sacerdotium*) and the imperial power (*imperium*), each autonomous in its own sphere to some extent, formed a unified whole as the parts of a single organism. The state with the emperor at the top was identified as an organic body.

The Russian church naturally inherited the political philosophy of Byzantium. But the church applied this philosophy to Russia itself rather late, during the rule of the Moscow Grand Prince Ivan the Third, after the fall of Byzantium, when the Moscow princes began to develop the awareness that they, as the autocratic rulers of the Orthodox populace, were the successors of the Byzantine (Roman) emperors.

But, before that happened, as a scholar of the Russian religious mind, George Fedotov, observed, the peculiarly Russian political phenomenon of a theocratic Orthodox Republic had been developed in the northwestern city-states of Novgorod and Pskov. These two city-states were governed by a democratic city assembly known as the *Veche*, which elected city officials, including the Archbishop of Novgorod, the head of the autonomous Novgorod Church. In addition to his religious functions, the Archbishop played a leading role in political affairs, presiding over the Council of Notables (*Sovet Gospod*), who conducted all the current affairs and prepared the most important proposals for the decisions of the Veche. As a mediator between the Veche and the prince (the head of the military forces), or between opposing parties within the Veche, the archbishop acted as a *de facto* President of the Republic, to use a modern analogy. The archbishop stood above the parties and symbolised the unity of the Republic. In order to preserve his independence, his name was drawn by lot from a list of candidates who had been elected by the Veche. (The All-Russian Sobor in 1917–18 used the same method in electing the Patriarch for the restored Patriarchate.)

The Novgorod Republic had a religious legacy, retaining for itself the name of Republic of St Sophia, Holy Wisdom of God. St Sophia was represented on earth by the archbishop.

The protection of Novgorod's liberties was one of the archbishop's most sacred duties. Thus the last Archbishop of Free Novgorod, Jonah, already advanced in age, went to Moscow to seek protection for the city from an intended military action of the Moscow Prince. 'Look with calm eyes on your subjects, and do not start to turn free men to slavery', Jonah exhorted the Grand Prince, Basil II.[3]

Fedotov pointed out that the 350 years of Novgorod republican experience cannot be dismissed easily. Novgorod was not just one city among many others. It was the political centre of an immense territory (from the Baltic Sea to the Urals and beyond) that was larger in size than all the other principalities of Great Russia, including Muscovy, put together.

The Novgorod territories gave birth to the most famous monasteries: Valaamo, Solovki, Kirillov, Ferapontov. Novgorod's trade with the Hanseatic League city-states made Novgorod the chief Russian window on Europe. Russians always treasured the memory of Novgorod as the expression of the most Russian tradition in Russian history. Thus when 1000 years of Russian statehood was celebrated in the nineteenth century, the monument to commemorate it was erected in Novgorod.

Novgorod's rich democratic experience did not find expression in a political theory to be passed on to posterity. As Fedotov observed, 'these expressions of the religious ideal of freedom in Orthodoxy, unfortunately, were not developed in canonical treatises. The spirit of freedom was left to the pages of the ancient chronicles and in part to the local cults.'[4]

Due to historical circumstances that strengthened the autocratic tradition of the Muscovite Grand Princes, which was to prevail, the Novgorod political experience became a passing episode which left no visible imprint on Russian political development. Muscovy became the successor of the Mongol military empire, inheriting its autocratic rule, its political despotism and, gradually, its territories. The political philosophy which prevailed among the church leaders during this period helped to bring about this political transformation.

The Russian church in the Muscovy period inherited the Byzantine theory of the coexistence of two separate and equal powers— sacerdotium and imperium—but it failed to implement this theory in political practice. The victory of the Josephites in the beginning of the sixteenth century resulted in the emergence of a special form of

Russian national Caesaro-papism. Joseph, the influential superior of Volokolamsk monastery, favoured an integration of church and state, and upheld the divine right of kings. He shaped the new theology of church-state union, by equating service at the court of the Grand Prince with the divine service at the church. Josephites were strong supporters of the 'Third Rome' idea, seeing in Moscow the *only true* Christian kingdom on earth.[5] So it was not by accident that, two generations after Joseph, Ivan the Terrible blasphemously twisted Jesus' words (Jn. 17:3) by saying: 'I zealously endeavor to exhort people to the truth and the light so that they come to know the one true God who is glorified in the Trinity, *and that they may come to acknowledge the Sovereign given to them by God* (M. M.)'.[6]

Joseph's ecclesiastical utilitarianism paved the way to the state utilitarianism of the rulers of the Empire of Peter the Great. For Joseph the monastery was almost a state institution, which had to prepare hierarchs for the state church. Since the senior hierarchs of the Russian church were drawn exclusively from the Josephites, Joseph's political philosophy prevailed in the church hierarchy for two centuries, until Peter's revolution.

Thus one disciple of Joseph, Daniel, the Metropolitan of Moscow, practically surrendered the church position to state authority, and his other disciple, Metropolitan Makarii, applied the theory of secular intervention in church affairs.

Except for the unique example of patriarch Nikon, who tried in vain to introduce the papal idea of the superiority of spiritual over temporal authority into Russian practice, no other church leader in the seventeenth century has attracted our attention as a political thinker. After the schism of the Old Believers and the abolition of the Russian patriarchate under Peter the Great, and during the period of the so-called 'Babylonian Captivity of the Russian Church', church hierarchs have preferred to keep silent on all matters of political dispute. Few dared to defend even church rights,[7] which were gradually reduced, especially during the rules of Catherine the Great and Nicholas I, and under Pobedonostsev. As far as the Old Believers were concerned, they preserved the old Josephite philosophy, but they took it completely out of the realm of history and into the realm of eschatological Utopia.

The only hierarch who made a significant, though scandalous, contribution to church political thought during the Petersburg period was Feofan Prokopovich, a cynical and totally opportunistic engineer of Peter's church reforms.[8] His philosophy served a unique end: to extol the power of the Tsar and to give theological justification to the Tsar's limitless authority. Significantly, the very title of one of his pamphlets read:

An Historical Inquiry into what were the Reasons, and in what sense the Roman Emperors, both pagan and Christian, were called Pontifices or Bishops of Politheistic Law; and whether in Christian Law the Christian Sovereigns may be called Bishops or Hierarchs and in what sense.

Playing on the double meaning of the word 'Episcopos' (literally 'overseer'), just as he had played on the words 'Christ the Lord' (The Anointed), applying it to Tsar Peter, Feofan made the point that sovereigns could be called Bishops of Bishops.[9]

The Court theologian bishop Feofan Prokopovich pushed to absurd extremes a philosophy which had been introduced into the church consciousness by another court theologian and historian, Bishop Eusebius of Caesarea, who was the first to teach that 'the power of the emperor in the world is a reflection of God's power in heaven'. For Eusebius, God, the 'Supreme Governor of the whole universe, by His own will appointed Constantine . . . to be Prince and Sovereign'.[10]

The ecclesiastical system and political theology tailored by Pro-kopovich to suit Peter's ambitions was to persist without major changes throughout the entire so-called St Petersburg period of Russian history. Thus Articles 42 and 43 of the Fundamental Laws (*Osnovnye Zakony*) of Russian Empire, prepared by the rather liberal and enlightened statesman Speranskii, stated:

As a Christian Sovereign the Emperor is the supreme defender and guardian of the dogmas of the ruling faith and the overseer of Orthodoxy and all the good orders in the Holy Church. In this sense, the Emperor, in the law of succession to the throne [5 April 1797], was called the Head of the Church. The autocratic power was implemented in the Church Administration by means of the Most Holy Governing Synod which it had established. [1832 edition]

For Konstantin Pobedonostsev, the powerful Oberprocurator of the Holy Synod, the autocratic rule of the emperor was the highest form of authority. It must be total and indivisible.[11] This philosophy was shared by many church leaders even as late as the end of the nineteenth century. Thus Bishop Feofan the Recluse, one of the most popular spiritual writers in Russia at the end of the nineteenth century, maintained that the Tsar, appointed by God, represented the head of the whole body of society. Every member of society must be connected to the Tsar 'to show Him silent obedience in everything, because he pronounces the will of God, and must cling to him with thankful love'. All governmental institutions and civil officers were, for Feofan the Recluse, 'the arms, the legs, and the eyes of the Tsar'.[12] Another church ideologist of monarchical autocracy, Bishop Innokentii of Kherson, added a mystical flavour to this political philosophy by comparing the Tsar with Moses:

> People need to have a perpetual Mount Sinai where the will of the heavenly Lawgiver is ever announced; a perpetual Mount Tabor where the light of the Glory of God is ever reflected on the faces of the anointed representatives of the people. This Sinai, this Tabor is the Tsars' throne.[13]

But the beginning of the twentieth century witnessed the rapid disintegration of this political philosophy among church leaders.[14] The winds of liberty and the expectation of political and church reforms stirred up the so far silent minds of the church hierarchs. Many of them were dissatisfied with the Tsar's unwillingness to permit the convocation of an elected church council.

In 1917, after the abdication of Nicholas II, the Holy Synod hailed the Revolution as 'the hour of general freedom for Russia'.[15] Then it refused to uphold the autocracy and called for the Constituent Assembly to decide the future political system of Russia.[16]

The political neutrality of the Holy Synod was further affirmed by the All-Russian Sobor (church council). Even before the Bolsheviks' *coup d'état*, the sobor, foreseeing the approaching civil war, accepted a resolution which stated that 'the Orthodox Church, in accordance with its Holy tradition, does not participate in the struggles of political parties'.[17] By making this decision and by employing Free Novgorod's method of electing the church primate, the sobor indicated its intention to restore the Russian church to a position similar to that which the church had enjoyed in the Novgorod Republic.

The sobor restored the Patriarchate and elected Tikhon Belavin to be the Patriarch. But as a result of the Civil War and emigration on the one hand, and the arrest of the Patriarch and the Renovationist Schism in 1922 on the other, the ROC found itself divided into three major jurisdictions; to use the modern terminology: the Patriarchal Church, the Karlovtsy jurisdiction (the ROC outside Russia), and the Renovationist movement, headed by the Living Church organisation.

The Church split was influenced by political events. Two jurisdictions (the Karlovtsy and the Renovationists) were clearly formed along political lines.[18] What were the political philosophies that caused this split?

The position of Patriarch Tikhon was the same as the position of the Sobor that elected him: political neutrality. Or, rather, a position above political struggle. To be sure, Tikhon's pastoral letters, written at the time of the Civil War amidst the bloody persecution of the clerics, were filled with accusations against the Bolshevik regime. But these accusations were prophetic, devoid of immediate political implications. Even his first reaction to the news from the Sobor that he had been elected to Patriarch was to compare himself to the prophet Ezekiel, who had received a scroll to consume with the words, 'lamentations, wailings and moanings' written on it, and to Moses, who had complained before God that he was too weak to carry 'all these people' on his own shoulders.[19]

The Patriarch looked at the Revolution and the Civil War from a prophetic vantage point, seeing in them the punishing hand of God. The Patriarch did not want to become a partisan of any political side, because he realised the futility of human political efforts in such an hour of divine judgement.[20]

Even in 1919, Tikhon, in one of his pastoral letters, clearly stated that 'it is not up to the Church, but it is up to the people to decide on the form of the Government. The Church does not bind itself to any particular political system, since the latter has only relative historical significance.'[21]

Amidst the Renovationist's schism, Tikhon's official announcement from his confinement in 1923 that he was not a political enemy of the Soviet regime, and that he condemned the political activity of the Karlovtsy Synod, reflects the continuity of his previous neutral position.[22] Even Metropolitan Anastasii, a political opponent of Patriarch Tikhon who was one of the leaders of the Karlovtsy jurisdiction in the 1920s and its head for almost 30 years (1936–64), acknowledged the continuity in Patriarch Tikhon's political stand. The church under Tikhon, wrote Anastasii, 'maintains its total independence from the Government in Canons and Doctrine, but professes its sincere civil loyalty to the Soviet Regime, as the one permitted by God, thus logically rejecting the counter-revolution'.[23]

This position was further upheld and developed by the letter to the Soviet government written from Solovki labour camp by imprisoned Orthodox bishops in 1926, one year after the death of Patriarch

Tikhon.[24] One can call it an ideal model of the church's political philosophy under the Soviet regime. Long before the human rights movement in the Soviet Union emerged in the 1960s, the bishops' letter had announced its principles. Far from naive, knowing quite well that the Soviet regime was ideocratic and totalitarian and, therefore, had no room for any freedom of conscience, the bishops, nevertheless, preferred to define the relations between church and state in the legal terms of the Soviet constitution. The constitution separated the church from the state. The church abstained from all political activities.

> The Church is not concerned with the redistribution of wealth, since it has always considered this to be the prerogative of the State, for which actions the Church has not been responsible. The Church is not concerned with the political organization of authority, since it is loyal to the Governments of all the Countries within the borders of which its faithful live. It can get along with every political system, from the oriental despotism of Old Turkey to the Republic of the USA.[25]

The bishops' letter, nevertheless, stressed the point that the two different philosophies—the Christian world view of the church and the communist world view—have different political and social implementations. The 'Church believes that the principles of Morality, of Justice and the Law are absolute and unchangeable', whereas 'for Communist ideology they are conditioned by the class struggle'.[26] These ideological differences are insurmountable, and the church would not overcome them by reinterpreting its teaching to suit the regime. The letter condemns all attempts by the Renovationists to reinterpret communist foreign and domestic policy in terms of a social gospel preached by atheists. In this sense the verdict of the Solovki letter is equally applicable to similar pronouncements by the post-war Moscow Patriarchate (henceforth referred to as MP).

The letter of the bishops also states the right of the church to abstain from the approval of the political actions of its government, because 'approving of a government is as much meddling in politics as reproaching a government would be'.[27] The church also offers to its faithful members complete freedom of political self-determination. Each faithful has his own mind and conscience to define his own political philosophy. The church's total withdrawal from politics implies a refusal to watch over the political loyalty of church members. 'The Orthodox Church considers police surveillance and police reporting totally incompatible with the dignity of its pastors. Hence Church prosecution of its members and pastors for political activities is equally inadmissible.'[28]

The apparent political neutrality of the letter, which affirmed the total independence and integrity of the church body from any interference by the state, implies, nevertheless, the existence of the church's own political philosophy. In the authors' mind the church is above political struggle. It should remain in a position similar to the one it occupied in the Novgorod Republic. But gone were the days of theocracy. The Solovki Bishops' letter implies the aspiration for a democratic, pluralistic and law-abiding society, which tolerates independent social organisations, such as the church, and also provides room for them to function. By taking the Soviet Constitution literally, the bishops interpreted it not in an ideocratic and totalitarian way, as it has always been interpreted in the one-party political system, but in a democratic way, as if they were dealing with a law-abiding society.[29] By carefully keeping the church above political turmoil, the bishops have preserved its inner freedom and its dignity.

On the other hand, the Karlovtsy Synod has had a partisan political orientation from the very outset. The Non-monarchists were even expelled from the Karlovtsy Sobor, which established the jurisdiction of the Russian Church Abroad.[30] In the political thought of the Karlovtsy hierarchs, Russian Orthodoxy could not normally exist without an Orthodox state, headed by an autocratic ruler. The Karlovtsy Sobor of 1921 accepted the political programme of restoration of an autocratic monarchy in Russia and began agitating to bring the House of Romanov back to power. Even when the hope of a Romanov restoration faded, the idea that the church needed the imperial protection of an autocratic ruler remained. The ruler's own religious convictions were considered irrelevant. The need for an Orthodox autocratic ruler deteriorated into the need for any autocratic state authority which would promise to support the church. This political philosophy is illustrated by *The Address of Thanks to Adolf Hitler*, written by Metropolitan Anastasii, Head of the Karlovtsy Synod, from neutral Yugoslavia in 1939.

The head of the *émigré* church almost invited Hitler to invade Russia in a new crusade against the Soviets. Anastasii promised that a prayer for Hitler would be offered not only in the newly erected church which the Nazi government had allowed to be consecrated in Berlin, and not only 'throughout Germany, but also in all Orthodox Churches in Russia'.[31]

Quite ironically, Anastasii greeted Hitler as 'a leader in the world struggle for peace and truth'. He promised Hitler the prayers of 'the devout people of all nations desiring peace and justice'. (These expressions would become familiar in numerous addresses of the post-war MP hierarchs to Stalin and other Soviet leaders.)

Far from being an expression of politeness towards a representative of a secular power, the letter actually urges a crusade, promising Hitler the support of the church. The philosophy of identifying church interests with the national and political values of a state brought into a bizarre state of confusion the mind of Anastasii, who in his political aspirations relied on the autocratic leader of the nation which had been, throughout the long history of Russia, its main political opponent.[32] Only a blind nostalgia for the church's alliance with a strong authoritarian state could have dictated such a letter.

A similar philosophy was shared by the leaders of the Renovationist Schism in 1922, in Russia. Before the revolution, some of the renowned leaders of this schism had belonged to the most conservative circles. They were monarchists and nationalists. Thus the first schismatic with a 'revolutionary' orientation was the hieromonk Iliodor Trufanov, who declared himself 'Patriarch' and established an independent Church Synod in Tsaritsyn in 1920. Before the revolution, Iliador Trufanov was a famous activist in 'The Union of Russian People', and was very close to Rasputin.[33]

The chief organiser of the Living Church, the priest Vladimir Krasnitskii, had also belonged to the 'Union of the Russian People' before the Revolution. He was even appointed Rector of the Union's church in St Petersburg. In those days he was a staunch ideological opponent of socialism and wrote a paper entitled 'The Exposure of Socialism', in which he stated that socialism was an invention of the devil.[34]

The first Hierarch to become the head of the Renovationist Schism, Bishop Leonid Verninskii, was known before the Revolution as a staunch monarchist of extremely conservative political views.[35] The same could be said of the next leading hierarch, who headed the Renovationist Church for 12 years, Bishop Vitalii of Belevsk. He was an old man who before the Revolution had been known all his life as an extreme political conservative.[36]

One of the earliest memorandums of the Living Church, addressed to the Soviet government, suggested that an organisation consisting of an influential group of Orthodox clergy should be created and made a part of the state bureaucracy. A student of the Renovationist movement, Levitin-Krasnov, maintains that this idea was the cherished dream of all the Renovationist leaders and that they did everything possible to make it come true. If they failed to make the Living Church a part of the state bureaucracy, it was through no fault of their own. This philosophy was to survive the Living Church. Levitin maintains that this philosophy was shared fully by Protopresvitor Kolchitskii, the all-powerful Chancellor of the Office of the Moscow Patriarchate during the period between the end of the war and the beginning of de-Stalinisation in 1956.[37]

The official resolutions and acts of the Living Church have been very much in line with this philosophy. Thus the first All-Russian Conference of the Living Church, which took place in August 1922 in Moscow, voted to expel from their dioceses all opponents of the Renovationist movement (especially bishops) and to dismiss all Parish Councils which had not accepted the clerics of the Living Church. Three out of the six chief speakers at the Conference (Adamov, Diakonov, and Krasnitskii) were active members of the 'Union of the Russian People' before the Revolution. In his speech, Adamov proposed the defrocking of Patriarch Tikhon (who was under arrest at this time) and the dismissal of all bishops who had opposed the Renovationist movement.

Thus Feofan Prokopovich, who worked hand in hand with the State Secret Police (the 'Tainaia Kantseliaria' of Biron's government) to eliminate his ecclesiastical opponents, acted very much as a forerunner of the Living Church's leaders, who would use the Soviet GPU (the Secret Police, Glavnoe Politicheskoe Upravlenie) to eliminate their church opponents.[38]

It is interesting to observe how the two ecclesiastical extreme movements, the Leftist Schism (Renovationists) and the Rightist Schism (Karlovtsy Synod), with their only apparently different philosophies, have been influenced by the same political philosophy and the same past experience of the close alliance between church and state. Both fell into the same trap, the old temptation to seek the restoration of the church's position as a state institution. The monarchists from the Russian Church Abroad hoped to achieve their goals with the restoration of an autocratic monarchy. The Renovationists hoped to establish a leftist alliance of the church and the Soviet regime. Both hopes turned out to be political Utopianism.

Now the question must be asked, what was the political philosophy of the post-war Moscow Patriarchate.[39] The MPs presence on the international scene, and its leadership in the so-called 'Peace Movement' from 1948 until the present time, are a matter of record. It is quite evident that the MP has moved far from the position of political neutrality held by Patriarch Tikhon and the Solovki bishops' letter. What is the real political philosophy, if any, that this switch in views signifies?

One scholar, Konstantinov, has observed that the foreign policy of the MP over the years has reflected perfectly and precisely all the curves and zigzags of the Kremlin's policies.[40] The only difference is the screen of the so-called 'struggle for peace' behind which the MP parrots the foreign policy of the Kremlin. Konstantinov is not the only one to observe that every foreign affairs' statement of the MP reflects the political concerns of the Soviet government. The answer to the question about this much too suspicious closeness of the two positions—the MPs and the Soviets—was given by Patriarch Aleksii: 'The Russian Orthodox Church supports totally the peaceful Foreign Policy of our Government, not because the Church allegedly lacks freedom, but because the Soviet policy is a just one and it corresponds to the Christian ideals which the Church preaches'.[41]

Metropolitan Nikodim even introduced the notion of two atheisms: the atheism-hedonism of bourgeois society, which Christendom condemns, and communistic atheism as a world view based on moral principles compatible with Christian norms and therefore tolerable by Christendom.[42]

The numerous political statements on foreign policy matters made by the highest hierarchs of the MP in recent years, including our time of *glasnost'*, have also echoed the Soviet government's 'correct' line. Patriarch Pimen's recent letter on the occasion of the seventieth anniversary of the October Revolution, signed by all the members of the Synod of Bishops, furnished another proof that the hierarchy is still afraid of expressing, or even having, its own opinion.[43] In an open letter to the Patriarch and the Holy Synod, a group of Orthodox clerics and the faithful rightly observed that the policy of glasnost' and perestroika which has been expressed everywhere in the state press and the media still has no following in the MP. 'The letter of the Patriarch', they said, 'reflected the spirit of the remnants of Stalin's era. The Regime was described as the "benefactor" of the church. The letter sounded anachronistic at a time when the Soviet media openly spoke about Stalin's crimes. Even the officials of the Council for Religious Affairs accepted that believers' rights had been violated in the past.'[44]

Since all these pronouncements by the church's hierarchs under

Soviet control have not been sincere, it is important to explore the real political meaning behind these pronouncements. The policy of the post-war MP was shaped by two bishops of the pre-revolutionary mould who consequently became the two patriarchs of the ROC during and after the war: Sergii Stragorodskii and Aleksii Simanskii.

Before the Revolution, Sergii Stragorodskii was a liberal theologian who, nevertheless, felt perfectly at home in the bureaucratic Synodal Church structure under the Tsar's autocracy. A standing member of the Holy Synod since 1911, Metropolitan Sergii was one of the first senior hierarchs to join the Living Church.[45] Though Aleksii, the future Patriarch, successor to Sergii, never belonged to the Renovationists, he proved to be similarly opportunistic. As a vicar Bishop of Petrograd in 1922, Aleksii legalised the Living Church under pressure from the GPU, removing excommunication from three leaders of the schism, who had been excommunicated by Aleksii's arrested superior, Metropolitan Veniamin of Petrograd.[46]

Metropolitan Sergii returned from the Renovationists to the Patriarchal Church through penitence after the release of Patriarch Tikhon, when the failure of the Renovationists became evident. His politics, as a *locum tenens* of the Patriarchal Throne after the death of Patriarch Tikhon, were the subject of numerous studies.[47] His figure and policy were controversial and provoked various responses. Lev Regelson's study provides the key to Metropolitan Sergii's political thinking. Regelson maintains that Metropolitan Sergii almost usurped church authority to restore the centralised bureaucratic synodal structure. But the restoration of this structure was more in line with the politics of the Living Church than with the legacy of Patriarch Tikhon.[48] As Regelson pointed out, the Church Council of 1917–18 'reinstated the Patriarchate, and the Patriarchate affirmed the personal dignity of the Church's bishop, and, finally, the dignity of the bishop restored the previously destroyed conciliatory spirit (*sobornost'*)' of the ROC.[49] Renovationism, on the contrary, was an extremely reactionary movement in spite of its reforms, sharing the old political philosophy of church-state symphony and synodal-bureaucratic church government.[50]

Metropolitan Sergii, rejecting the innovations of the Living Church and its socialist political jargon, as well as its scandalous co-operation with the GPU, nevertheless preserved its political philosophy and its practice of centralised bureaucratic church organisation. Both the Living Church and Sergii's church government were surrendered to state control, and enjoyed its very limited and dubious protection.[51]

His contemporaries, priests and bishops, accused Sergii, saying that 'he had renounced Church freedom and at the same time had preserved the fictions of canonicity and Orthodoxy'.[52]

It is noteworthy that the book *Patriarch Sergii and his Spiritual Legacy* contains a favourable reference to the authority of Feofan Prokopovich. Outlining a prospected programme for religious instruction, and emphasising the need to train pastors as 'exemplary members of society' and 'model citizens', the book cites Prokopovich's appeal to the priests of his time to serve the state with devotion.[53]

Even a Soviet student of the ROC who had studied its policy from a communist perspective maintained that the church organisation restored by Sergii under the name of the Moscow Patriarchate combined the traditional Orthodox forms with the political opportunism of the Renovationists.[54]

A centralised church government with an autocratic patriarch totally controlled by the government helped to surrender the church to the totalitarian regime and to deprive it of its freedom.

The rudiments of the church's freedom and independence, introduced by the All-Russian Sobor, and preserved by Patriarch Tikhon and by the bishops that remained faithful to his testament, disappeared when the old philosophy of alliance with the state, albeit a state inspired by atheistic and anti-clerical ideology, prevailed. The church leaders with the old imperial mentality returned the church to its familiar course.

Thus we can discern in the background of the ROC policy of our century two ecclesiastical trends in Russian history which we can designate as 'the Novgorod legacy' and 'the Moscow legacy'. The All-Russian Sobor, Patriarch Tikhon and the imprisoned Bishops (in the Solovki camp) restored the ROC to the dignity of a free spiritual body, above political struggle. Their position clearly favoured law, order, and a structure of political freedom that would guarantee the freedom of the church to remain faithful to its spirit of sobornost'. It was 'the Novgorod legacy' which they had in mind, realising, however, that the time of the Orthodox theocracy had passed. Therefore the Solovki bishops' letter insisted on the implementation of a Soviet law on the separation of the church from the state. To their thinking the model of a theocratic Orthodox republic was replaced by the vision of a modern democratic pluralistic society, which respects the freedom of the individual and of association and would respect the freedom of the church.

The Karlovtsy Synod, the Renovationists, and the post-war MP—all remained linked to the 'Moscow legacy', the tradition which subjugated the church to the authority of the state and its immediate political interests. Today it seems that ROC political conservatism and its total subjugation to state policy is overwhelming.

But what we call the 'Novgorod legacy' is not totally dead. It has strong supporters among some clerics and faithful. It is this philosophy that has influenced the emergence of church dissent and the ROC's involvement in the Human Rights Movement.[55] Today it is this philosophy that inspires church activists who have launched independent publications in order to shape a new church position in the ecclesiastical as well as in the political arena.[56] The general awakening of public democratic activity in the beginning of this century inspired the same attitude among church leaders and resulted in the All-Russian Council and the restoration of the Patriarchate. One can hope that the contemporary awakening of public political activism under perestroika will also eventually reawaken the aspirations for freedom among the hierarchs of the ROC, and that they will remember the forgotten 'Novgorod legacy' left to them by their predecessors, confessors and martyrs.

NOTES

1. Henceforth referred to as ROC.
2. A. Levitin-Krasnov, V. Shavrov, *Ocherki po istorii russkoi tserkovnoi smuty*, 3 vols (Küsnacht: 1977) vol. I, p. 96ff, 162ff.
3. G. P. Fedotov, *The Russian Religious Mind (II)*, in *The Collected Works of G. P. Fedotov*, 4 vols (Belmont: 1978) vol. IV, pp. 186–93.
4. G. P. Fedotov, *The Russian Religious Mind (II)*, p. 194.
5. J. H. Billington, *The Icon and the Axe, An Interpretive History of Russian Culture* (New York: 1970) pp. 92–3.
6. G. P. Fedotov, *St Filipp, Metropolitan of Moscow—Encounter with Ivan the Terrible*, in *The Collected Works of G. P. Fedotov*, 4 vols (Belmont: 1978) vol. I, p. 143.
7. See A. V. Kartashev, 'Delo Arseniia Matsievicha', in his *Ocherki po istorii Russkoi Tserkvi*, 2 vols (Paris: 1959) vol. II, pp. 456–80.
8. G. V. Florovskii (Archpriest), *Puti russkogo bogosloviia*, 2nd edn (Paris: 1981) pp. 82–105.
9. G. V. Florovskii, *Puti russkogo bogosloviia*, pp. 86–7.
10. Eusebius, *Life of Constantine*, NPNF, v. I, l. 24–31.
11. See K. P. Pobedonostsev, *Reflections of a Russian Statesman*, trans.

R. C. Long (Ann Arbor: 1965) pp. 254, 27–8, 32–58.

12. Bishop Feofan the Recluse, *Put' ko spaseniiu: Nachertanie khristians-kogo nravoucheniia*, 2nd edn (Moscow: 1895) pp. 514–18.

13. V. M. Skvortsov, *Tserkovnyi Sovet i gosudarstvennyi razum, (sbornik tsitat)*, Spb., 1912 quoted from L. Regelson, *Tragediia Russkoi Tserkvi 1917–1945* (Paris: 1977) pp. 21–2.

14. See P. Walters, 'The Russian Orthodox Church', in *Eastern Christianity and Politics in the Twentieth Century*, ed. P. Ramet (Durham, NC: Duke University Press, 1988) pp. 65–7; for a detailed study of the bishops' mood, see J. W. Cunningham, *A Vanquished Hope, The Movement for Church Renewal in Russia, 1905–1906* (New York: 1981).

15. P. Walters, 'The Russian Orthodox Church', p. 68.

16. L. Regelson, *Tragediia Russkoi Tserkvi 1917–1945*, pp. 25–7.

17. L. Regelson, *Tragediia Russkoi Tserkvi 1917–1945*, p. 28.

18. See D. Pospielovsky, *The Russian Orthodox Church under the Soviet Regime, 1917–1982*, 2 vols (New York: 1984) vol. I, pp. 43–92, 113–33.

19. L. Regelson, *Tragediia Russkoi Tserkvi 1917–1945*, p. 33.

20. A good insight into the Patriarch's mind is given in several sermons of Fr. Sergii Bulgakov. 'Slovo o patriarkhe Tikhone, 1923, 1923, 1925' in Sergii Bulgakov (Protopop), *Slova, poucheniia, besedy* (Paris: 1987) pp. 463–82.

21. Circular letter of Patriarch Tikhon to the archpastors of the ROC, calling on them to avoid involvement in political struggle. (Letter of 25 Sept./8 Oct. 1919.) Order of Highest Church Authorities no. 21–22. Quoted from L. Regelson, *Tragediia Russkoi Tserkvi 1917–1945*, pp. 262–4.

22. See the text in A. Levitin-Krasnov, V. Shavrov, *Ocherki po istorii russkoi tserkovnoi smuty*, vol. II, pp. 152–6.

23. 'Pis'ma mitr. Anastasiia k G. N. Trubetskomu', in *Vestnik Russkogo Khristianskogo Dvizheniia*, 151 (1987) pp. 227–37 (229–30).

24. 'Obrashchenie pravoslavnykh episkopov iz Solovetskikh ostrovov k Pravitel'stvu SSSR', in *Vestnik Russkogo Khristianskogo Dvizheniia*, 152 (1988) pp. 193–206.

25. Ibid., p. 194.

26. Ibid., p. 196.

27. Ibid., p. 202.

28. Ibid., p. 203.

29. One can easily see the political implementation of this philosophy, by comparing it with the ideology of the Human Rights movement which was developed in the late 1960s and the 1970s by Soviet dissidents. See, D. Nelidov, 'Ideocratic Consciousness and Personality'; V. Chalidze, 'Important Aspects of Human Rights in the Soviet Union'; M. Meerson-Aksenov, 'The Dissident Movement and Samizdat', in *The Political, Social and Religious Thought of Russian 'Samizdat'—an Anthology*, ed. M. Meerson-Aksenov and B. Shagrin (Belmont: 1977).

30. See the story of the expulsion of the former Duma Chairman, Michael Rodzyanko from Karlovtsy Sobor in D. Pospielovsky, *The Russian Church under the Soviet Regime, 1917–1982*, vol. I, pp. 116–17.

31. Published in D. Pospielovsky, *The Russian Church under the Soviet Regime, 1917–1982*, vol. II, appendix 5, pp. 491–2.

32. 'We have learned from most reliable sources,—writes Anastasii,—that the faithful in Russia, groaning under the yoke of serfdom, await their deliverer and pray to God unceasingly that He will preserve you, guide you and grant you His all-powerful help. Your great achievements on behalf of the German people and towards the greatness of the German Empire have made you an example worthy of imitation, a model of devotion to one's own people and one's Fatherland, and of how one must stand up for one's national and spiritual values. These values also find their consecration and immortalization in our Church ... You have erected a House to the Heavenly Lord. May He bless your national building labours—the creation of your Empire ... In the name of the Bishop's Synod of the Russian Orthodox Church abroad.' Ibid.

33. A. Levitin-Krasnov, V. Shavrov, *Ocherki po istorii russkoi tserkovnoi smuty*, vol. I, pp. 52–3.

34. Ibid., pp. 64–6.

35. Ibid., pp. 88–9.

36. Ibid., p. 98.

37. In this memorandum, prepared by the priest Kalinovskii, one of the four initial members of the Central Committee of the 'Living Church', and sent to VTZIK (All-Soviet Central Executive Committee), leaders of the 'LC' suggest: (1) that those Orthodox clerics and laymen who are loyal to the Soviet Regime be selected in order to 'protect them' from the Hierarchy faithful to the Patriarch Tikhon; (2) that these people be organised into the All-State union for the purpose of elaboration of the joint church-state platform; (3) that this union be appointed to watch over the Patriarchal office and to implement all state decisions which are not harmful to the religious and moral feelings of the Orthodox populace. The memorandum was published in issue no. 2 of the journal *Zhivaia Tserkov'*, pp. 128–129.

38. On Feofan's involvement with the Secret Police, particularly in the time of the 'Bironovshchina', see A. V. Kartashev, *Ocherki po istorii Russkoi Tserkvi*, vol. II, pp. 395–99, and G. V. Florovskii, *Puti russkogo bogosloviia*, pp. 89–90.

39. Henceforth referred to as MP.

40. D. Konstantinov, *Gonimaia tserkov'*, Vseslavianskoe Izdatel'stvo (All-Slavic Publishing House, New York: 1967) p. 89. See also W. Fletcher, *Religion and Soviet Foreign Policy, 1945–1970* (London: 1973).

41. Dneprov, 'Vsenarodnoe Sobranie, *Zhurnal moskovskoi patriarkhii* (1955) 6, p. 27.

42. Archbishop Nikodim, 'Mir i svoboda', *Zhurnal moskovskoi patriarkhii* (1963) 1, pp. 39–44. Quoted from D. Konstantinov, *Gonimaia tserkov'*, pp. 108–09.

43. See *Zhurnal moskovskoi patriarkhii* (1987) 11.

44. 'Pis'mo gruppy sviashchennikov i mirian patriarkhu Pimenu', *Vestnik Russkogo Khristianskogo Dvizheniia*, 151 (1987) pp. 211–15.

45. A brief biography with insight into his character is given in A. Levitin-

Krasnov, V. Shavrov, *Ocherki po istorii russkoi tserkovnoi smuty*, vol. I, pp. 166–70.

46. See A. Levitin-Krasnov's 'Neopublikovannaia stranitsa iz zhizni patriarkha Aleksiia' in *Ocherki po istorii russkoi tserkovnoi smuty*, vol. I, pp. 103–06.

47. See D. Pospielovsky, *The Russian Church under the Soviet Regime, 1917–1982*; L. Regelson, *Tragediia Russkoi Tserkvi 1917–1945*; N. Struve, *Les Chrétiens en URSS* (Paris: 1963) pp. 36–70; *Patriarkh Sergii i ego dukhovnoe nasledstvo* (Moscow: 1947).

48. L. Regelson, *Tragediia Russkoi Tserkvi 1917–1945*, pp. 96–195.

49. Ibid., p. 70.

50. Ibid., p. 96.

51. 'Despite Sergii's Declaration, he was never given the opportunity until the Second World War to give any practical demonstration to his loyalty. All religions suffered savage and comprehensive persecution during the late 1920s and 1930s . . . By 1939 the Orthodox church had virtually ceased to exist as an institution . . .', P. Walters, 'The Russian Orthodox Church', p. 75.

52. Ibid., p. 146.

53. 'Patriarkh Sergii i ego dukhovnoe nasledstvo', Moscow, 1947, p. 400. Quoted from Nadezhda Teodorovich, 'Curricular Changes in Soviet Theological Schools' in *Religion in the USSR*, Institute for the Study of the USSR, Munich, Series I, no. 59, July 1960, p. 45.

54. See A. A. Shishkin, *Sut' i kriticheskaia otsenka 'Obnovlencheskogo' raskola russkoi pravoslavnoi tserkvi* (Kazan': 1970).

55. See ch. 'Pravoslavnye' in L. Alekseeva, *Istoriia inakomysliia v SSSR. noveishii period* (Benson: 1984) pp. 217–36.

56. See, for instance, the journal *Vybor* edited by Aksiuchits and Anishchenko, and *Biulleten' khristianskoi obshchiny* published by Ogorodnikov.

14 The Rise of the Ukrainian Autocephalous Orthodox Church, 1919–22

Bohdan R. Bociurkiw

The emergence of the Ukrainian Autocephalous Orthodox Church (UAOC) in post-revolutionary Ukraine and its final constitution at the All-Ukrainian Sobor in October 1921 represents a major divide in modern Ukrainian ecclesiastical history, at the confluence of national, social and religious revolutions triggered by the overthrow of the Tsarist regime in 1917.

The legacy of the long Russian domination over the Ukrainian Orthodox Church not only placed the latter outside the mainstream of Ukrainian cultural and political revival; it also made the church into an ideological and institutional weapon determined to block the progress of the Ukrainian people toward nationhood and political independence.[1]

The extent of alienation of the established church from Ukrainian society was reflected in the ethnic make-up of the episcopate in the nine 'Ukrainian' dioceses in 1915: of the nine diocesan bishops eight were Russians and only one ethnic Ukrainian; among the 15 vicar bishops only two were of Ukrainian origin.[2]

Russified theological schools and monasteries in Ukraine zealously guarded against the infiltration of 'Ukrainophile' influences. They produced a clergy that with few exceptions was alien to Ukrainian national and social aspirations. This also reflected the degree of submergence of the national identity of the Ukrainian masses and the weakness of the Ukrainian national movement. Thus, according to the 1897 imperial census, Russians who represented only 4.3 per cent of the population in Right-Bank Ukraine (the Kiev, Podillia and Volhynia *gubernii*), constituted 48.5 per cent of all the priests and male monastics in that region; in Left-Bank Ukraine (the Chernihiv,

Poltava and Kharkiv gubernii), where Russians comprised 13.3 per cent of the population, they accounted for 31.3 per cent of the male clergy; while in the southern gubernii of Katerynoslav, Kherson and Tavriia, 64.0 per cent of the priests and male monastics were Russian (but only 21.4 per cent of the population).[3]

Catalysed by the revolution of 1917, the Ukrainian church movement emerged as a reaction against this state of affairs in the church. It was nourished by a combination of indignant nationalism, ecclesiastical radicalism, and fundamentalist religious zeal. On the one hand, the movement represented a projection of renascent Ukrainian nationalism upon the ecclesiastical–religious scene. With the political forces of the day, it shared the ultimate aim of the Ukrainian revolution—the recovery of the Ukraine's national identity, heritage and freedom through emancipation from Russian control. On the other hand, paralleling the evolution of the aspirations of the Ukrainian revolution from federalism to independence, the Ukrainian church movement progressed from its initial aspirations for ecclesiastical autonomy and Ukrainianisation of the liturgy toward demands for the autocephaly of the Ukrainian Church. In the Ukrainian context, it expressed the aspirations of the progressive movement within the Russian Orthodox Church for the democratisation of the Church on a conciliar basis; an equalisation in the status of the white and black clergy and the curtailment of episcopal domination; the renovation of the Church, especially at the parish level; and the establishment of harmony between the Church and the aspirations of the people.[4]

Arrayed against the national church movement was virtually the entire episcopate of Ukraine. The episcopate was supported by the ecclesiastical administrative apparatus and nearly all the monastic clergy, and commanded the considerable material resources of the local church. This formidable force, containing some of the outstanding representatives of political reaction and militant clericalism in Russia was headed in 1917–18 by Metropolitan Antonii Khrapovitskii. A powerful figure with considerable gifts of leadership and persuasion, of vast ambition and authority, he maintained a remarkable hold on the loyalties of the ecclesiastical elite in Ukraine.[5] This stratum's perception of the Ukrainian problem was shaped by a combination of Russian nationalism, conservatism, and complete misunderstanding of the dynamics of the Ukrainian revolution. Hence, their disdain and ridicule of the Ukrainian language as either a crude dialect of 'Little Russian' peasants or a 'Galician invention';

their notion of the Ukrainian people as an integral part of the Russian nation, without a distinct past or future; their view of Ukrainian nationalism as an artificial and unpopular creation of misguided intellectuals and enemy-inspired troublemakers; and their opinion of the Ukrainian church movement as an exclusively politically-inspired venture of a handful of malcontent priests and radicals devoid of true faith and alien to the pious masses.[6]

At the same time, the canonical framework and the hierarchical structure of the Orthodox Church supplied the Russian episcopate, as the exclusive repository of the apostolic succession and of canonical authority, with formidable weapons against the opponents of the status quo. Not only could the bishops resort to ecclesiastical sanctions against the 'anti-canonical' acts of the clergy and believers at will; they also had the forces of mass inertia and habit on their side, the conservative spirit of the church, and in particular the vigorous support of powerful nationalist and reactionary Russian elements strategically entrenched in Ukrainian cities.

The Ukrainian revolution provided the autocephalist movement with the historically tested, if not canonical, alternative of relying on state legislation and administrative measures to establish harmony between the Church and Ukrainian national interests. Unfortunately for the movement, the Central Rada government, which probably stood the best chance of enforcing the Ukrainianisation of the Church, intervened belatedly and only half-heartedly in support of this cause. The Hetmanate, though taking a positive attitude toward ecclesiastical affairs and professing sympathy for the nationalisation of the Church, was too dependent on the acquiescence of conservative Russian strata to break the open defiance of the Ukrainian cause by the Russian episcopate with state power. Eventually, in a futile attempt to salvage his regime, Skoropads'kyi sacrificed the cause of the emancipation of the Ukrainian Church along with Ukrainian independence. The Directory acted promptly and forcefully to implement the objectives of the Ukrainian autocephalist movement by law in January 1919, but the Directory's life-span was simply too short to implement effectively its decree on autocephaly. Of the several causes that prevented the autocephalists from breaking the opposition of the ecclesiastical authorities, the instability of the Ukrainian national government was the most obvious.[7]

As the Russian-Ukrainian struggle for the control of the church increased in bitterness, the chances for a compromise solution espoused by Russian Church liberals—broad autonomy of the Ukrainian Church under the limited authority of Moscow, coupled with a gradual Ukrainianisation of the Church—rapidly decreased with the polarisation and growing rigidity of the attitudes of the contending camps. The two major documents of this period—the 'autonomous' statute as finally adopted in November 1918 by the All-Ukrainian Church Sobor,[8] and the January 1919 Ukrainian government decree on autocephaly[9]—illustrated the irreconcilability of the positions taken on the one hand by the Moscow Patriarchate and its spokesmen in Ukraine, and on the other by the Ukrainian autocephalists and their governmental supporters. Neither of these two documents could be said to have finally settled the controversy. With some support from Russian church liberals, the Ukrainian side persistently denied the validity of the 1918 statute on such grounds as the arbitrary composition and procedures of the All-Ukrainian Sobor and the failure of the statute to secure the required approval of the state. The supporters of the Moscow patriarchate rejected the Directory's law on autocephaly as a unilateral act of the Ukrainian government that had never been approved by the canonical leadership of the Church. While the Bolshevik victory prevented the implementation of the 1919 decree on autocephaly, the former document—the 1918 statute as amended by the Patriarch—was of minor practical significance in guiding the internal affairs of the Russian Orthodox Church in Ukraine after 1921.

As hopes for the survival of Ukrainian statehood faded away, the Ukrainian autocephalist movement came to face a momentous decision. Frustrated in its attempts to de-Russify the Church from above, it could either admit defeat and disband, and perhaps work slowly toward these aims within the church, or resort to a church revolution, sever its canonical links with the Russian Church and form a separate church organisation that would undertake the Ukrainianisation of the church from the grass roots by winning over Ukrainian believers and progressively depriving the Russian Church of its parishes in Ukraine.

The Russian Orthodox Church in Ukraine emerged from the Civil War in a difficult and vulnerable position. Compromised in the eyes of the victorious Bolsheviks by its close collaboration with the Russian Whites, the Church had by 1920 lost most of its diocesan bishops, including such prominent ecclesiastical leaders as Metropolitans Antonii of Kiev and Platon of Odessa, Archbishops Evlogii of Volhynia and Feofan of Poltava, who accompanied the remnants of the Denikin-Vrangel' armies into exile, where they formed the core of the anti-Soviet Karlovtsy Sobor. While in most of the Ukrainian dioceses the vacant sees were soon filled by vicar bishops, the 'autonomous' Ukrainian Church remained without a canonical head until August 1921, when Metropolitan Mikhail (Ermakov) arrived in Kiev as the first in a series of patriarchal exarchs for Ukraine. In the meantime, in 1919–21, the Kievan Metropolitanate was administered by the Kievan Ecclesiastical Administration (Sobor of Bishops)—a council of the see's vicars.[10] According to the rules adopted in 1918 by the All-Ukrainian Church Sobor and confirmed in the Patriarchal grant of autonomy, the Metropolitan of Kiev was to be elected by a Ukrainian Sobor, but only upon the death or resignation of the previous occupant of the see; as neither of these conditions existed at that time, the Patriarchate resorted to the appointment of an exarch for Ukraine, a temporary measure that was destined to continue to the present day. Metropolitan Mikhail was a Russian with a limited knowledge of Ukrainian conditions.[11] However, in his new position, he managed to establish some order in the local ecclesiastical organisation, but failed in his main task of averting the autocephalist revolution in the Church. Like his predecessor—the interim Kievan Sobor of Bishops—Mikhail took an irreconcilable position toward the 'Ukrainian schism' and by rejecting the request of the 1921 Sobor for a canonical Ukrainian bishop assumed partial responsibility for the final break of the Ukrainian movement with the Patriarchal Church.

The return of the Bolsheviks in 1920 brought the Church in Ukraine into the mainstream of the three-year-old conflict between the Church and the new regime. With the Soviet Ukrainian government now following the RSFSR in carrying out anti-religious legislation, the pressure on the Orthodox Church and other religious communities in Ukraine increased rapidly. The implementation of the Separation Decree, promulgated on 22 January 1919, and the expropriation of ecclesiastical property left the Exarchate and the diocesan administrations in a precarious extra-legal position, with the bishops and clergy placed in material dependence on the atomised 'groups of believers' and left at the mercy of the Soviet administration and police. A number of monasteries and convents were disbanded by the authorities. Ecclesiastical publications ceased to appear and theological education came to a virtual standstill.

The Separation Decree moved the centre of gravity from the Russian Orthodox hierarchy to the laity who were more responsive to

Ukrainian influences than the higher strata of the church. At the same time, the new law cast the Soviet authorities in the role of arbiter in this intra-church conflict.[12]

It is unlikely that the Ukrainian autocephalists had any illusions about the Bolshevik attitude toward religion; nevertheless, the new regulations on religious activities offered the Ukrainian movement an opportunity to proceed with a de-Russification of the Orthodox Church 'from below' by organising Ukrainian 'twenties' (groups of a minimum of 20, later 50 laymen required under Soviet law for the registration of a parish and the lease of a nationalised church building) and thus taking over individual churches and parishes. The Soviet authorities, for their part, welcomed this opportunity to weaken from within their principal ecclesiastical adversary—the Russian Orthodox Church. In this manner, three Ukrainian parishes were formed in Kiev by mid-summer 1919, despite opposition on the part of the administrator of the Kiev diocese, Bishop Nazarii (Blinov) of Cherkasy.[13] Among the 'Ukrainianised' churches was the oldest venerated Ukrainian shrine, St Sophia's Cathedral, which henceforth became the centre of the autocephalist movement.

To meet indiscriminate anti-Ukrainian agitation on the part of the local Russian clergy, who charged the national church movement with Bolshevik, Uniate or Protestant tendencies, the Ukrainian parishes of Kiev issued a joint public declaration titled: 'What are the Vital Objectives of Orthodox Ukrainians?' In denying the above charges, the declaration listed three principal objectives of the movement: (1) the introduction of the Ukrainian language into church services and the revival of native religious rites and traditions; (2) a return to the *sobornopravnist'*, that is, a conciliar system of ecclesiastical government, including the election of bishops and clergy by laymen and the participation of the latter in all phases of church life; and (3) the autocephaly of the Ukrainian Orthodox Church within the ecumenical Orthodox Church.[14]

Meanwhile, on 17 April 1919, the leaders of the lay movement constituted themselves as the All-Ukrainian Orthodox Church Council (*Rada*), thus resuming the name under which the movement had been launched in 1917.[15] A year later, after the Bolsheviks had recaptured Kiev, the All-Ukrainian *Rada* followed the new Soviet regulations and registered a statute of the 'Union of Ukrainian Parishes' which provided for a nationwide organisation of parishes with a hierarchy of councils (*rady*).[16] It was the first church statute that was legalised by the Soviet Ukrainian Government.

The local Orthodox episcopate assumed a hostile attitude towards the questions of the Ukrainianisation of parishes and church services. The two-year-old conflict was further aggravated by the tactics of the *Rada*, which not only by-passed the episcopate and dealt directly with the authorities, but also assumed *de facto* jurisdiction over the Ukrainian parishes, instructing them not to submit to the bishops' authority and to remove any mention of the Patriarch's name from the liturgy.

Yet for some time, the *Rada* avoided a complete break with the Russian episcopate. For his part, Patriarch Tikhon urged moderation and patience on both sides. But the dispute over the Kievan St Sophia's Cathedral, which had been taken over by a newly-organised Ukrainian parish against episcopal opposition, precipitated a split in the Church. On 30 April 1920 Bishop Nazarii suspended all the clergy of the Ukrainian parishes affiliated with the *Rada* and prohibited all services in the Ukrainian language.[17]

It is difficult to determine whether or not the bishop's action was a premeditated attempt to force the Ukrainian church movement into the position of a non-canonical, schismatic sect; he might have hoped that such a wholesale prohibition would shock the clerical members of the movement into submission to the episcopate. Whatever motivated Nazarii's move, its immediate consequence seemed to be the final break between the Russian Orthodox Church and the Ukrainian movement, and the formal proclamation by the latter of an independent Orthodox Church.

On 5 May 1920, on the eve of the entrance of the allied Polish and Ukrainian troops into Kiev, an enlarged meeting of the *Rada* decided to accept the challenge and to break off all ties with the Russian Church. The fateful decision of the *Rada* was communicated to the Ukrainian community in a lengthy manifesto ('The First Letter'), a 'declaration of independence' of the Ukrainian Autocephalous Orthodox Church.[18]

Despite its revolutionary tone, the proclamation of Ukrainian autocephaly met with a favourable response from the Ukrainian community. In early June, a conference of the representatives of the Kievan and adjoining Ukrainian parishes ratified this decision of the All-Ukrainian *Rada*, and elected first candidates for bishops; it was hoped that perhaps one of the foreign Orthodox Churches might be persuaded to consecrate the episcopate for the Ukrainian Church.[19] In the meantime, the Autocephalous Church began to expand rapidly beyond the Kievan gubernia, the stronghold of the movement. Within a few months, new Ukrainian parishes had sprung up in most of the larger Ukrainian cities (Vinnytsia, Kam"ianets', Zhytomyr, Chernihiv, Odessa, Mykolaiv, Kherson), as well as in the country.[20]

In the countryside, Ukrainian autocephalists attracted some followers from the left-wing Ukrainian parties, especially members of the UKP (Ukrainian Communist Party) frustrated by the Ukrainophobia of the ruling Bolshevik Party.[21] It was thanks to their members' support that the Ukrainian Church movement succeeded in getting the endorsement of the Kiev district congress of *komnezamy* (Committees of Poor Peasants) in August 1920. Its resolution, that divine services in all churches of the Kiev district be celebrated in Ukrainian, was widely disseminated by the autocephalists to intensify pressure for the Ukrainianisation of the parishes, until the embarrassed Soviet authorities intervened in mid-1921 to eliminate autocephalist influence in the komnezamy.[22]

Although it won considerable support among the laity, the Autocephalous Church attracted almost no new converts from the Orthodox clergy. Since no bishop would ordain priests for the Ukrainian Autocephalous Church, the latter was faced with a serious shortage of priests as the number of its parishes continued to grow. The future of the church therefore depended upon a successful solution to the problem of the Ukrainian episcopate—the chief problem of the movement from its very inception.

It was in the summer of 1920 that the All-Ukrainian *Rada* found what seemed to be a happy solution. Through the 'Ukrainian Church Brotherhood' in Poltava, another hitherto independent centre of the national church movement, the *Rada* established contact with the newly-appointed administrator of the local diocese, Archbishop Parfenii Levyts'kyi, a Ukrainian well known for his past sponsorship of the translation of the Gospels into Ukrainian.[23] In August, the *Rada* sent Parfenii a delegation that was headed by its chairman, M. Moroz and the spiritual leader of the Autocephalous Church, Archpriest V. Lypkivs'kyi. Supported by the local brotherhood, the delegates persuaded the archbishop to assume leadership over the Ukrainian Church. On 21 August 1920, Parfenii—now accorded by the movement the title of the 'All-Ukrainian Archbishop'—wrote a declaration in which he blessed the work of the *Rada* and its parishes 'for the creation of a living, conciliar (sobornopravna) and free Ukrainian Church, native to the Ukrainian people by its language, traditions and rites'. For the sake of 'peace within the church and the preservation of unity of the Christian flock,' Parfenii agreed to assume 'care' of the autocephalist parishes and promised to ordain new Ukrainian priests, but he declined the *Rada*'s request to consecrate a bishop for the Ukrainianised parishes as 'untimely'.[24]

Parfenii's identification with the cause of the *Rada* added to the canonical respectability and popular appeal of the Autocephalous Church. During the few subsequent months, the archbishop ordained some thirty priests for the rapidly multiplying Ukrainian parishes; some hitherto 'neutral' clergymen now joined the autocephalists.[25]

In the meantime, Archbishop Parfenii found himself under growing pressure from the Kievan bishops and Patriarch Tikhon to break his relations with the autocephalists. Following his agreement with the *Rada*, Parfenii wrote to Bishop Nazarii on 24 August: 'It is no problem if they [the autocephalists] pray in Ukrainian. But it would be an irreparable tragedy if they leave the Church.' He begged Nazarii 'not to hinder Ukrainians from celebrating [the liturgy] in Ukrainian' and to lift his suspension of the Kievan clergy. Parfenii also urged him to ordain candidates presented by the Ukrainians. Nazarii's bitter reply of 7 September reiterated the autocephalist 'sins', thereby rejecting Parfenii's pleas. Later in the fall, responding to Nazarii's complaint, Patriarch Tikhon wrote to Parfenii urging him to put an end to his interference in the affairs of the Kievan diocese. Nazarii's suggestion of several measures 'for the restoration of ecclesiastical peace in Ukraine' were approved by Patriarch Tikhon in December 1920. Far from meeting the autocephalist demands, the concessions included the establishment in Kiev of a committee of experts which would undertake to translate liturgical and other texts from Church Slavonic into Ukrainian; at the same time, the clergy of the Kievan diocese were allowed to adopt a Ukrainian pronunciation of Church Slavonic and to read the Gospel in Ukrainian during the liturgy.[26]

While Parfenii would not formally repudiate the All-Ukrainian Church Rada, he ceased, as of January 1921, to ordain the *Rada*'s candidates for the priesthood.[27] In February, a sobor of bishops in Kiev decided to defrock all the autocephalist priests and to order an immediate dissolution of the *Rada*.

In response, the *Rada* convened on 27–28 March 1921, a 'pre-sobor conference' of rural parish representatives of the Kiev region. The gathering declared 'the so-called Holy Sobor of Bishops of the Entire Ukraine' as devoid of any authority over the Ukrainian Church in view of the *Rada*'s May 1920 proclamation of Ukrainian autocephaly. Declaring the Kievan see vacant, the conference authorised the *Rada* to invite Archbishop Parfenii to take over the direction of the Kiev metropolitanate and have him elected to this see at the Kiev guberniia sobor in May. At the same time, the gathering voted, in departure from the existing canons, to make married candidates eligible for the episcopal ordination and to allow remarriage and divorce of the clergy.[28]

The April meeting was followed by a church conference of the Kiev guberniia, which met on 22–26 May under the chairmanship of Mykhailo Moroz. Closely watched by both the Soviet authorities and the Russian Church for indications of the dynamics and direction of the Ukrainian autocephalist movement, the meeting attracted 412 delegates, including 58 priests and 12 deacons, as well as representatives from other Ukrainian guberniia. Conspicuously absent was the 'All-Ukrainian Archbishop' Parfenii of Poltava, though, according to Lypkivs'kyi, the delegates were assured by his 'representative' of Parfenii's continuing support. Despite the absence of bishops, the conference assumed the name and prerogatives of a church sobor and declared that it could alter church canons to correspond to changed circumstances. The Kiev sobor then proceeded to ratify the autocephaly of the Ukrainian Orthodox Church and the resolutions of the April conference; it approved the conciliar structure of the church based on a hierarchy of church councils headed by the All-Ukrainian *Rada* which limited the authority of bishops within the Ukrainian Autocephalous Church to spiritual leadership. Declaring the Kievan see vacant, the gathering elected Archbishop Parfenii as Metropolitan of Kiev and a reformist Bishop, Antonin (Hranovs'kyi)—a Ukrainian living in involuntary retirement in Moscow—as Parfenii's deputy. The Kiev sobor elected nine priests and one layman as candidates for bishops (about a half of whom were married), and announced the convocation of an All-Ukrainian Sobor of the Ukrainian Autocephalous Orthodox Church (UAOC) for October 1921.[29]

The decisions of the Kievan guberniia sobor of 22–26 May 1921 precipitated a final rupture between Archbishop Parfenii and the UAOC. In his report to the Sobor of Bishops of the Entire Ukraine, dated 15 June 1921, Parfenii declared that the Kiev sobor took place without his permission or blessing, that he was elected as 'All-Ukrainian Archbishop' 'without his knowledge and consent', that he did not accept the title conferred upon him, and that he could not accept resolutions of the sobor on such matters as the abolition of canons, on the Kievan episcopate or on the administration of the Ukrainian Church, which he considered 'a radical departure from the teaching and practice of the Orthodox Church'.[30] Parfenii's declaration was given wide publicity by the Sobor of Bishops, hurting the autocephalist cause among the conservative-minded Ukrainian clergy and widening the differences over the Ukrainian church movement's future strategy within the All-Ukrainian *Rada* itself.

Bishop Antonin (Hranovs'kyi), who had for some time maintained contacts with the All-Ukrainian Church *Rada* and encouraged its Ukrainianisation efforts,[31] was now approached by the *Rada* to assume the canonical leadership of the UAOC. Antonin did not repudiate his election as Parfenii's deputy at the May sobor, and, according to V. Lypkivs'kyi, agreed to assume the Kievan post, but when a *Rada* representative was sent to Moscow to help him with the move to Kiev, he changed his mind and declined the post.[32] As it later turned out, he was not sympathetic to the idea of married bishops and considered the 'self-ordination' of bishops by clergy and laymen a major tragedy for the Ukrainian Church.[33]

The radicalism of the Kiev Sobor majority was reinforced and given theological foundation by Volodymyr Chekhivs'kyi, a former premier of the Ukrainian government, who had been co-opted by the All-Ukrainian *Rada*. Having broken with the oppositionist Ukrainian Communist Party (UKP) over its attitude toward religion, Chekhivs'kyi had declined to accept a unanimous episcopal nomination at the May Sobor, but had emerged as the chief ideologist of the UAOC and the principal proponent of even more extensive canonical reforms. On the other hand, the conservative minority in the autocephalist leadership (priests Ksenofont Sokolovs'kyi, Serhii Pylypenko and Pavlo Pohorilko) were pressing the *Rada* to seek the ordination of Ukrainian candidates by the bishops of the Russian Church or the newly autocephalous Georgian Orthodox Church. When, on 15 August 1921, the Sobor of Bishops met in Kiev under the newly-appointed patriarchal 'Exarch of Ukraine', Metropolitan Mikhail (Ermakov), the All-Ukrainian Rada approached the bishops to create an extraterritorial diocese for Ukrainian autocephalists and to ordain the *Rada*'s candidate as bishop for such an eparchy.[34] After the rejection of its request, the *Rada* dispatched two widowed episcopal candidates for bishops (Pavlo Pohorilko and Stepan Orlyk) to Georgia, to seek ordination by the Georgian Patriarch-Catholicos;

but the hostilities between Soviet Russia and independent Georgia prevented the two priests from travelling beyond Kharkiv. In desperation, they visited the two Ukrainian archbishops—Parfenii of Poltava and Ahapit (Vyshnevs'kyi) of Katerynoslav—but having failed to convince the hierarchs to ordain them, they returned to Kiev on the opening day of the All-Ukrainian Sobor, 14 October.[35]

The First All-Ukrainian Church Sobor, which convened in the St Sophia Cathedral in Kiev on 15 October 1921, brought together over 400 delegates representing nearly all Ukrainian gubernii and the Kuban' region. Among the delegates were 64 priests and many leading representatives of the Ukrainian intelligentsia.[36] The *Rada* had also sent out invitations to all bishops, but Exarch Mikhail announced that any bishop or priest participating in the Sobor would be expelled from the Church. As a result, no bishop attended the Sobor. Given the situation, two questions were paramount in the delegates' minds: (1) in the absence of even a single bishop, was this gathering a canonically valid sobor, empowered to speak for the Ukrainian Orthodox Church? and (2) without any bishops present, could it ordain new bishops for the Church?

A frantic, eleventh-hour attempt was made by the Sobor to persuade the Kievan Exarch, Metropolitan Mikhail to consecrate a bishop for the Autocephalous Church. Invited by a special delegation, the Exarch did indeed appear at the Sobor, but only to deny its canonical validity and to repeat his refusal to ordain autocephalist episcopal candidates.[37] For most of the Sobor delegates, this put an end to any illusions about the possibility of a compromise with the Russian hierarchy.

After a prolonged debate, the spiritual leader of the movement, Archpriest Vasyl' Lypkivs'kyi, won the recognition of the Sobor's validity, having argued that its members represented the entire Ukrainian Church and that they gathered in Christ's name and with a firm belief in the presence of Christ and the Holy Spirit amongst them.

Volodymyr Chekhivs'kyi, the Church's most prominent lay ideologist, argued that since bishops in the apostolic times were consecrated by presbyters, the exclusive assumption of this right by the bishops represented a violation of the apostolic practice. Since the grace of the Holy Spirit resides in the entire Church, it should have the right to ordain its episcopate through its Sobor representatives, despite the fact that none of them were bishops; after all, this would be consistent with the ancient practice of the Alexandrine Church.

Speaking for the conservative minority, Archpriest Ksenofont Sokolovs'kyi rejected Chekhivs'kyi's arguments as a departure from long-established church canons and warned the Sobor against what he called a 'Protestant deviation' and 'betrayal of Orthodoxy'.[38] When the majority of the Sobor delegates accepted Chekhivs'kyi's arguments, the minority—perhaps as many as one third of the delegates—led by Sokolovs'kyi and Pavlo Pohorilko, walked out of the Sobor.[39] Among the 'secessionists' were about a half of the priests, including the supporters of Archbishop Parfenii of Poltava (the circle of Archpriest Feofil Buldovs'kyi).

Having declared itself the genuine voice of the Ukrainian Church 'inspired by the Holy Spirit', the 1921 Sobor resolved that it should have 'the right to change those canons of the Orthodox Church which, although established by the first seven Ecumenical Councils and justified in the past, could no longer meet the present vital needs of the Ukrainian Church or further its organic development'.[40]

This was indeed a momentous decision, for the Sobor thereby assumed the prerogatives of the ecumenical councils and thus broke away from the established canonical framework of the Orthodox Church. All the subsequent innovations in ecclesiastical rules introduced by the Kiev Sobor followed from this relativistic, instrumental notion of the canons.

The Sobor proceeded to restructure the constitution of the Ukrainian Church so as to make it more egalitarian and conciliar. The All-Ukrainian Sobor, it resolved, exercised the fullness of ecclesiastical authority despite the fact that the 'Ukrainian Church has no bishops and is presently an orphan'.[41] In order to reconstitute the hierarchy of the Church, 'the Sobor shall elect the Metropolitan of Kiev and All Ukraine and bishops for the individual regions of Ukraine'. The Sobor also made all church offices elective; the episcopal organisation of the Church was replaced by a loose hierarchy of the lay-dominated, self-governing church councils (*rady*), from the All-Ukrainian Orthodox Church Council heading the Church between the sobors, down to the regional, district and parish church councils. The bishops and the clergy were to serve merely as honorary chairmen of the *rady*. The Kiev Sobor also declared that married priests would have the same right as the monastic clergy to be elevated to the episcopacy. Rules governing the clergy were liberalised, granting them the right of divorce and remarriage, and allowing them to wear civilian clothes outside the church, shave their beards and cut their hair.

The Sobor confirmed the autocephaly of the All-Ukrainian Orthodox Church proclaimed by the Ukrainian Church Rada in May 1920, and repudiated the seventeenth-century annexation of the Kiev metropolitanate by the Moscow Patriarchate as an 'immoral, anti-canonical', and illegitimate act of violence.

The gathering also decreed the complete Ukrainianisation of church life, including a broad utilisation of folk art and folk music in church rites, and the revival of the traditional Ukrainian religious customs. It also provided for extensive lay participation in all phases of ecclesiastical life and emphasised the need for further development of church brotherhoods—the traditional form of lay participation and influence in the life of the Church—and the development of lay preaching (*blahovisnytstvo*).[42]

As for the church's relationship to the state, the Sobor accepted the official separation of the Church from the state as being 'in accordance with the teachings of Christ', and welcomed the granting of 'religious freedom in the Ukrainian Soviet Socialist Republic'. At the same time, the gathering committed the Church to an apolitical platform: 'Whoever introduces elements of coercion, of social, class, political or national oppression into the life of the Church should be excluded from the Church until he repents'.[43]

In accordance with its new canons, the Sobor unanimously elected Archpriest Vasyl' Lypkivs'kyi as Metropolitan of Kiev and All Ukraine. On 23 October, he was consecrated at the St Sophia Cathedral by some 30 priests and 12 deacons, as well as by lay members of the Sobor. Before the Sobor adjourned, on 30 October, five more bishops were consecrated by Metropolitan Lypkivs'kyi, with the participation of the Sobor: they were Archbishop Nestor Sharaievs'kyi for the Kievan diocese, and bishops Ivan Teodorovych (for the Vinnytsia diocese; subsequently he was dispatched to head the UAOC diocese in North America); Iurii Mikhnovs'kyi (Chernihiv); Oleksandr Iareshchenko (Poltava and Lubny); and Stefan Orlyk (Nizhyn).[44] In addition, a large number of priests were ordained and were assigned to newly-formed autocephalist parishes.

The first All-Ukrainian Sobor of 1921 represented a radical break with the canonical status quo, a break, which, at least as far as the mode of ordaining the episcopate was concerned, was less a matter of choice than the consequence of the unfavourable circumstances attending the birth of the new Church. What emerged from the reforms adopted at the 1921 Sobor was a new Church which, while professing to be Orthodox, severed its canonic links with other Orthodox Churches. Its canons, doctrines and organisation combined elements of Orthodoxy with such seemingly 'Protestant' features as an elected, married episcopate; less rigid distinctions between priesthood and lay believers; lay preaching; conciliar self-government at all levels of the Church; and a pragmatic approach to the Orthodox canons.

The new Church spread rapidly after the 1921 Sobor. Within a year, the Ukrainian Autocephalous Church had 734 parishes (not including the Katerynoslav guberniia), and by May 1924 it reached its peak strength of 1 199 parishes in the Ukrainian SSR alone.[45] Russian opponents of the UAOC estimated its following during the 1920s at three to six million faithful.[46]

The Russian Orthodox Church in Ukraine responded to the All-Ukrainian Sobor of October 1921 in two ways: it launched a massive attack among the clergy and believers against the legitimacy of the Sobor-ordained episcopate which were labelled the 'self-consecrated' (*samosviaty*) and declared the Ukrainian Autocephalous Orthodox Church a heretical schism; at the same time, the Exarchate tried to neutralise the appeal of the Ukrainian autocephaly by accepting and promoting those Ukrainian priests who broke with the UAOC over the issue of 'popular ordination' of bishops in violation of the church canons.

After the 1921 Sobor, Exarch Mikhail issued a pastoral letter condemning the 'false hierarchy' as 'enemies of the altar, . . . and traitors to the faith'; he called upon the believers to 'beware of the fraud and reject false hierarchy so as not to become sectarians'.[47] Similar repudiations of the UAOC were issued by individual bishops, including Parfenii of Poltava.[48]

To capitalise on the split in the ranks of the Ukrainian clergy and to blunt the Autocephalist arguments about the lack of Ukrainian bishops, the Sobor of Bishops proceeded to ordain, in late October 1921, the leading critic of 'Protestantism' within the UAOC, Ksenofont Sokolovs'kyi as Bishop Ioannikii of Bakhmut, vicar of the Katerynoslav diocese. Some time after, the Exarchate ordained another Ukrainian priest (though not a supporter of the Ukrainian autocephaly), Hryhorii Lisovs'kyi, as Bishop of Lubny, who succeeded to the Poltava see after Parfenii's death in 1922.[49]

In 1923, two supporters of 'canonical autocephaly', Feofil Buldovs'kyi and Serhii Labuntsev, were ordained as bishops of Lubny and Pryluky respectively, vicars to the Poltava bishop, Hryhorii Lisovs'kyi. Another secessionist from the 1921 Sobor, Pavlo Pohorilko, joined the Renovationists (*obnovlentsy*) and was elected in February 1923 to their 'Supreme Ecclesiastical Administration' in Kharkiv. Later that year, he was consecrated by Metropolitan Antonin Hranovs'kyi in Moscow as a vicar bishop for Podillia. After the Renovationist 'All-Russian Sobor' in 1923 failed to approve Ukrainian autocephaly, Pohorilko seceded from the Renovationist Church, leading a considerable number of Podillia parishes into a new autocephalist group known as the 'Fraternal Union of the Ukrainian Orthodox Parishes of the Autocephalous Church' (*BOUPPATs*).[50]

In the meantime, the capture of the patriarchal administration in Moscow by the regime-supported 'Living Church' in spring 1922 suddenly transformed the Exarchate's attitude towards autocephaly of the Church in Ukraine. Now, to prevent the Living Church takeover of the Exarchate, its bishops evidently decided to resort to a tactical device of 'provisional autocephaly' for as long as the Patriarchal administration was paralysed. Prevented by the authorities from convening an All-Ukrainian Sobor in September 1922, the Exarchate held a 'Sobor Conference' in Kiev which recommended to the 'Sobor of Bishops of the Entire Ukraine' that it proclaim 'as early as possible' in a 'legal-canonical manner' (1) autocephaly for the Orthodox Church in Ukraine, (2) a broad conciliar principle of ecclesiastical government, and (3) Ukrainianisation of church services and ecclesiastical life, but 'without coercion'. While the episcopate could now claim the benefits of independence from Moscow without actually proclaiming autocephaly, they took a procrastinating attitude on the issues of conciliarism and Ukrainianisation.[51]

Patriarch Tikhon's release from house arrest in 1923 and his resumption of the leadership of the Church has ended the 'provisional autocephaly' of the Exarchate.

After Tikhon's death the bishops supporting 'canonical' autocephaly and Ukrainianisation—Feofil Buldovs'kyi, Ioannikii Sokolovs'kyi, Pavlo Pohorilko, Serhii Labuntsev and at least one other bishop—met in Lubny in May 1925. They proclaimed themselves as the 'Sobor of Bishops of the Entire Ukraine'; invoking unfulfilled resolutions of the September 1922 'Sobor Conference', they decreed autocephaly of the Orthodox Church in Ukraine and formally renounced the authority of the Moscow Patriarchate over the latter. This Conciliar-Episcopal (*soborno-iepyskops'ka*) Church (labelled by its opponents 'The Lubny Schism'), which did not attract a large following, survived in the Left-Bank Ukraine until the mid-1930s.[52] The Renovationist (Synodal) Church, which—with government support—spread into Ukraine by 1922–23, eventually adopted for tactical purposes an autocephalous status in May 1925 and explicitly repudiated the annexation of the Ukrainian Church by the Moscow Patriarchate in the mid-1680s,[53] but it retained its predominantly Russian character as well as its place in the all-Union Renovationist centre, soon renamed the Synod of Orthodox Churches in the USSR.

At the start of the movement for Ukrainian Autocephaly, it seemed that the regime did not expect that the movement would get out of hand, develop a mass following and transform itself from a faction in the Orthodox ranks into a national church, preaching a revolutionary gospel that combined a revitalised Christian message with Ukrainian nationalism and social radicalism. The rapidly rising popularity of the new church made the authorities more suspicious of the political implications of the Autocephalist ideology.

On 20 October, just before the end of the 1921 Sobor, the All-Ukrainian Congress of Guberniia Administrative Department Chiefs and Heads of Militia had resolved that '*the Ukrainian Autocephalous Church which hides behind a false democratic facade is more dangerous to the proletariat than the [Russian] Orthodox Church which celebrates liturgy in the Church Slavonic language*, because the former lulls the class self-consciousness of the proletariat. While it hypocritically applauds the Soviet regime for the separation of the church from the state, . . . it attempts to appropriate for itself the rights of the Soviet authorities'.[54]

The opponents of the Ukrainianisation dominated the CP(b)U Central Committee plenum which met on 6 February 1922 and passed a resolution that attacked the Ukrainian Autocephalous Church, along with Ukrainian schools, 'Prosvita' reading clubs, and co-operatives as four 'nationalist citadels':

> Having suffered defeat in an open battle with the proletariat and the village poor of Ukraine, Ukrainian counter-revolution is gradually capturing into its hands all kinds of Ukrainian schools. The very same elements, especially teachers, assume leadership of the movement for the so-called Autocephalous Ukrainian Church

where, under a pretext of combating the Russian Orthodox Church, a second nationalist citadel is being created . . .[55]

The nature of Soviet interest in the UAOC can well be seen from a March 1922 questionnaire circulated by the Commissariat of Justice to all its gubernii subdivisions in Ukraine: nine out of its 11 questions concerned the Autocephalous Church, including its expansion, social base, political orientation ('open or secret connection with the Petliurites'), and its interrelations with the Russian Church (*ekzarkhisty*).[56] Even before the autocephalist Sobor ended its sessions in late October 1921, the Soviet Ukrainian press began to attack the UAOC for the alleged 'betrayal of its revolutionary platform'. Writing in June 1922, in the official daily organ of the Kharkiv government, *Visti*, V. Ellan-Blakytnyi openly accused the autocephalists of 'counter-revolutionary' tendencies.[57] The press attacks continued through the 1920s, reaching their peaks in the autumn of 1922 and in 1926. At first, the aim of this campaign was to intimidate the leaders and the adherents of the UAOC into joining the so-called Living Church; and, subsequently, to paralyse and split the Church and ultimately destroy it from within through a succession of so-called 'progressive' and 'loyalist' schisms to which the authorities and the GPU were prepared to offer their open support. Even if eventually the regime was able to 'persuade' several autocephalist bishops and groups of priests to launch a splinter 'Active Christian Church' (1923–26), it soon saw that it was another matter altogether to 're-educate' the large lay following of the Ukrainian Autocephalous Orthodox Church; indeed, the latter overwhelmingly repudiated the 'Active Christian Church' faction. The autocephalist laity and conciliar grass-roots democracy thus proved to be the Church's most reliable bulwark against takeover by the so-called 'progressives'.[58]

Among the factors contributing to the rise of the Ukrainian Autocephalous Orthodox Church by far the most important was the Ukrainian revolution of 1917–19 in its political, national and social dimensions. It could not but affect the Ukrainian Orthodox believers, challenge their perception of the Russian Orthodox Church and its relationship to the Ukrainian cause, and inspire part of the Orthodox clergy and lay intelligentsia with an ideal of an independent, national and popular church in a new 'symphonic' relationship with the Ukrainian state. The ensuing conflict between the autocephalist movement and the Russian episcopate in Ukraine was but a reflection of the larger confrontation between emergent Ukrainian nationalism and Russian imperial nationalism of which the church remained the most important institutional base. Similarly, with the Bolshevik defeat of the Ukrainian state, the Ukrainian Autocephalous Church became the most important institutional expression of the continuing Ukrainian aspirations for independence from Russia.

The jurisdictional and canonical barriers to autocephaly erected by the Russian episcopate in Ukraine served both to limit the effectiveness and radicalise the methods of the national church movement. The influx into the ranks of the UAOC of the frustrated elements of the UKP (led by Volodymyr Chekhivs'kyi) eventually helped to bring about the victory of the radical reformist forces within the Church at its 1921 Sobor. The refusal of the Exarchate to make any meaningful concessions to Ukrainian demands played into the hands of the opponents of 'obsolete canons'.

Soviet takeover of Ukraine and the clear priority placed by the victorious Bolshevik regime on 'smashing' the power of the former state church facilitated the 'grass-roots' revolution by the Ukrainian autocephalists; they exploited the new Soviet legislation on religion enabling them to 'register' Ukrainian parishes and obtain from the authorities nationalised church buildings. Eventually the same laws were turned by the regime against the UAOC.

The ecclesiastical revolution culminating in the 1921 Sobor was more than a strictly religious phenomenon. The autocephalist reinterpretation of Orthodox doctrine sought to provide religious legitimation for the cause of the Ukrainian national and social liberation, while the structural changes within the Church clearly reflected the movement's egalitarian, populist orientation. The influence of the autocephalist movement extended far beyond the confines of the UAOC whose canonical radicalism had alienated nearly all 'old' clergy and many believers. 'Conservative' members of the movement who had seceded from the 1921 Sobor carried the ideas of autocephaly and Ukrainianisation, if not of conciliarism, into the ranks of the Exarchate; eventually as regularly ordained bishops they provided in 1925 what they believed was a 'canonical alternative' to the UAOC. Even the regime-sponsored Renovationist Church in Ukraine considered it expedient to assume a guise of a Ukrainian autocephaly.

Forcible suppression by the Stalin regime of the UAOC[59] and Buldovs'kyi's 'conciliar-episcopal' church did not signal the end of Ukrainian striving for an autocephalous Ukrainian church; this was shown by its revival, alongside with Autonomous Church (*Ex-*

archate), during the short wartime German occupation and by the continuing if jurisdictionally fragmented existence of the Ukrainian Autocephalous Orthodox Church in Ukrainian Diaspora in the west where it has eventually overcome the canonical radicalism of the 1921 Sobor.

NOTES

1. On Russification of the Orthodox Church in Ukraine see Ivan Vlasovs'kyi, *Narys istorii Ukrains'koi Pravoslavnoi Tserkvy*, vol. III (New York: Bound Brook, NJ, 1957).

2. Sviateishii Pravitel'stvuiushchii Sinod, *Spiski sluzhashchikh po Vedomstvu Pravoslavnago ispovedaniia za 1915 god* (Petrograd: 1915).

3. Bohdan Krawchenko, *Social Change and National Consciousness in Twentieth-Century Ukraine* (London: 1985) p. 4. The data on ethnic composition of the Orthodox clergy in Ukraine have been calculated by Krawchenko on the basis of the 1897 census and appear in Table 2 of his 'A Social Profile of the Orthodox Clergy in Russian-Ruled Ukraine Before the Revolution', presented at the annual meeting of the American Association for the Advancement of Slavic Studies at Boston in November 1987.

4. See Serhii Shelukhyn, 'Vo istynu voskrese!', *Nova rada* (Kiev), no. 11 (11–24 April 1917).

5. See Nikon (Rklitskii), Bishop, *Zhizneopisanie Blazhenneishago Antoniia, Mitropolita Kievskago i Galitskago* (New York: 1958), especially vol. 4.

6. These attitudes are best reflected in a message issued in November 1918 by 17 bishops attending the Autumn session of the All-Ukrainian Sobor in Kiev, reproduced in *Golos Kieva*, 22 November 1918.

7. See my 'Politics of Religion in the Ukraine: The Orthodox Church and the Ukrainian Revolution, 1917–1919', Kennan Institute for Advanced Russian Studies (Washington, DC: 1986) Occasional Paper no. 202.

8. The Statute is reproduced in full in Dmytro Doroshenko, *Istoriia Ukrainy 1917–1923 rr.*, vol. 1 (Uzhhorod: 1930) pp. 328–30.

9. Full text appeared in *Trybuna* (Kiev), 2 January 1919.

10. A. Pokrovskii, 'Avtokefaliia Pravoslavnoi Tserkvi na Ukraine', in *Ukrains'kyi Pravoslavnyi Blahovisnyk* (Kharkiv: 1925) (hereafter *Ukr. Prav. Blah.*) no. 15, pp. 4–5.

11. A native of St Petersburg, Ermakov graduated from the Kiev Theological Academy in 1887 and returned to Ukraine to head the Volhynia Theological Seminary in 1893; in 1899 he was ordained a vicar bishop for the Chernihiv diocese but later that year was made Bishop of

Kovno. His last position was that of Archbishop of Grodno, a diocese that ended up in Poland after the Treaty of Riga.

12. See [Ukrainian SSR] Narodnyi komissariat iustitsii, *Tserkov' i gosudarstvo: Sbornik postanovlenii, tsirkuliarov po otdeleniiu tserkvi ot gosudarstva, otchetov i raz"iasnenii Likvidatsionnogo otdela NKIu* (hereafter *Tserkov' i gosudarstvo*) (Kharkov: 1922) pp. 3–11.
13. Vasyl' Lypkivs'kyi, Metropolitan, *Istoriia Ukrains'koi Pravoslavnoi Tserkvy. Rozdil 7: Vidrodzhennia Ukrains'koi Tserkvy* (hereafter Lypkivs'kyi, *Istoriia*) (Winnipeg, Man.: 1961) pp. 15–19.
14. *Tserkva i zhyttia* (Kharkiv: 1927) nos. 2–3, pp. 238–9.
15. Iu. Samoilovich, *Tserkov' ukrainskogo sotsial-fashizma* (hereafter Samoilovich, *Tserkov'*) (Moscow: 1932) p. 83.
16. Ivan Vlasovs'kyi, *Narys istorii Ukrains'koi Pravoslavnoi Tserkvy*, (hereafter Vlasovs'kyi, *Narys*), vol. IV, part I (New York-Bound Brook, NJ: 1961) p. 83.
17. Ibid., p. 24.
18. *Tserkva i zhyttia* (1927) no. 1, pp. 120–3.
19. Lypkivs'kyi, *Istoriia*, p. 27.
20. Samoilovich, *Tserkov'*, p. 94.
21. See *Kak i pochemu Ispolkom Kominterna raspustil UKP* (Kharkov: 1925) p. 39.
22. *Tserkov' i gosudarstvo*, pp. 14–15.
23. Vlasovs'kyi, *Narys*, vol. III (1957) pp. 298–9.
24. *Tserkva i zhyttia* (1927) no. 11, pp. 123–4; Lypkivs'kyi, *Istoriia*, p. 28.
25. Lypkivs'kyi, *Istoriia*, p. 29.
26. 'Materiialy do istorii borot'by za avtokefaliiu Ukrains'koi Tserkvy' (hereafter 'Materiialy do istorii'), *Relihiino-naukovyi vistnyk* (1923) no. 7–8, pp. 43–6.
27. Lypkivs'kyi, *Istoriia*, p. 29.
28. 'Materiialy do istorii', pp. 47–55.
29. Iosif (Krechetovich), Archbishop, *Proiskhozhdenie i sushchnost' samosviatstva lipkovtsev* (hereafter Archbishop Iosif, *Proiskhozhdenie*) (Kharkov: 1925) pp. 14–19.
30. *Tserkov' i gosudarstvo*, p. 16.
31. I. Tsyba, 'Tserkovno-vyzvol'nyi rukh na Ukraini 1917–1921 rr.', *Relihiino-naukovyi vistnyk* (1922) no. 2, p. 21.
32. Lypkivs'kyi, *Istoriia*, p. 32.
33. Anatolii Levitin-Krasnov and Vadim Shavrov, *Ocherki po istorii russkoi tserkovnoi smuty*, vol. III (Küsnacht: 1978) pp. 249–50.
34. Archbishop Iosif, *Proiskhozhdenie*, p. 24.
35. Lypkivs'kyi, *Istoriia*, pp. 32–4.
36. V. Potiienko, *Vidnovlennia iierarkhii Ukrains'koi Avtokefal'noi Pravoslavnoi Tserkvy* (hereafter Potiienko, *Vidnovlennia*) (Neu Ulm: 1971) p. 23.
37. Lypkivs'kyi, *Istoriia*, pp. 38–9.
38. Ibid., p. 40.
39. Vlasovs'kyi, *Narys*, vol. IV, part I, p. 118.
40. *Diiannia Vseukrains'koho Pravoslavnoho Tserkovnoho Soboru v Kyievi 14–30 zhovtnia n.s. 1921 r.* (Frankfurt/Main: 1947) pp. 3–4.
41. Ibid., pp. 7–8.

42. Ibid., pp. 3–31.
43. Michel d'Herbigny, SJ (ed.), 'Dossier américain de l'Orthodoxie Panukrainienne. Dix-huit documents inédits traduits de l'ukrainien par le prince Pierre Volkonsky et le pére Michel d'Herbigny, SJ', in *Orientalia Christiana*, vol. I (July–September 1932) no. 4, p. 119.
44. Lypkivs'kyi, *Istoriia*, pp. 41–2; Potiienko, *Vidnovlennia*, pp. 38–43.
45. The data have been compiled from the minutes of the October 1922 and May 1924 plenary sessions of the All-Ukrainian Orthodox Church *Rada*: 'Protokoly zasidan' Velykykh Pokrivs'kykh Zboriv Vseukrains'koi Pravoslavnoi Tserkovnoi Rady, 22–29.X.1922' (mimeographed copy in Osteuropa Institut, Munich); and 'Protokol Velykykh Mykil's'kykh Zboriv VPTsR, 25–30.V.1924 (mimeographed copy in the archive of Metropolitan Ivan Teodorovych, Philadelphia).
46. The first estimate was given in Archbishop Iosif, *Proiskhozhdenie*, p. 1; and the second—in Bishop Serafim (Ladde), 'Die Lage der orthodoxen Kirche in der Ukraine', *Eiche*, x (1931), no. 1, pp. 11–40.
47. Archbishop Iosif, *Proiskhozhdenie*, p. 28.
48. Lypkivs'kyi, *Istoriia*, p. 31.
49. Metropolitan Manuil (Lemeševskij), *Die Russischen orthodoxen Bischöfe von 1893 bis 1965* (edited and updated by P. Coelestin Patock, OSA), vol. II (1981) p. 372; Friedrich Heyer, *Die Orthodoxe Kirche in der Ukraine von 1917 bis 1945* (Köln-Braunsfeld: 1953) p. 91.
50. 'Novyi raskol sredi ukrainskikh tikhonovtsev', *Ukr. Prav. Blah.* (1926) no. 1, p. 9.
51. 'Avtokefaliia Pravoslavnoi Ukrainskoi Tserkvi v soveshchanii deputatov Kievskogo Sobora 1922 goda', *Golos Pravoslavnoi Ukrainy* (Kharkov: 1925) no. 3, pp. 3–5.
52. In 1930, the Conciliar-Episcopal Church had in its jurisdiction some 350 parishes, *Bezvirnyk* (Kharkiv: 1931) nos. 9–10, pp. 49–54.
53. *Golos Pravoslavnoi Ukrainy*, no. 10 (1925) p. 3.
54. *Tserkov' i gosudarstvo*, p. 29.
55. Ukrainian SSR, Ministerstvo Kul'tury Ukrains'koi RSR *et al.*, *Kul'turne budivnytstvo v Ukrains'kii RSR. Vazhlyvishi rishennia Komunistychnoi partii i Radians'koho uriadu 1917–1959 rr.: Zbirnyk dokumentiv*, vol. I (1917–June 1941) (Kiev: 1959) p. 150.
56. Circular no. 53 of the Liquidation Department of the Commissariat of Justice of the Ukrainian SSR, reproduced in *Sbornik tsirkuliarov po Narodnomu Komissariatu Iustitsii s l-go dekabria 1921 goda po l-e iulia 1922 goda. Vypusk 4-yi* (Kharkov: 1922) pp. 104–05.
57. See Vasyl' Ellan-Blakytnyi, 'Zle pryladzhena mashkara', reproduced in Vasyl' Ellan, *Tvory*, vol. I (Kiev: 1958) pp. 271–2.
58. It was not accidental that, when the GPU staged a 'self-dissolution' of the Ukrainian Autocephalous Orthodox Church in late January 1930 and allowed its replacement later that year by a 'Ukrainian Orthodox Church'—the main victims of this forcible 'reorganisation' were *rady* (lay-dominated church councils) and the entire principle of conciliarism.
59. See my article 'The Soviet Destruction of the Ukrainian Orthodox Church, 1929–1936', in *Journal of Ukrainian Studies* (Summer 1987) no. 22, pp. 3–21.

15 The Renovationist Coup: Personalities and Programmes
Philip Walters

Who were the Renovationists, and what did they want? There is clear continuity between the Renovationist movement and the church renewal movement of the years before the Revolution. Firstly, there was continuity of ideas between some of the Renovationists and members of the pre-revolutionary 'church intelligentsia' who were beginning to distinguish themselves from the atheist or anti-clerical intelligentsia of the nineteenth century by their reconciliation with religion.[1] Secondly, individuals who were later to be active in Renovationism participated in various pre-revolutionary social and political groupings involving clergy—notably the 'Group of 32' priests of the 1905 Revolution, and the 'League of Democratic Clergy and Laymen' founded in March 1917.

Two types of concern were thus inherited by the Renovationists. Firstly, there was a concern with liturgical reform and spiritual revival in the context of, or indeed as contributing to, the current social transformation towards a just society. Secondly, there was a concern to voice the cause of the ordinary 'white' parish clergy and to press for the realisation of their rights. Clearly these two concerns could overlap: the League of Democratic Clergy and Laymen, dominated as it was by 'white' clergy, was working for a programme of political, social and economic reforms which would involve relating the Gospel directly to issues of social justice.[2] But when securing the rights of the white clergy as a particular 'class' became the overriding concern of the Renovationist group 'Zhivaya tserkov'', the methods used were quickly seen to be compromising the aims of others in the Renovationist movement. It is perhaps symptomatic that leading figures in the 'Zhivaya tserkov'' group like V. D. Krasnitskii and S. V. Kalinovskii had before the Revolution been associated with extreme right-wing radicalism (the Black Hundreds and the League of the Russian People).

Disparate as the aims and incompatible as the methods of the various Renovationists turned out to be, these individuals did nevertheless succeed in co-operating to achieve power in the church. What held them together at this stage in the consolidation of the Soviet political and social system? The unique ideological climate of the early years of NEP was doubtless a factor. A dialectical understanding of social evolution, which demonstrated that the new socialist state was to be welcomed as embodying essentially Christian ideas,[3] was now combined with a more explicitly étatist and indeed nationalistic understanding of the current situation as expounded by the 'smenovekhovtsy'.[4] In these ambiguous circumstances, a movement which seemed to be successfully reconciling itself with a 'new' reality and moving towards a triumphant yet 'new' symphony of church and state was likely to attract radicals from both 'right' and 'left'.

In these circumstances then, the Renovationists were able to stage an ecclesiastical coup in May 1922. Obviously they would not have been able to do so without the, at least, tacit approval of the government. So what was the agenda of the Soviet authorities?

Firstly, the general social strategy which constituted NEP could justify an ecclesiastical policy such as the authorities now began to pursue. Under NEP, Soviet society was envisaged as comprising three main groups or classes; the proletariat; the peasantry; and the 'new bourgeoisie' of 'nepmen' and kulaks. Of these groups only the first two were regarded as permanent: those in the third group would eventually be surplus to requirements and now enjoyed the status of 'incongruous, and barely tolerated, intruders'.[5] The new church policy (from Spring 1922) was called by Trotskii an 'ecclesiastical NEP':[6] while there was ultimately no place for religion under socialism, concessions could at the moment be made to religious believers who were opposed to the pre-revolutionary established 'feudal' ecclesiastical order. The government could justify making concessions for the moment to Protestant denominations, and in the same way it could condone the appearance of 'protestants' within the Orthodox Church. 'Just as it had proved necessary to make concessions to buyers and sellers of commodities, so it was necessary to conciliate in some measure those who still clung to the practices of the church'[7] in order to ensure the ultimate survival of the Soviet system. Of course the broad strategy of NEP thus outlined would be likely to undergo all kinds of modifications in practice; and this was in fact the case as far as the government's tactics towards the Orthodox Church were concerned, to a considerable extent because there were disagreements at the highest level about anti-religious work in general, as we shall see in a moment. But we should at this point note that the general conceptual framework of NEP was likely to encourage the appearance within the church 'reform' movement of individuals whose motives had an admixture of what Levitin calls 'poshlost''—'vulgarity'. The characteristics criticised in the nepmen—opportunism, careerism, the desire to make a quick personal profit—were characteristics shared by many of those involved right from the start in the Renovationist movement.

Let us now look in more detail at the policy of the Soviet government towards religion specifically. During the first half of the 1920s this had not yet resolved itself into one generally accepted strategy. It is clear that its fluctuations reflected not only genuine disagreements about the effectiveness of particular tactics but also aspects of the power struggle which Trotskii eventually lost.[8]

Article 13 of the Party Programme, adopted at the Eighth Party Congress in 1919, expressed for the first time the explicit aim of the Party to uproot religious ideas amongst the masses. The Tenth Party Congress in 1921 issued a resolution calling for a comprehensive programme of anti-religious propaganda amongst the workers, using the mass media, films, books, lectures and similar instruments of enlightenment. In August 1921 a plenary meeting of the Central Committee issued an eleven-point instruction on how to interpret and apply Article 13. It made a distinction between uneducated and educated believers. The former can be admitted to the Party if despite being believers they have proved their devotion to communism. Anti-religious work is conceived as a long-term educative process rather than as 'destructive and negative'. As such it is clearly in line with the general ideology of NEP, and reflects the views of such men as Emel'yan Yaroslavsky (who at the Tenth Party Congress in 1921 was appointed a member of the all-powerful Central Committee Secretariat, already under the control of Stalin who a year later became its General Secretary) and Anatoli Lunacharsky (who was later to participate in public debates with Aleksandr Vvedensky, a leading Renovationist, in a form of Christian-Marxist dialogue), rather than those of Trotskii who tended to dismiss religion as a matter of superstition and who held that a few sharp shocks administered against religious institutions would soon persuade the masses to embrace atheism. It was Trotskii who in 1921 was in favour of having Patriarch Tikhon shot, against the advice of Lenin who feared the danger consequent on creating such a prominent martyr.

Nevertheless, it was Trotskii who was evidently in charge of policy towards the churches in 1922. Early 1922 saw the campaign to seize church valuables in full swing. Figures have been quoted to demonstrate that the government expected to raise at best only a tiny proportion of the total sum to be used to aid the starving from the sale of the seized church treasures.[9] The campaign was as much as anything else the exploitation by the government of a chance to make an example of the Russian Orthodox Church. The authorities expected resistance from the faithful which would in turn give them an opportunity to visit heavy penalties on the resisters. In the course of searches in churches and monasteries, items could be discovered, or be said to have been discovered, which would discredit or incriminate the faithful.[10] Overall, the way in which the campaign was conducted can hardly be said to have corresponded to the spirit of the instruction of August 1921.

Intensified campaigns against heterodoxy in many areas of endeavour made themselves felt during 1922. One writer ('M. B. B.') ascribes responsibility for these to the 'left' communists led by Trotskii and others who were afraid that the spirit of NEP might endanger the whole revolution, and he sees these campaigns as 'permanent revolution' being carried on not on the international scene but against internal enemies.[11] As part of the general cultural revolution he discerns a 'gigantic antireligious propaganda campaign' which according to him began in Spring 1922.[12] He quotes Nadezhda Krupskaya as deploring the excesses involved—tearing crosses off children's necks, shooting at icons.[13]

It is clear, then, that there were differences at the highest level over the anti-religious strategy and that the onset of NEP brought these differences into sharper focus. Some have been happy to state unequivocally that the Renovationist Coup of May 1922 was Trotskii's idea; others have concurred, but uneasily, feeling that it is hard to reconcile with his disdain for subtle policies in this field. It is arguable, however, that as a policy it offered something to the apologists of both short- and long-term anti-religious strategies. The following scenario is plausible: the short-term strategists would be relying on the continuing effectiveness of the church valuables purge, and would be prepared to pursue this with the help of some ambitious clergy from Petrograd who would be happy to seize power in the church and conduct a purge of their own; while the long-term strategists would welcome the chance of putting in place a church leadership loyal to the Soviet experiment which would then put little resistance in the way of a long-term programme of atheist education. And of course to all types of anti-religious strategist the benefits of simply promoting a schism within the church would be self-evident.

It may be symptomatic of the tactical manoeuvring going on amongst the Soviet leadership that responsibility for seeing the coup through to a successful conclusion was transferred from the Commissariat of Justice to the GPU, in the person of Evgeni Aleksandrovich Tuchkov. On 8 May 1922 three Renovationist priests, Vvedensky, Belkov and Stadnik, arrived in Moscow from Petrograd to join Krasnitsky who had arrived a few days earlier. They were coolly received by the Moscow Renovationists, who had been testifying at the recent trial of 17 individuals accused of opposing the appropriation of church treasures—notably by Bishop Antonin Granovsky. Tuchkov arranged for the arrivals from Petrograd, together with the Muscovite Kalinovsky, to meet the imprisoned Patriarch Tikhon on 12 May. Over the next few days the coup was effected, and announced in the second issue of the journal *Zhivaya tserkov'*.[14]

> Pointing out that under the leadership of Patriarch Tikhon the Church is experiencing total anarchy and that it has undermined its authority and influence over the masses as a result of its counter-revolutionary politics and in particular by its resistance to the appropriation of church valuables, the group of clergy demanded that the Patriarch call without delay a Local Council to organise the Church and that he withdraw completely from church administration pending the Council's decisions.[15]

Until Tikhon's nominated successor Agafangel should arrive in Moscow, the Renovationists would set up a Higher Church Administration (Vysshee tserkovnoe upravlenie). Agafangel was in fact prevented from reaching Moscow and the VTsU remained in power as the church administration now favoured by the government.

The 'renovated' Orthodox Church evidently excited considerable interest and was initially successful in gaining the endorsement of leading clergy. An article in *Izvestiya* illustrates the government's satisfaction at this state of affairs:

> We are watching with great attention and interest how this church movement is proceeding throughout the length and breadth of Russia. The very fact that the provincial press is devoting a lot of space to discussing this movement shows that it has become a matter of more or less lively concern everywhere and that every-

where it is producing an active response not only among the believers in the population but in the masses who are normally indifferent to religious matters.[16]

On the eve of the Renovationist Congress in August 1922 the government issued a decree obliging all 'associations not serving purposes of material gain' to seek registration with the state authorities. Those which failed to secure registration were to be closed down. On the basis of this decree the government was able to deny registration to Patriarchal churches, then hand them over to the Renovationists. E. H. Carr comments that 'these developments were significant as constituting the first formal recognition of religious bodies by the Soviet State'.[17] In these circumstances many leading bishops, including Sergii Stragorodsky, the future Patriarch of the Russian Orthodox Church, came out in support of the VTsU. There was a great deal of unclarity about Patriarch Tikhon's real intentions, and the clergy were generally under the impression that they were faced with a choice between either supporting the VTsU or endorsing chaos in the Church.[18]

The earliest statements of the aims of the Renovationists, as they appeared in the first two issues of *Zhivaya tserkov'*, contained elements representing all sections of the movement. Thus for example the forthcoming Council was urged, amongst other things, to replace conservative church doctrine with a dynamic creativity, and also to sanction the elevation of white married clergy to episcopal office. One thing which united all the Renovationists was opposition to capitalism. 'From a Christian point of view', wrote Vvedensky, 'capitalism is a great moral injustice'.[19] One commentator, summarising the essence of the 'church revolution' on the basis of information supplied by individuals as various as Bishop Antonin Granovsky, Vvedensky and Kalinovsky, wrote that Renovationists hold that Christian love 'will not be reconciled with socio-economic inequality or the exploitation of man by man, with the existence of capitalism in a Christian world: they therefore welcome Soviet power, which is striving to replace capitalism with communism . . .'[20]

It was in the area of future relations between the various ranks of clergy, however, that different views amongst the Renovationists were already becoming apparent. Vvedensky's opinion was that a hierarchy must exist in the church, and hence bishops must be retained; but a bishop must not be a 'despot', but rather a 'mystical centre' in a diocese conceived of as a 'community': 'each diocese can work out its own form of existence'.[21] V. N. L'vov (the former Procurator of the Holy Synod, who joined the schism at the time of the May coup) argued that

> without an episcopate the Orthodox church cannot exist; this would be protestantism . . . As far as running the Orthodox Church is concerned the clergy plays no independent role . . . the priest is inseparable from the parish, he is part of the parish, and not an independent element in the church administration. There are only two such independent elements: the bishop and the people . . . the clergy has come to occupy a place between the bishop and the people and claims to play an independent role . . . All this is incorrect and does not correspond to the spirit of the early church . . .[22]

In the very next article in the same issue of the journal a completely different view is expressed by Krasnitsky: the retirement of Patriarch Tikhon 'means the end of the primacy of monks in the church—the transfer of power in the Russian Orthodox Church into the hands of the white parish clergy'. Everywhere, he asserts, monastic bishops are handing over the reins to 'representatives of progressive groups of white parish clergy'.[23] One point of agreement is clearly that the rank of bishop should no longer be available exclusively to unmarried monastics; but there is equally clearly little consensus about the relative roles of bishops, priests and laymen in the running of the Renovationist church.

The single-minded champion of the rights of the white parish clergy was Vladimir Dmitrievich Krasnitsky. Unlike other Renovationist leaders he had no sort of 'dissident' record: as a student he had been reliable and obedient. He was the author of a dissertation entitled *Socialism Unmasked (Oblichenie sotsializma)* based on the contention that 'socialism is of the devil'. While still a student he joined the Union of Russian People.[24] Levitin says that: 'Krasnitsky was a careerist—a man who would always bet on the horse that had the best chance of winning'.[25] His writings as leader of the 'Living Church' faction are couched in combative terms which seek to identify enemies and rally the loyalists, and are reminiscent in this sense of much secular revolutionary propaganda. Vvedensky was incapacitated for some time in consequence of being hit on the head by a stone thrown by an angry *babushka*. Krasnitsky uses this incident to imply that there is an anti-revolutionary conspiracy, to issue dire

warnings to those responsible and to honour the Renovationists' first
martyr:

> Let those who aimed the stone at the head of Fr Vvedensky
> remember that this preacher of love who is so indulgent to his
> enemies will be replaced by men who will crush their counter-
> revolutionary plans with an iron rod: the stone thrown at Fr
> Aleksandr will rebound on the heads of those who directed the arm
> of this dark fanatical woman.[26]

Krasnitsky excited misgivings from the moment he first appeared
amongst Renovationist circles in Petrograd early in 1922. 'I'd like to
know where this fellow has sprung from', Vvedensky is reported to
have said. 'He's never been a member of any renovationist group,
none of us know him, but he suddenly appears at one of our
meetings. Why? What for? He's clearly up to something.'[27]

Krasnitsky was doubtless a willing instrument in the hands of
Tuchkov and the GPU. Nevertheless, Levitin is able to discern much
which was good in him. He believes that Krasnitsky was a sincere
Christian, pointing to the fact that when his career came to an end as
suddenly as it began he chose not to renounce the faith (unlike, for
example, Kalinovsky or Platonov) but to carry on a difficult existence
as the priest of a cemetery chapel. Levitin sees the main idea
motivating Krasnitsky as that of the unity of church and state.[28]
Levitin is also of the view that Krasnitsky 'had a real love for the
white clergy from whose ranks he sprang'.[29] Certain it is that the
white clergy had a huge reservoir of resentment. When the first flush
of Renovationist success was over, it was clear that while the majority
of bishops and the masses of the faithful were still loyal to, or
returned to, the Patriarchal church, the majority of the white clergy
remained with the Renovated church.[30]

Krasnitsky's Living Church group, with the backing of the GPU,
very quickly achieved control of the whole Renovationist movement.
The Living Church then set about attacking 'counter-revolution' in
the parishes and dioceses.

> Unnoticed, the 'Living Church Group', the living nerve of the
> whole ecclesiastical transformation, is being organised . . . Every-
> thing connected with the old order which subordinated the Church
> to the class-based landowning state—everything must be done
> away with. Decisively and irrevocably, everything must be cut out
> of church theory and practice which supports the hegemony of the

rich and titled over ordinary working people . . .'[31]

The October Revolution was not without its significance for them: they decided to seize power. With this aim the Central Committee—yes, they have their Central Committee too—they're real revolutionaries!—the Central Committee of the 'Living Church' group sent a circular round the dioceses: 'organise local "Living Church" groups immediately on the basis of recognition of the justice of the social revolution and of international workers' solidarity'.[32]

The methods employed by Living Church representatives included denunciation, and shortly opponents of the Living Church began to experience arrest and exile. 'Nobody compromises us like Krasnitsky', commented Vvedensky.[33] From time to time reports in the papers show how close the co-operation was between the security organs and the Living Church: 'Bishop Gennadi has been arrested, for concealing church valuables, engaging in counter-revolutionary activity and *persecuting supporters of the Living Church*'.[34]

As far as the bishops were concerned, Krasnitsky was prepared to concede that there were some who were liberal-minded, but he compared them to Kerensky, destined soon to yield before the power of the radicals—the white parish clergy. 'The Revolution drove the landowners off their estates and the capitalists out of their palaces, and it is going to drive the monks out of their bishops' residences too. It is time to settle accounts for all the suffering the white clergy has undergone at the hands of the despots—the monastic bishops.'[35] In Levitin's view, Krasnitsky really wanted to abolish the episcopate altogether, leaving priest and deacon as the only ranks in the hierarchy, but couldn't state this openly. Instead he began replacing monastic bishops with married bishops who owed their careers to him and would, by dint of being married, be compelled to stay loyal to the Living Church.[36] Between 3 June 1922 and May 1923 53 bishops were ordained from the ranks of the white clergy.[37]

The Living Church was firmly opposed to any role for the laity in the running of church affairs. The Living Church programme envisaged laymen playing a role only if they were members of a local Living Church group, where they would have to submit to parish discipline and take only such action as was sanctioned by their priest. 'The cornerstone of this whole movement', comments Bonch-Bruevich, 'is to pursue the interests not of the "laity", but of that same clergy, except that "white" has replaced "black"—but of course this white is no less black than the black'.[38] One of the reforms introduced by the Local Council of 1917–18 had been to give laymen a greater role in parish councils, where they had generally turned out to be supporters of the Patriarchal system. The Living Church intended to correct this tendency. In those parishes where the lay presence was already articulate and well organised there was resistance to the policies of the Living Church; in the less well organised parishes the Living Church did correspondingly better.

The Living Church was, then, a clerical 'party' which seized power in the Church by revolutionary means in the name of a particular class, just as the Bolsheviks had seized power in the state, and which then consolidated its hold through the agency of local cells. The limited nature of its aims has however excited censure not only of its methods but also of those very aims themselves. The Living Church had little interest in the spiritual and social regeneration which as we noted earlier were the priority of other Renovationist groups. For Stratonov it represented:

> a clearly expressed 'priestly reaction' against reforms introduced by the Local Church Council of 1917–18. Behind its revolutionary slogans and hysteria lay the blackest reaction, aiming to transform the church into an area of privilege for the white clergy: to control and exploit the rest of church society. This movement was also reactionary as far as the organisation of church power was concerned, returning it essentially to a synodal form of government.[39]

It is in my view misleading to speak here of 'reaction'—after all, the white clergy as such had never held power in the church and were now giving vent to frustrations built up over several generations. Nevertheless it is true that objectively the policies of the Living Church could easily have led to a new type of established 'state church'. The restoration of the Patriarchate in 1917 had symbolised the aspiration of the church to free itself from the clutches of a conservative state exercised through the Holy Synod and its Procurator: in Levitin's view the Living Church now stood simply for 'a particular kind of reversion to Pobedonostsevism under Soviet conditions'.[40] We may reflect again on the ambiguous implications of the ideological climate prevailing under NEP.

It was not necessarily obvious to the general public in the first months after the Renovationist coup that many of the Renovationist leaders had serious reservations about the aims and methods of Krasnitsky and his group. The most imposing individual amongst these leaders was the Moscow-based Bishop Antonin Granovsky, who possessed natural authority and charisma: his huge build, thunderous voice, and physical strength were widely appreciated. It suited the purposes of the Living Church group to maintain him as the front man in the movement. One Western observer, describing the 'Initiative Group' involved in the events of May 1922, writes that 'the most notable figure amongst them was, and is, Bishop Antonin . . .'[41]

Before the Revolution, Antonin had been in constant trouble with his superiors for his support for reforms in the practices and teachings of the Church. As a member of the St Petersburg Theological Censorship Committee he had spoken in favour of complete freedom of the press and the abolition of censorship altogether. His 'dissident' stand before 1917 no doubt contributed to the reputation he had built up for instability, even madness. Summarising sundry comments to this effect, one writer says that 'all in all he was an unquiet, unstable personality, without a strong character, without clear ideas, lacking real links with Orthodox tradition. His liberal and modernistic views were often determined by his moods'.[42] However, Levitin paints quite a different portrait of the bishop, based on his own deep regard and love for him: he emphasises Antonin's great learning, his deep insight into hypocrisy and falsehood, which he would deflate with crude peasant humour, and above all his unswerving devotion to seeking the truth. Certainly Antonin's conduct in the critical years we are considering gives substance to Levitin's assessment, and if Antonin ended up as a completely isolated figure this was as much a consequence of the strengths as of the weaknesses in his character.

Antonin in fact stood for the purest and most idealistic aspirations in Renovationism. His aim was to bring about moral improvement in individuals as the necessary basis for the reform of society as a whole. His slogan was 'the communisation of Life' ('kommunizatsiya zhizni'). 'The word "communisation" appeared in his theological system a long time before the October Revolution and completely independently of Communist ideology.' At the basis of his system lay the idea of 'multiple unity' ('mnozhestvennoe edinstvo'). 'The communisation of life is the free unity of free individuals redeemed by the blood of Christ, and the cradle for this is the Church'. He welcomed the Revolution but rejected both its methods (such as denunciations) and its militant atheism. 'Soviet power is not just non-religious, but anti-religious', he warned.[43] As far as practical reforms in the liturgy are concerned—using a language comprehensible to the layman

(Russian instead of old Church Slavonic), participation of the congregation in the liturgy, celebration of the liturgy in the middle of the congregation—Levitin finds all Antonin's proposals later embodied in the reforms of the Second Vatican Council.[44]

It was Antonin, then, who naturally opened the first great Renovationist event: the Congress (S″ezd) which began on 6 August 1922. 'We would like to think', he said, 'that you have been brought here not by clerical, caste or profit-seeking motives but by Christian Socialist ideals. My desire is that people should be united not in the name of material interests but in the name of ideas.'[45] Krasnitsky was then elected Chairman of the Congress. His first act was to order the expulsion from the chamber of all monks, including Antonin. The Congress then passed a resolution concerning monastic bishops: they were to be required to submit to the rulings of the VTsU on pain of removal from their posts. The monks expelled earlier were then allowed back in: all returned except Antonin.

The Congress devoted a lot of time to organising the finances of the Living Church, which was experiencing a severe financial crisis: the faithful were no longer giving voluntarily on the scale required. A resolution was passed that in each diocese the income from sales of candles and fees for funerals would be gathered together and half of the total given to the VTsU. This would create a substantial 'church-NEP trust'.[46] Anti-religious writers drew their own conclusions about this move.

> Having more or less disposed of their main opponents—the monks and the white clergy supporting them—these quarter-revolutionaries of the priestly calling want to gain control of one of the main levers of power in our age and even in our socialist society. The struggle for material resources, for money, for the parish cashbox—this is the real basis for this whole struggle with the parish councils, which up to now have had control of church funds and thus have held the parish clergy in their hands.[47]

The Congress also passed a resolution on the organisation of parishes: to expel all opponents of the Living Church, especially hierarchs; to dissolve parish councils which would not accept priests recognising the VTsU and to substitute new councils; and to compel incumbent priests of churches formerly belonging to monasteries and convents to recognise the VTsU. 'It is difficult', writes Levitin, 'to express more clearly and precisely the inner essence of the Living Church. This essence is modernised Pobedonostsevism'.[48]

Immediately after the Congress, Bishop Antonin announced the formation of his own Renovationist group, the 'Union of Church Renewal' ('Soyuz tserkovnogo vozrozhdeniya'). Antonin remained the figurehead of the whole Renovationist movement until June 1923, but he and his new group withdrew more and more from direct involvement in church politics, devoting themselves instead to constructing a small, closely-knit religious movement, or indeed sect, consisting of sincere spiritually and morally pure individuals. 'I don't need priests,' said Antonin, 'let the priests go and dance around the skirts of the Living Church and SODATs—that's their road—I need people, not priests'.[49] (SODATs was a second splinter group within Renovationism, founded in the autumn of 1922 by Vvedensky.)

The resolutions of the Congress were greeted with hostility by the mass of the faithful; and even the parish clergy were in general not prepared to accept the new financial arrangements. In twelve dioceses the majority of the clergy now came out in support of Antonin, as did many of the hierarchy who had initially supported the Living Church, including Sergii Stragorodsky. During the autumn this evaporation of support forced Krasnitsky to capitulate. From now on all Renovationist tendencies were to be allowed equal representation in the VTsU. Krasnitsky was disconcerted to find in this context that the Soviet authorities had no objections to the schism within a schism. In the autumn he made an attempt to unseat Antonin, and called in the GPU to make sure he left the Moscow diocese, but the GPU replied that according to the law on separation of church and state they had no basis for any intervention in internal church affairs.[50]

The Renovationists in Petrograd, led by Vvedensky, also came out in opposition to Krasnitsky and the policies of the Living Church, specifically to the proposed financial centralisation and to the marginalisation of laymen. Aleksandr Ivanovich Vvedensky had been involved in religious radicalism from his youth. His rise to preeminence in the Renovationist movement began in the autumn of 1922 when as part of a renewed energetic anti-religious campaign he appeared in public debates with atheist apologists such as Lunacharsky, usually getting the better of the argument by virtue of his passion and oratorical skill. At that time too he founded the second splinter group within Renovationism, 'The Union of Communities of the Ancient Apostolic Church' ('Soyuz obshchin drevne-apostol'skoi tserkvi');[51] and later, after the demise of Krasnitsky and the withdrawal of Antonin, he became the recognised leader of the whole

Renovationist movement until it finally petered out in the 1940s.

While Bishop Antonin was an ascetic, a puritan, Vvedensky was an exalted aesthete, even a decadent, passionately committed to creativity. His roots lay in the New Religious Consciousness of Merezhkovsky, Gippius and others. 'His passionate desire for truth', writes Levitin,

> and a sense of the inescapable senselessness of everyday life, were flooded by his immense oratorical talent, and this produced tremendous sermons which galvanised his listeners; at the same time the confusion of his thought and the mixture of moral values in him, typical of decadence, promoted a shocking lack of principle.[52]

Levitin attempts to fathom this paradoxical combination in Vvedensky of exalted, passionate aspiration and a propensity for completely unprincipled action. Vvedensky was a powerful orator, but 'when he left the podium he was taken over by vulgar, petty, vainglorious interests . . .'[53]

> It is a great mystery how A. I. Vvedensky—a good, kind man, and at the same time genuinely religious—was capable with such incomprehensible ease of wading through human grief, tears and blood. Perhaps the key is to be found in the intoxicating effect which success had on him—'You know, it is good to be someone who triumphs' . . . This pathological thirst for success was linked in some peculiar way with his religious impulse. In 1939 he wrote in his diary: 'If you take my inner life it is full of light, and the greatest expression of this is success, sometimes triumphant success . . .'[54]

Bishop Antonin commented, 'He's a sinner, a great sinner. What's a man like him doing trying to reform the Church? He needs to reform himself first.'[55]

Without indulging in psychological speculation, we should just note that the two elements in Renovationism, the idealistic and the self-interested, were here embodied in one individual and that it was this individual who remained at the head of the whole movement until its demise.

From late 1922 all the efforts of the various Renovationist groups were concentrated on preparing for a full Council (Sobor). This was originally to have been held in the summer of 1922, but after the Congress Krasnitsky saw it as his priority to purge the episcopate first. Meanwhile, as we have seen, a new energetic anti-religious campaign began in the autumn of 1922 and reached a peak around Easter 1923.

The long-awaited trial of Patriarch Tikhon was announced for 11 April, but did not take place. A new date was fixed: 24 April; but this too passed without further developments. The Council was held between 29 April and 9 May, and was judged a triumph. Bishop Antonin, presiding, was faced with a personal crisis: a married bishop was elected Executive President and his own role was defined as that of Honorary President. In the end he accepted this situation. In the opinion of Levitin, his greatest fear was that he would be left isolated. In the event, he was isolated anyway. At the end of June Krasnitsky relieved him of his post and forced him into retirement.

The trial of Patriarch Tikhon had still not taken place. Then on 26 June came devastating news: he had been released, and had renounced his former anti-Soviet stance. Obviously a change in government policy had been consolidated during the previous two months.

The persecution of the Orthodox Church and in particular the treatment of Patriarch Tikhon had for some time been attracting critical comment from abroad. The atheist journal *Bezbozhnik*, reporting the loyal declaration of the Council of 1923, asserted that 'of course these decisions are of immense importance—from now on no-one dares to say that the Soviet government persecutes the Church, persecutes religion',[56] but the fact of the matter was that the Living Church was being widely dismissed by foreign observers as a tool of the Soviet government. On 8 May 1923 the Curzon Ultimatum formalised the misgivings of the British government, noting persecution of religion as one of the factors hindering the establishment of proper relations between Britain and the USSR.

The Curzon Ultimatum was not of course the direct cause of the change in anti-religious tactics, however.

> Already from the beginning of May a significant reduction in anti-religious propaganda was noticeable, and this was particularly striking after the hysterical anti-Christmas and anti-Easter propaganda campaigns. The central press virtually stopped publishing anti-religious articles and there was less and less to be read even about the Patriarch.[57]

Other directives from the Central Committee during May and June were concerned with putting a brake on the arbitrary closure of churches.[58] The cause of these developments is to be found in the deliberations of the Twelfth Party Congress of 17–25 April 1923.

A special section of the resolutions of this Congress was devoted to anti-religious agitation and propaganda. The resolutions pointed out that the conditions which Marx identified as giving rise to religious feelings had not yet been eradicated, and that therefore propaganda must continue, but that crude methods and coarse mockery which would offend believers and increase their fanaticism must be avoided. Increasing economic difficulties were making themselves felt—they led to strikes during the summer of 1923—and it was now seen as essential to work to strengthen the 'link' between the proletariat and the peasantry in the interest of NEP, and to rally and unite rather than estrange and divide. By now, the Soviet authorities had had time to appreciate the fact that the Living Church held no appeal for the peasant masses and that it no longer made sense for the government to commit itself to the support of the Renovationists.

The type of anti-religious activity recommended by the Congress bore the hallmark of the Yaroslavsky school. On 27 May 1923 the journal *Bezbozhnik* carried an article by Yaroslavsky in which he called for improved relations between believers and non-believers among the workers.[59]

There was of course more to these decisions than the simple desire to conciliate the peasants: they were also symptoms of the continuing power struggle in the leadership. The Congress had considered a background document on the work of the Central Committee in the field of anti-religious propaganda which noted both the success of the campaign to seize church valuables and the effectiveness of the Living Church in confounding reactionary clergy and winning over the believing masses. The positive tone of this document contrasted sharply with the tone of the opening report by Zinoviev on the work of the Central Committee on 17 April. 'We have gone too far,' he asserted, 'much too far . . .' 'We need serious anti-religious propaganda, we need serious preparation in schools and appropriate education for young people.'[60] The background document is Trotskiist in tone. Since January 1923 Trotskii had been increasingly isolated in the Politburo. In late 1922, according to Trotskii, Stalin had succeeded in appointing Yaroslavsky as Trotskii's deputy in the department of anti-religious propaganda.[61] Now at the Twelfth Party Congress those who followed Zinoviev in urging the necessity to conciliate the peasantry were also expressing their opposition to Trotskii.

The battle over anti-religious strategy as it played itself out in the years 1923–6 in fact involved three factions. The 'leftists', including Trotskii, favoured hard-line tactics to destroy what they saw as a relatively superficial phenomenon. The 'rightists' (whom we have not so far had occasion to mention, since their beliefs necessarily meant that they did not propose any active strategy at all) believed that religion would eventually wither away of itself by a process of 'samotek'. The 'centrists', including Yaroslavsky, stood for a long-term strategy of anti-religious education.[62] We should note that in this struggle Yaroslavsky, in typical Stalinist style, was adopting the middle ground and posing as a moderate, but that later on he was able from this central position to defeat his rivals on both 'right' and 'left' and effect his own anti-religious policy from 1929 which exceeded all previous efforts in its extremism.

Conciliation of the peasantry remained the central element in party policy from 1923 to 1925, and this was also the period of greatest toleration for the Patriarchal Church as an institution. As far as the Renovationist Church was concerned, the government was now attempting to effect a reconciliation between it and the Patriarchal Church in such a way that the latter would be forced to accept a leadership which would do what it was told. The aim was now a form of *hidden* schism; the infiltration of Trojan horses within that church to which the believing population had demonstrated its continuing allegiance. This is what lay behind the extraordinary announcement in *Izvestiya* on 24 May 1924 that Patriarch Tikhon had invited none other than Krasnitsky to help him to run the Church and stamp out counter-revolutionary activity. It is not clear whether Tikhon did in fact agree to this, and in any case he repudiated the arrangement in June. It is symptomatic of the fact that the government felt it could not afford to antagonise the faithful too blatantly at this time that Tikhon suffered no serious repercussions for his firm stance.

The mass of believers continued to remain doggedly loyal to the Patriarchal Church in its unrenovated state. We can detect a certain amount of wishful thinking in the comments of an atheist writer in 1926:

The renewal movement has dealt a terrible blow to the church. In unmasking the counter-revolutionary decay, venality, mendacity and cunning of the Tikhonites the Renovationists have clearly shown the terrible harm done by religion. It should be emphasised that thinking workers and peasants . . . have become atheists. They have not joined the Renovationists, since they see there the same church, cleaned up on the outside, but essentially unchanged. The Renovationist clergy have not stopped the rise of atheism, have not provoked a religious upsurge amongst the masses; in destroying the Tikhonites, they have destroyed themselves.[63]

This writer was correct in his conclusion about the Renovationists themselves; but not, as time has proved, about the Patriarchal Orthodox Church.

NOTES

1. The Renovationist Titlinov provides a conspectus of the ideological precursors of Renovationism in B. V. Titlinov, *Novaya tserkov'* (Petrograd: 1923) pp. 41–50. Somewhat indiscriminately, he brings in the Slavophils, Dostoevsky, Solov'ev, Tolstoy, a gallery of early twentieth-century religious thinkers and those who participated in the Religio-Philosophical meetings of 1902–03. Needless to say, not all these figures shared the later views of the Renovationists to the same or indeed any extent. See also Dimitry Pospielovsky, *The Russian Church under the Soviet Regime*, vol. I (New York: 1984) pp. 85–6.
2. Levitin and Shavrov see 'bourgeois vulgarisation' of the church reform programme setting in as early as 1905: 'One can readily see Vladimir Solov'ev's great conception of a universal, all-embracing spiritual renewal being supplanted by demands to defend the rights of the parish clergy'. Anatoli Levitin and Vadim Shavrov, *Ocherki po istorii russkoi tserkovnoi smuty* (Küsnacht: 1978) part I, p. 6. A similar view is expressed by the priest Evgeni Belkov in his 'Predvestniki zhivoi tserkvi', *Zhivaya tserkov'* (23 May 1922) no. 2, pp. 10–11.
3. See Titlinov, op. cit., pp. 69–76.
4. See Pospielovsky, op. cit., vol. I pp. 85–9; Levitin and Shavrov, op. cit., part I, pp. 137–8. 'The contemporary church reform movement is a particular type of accommodation to NEP by the clergy', writes Ya. Okunev, 'Smenovekhovtsy v tserkvi', in *Kommunist* (22 November 1922) no. 268, p. 2.
5. E. H. Carr, *Socialism in One Country*, vol. I (Harmondsworth: Pelican, 1970) p. 103.
6. See L. Trotsky, *Literatura i revolyutsiya* (1923) p. 29.
7. Carr, op. cit., vol. I, p. 53.
8. See Joan Delaney, 'The Origins of Soviet Antireligious Organisations', in Richard H. Marshall (ed.), *Aspects of Religion in the Soviet Union 1917–1967* (University of Chicago Press: 1971) pp. 103–39; Dimitry Pospielovsky, *A History of Marxist-Leninist Atheism and Soviet Anti-Religious Policies* (vol. I of *A History of Soviet Atheism in Theory and*

Practice, and the Believer) (London: Macmillan, 1987); M. B. B., 'Der misslungene Versuch zur Vernichtung der Russisch-Orthodoxen Kirche in den Jahren 1922–1923 und die Niederlag e des linken Kommunismus', in *Ostkirchliche Studien*, vol. 22 (September 1973) no. 2/3, pp. 105–49.

9.   M. B. B., op. cit., pp. 127–31.
10. See for example reports in the Renovationists' journal. One states that during a search at the nunnery of the Annunciation in Kherson 'large quantities of powder, eau de Cologne, pomade, toilet soap and corsets were discovered'. More seriously, a search at the premises of the former secretary of Metropolitan Antoni Khrapovitsky revealed correspondence between the Metropolitan and the hetman Skoropadsky and a German general. *Zhivaya tserkov'* (15 June 1922) no. 3, p. 3.
11. M. B. B., op. cit., p. 109.
12. Ibid., p. 131. See also Alexander Kischkowsky, *Die sowjetische Religionspolitik und die Russische Orthodoxe Kirche*, 2nd ed. (Munich: 1960) p. 48.
13. N. Krupskaya, *Leninskie ustanovki v oblasti kul'tury* (Moscow: 1934) p. 198.
14. The first issue of this journal, dated 'May 1922', appeared before the critical events just described. It was edited by S. V. Kalinovsky. The second issue, dated 13 May, was still edited by Kalinovsky, but now in the name of the Higher Church Administration. The third issue, dated 15 June, was edited by Krasnitsky, in the name of the '"Living Church" Group'. These developments reflected the rapid assumption by the 'Living Church' faction led by Krasnitsky of the dominant position in the Renovationist movement.
15. 'Vremennoe samoustranenie sv. patriarkha Tikhona ot upravleniya', in *Zhivaya tserkov'* (23 May 1922) no. 2, p. 1.
16. M. Gorny, 'Vokrug "Zhivoi tserkvi"', *Izvestiya* (7 July 1922) reproduced in *Zhivaya tserkov'* (1–15 July 1922) no. 4, pp. 7–8 (quote p. 7).
17. E. H. Carr, op. cit., vol. i, pp. 51–2.
18. Johannes Chrysostomus, *Kirchengeschichte Russlands der neuesten Zeit*, vol. i (Patriarch Tikhon 1917–1925) (Munich and Salzburg: 1965) pp. 204–07.
19. A. Vvedensky, 'Chto dolzhen sdelat' gryadushchii sobor?', in *Zhivaya tserkov'* (23 May 1922) no. 2, pp. 4–6 (quote p. 5).
20. Iv. Tregubov, 'Tserkovnaya revolyutsiya, ee vragi i druz'ya (po dannym, poluchennym ot ep. Antonina, prot. Vvedenskogo i svyashch. Kalinovskogo)', in *Zhivaya tserkov'* (15 June 1922) no. 3, pp. 13–14 (quote p. 13).
21. A. Vvedensky, 'Chto dolzhen sdelat' . . .', p. 5.
22. Vladimir L'vov, 'K soboru', in *Zhivaya tserkov'* (1–15 July 1922) no. 4, pp. 2–5 (quote pp. 3 and 4).
23. Prot. V. Krasnitsky, 'Monasheskii vopros', in *Zhivaya tserkov'*, no. 4, pp. 5–6 (quote p. 5).
24. Levitin and Shavrov, op. cit., part i, pp. 64–5.
25. Ibid., p. 66.
26. V. Krasnitsky, 'Pervomuchenik tserkovnogo obnovleniya', in *Zhivaya tserkov'* (15 June 1922) no. 3, p. 15.

27. Levitin and Shavrov, op. cit., part I, p. 65.
28. Ibid., p. 66.
29. Ibid., p. 131.
30. Irinarkh Stratonov, *Russkaya tserkovnaya smuta, 1922–1931 gg.* (Berlin: 1932) p. 67.
31. 'Ot redaktsii', in *Zhivaya tserkov'* (15 June 1922) no. 3, pp. 1–2 (quote p. 2).
32. Vladimir Bonch-Bruevich, *'Zhivaya tserkov' i proletariat* (Moscow: 1924) p. 26 (first published in the journal *Molodaya gvardiya* no. 6–7, Oct–Dec. 1922).
33. Levitin and Shavrov, op. cit., part I, p. 97.
34. *Kommunist* (17 August 1922) no. 188, p. 3, quoted in Levitin and Shavrov, op. cit., part I, p. 136. The italics are Levitin and Shavrov's.
35. Prot. V. Krasnitsky, 'Gruppa progressivnogo dukhovenstva i miryan "Zhivaya tserkov'"', in *Zhivaya tserkov'* (15 June 1922) no. 3, p. 11.
36. Levitin and Shavrov, op. cit., part I, p. 134.
37. Ibid., p. 143.
38. Bonch-Bruevich, op. cit., p. 27.
39. Stratonov, op. cit., p. 54.
40. Levitin and Shavrov, op. cit., part I, p. 129.
41. Captain Francis McCullagh, *The Bolshevik Persecution of Christianity* (London: 1924) p. 30.
42. Chrysostomus, op. cit., vol. I, p. 214.
43. Levitin and Shavrov, op. cit., part I, pp. 150–1.
44. 'Tserkov' v Sovetskom Soyuze' (interview with Levitin'), *Russkaya mysl'* (5 December 1974) no. 3028, p. 5.
45. Levitin and Shavrov, op. cit., part I, p. 160.
46. Ibid., p. 164.
47. Bonch-Bruevich, op. cit., pp. 31–2.
48. Levitin and Shavrov, op. cit., part I, p. 163.
49. Ibid., part II, p. 70.
50. Ibid., part I, pp. 185–6.
51. It is beyond the scope of this paper to examine precisely which issues united Vvedensky and Granovsky and which divided them. Vvedensky, it seems, was interested primarily in *doctrinal* innovation while Granovsky was concerned with innovation in *liturgical practice* and in *moral reform*. Vvedensky was also opposed to the preservation of a celibate monasticism and while agreeing that bishops were essential to the church held that they should be drawn from the white clergy. There was of course also the clash of temperament.
52. Levitin and Shavrov, op. cit., part I, p. 14.
53. Ibid., part II, p. 33.
54. Ibid., part I, pp. 106–07.
55. Ibid., part I, p. 215.
56. Quoted in S. V. Troitsky, *Chto takoe Zhivaya Tserkov'* (Warsaw: 1928) as reproduced in W. C. Emhardt, *Religion in Soviet Russia: Anarchy* (Milwaukee and London: 1929) pp. 353–4.
57. M. B. B., op. cit., p. 136.
58. Pospielovsky, *A History of Marxist-Leninist Atheism* . . . , p. 38.
59. Delaney, op. cit., pp. 112–15.

60.   *Stenograficheskii otchet 12 s"ezda* (Moscow: 1968) p. 44. See M. B. B.,
       op. cit., pp. 136–7.
61.   E. H. Carr, *The Interregnum 1923–1924* (Harmondsworth: Pelican,
       1969) p. 26.
62.   Delaney, op. cit., pp. 119–21.
63.   Valentin Rozhitsyn, *Tikhonovtsy, obnovlentsy i kontr-revolyutsiya*
       (Moscow-Leningrad: 1926) p. 7.

16 The Survival of the Russian Orthodox Church in her Millennial Century: Faith as *Martyria* in an Atheistic State[1]

Dimitry V. Pospielovsky

> 'The Night will be very long and very dark'
>
> Patriarch Tikhon's last words on his death bed, 1925.

It is hardly necessary to reiterate here the legal status and the realities in which the Orthodox Church, from the very first days of the Bolshevik rule, and all religious faiths of the USSR later, have had to exist. To put it briefly, as early as January 1918 the church was disenfranchised, deprived of the status of a juridical person, and along with that stripped of all her real estate, of all church buildings, schools, monasteries, residences for the clergy, bank accounts, as well as of the right to own any of these, of the right to teach religion either to children or adults, in state schools as well as in private ones. Nor could parishes organise and run any Sunday schools. The hierarchical structure of the church had henceforward no legitimate status. The state recognised only groups of laity who could lease a church building from the state for worship or a house in which to settle a priest with his family. The legislation of 1929, furthermore, deprived the believers of the right to engage in religious propaganda, that is to publicly debate with the atheists and to defend religion when the latter attacked it. Various laws of that year banned even special church services for particular groups of believers, for example women, youths and school children. They forbade the priests to organise any clubs or hobby groups attached to churches, for example music or art circles, or lovers-of-nature groups taking hikes into the country. The Church was equalised with private enterprise, and with the attack on the latter in the collectivisation and industrialisation drive of 1929–33 came a wholesale liquidation of churches and clergy, particularly in the countryside. With varying intensity of terror and despite brief periods of respite the all-out destruction of the church continued through 1939, so that only several hundred functioning churches of all religions survived by 1940 on the original Soviet territory. Some 500 bishops, at least 40 000 Orthodox clergy, at least an equal number of monastics, plus unknown thousands of believers had been killed or had died in Soviet prisons and camps by the beginning of World War II.[2]

Although Stalin allowed the church a limited restoration after 1943, and currently policies towards the church have been considerably relaxed, the laws have so far not been changed. Technically the church continues to have no real legal status, no means of legal security against any arbitrary encroachments by the state which is officially committed to atheism to the present day.

And yet, the church exists, and in the words of one contemporary Moscow priest:

> . . . a new generation of young intellectuals has begun to turn to the Church . . . through much suffering and deep rethinking they have found their way to conversion to Christ . . . Faith and the Church for them . . . are inseparable from martyrdom, with educational and professional sacrifices.
>
> The Lord sees that these sixty years of our history have produced a thousand times more saints than the whole of the Russian history, that *living* saints are currently treading Russia's soil.[3]

How did the church survive? How has she managed to pass on the message, the teaching, the faith? A pious Russian will simply say: 'God's miracle, God's will'. And miracles abound in many Soviet believers' autobiographies and memoirs, most of which even a sceptical mind will accept as rationally inexplicable. Here is a case in point.

The author is the wife of a pre-revolutionary lawyer who, after living through the apocalyptic horrors of the revolution and the civil war feels called to the priesthood. After his ordination he soon finds himself behind bars, in prisons, camps and exile. The author who also spent many years in prisons for her faith sees their whole life as a chain of miracles, miracles of being saved from starvation, from prison by unknown persons literally met in the streets upon release from prison. One such ordeal takes the family to a famous Moscow priest, Fr. Ivan Kedrov. The deacon's daughter at Fr. Kedrov's church, Olga, while working for a Soviet institution had lost her faith in God under the impact of the anti-religious propaganda, but later became disillusioned with the official ideology. Feeling empty and guilty, she decided to take her life.

As she was writing her pre-suicide letter to her former confessor, Fr. Kedrov . . . she suddenly heard a voice: 'Stop it, go to my father; he'll tell you what to do, and you'll once again become his spiritual daughter'. Olga turned around and saw a young girl smiling at her. Olga began to shout: 'Who are you? You've no right to interfere; this is my decision . . .' 'I'm Father Kedrov's daughter, Vera', replied the girl, 'my father loves you; go to him without fear, don't cry'. Vera put her hand on Olga's head. Olga suddenly felt peace and bliss. 'But I'm Judas', she replied. Vera moved her arm, and suddenly Olga saw three crosses on a hill: 'You see the thief and murderer next to Jesus? And what did the Lord tell him?'

The vision disappeared. Olga sat petrified. Then she rushed to Fr. Kedrov, begging him to show her his family photographs. In one of them she recognised Vera, and asked who she was. The Priest told her she was his deceased daughter. On hearing Olga's story he took her first to church for a prayer and absolution, then to Vera's grave. After this experience Olga soon took the veil in a convent (probably a secret one, because already by the late 1920s very few overt convents remained).[4]

But God is not a juggler. Miracles are super-natural, not anti-natural. Moreover, as in Olga's case above, God works through human freedom, not against it. The above memoir sees the purpose of the ordeals and miracles in her and her family's life in strengthening their faith in God and love for fellow-man. Behind the miracles, indeed behind the very miraculous survival of faith in the atheistic world, there are God's people and their actions. And the aim of this paper is to show what people and what actions helped to save the church in Russia and to provide for the continuity of the faith.

At the time of the Bolshevik Revolution a full local council of the whole Orthodox Church of Russia was in session, the first such council since 1700 when Peter the Great had banned all church councils and subordinated the church to a department of state. Despite all the repeated attempts of the church to regain her autonomy, none of the tsars to the fall of the monarchy in March 1917, allowed a reversal of the very harmful acts of Peter the Great.[5]

The 1917–18 local Council restored the conciliar principle of Church administration and elected a very popular bishop, Tikhon, the Patriarch, that is the temporal head of the whole Russian Church.

It was Patriarch Tikhon and the Council who issued an encyclical in January 1918 which, in response to Bolshevik terror, excommunicated all those engaged in shedding innocent blood and persecuting the church, but then appealed to the faithful to offer non-violent resistance, form unions and brotherhoods of Christians to defend the church, 'to contrapose the force of spiritual inspiration against the external force of brutal power'.[6]

Such unions indeed were formed. Sixty to seventy thousand people joined them in such cities as Petrograd and Moscow and proportionally similar numbers in most towns, cities and even villages. They organised mass church processions across towns and cities in protest against the persecutions and attempted closures and state confiscations of churches. They organised the feeding of the clergy, classified by the Soviet government as a parasitical class and therefore receiving starvation level ration cards or none at all. They protected the clergy by providing sizeable groups of bodyguards, armed with clubs at best, against the machine guns of the Reds. In this first unequal confrontation of 1918–20 several thousand clergy and monastics and at least 12 000 lay religious activists were killed, but the church survived, and even began to grow after 1921, with the first mass disappointments in the Bolshevik promises of a paradise on earth. The growth of the church was particularly noticeable in the larger urban centres, where the formerly radical and highly secular intelligentsia, active in leftist, mostly socialist parties before the revolution, now began to return to the church.[7] Thus began a new era in the life of the national church: where during most of the first nine centuries of the church's existence nominal membership in the church was practically an automatic attribute of being Russian, in the millennial century that national church began to revert to the status of her first decades on the Russian soil—to being again a church of converts.[8]

This statement may cause some eyebrows to rise, particularly since relatively recent Soviet sociological surveys, for whatever they are worth, claimed that over 80 per cent of contemporary Orthodox believers inherited their faith from their childhood.[9] But in a society lacking regular religious education, literature and organisations, conversion ought to be seen in a wider context.

For instance, when in 1917 practising one's religion and taking the sacraments ceased to be obligatory for all Russian soldiers baptised Orthodox, the proportion of such observants declined from nearly 100 per cent in 1916 to less than 10 per cent communicants in 1917.[10] Thus, when churches began to fill again in the 1920s, and new churches were built or old ones re-opened,[11] we are dealing with a process of re-conversions. When the leader of the League of Militant Godless reluctantly admitted in 1938 that some 50 per cent of the population were religious believers, a good half of them may have been atheists at one or other point in their lives before consciously returning to the faith.[12] When the initiator of the abortive 1960s campaign to reopen a church in the industrial city of Narofominsk, turned out to have been the very same person who as a young activist of the Militant Godless led the destruction of a local church in the 1930s and danced around the bonfire of icons—as reflected in a contemporary Soviet magazine photograph—we are witnessing a case of conversion of an ordinary uneducated worker woman, although she had been baptised in her infancy.[13] In the words of the late Fr. Vsevolod Shpiller, one of Moscow's most intellectually influential priests of the recent past:

> our Church has more members than perhaps any other, . . . who have come to the Church through the personal experience of 'a conversion crisis'. In their childhood their *entourage* was . . . often antireligious . . . Then suddenly they saw the Church in her beauty and truth . . . and came to her . . .[14]

It is in this sense that the post-revolutionary Orthodox Church has been a church of conversions. She has also been a church of martyrdom from the first years of Bolshevism to the present, in one form or another. Here we could present lists of sadistic scalping, beating to death, amputation of limbs and then bleeding to death and drowning of bishops, priests and church activists. But one of the most striking cases was the 1922 trial and execution of Metropolitan Veniamin of Petrograd. Striking, because this was a clear case of liquidation of an innocent churchman whose only crime was that he had been much too popular, particularly among the youth and the working classes of the city, and this dangerously undermined the anti-religious campaign and its propaganda stereotypes, as well as the regime's support for the pro-Soviet, so-called Renovationist, schism in the Orthodox Church. The court room was packed with over 3000 people each day of the trial. Although a large proportion of the audience consisted of organised mobs of communists and *komsomols*, the saintliness of the bishop was so compelling, that all of them rose every time the bishop entered or left the hall, giving his blessing to the people.

Metropolitan Veniamin's defence counsel, Gurovich, who had proved the innocence of his client, stated that as a Jew he was particularly grateful for the opportunity to defend that holy man and to thus repay the Orthodox Church for her help to the Jews at the height of the anti-semitic campaign in Russia before the revolution.[15] Moreover, he warned the Bolsheviks that by murdering the bishop they were creating saintly martyrs who have always only strengthened the church; and that the regime's support for the Renovationists would backfire, because the nation could follow a Saul turning into Paul, the martyr; but it would not follow those 'who deserted from the camp of the martyrs to the camp of the winners'.[16] Indeed, the Renovationist adventure would soon prove a failure precisely because the faithful abandoned them. But who knows, how many of those young communists in the court-room who had been his enemies at first but then rose for the bishop's blessing, applauded the speech of the defence lawyer and probably added their tears to the general sobbing in the hall when the execution verdict was read, how many of them eventually turned to God?

Or, let us take the case of Bishop Makarii of Viaz'ma. Along with a number of clergymen and officials of pre-revolutionary Russia, one summer night of 1918 he was taken out for execution. There, in the open field he asked the executioner to be spared for the last bullet, so that he could bless and spiritually strengthen each victim before the execution. The Bishop's behaviour could not but affect the executioner's will to fulfil his orders, particularly when the turn came to shoot the Bishop. Although in pitch darkness and at a distance, the Bishop perceived the soldier's hesitation, and he addressed him: 'My son, let your heart not trouble you. Do as you were told by those who sent you here.' This story the executioner later shared with his doctor. Ever since that night the soldier saw the Bishop in his dreams every single night of his life until he died of a very mild form of TB, having no will to live. 'How can I go on living after that?', the soldier said to his doctor.[17]

A group of Soviet geologists working in the Siberian Taiga in 1933, pitched their tents not far from a concentration camp. One day they discovered a freshly dug trench close to their tents and saw a detachment of soldiers leading a largish group of prisoners to the trench. The soldiers ordered the geologists to get into their tents and explained, they were going to liquidate Orthodox priests, 'an element alien to the Soviet system'. This was the only justification. In a few minutes the geologists could hear one and the same command repeated 60 times: 'Say there is no God and your life will be spared'. And the same reply repeated 60 times: 'God exists!', followed by a shot. Not a single priest chose to spare his life.[18] How many of those geologists had been non-believers and how many of them were converted by the martyrdom of those 60 priests? For it was not in vain that at least someone of the witnesses passed this information on to our contemporaries 50 years after the event.

A certain Alexander, a former prisoner of the Kolyma death camps, remembers four priests who shared the same huge tent with him, several Orthodox Christians imprisoned for their faith and a large number of regular criminals, including ordinary murderers. One of the four priests, Sergii, observed the hesychastic rule of silence. About the only words he uttered were whispers of prayers: after a whole day of hard manual labour, insufficient food and cold, he would spend almost the whole night in prayer. This caused the wrath of the criminals complaining that that interfered with their sleep. One day the soldiers took three priests and the Christian laymen away; only Fr. Sergii of that group remained in the tent. Suddenly some mystical fear and a sense of terror gripped the criminals. At this point Fr. Sergii suddenly began to speak:

> . . . and all the murderers and robbers listened in utter silence, trying to catch every word he uttered. Fr. Sergii spoke of the poverty and vanity of our existence, of the eternal bliss awaiting everybody who repents. 'All this was so new and unusual for the listeners', writes Alexander, 'that it was felt that through his lips it was Someone Else who spoke'.

Some hours later only one of the three priests and lay Christians returned to the camp. It was Fr. Rafail, who recounted how all of them were first warned that unless they agreed to renounce Jesus, they would be shot. Everyone of the group individually confessed his unswerving faith in God, whereupon they were led into a field and ordered to dig a ditch. Then everyone was shot in the head, including the laity, but Fr. Rafail, who was ordered to fill up the ditch, was then brought back to the camp. The time of the terror that had befallen the prisoners described by Alexander coincided with the shooting of that Christian group several miles away.[19]

Here we see an obvious case of a missionary dissemination of faith through martyrdom obviously affecting not only Alexander, who admits in a *samizdat* memoir over 40 years later that the experience shook up his spiritual life forever, but it also directly affected hardened criminals.

This brings us to the subject of the role of the *startsy* or elders and spiritual fathers, in the transmission and dissemination of faith in Soviet conditions, for Alexander's brief description of Fr. Sergii leaves no doubt that he was a *starets*, a monastic spiritual father and adviser to a hungry flock.

One of the most famous recent startsy was Fr. Tavrion (Batozsky). Deceased in 1978 at the age of 80, he had spent nearly 30 years in camps, prisons and internal exile for his service to the church and to believers. Shortly before his death he said to a visiting Orthodox bishop from England:

> If you only knew how grateful I am to God for my wonderful life! Imagine, the good Lord had entrusted such a responsible pastoral work among prison inmates to me when I was still so young [27 years old at the time of his first arrest in 1925]. If I had not landed in those camps, how many people would never have heard the word of God![20]

The issue of the relationship of prisons to the survival and mission of faith is in itself a fascinating subject. Many ex-prisoners, including Alexander Solzhenitsyn, have found their faith while in prisons and in direct relationship to their ordeals. Vladimir Osipov was a prisoner of conscience in the 1960s and once again from the mid-1970s to early 1980s, and used to be a Marxist before his first imprisonment but has become an Orthodox Christian while in a concentration camp. He points to such factors as: a cathartic experience of the impasse of materialism, the reading of Dostoevsky while in the labour camps, and the ability to view the Soviet society from a prison more reflectively, as if from a distance, as ways to a faith in the Supernatural. Others speak about the existential choice that the prison puts before every inmate: co-operate with the authorities, report on your comrades, and you'll receive better treatment and early release; refuse to compromise, and you'll be tortured with hunger, punishment cells, loss of health and perhaps even a premature death. The latter choice is inexplicable in terms of materialism and moral relativism; its justification lies plainly in the sphere of religious morality based on the absoluteness of good and evil.[21] Another prison veteran, a medical doctor, pondering over the question, why 'a vast majority' of prisoners of conscience become 'firm, unwavering believers in God', comes to the following conclusion which is quite incompatible with a secular consumerist attitude to life. 'Man has been created only in order to think', and prison, where time loses all sense, is the ideal place for prolonged, profound thinking, for there man is free from the daily concern for his own and his family's material existence: 'Nowhere else is there such a freedom for thought, such a deliverance from all worldly concerns'.[22]

And throughout the period from the 1920s to the early 1950s no other part of Soviet society had such a high density of priests, bishops and theologians as its punitive establishments. No doubt, there they continued their mission and, given the above testimonies, were probably most successful at it.

Whether monastic or non-monastic, whether in camps or at large, startsy and generally spiritual fathers of undisputed moral authority, became the natural leaders and organisers of church brotherhoods. These mushroomed across Russia soon after Patriarch Tikhon's January 1918 appeal to believers to form spiritual unions and brotherhoods to preserve the church and the faith under the atheistic regime. Sometimes, particularly after the Revolution, the term 'brotherhood' stood for a church society of both sexes. Some church brotherhoods of that kind had existed from the pre-revolutionary times, but it was after 1918, with the closure of church schools, publishing enterprises and libraries, that the Christian enlightenment, mutual aid and missionary role of these brotherhoods became particularly important. Priests often divided members into senior and junior brothers and sisters, because numerically the brotherhoods were too large to allow pastoral individual work with each member. The priests used to work with the senior ones, training them to lead the junior members. After Sunday liturgies in the parishes with such brotherhoods, benches used to be brought into the church. The priest would read something from the Scriptures or writings of the Church Fathers, which would develop into a general discussion. Members were told to keep diaries where they noted details of their spiritual life, issues and questions arising therefrom. These were to be discussed with the senior brothers and sisters, or, when the senior adviser found him- or herself incapable of solving a problem, they would be directed to the spiritual father. Brotherhood members were entrusted with religious education of parish children. Even children and youth camps in the country were organised in the 1920s for that purpose. Veterans of these brotherhoods say that their priests and elders had prepared them for future trials. The spiritual training allowed them morally and spiritually to survive the camps and prisons, and to carry on the dissemination of the word of God both in prisons and on return to normal life after release. The brotherhoods engaged also in charity, particularly helping the families of those in prisons or otherwise persecuted. They also helped the imprisoned clergy.

Once all this had become illegal in 1929, 'the life of the Church went underground . . . Not the Church, but her life, her activities.'[23] This remains true to a great extent to this day, particularly where mission and preparation for conversion are concerned. Take the case of a recent high-school graduate described by himself. While in his last school year (that is 17 years old), he met a Christian family. There he always encountered large gatherings of people, thanks to whom he realised 'that Christianity is a *living* faith, not just a set of rituals'. There, apparently, he was given a brochure on the Lord's Resurrection which, 'for the first time allowed me some minimal appreciation of the Christian experience'. Gradually he realised 'the senselessness of atheism', the impotence of man without God; even thoughts of committing suicide went through his head before he described all his 'experiences of the last nine or ten days' in a letter delivered to a priest by his new acquaintances. Apparently, the same friends arranged a meeting between the young man and the priest. A week later he was baptised. He concludes: 'My whole life now is a life in the Church; my falls, misfortunes and happiness are all defined by my relationship to Christ. The main thing was my conversion. It is the beginning, the birth.'[24]

To sum up the above story in terms of the contemporary Soviet law, all the activities there described, except for the final act of baptism, fall under the category of illegal religious propaganda and dissemination of hostile literature, punishable by imprisonments and fines.[25] This confirms the above quotation that all the active life of the church—such as education and mission—is carried on in the underground or the catacombs, coming up into the open only for acts falling directly into the liturgical sphere: communal or private church services and sermons. The Christian family and the group of people who brought the youth to the doorstep of the church were undoubtedly members of such brotherhoods of our own days.

Their teaching ability is no accident. According to the available literature, paradoxically, although Soviet teachers are required by law to be active atheists, the brotherhoods—right from their beginnings and throughout the Soviet period—produced many outstanding pedagogues. A case in point was Dr Vera Vasilevskaia. A scholar in the field of child psychology and education theory, she was an adult convert to Orthodox Christianity of nominally Jewish background and an aunt of the present-day charismatic Moscow priest, Father Alexander Men'. Vasilevskaia left very penetrating memories about Fr. Seraphim Batiukov, the priest who had secretly converted her and most of her family in the 1930s, a famous starets and brotherhoods' leader.[26]

Logic and recent evidence suggest that the remnants of the pre-war brotherhoods have contributed considerably to the continuity of the church and to the inheritance of Christian teachings by our contemporaries. As the case with the above young student and other samizdat material indicates, the 1970s and 1980s have seen not only the survival but also the rebirth of some forms of Christian brotherhoods on the fringes of the official Orthodox Church. Some call themselves brotherhoods, others, religious seminars. One of the early documents of reborn brotherhoods belongs to the very early 1970s. It speaks about the formation of miniature brotherhoods of newly converted intellectuals. Their aim is to revive the Christian way of thinking, to repent for their own and their parents' sin of abandonment of the church in her hardest hour, and to struggle for the restoration of the legal rights of the church and the believers in the USSR.[27]

Undoubtedly such unofficial religious seminars as that of Alexander Ogorodnikov, dispersed some nine years ago by the KGB with the incarceration of Ogorodnikov himself and other main activists, such as Vladimir Poresh, Tatiana Shchipkova, Popkov, Ermolaev, Argentov and others, have been but a continuation and renewal of the brotherhoods. The Ogorodnikov seminar, while growing in numbers, began to have its sessions in various cities besides Moscow—for example Ufa in the Urals, Smolensk in west Russia—in order to evolve into a network of small, local, tightly knit and apostolically active Christian communities, studying Christianity not only in theory, but applying it to their daily life, which would include active mission and proselytising. They even hoped to eventually organise Christian summer camps for children and tried to set up a rural agricultural Christian commune. All that was not only denied to them by the Soviet authorities but, as mentioned above, most of its active members soon found themselves with long terms of imprisonment in strict regime camps. Ogorodnikov eventually spent almost eight years in concentration camps until his amnesty in 1987.

Currently such seminars are unofficially tolerated as long as they do not try to actively proselytise outside their group or add any social activities to their agenda—the law denying the church any activities beyond the walls of the temple continues to be observed by the state rather strictly. Seminars or Christian brotherhoods as groups of theological or religio-philosophic self-education, have lately mushroomed in the country with the regime's greater laxity towards the so-called non-formal societies. There are several dozen such study groups in Moscow alone, and probably well over 100 across the country, producing at least two serious religious samizdat journals in Moscow alone—Ogorodnikov's ecumenical *Christian Community Bulletin*, and Viktor Aksiuchits's and Gleb Anishchenko's *Choice* ('a literary-philosophical journal of Russian Christian culture'). The church unofficially supports the seminars, individual priests meet regularly with their leaders, instruct them, advise them as to the agenda of discussions, provide them with the necessary literature and bibliographies for further reading; and quite openly celebrate special services in churches for the seminars, for their spiritual health and success in disseminating the word of God among the young.[28] Thus, although still unofficially and, perhaps not yet universally, the gap between these fringe groups of Christian neophytes and seekers on the one hand, and the overt and official Orthodox Church on the other seems to be on its way to being bridged. Yet, whatever the 'behind the scenes' help of the professional clergy, the contemporary seminars and brotherhoods are formed by laymen, mostly neophytes, still rather uncertain in their identification with the church, needing probably even closer clerical guidance than their predecessors who had been raised within the church, and had studied religion in pre-revolutionary general education schools. Many samizdat authors point to the difficulty of truly inducting or reinducting neophytes into the church without proper pastoral guidance and appropriate litera-ture, even though they may have been consciously baptised as adults. Consequently, neophytes often fall into one or the other extremity: some become practically idolators of the ritual aspects of Orthodox Christianity, others place their theological discoveries above the church, believing that church worship is meant for uneducated old women. For a baptised intellectual it can be enough to belong to Orthodox culture as expressed through the literature of Dostoevsky and other Russian writers, the philosophy of Soloviov or Berdiaev, the theology of Florovsky or Florensky, and the iconographic art of Rublev. Only proper pastoral and theological guidance, claim these authors, can cure the neophytes of both temptations.[29]

Such are the channels of the transmission and inheritance of the church in Soviet conditions. Are they sufficient? Are we really talking about a church of the masses or about one for the selected few? What are the numbers, and how effective is the faith thus inherited?

These questions are very difficult to answer satisfactorily.

Soviet official studies of believers, largely based on interviews and sociological field surveys carried out by the atheistic establishment, claim that religious believers are predominantly very old people of very low educational level and that their faith is very vague and primitive, while their numbers are constantly declining with the rise of educational standards in the country.[30]

Numbers and proportions of believers in the total population of the Soviet Union are a highly controversial issue. Already in the 1920s many Soviet atheistic publications were claiming that only 11 per cent of urban working-class children were being brought up in faith in God by their parents. Yet, in 1938 they admitted that one third of the urban and two-thirds of the rural population were religious believers. Surveys carried out under the German occupation of the western parts of the USSR, showed only 1 to 2 per cent as avowed atheists. Official Soviet surveys of the 1960s–1970s claim that believers constituted 10 to 25 per cent of the urban population and 15 to 40 per cent of the rural one. A bishop in the Soviet Ukraine in a letter to Brezhnev of 1977 claimed that believers constituted 'a good half of the population'.[31]

Father Innokentii of the Leningrad Theological Academy in a rare dialogue published in a Soviet sociological journal warned against the acceptance of Soviet published figures at face value, because they are based on data submitted by the officials of the Soviet Council for Religious Affairs, which in turn are gained from the parish wardens' reports who know that the state officials want figures which would testify to the decline of religious practices. Therefore in both stages of reporting such figures are deliberately slanted downwards. He accepts the approximation of about 20 per cent of the total population of the USSR as being practising members of the Orthodox Church (some 55 million), but says that, depending on the area, the figure varies from less than 10 per cent to over 60 per cent (in the rural areas of western Belorussia, for instance). In the last 10 to 15 years, he continues, there has been a marked change in the profile of the believers. On the one hand, there has been some decline in regular church attendance. On the other, there has been a marked increase in the under-fifty age group, as well as of youths attending churches. Among these latter categories there are considerably more males than in the above-sixty age group, while in the under-thirty age group the proportion of both sexes is about equal. The decrease has been at the cost of the over-sixty generation which consisted mostly of women not only because women are more religious than men, but because the males of that generation had been decimated by the war, and also 'by the socio-cultural hurricanes of the 1920s–30s'. These old women had been religious by inheritance, but their cultural-educational level had been so low that many of them failed to pass on their faith to their offspring. Only regarding that passing generation of churchwomen is there any accuracy in the claims that the educational level of religious believers was much lower than the national average. As to the under-sixty age group, their educational level is no lower than that of the national average. The point, according to Fr. Innokentii, is that it is the families of Christian intelligentsia who succeeded in transmitting religious faith to their children and grandchildren in the absence of religious schools. The other, and a rapidly growing proportion of believers, making up about one third of regular church attendants in the major cities today, consists of adult converts, again mostly well-educated young people.[32]

Both Fr. Innokentii and other representatives of the Russian Orthodox Church emphasise also that the growing proportion of young neophytes is clearly visible only in those major cities where there are numerous churches, that is where a certain security of anonymity is available. In cities where there are only one or two churches, a young Christian will rarely risk his or her educational or professional career by openly demonstrating faith in church where he or she can be easily spotted. He or she will travel many hundreds of kilometres to Moscow, Leningrad, Kiev, or to a far away village where no one knows the person, rather than be exposed as a religious believer in one's town of residence, work or study. This further bedevils any accurate calculation of believers and new converts.[33]

Then, writes Fr. Innokentii, there is the large but incalculable category of what Soviet religiologists call 'waverers': 'people who attend the church from time to time, but know very little about the faith . . . Yet, they consider it their duty to baptise their children' but because of their secular and liberal attitude to family life they avoid getting married in church, knowing that the Gospel teaches inviola-bility of the marriage sacrament. Hence the discrepancy between the percentage of infant baptisms and church weddings.[34] But how widespread is the practice of infant baptism? According to Soviet publications, some 35 per cent of all babies born lately in the USSR have been baptised, which, at least potentially, would give a population of about 100 million baptised souls in an overall Soviet population of about 280 million. The official church figure presented at the 1988 Local Council of the Russian Orthodox Church is 30 million persons baptised between 1971 and 1987, in 16 years, or during a little less than a quarter of the average life-span of a generation. Given Fr. Innokentii's informed opinion that up to one third of the younger generations of believers are converts—and according to most observations the predominant age of conversions is 25–30—we can assume that of the 30 million souls baptised in the Orthodox Church in a sixteen-year period, 10 million were adults. Then the 20 million can be multiplied by four (16 years × 4 = 64, the average span of male life in the USSR), while the 10 million adults could be multiplied by $2\frac{1}{2}$ (70 years being the approximate age span expectation for those who have survived to 25–30). The total will be 105 million, which would be the lowest possible potential of the projected Orthodox population, assuming that the current baptismal dynamics remain constant. Add to that Roman Catholics, Protestants, other Christians, not to mention Moslems and other significant non-Christian faiths of the USSR, and the total will be considerably in excess of the 100 million religious believers of all faiths—a calculation made on the basis of official Soviet estimates. As the historically organised sector of the Soviet population roughly amounts to 200 million, the rate of the baptised (Orthodox) among them would be about 55 per cent. This coincides with unofficial and samizdat estimates, and with a Soviet 1960 survey of children in a Soviet young pioneer camp, among whom the rate of baptised children was found to have stood at 53 per cent. But surely the figure among young pioneers would have been lower than across the nation, as many Christian children evade the organisation and particularly its camps with their intensive anti-religious education. Moreover, there has been a general rise of people turning to religion since the 1960s.[35] Thus, in terms of the rate of baptised souls the Soviet Union compares well with many contemporary western countries and shows no decline of religion.

What remains to be investigated is the Soviet atheistic propaganda claim that the content of the current believers' faith is very vague and confused from the theological point of view; that a faith in rituals often replaces theology and reversals to paganism are noticeable, particularly in the areas which had been converted relatively recently.[36] That, of course, stands to reason in view of the absence of any regular religious education of the laity, lack of appropriate literature and the dire shortage of well-educated clergy: there are only three undergraduate theological seminaries and two graduate theological academies; and they are not allowed to produce proper textbooks for their students. Lately, both problems have been repeatedly mentioned by leading Soviet clergymen,[37] while a bishop stated at a diocesan conference in 1987 that the laity was suffering from many superstitions which they mixed into their religious faith, and from ignorance of the true faith. He appealed to the clergy to instruct their flocks accordingly, particularly parents and children, and to pay more attention to theologically educative sermons.[38] The neophytes themselves complain that they 'have been baptized into Christ', but 'not clothed into Christ', badly needing pastoral guidance.[39] This must be even truer of the masses who have inherited the faith more as a tradition, as a gut feeling, rather than as a conscious choice. Although their proportion in the religious sector of the population may be declining, according to Fr. Innokentii, they still constitute a majority of the flock at an average parish and a majority of those who baptise their children.[40] Nor do the catastrophic rates of alcoholism, divorce, irregular sex life and crime indicate a deep imprint of Christ's teachings on the masses (or on considerable proportions of the intelligentsia).

As Fr. Innokentii points out, the successful transmission of faith in the families of the intelligentsia and the rapidly rising numbers of converts leave no doubt that the church is by no means a dying phenomenon. But her real spiritual and moral weight—her ability to morally revive the society in her second millennium—will largely depend on whether the church will have succeeded in obtaining those rights which will allow her to take full pastoral care of the neophyte groups, to teach and to lead the Christian brotherhoods which are spontaneously appearing to the fullness of church life. Much will also depend on the restoration of the social prestige of the official church and her clergy; and this will come only after the clergy have been allowed to speak with their own voices on social questions, rather than automatically repeating official policies dictated to them by state agents.

NOTES

1. This is a revised and updated version of this author's paper originally
    written by him in Russian, delivered at the Russian Orthodox Church
    Millennium Conference organised by the Lutheran Academy in Bavar-
    ia (Tutzing: May 1987) and published in *Grani* (Frankfurt/Main) no.
    147 (January–March 1988). An even earlier version appeared in
    samizdat in Alexander Ogorodnikov's *Biulleten' khristianskoi
    obshchestvennosti* (Moscow: 1987).
2. On disenfranchisement of the Church in 1918 see D. Pospielovsky, *A
    History of Soviet Atheism in Theory and Practice and the Believer*, vol.
    1, *A History of Marxist-Leninist Atheism and Soviet Antireligious
    Policies* (London: Macmillan, 1987) pp. 27–9; on anti-religious legisla-
    tion, ibid., pp. 132–53. On the clergy toll see ibid., vol. 2, *Soviet
    Antireligious Campaigns and Persecutions* (London: 1987) pp. 66–8.
3. 'Slovo O. V. Borovogo', *Russkoe vozrozhdenie* (New York, Moscow,
    Paris: Preparatory Committee for the One Thousandth Anniversary of
    the Baptism of Russia) (1980) no. 9, pp. 38–43.
4. 'Puti tvoi, Gospodi', anonymous ms. (46 pages). Keston College
    Orthodox *Samizdat* Archives, Keston, Kent, England. There are many
    miraculous elements also in the memoirs of Vera Vasilevskaia, men-
    tioned below. She is a well-known and highly reliable source: an
    outstanding pedagogue and scholar in the field of child psychology, the
    deceased aunt of one of Moscow's most outstanding priests, Fr.
    Alexander Men'. Metropolitan Anthony (Bloom) of London, a medic-
    al doctor and neuro-pathologist by training, once remarked that
    miracles become particularly obvious and visible in extreme situations;
    they are like crutches sent to human beings as a last resort (public
    discussion after D. Pospielovsky's lecture at the Orthodox Forum
    Centre, London, February 1987).
5. On the frustrated efforts in the immediate pre-1917 period see James
    W. Cunningham, *A Vanquished Hope* (St Vladimir's Seminary Press:
    1981) *passim*.
6. Lev Regelson, *Tragediia Russkoi Tserkvi* (Paris: YMCA Press, 1977)
    pp. 225–6. Although most of the terror, particularly against the church,
    was the work of Bolsheviks, hence, *de facto* the excommunication
    encyclical was mostly addressed at them, the Patriarchate was very
    careful to observe its impartiality in a struggle where the faithful were
    to be found on both sides of the front. It ordered funeral services for
    casualties of both sides and strictly censured priests who publicly
    welcomed the Whites. The Patriarch also refused to give his blessing to
    the Whites, and announced a civic loyalty to the Soviet regime as early
    as September 1919, when the Whites were still on the offensive and
    within less than 200 miles of Moscow.
7. 'Puti tvoi' and multiple other sources, both official and unofficial.
    There is no consensus as to the exact year when this process of return
    to the church began. As far as the intelligentsia is concerned, it began
    at least 15 years before the revolutions of 1917. The most famous of

these were the philosophers, publicists and future theologians—almost all former Marxists, some former leading theorists of Marxism, for example Petr Struve and S. Bulgakov—who would constitute the so-called Russian Religio-Philosophic Renaissance. But that was a trickle. In the 1920s the intelligentsia re-conversions to Orthodox Christianity became almost a flood. But even in the rural areas, according to contemporary Soviet sources, there appeared an absolute growth of religious temples of all confessions in the second half of the 1920s; in the Russian republic it expressed itself in the increase of all temples from 31 678 in 1927 to 32 539 in 1928, of which Orthodox churches constituted 71.5 per cent in 1927 and 72 per cent in 1928. See Pospielovsky, *Russian Church under the Soviet Regime, 1917–1982* (Crestwood, NY: St Vladimir's Seminary Press, 1984) pp. 99–102; V. D. Kobetsky, 'Issledovanie dinamiki religioznosti SSSR', *Ateizm, religiia i sovremennost'* (Leningrad: 1973) pp. 116–27.

8.   For a church estimate on the percentage of adult converts in the contemporary Russian Orthodox Church, see note 32 below.

9.   Pospielovsky, *A History of Soviet*, vol. 3, *Soviet Studies on the Church and the Believer's Response to Atheism* (London: Macmillan, 1988) pp. 191–2. As pointed out in note 32 below, the church's estimate on the rate of adult converts is considerably bigger than the state's. But a Soviet religiologist's comment following Fr. Innokentii's article admits that the latter is much more reliable than the Soviet atheistic 'scholarship'.

10.   L. Emeliakh, 'Atheizm i antiklerakalizm narodynkh mass v 1917 g.', *Voprosy istorii religii i ateizma*, vol. 5 (Moscow and Leningrad: 1958) pp. 64–7. The samizdat biographical novel *Ostraia Luka* claims that the process began as the people became tired of World War I and blamed priests for it. Around 1922 the author shows the beginning of the reversal of the process, a return to the church. Anonymous ms., Keston College Orthodox Samizdat, Archives, p. 163.

11.   F. Oleshchuk, *Kto stroit tserkvi v SSSR* (Moscow, Leningrad: n.d.) p. 6.

12.   Pospielovsky, *Russian Church*, p. 172.

13.   Pospielovsky, *A History*, vol. 3, pp. 236–7.

14.   Pospielovsky, *Russian Church*, p. 328.

15.   Pospielovsky, *A History*, vol. 2, 'Antireligious Campaigns and Persecutions' (London: Macmillan, 1987) pp. 53–4. What he meant was in particular the fraudulently organised trial in Kiev in 1913 of a Jewish worker Beilis, accused of a ritual murder of a Christian youth. The Orthodox Church provided the defence with its theological expertise to prove that Jews could not engage in any ritual murder, thus destroying the case of the prosecution and securing Beilis' acquittal.

16.   Regelson, p. 300; Pospielovsky, *A History*, vol. 2, pp. 52–3.

17.   Pospielovsky, ibid., p. 7.

18.   Ibid., pp. 82–3.

19.   Ibid., p. 83; and vol. 3, pp. 231–2.

20.   Ibid., vol. 3, p. 231; Metropolitan Anthony's testimony at the Orthodox Forum Centre, London, 13 February 1987.

21. Solzhenitsyn, *Gulag Archipelago*, vol. 2, part 4, chapter 1; Michael Scammell, *Solzhenitsyn. A Biography* (London: Hutchinson, 1984) pp. 302–03; Osipov, 'Ploshchad' Maiakovskogo, stat'ia 70', *Grani* (Frankfurt/Main: 1971) no. 80, pp. 119, 131–2; 'Formuliar', anonymous ms., Keston College Orthodox Samizdat Archive, pp. 1–2; S. Fudel', 'U sten Tserkvi', *Nadezhda. Khristianskoe chtenie* (Russia: Samizdat; Frankfurt/Main reprints) (1979) no. 2, p. 234; Vladimir Tel'nikov, recorded public talk at Radio Liberty on his arrival from the USSR, Munich, 28 March 1972.

22. Pospielovsky, *A History*, vol. 3, p. 247.

23. Natal'ia Kiter, 'Ispovedniki i mucheniki 30-kh godov' (from the Hoover Institution Archives), *Vestnik RkhD* (1987) no. 150, p. 243.

24. 'Istoriia odnogo obrashcheniia', *Nadezhda* (1980) no. 4, pp. 295–300.

25. The articles most commonly applied for religious 'offences' have been: Article 142 of the Criminal Code: 'Breaking the law on the separation of Church from the State and School from the Church'—for unauthorised teaching of religion, catechisation, religious seminars and study groups.

Article 1901: 'Dissemination of knowingly false insinuations undermining the Soviet state and social order'—passing on religious or any other literature not authorised for publication in the USSR has been punished in cords under this article.

Article 162: 'Participation in banned enterprises', such as illegal publication or xeroxing of religious literature.

Open criticism of Soviet religious legislation as well as any other acts of the Soviet Government has on some occasions been tried according to the extremely severe Article 70: 'Antisoviet agitation and propaganda' with punishments of up to 10 years at hard labour followed by up to five years of internal exile. Among churchmen sentenced by means of this article have been Fr. Gleb Yakunin, Deacon Vladimir Rusak and the lay Orthodox Christian Vladimir Osipov (twice).

26. Pospielovsky, *A History*, vol. 3, pp. 229–30.

27. I. Denisov, 'Slovo otstupnikov', in *Vestnik RSKhD* (1971) no. 99, pp. 112–21.

28. Gleb Anishchenko, 'Nekotorye problemy pravoslavnoi periodiki', in *Russkaia mysl'* (22 January 1988) p. 10.

29. Pospielovsky, *A History*, vol. 3, pp. 227–8, 243–7; anonymous, 'O Russkoi pravoslavnoi Tserkvi' (Moscow: Samizdat, 1986) Radio Liberty Archive: AS5911, pp. 25–8.

30. Pospielovsky, *A History*, vol. 3, pp. 197–216, 251–60, and generally chapter 10; see also, 'Dialog', in *Sotsiologicheskie issledovaniia* (July–August 1987) no. 4, pp. 28–49.

31. Pospielovsky, *A History*, vol. 3, p. 196.

32. S. N. Pavlov (Hieromonk Innokentii) 'O sovremennom sostoianii Russkoi pravoslavnoi Tserkvi', *Sotsiologicheskie issledovaniia* (July–August 1987) no. 4, pp. 36–41.

33. Ibid., pp. 38–9; oral statements to this effect by Russian clergy at a conference in January 1988.

34. Pavlov, 'O sovremennom', p. 40.

35. Report of Metropolitan Vladimir (Sabodan), Chancellor of the

Moscow Patriarchate, at the Local Council, 6–9 June 1988. Ms., Department of Foreign Church Relations, 1988. Russian, Order no. 247, p. 1. On individual reports and on the pioneer camp survey see Pospielovsky, *A History*, vol. 3, pp. 192–3.

36. Ibid., pp. 197–216, 251–60.
37. 'Iz zhizni dukhovnykh shkol. Interv'iu predsedatelia Uchebnogo komiteta arkhiepiskopa Alexandra', in *Zhurnal Moskovskoi patriarkhii* (May 1987) no. 5, pp. 21–2; 'Zasedaniia rukovodstva Uchebnogo komiteta i Dukhovnykh shkol', in *ZhMP* (November 1987) no. 11, pp. 31–3.
38. 'Iz zhizni eparkhii. Smolenskaia eparkhiia', in *ZhMP* (1987) no. 11, pp. 38–40.
39. 'O Russkoi pravoslavnoi Tserkvi', pp. 14, 18–20; Pospielovsky, *A History*, vol. 3, pp. 228–32, 251–60.
40. Pavlov, 'O sovremennom', pp. 36–40.

17 Are the Furov Reports Authentic?
Raymond Oppenheim

INTRODUCTION

The leadership of the Russian Orthodox Patriarchate of Moscow is often criticised for its subservience to the Soviet authorities, for its slavish support of the foreign policy goals of the Soviet Union, and for its timid willingness to accept constant interference in its internal affairs by Communist bureaucrats. In defence of the church's response to Soviet pressure, the apologists have usually made the obvious point that co-operation has meant continued existence.

There have been very few opportunities to catch a glimpse of the control mechanism used by the Communist Party to impose its will upon the church hierarchy. There has been a great deal of dissident criticism of the bishops, and much speculation based on secondary sources. Actual documents are rare indeed. A single, dramatic exception to this lacuna exists—the so-called 'Furov Documents'. These reports appear to be an in-house collection of papers, gathered or written by Vasiliy Grigorievich Furov, Deputy Chairman of the State Committee for Religious Affairs (usually abbreviated as CRA).

If Furov's reports are genuine, we can explore insights, never revealed before, into the actual way in which the state has attempted to control the church. It is also possible to study, through the eyes of Soviet bureaucrats, the degree to which the bishops and other church leaders have attempted to resist this control. Perhaps of greatest interest to students of religion in the Soviet Union, is the new perspective on the men themselves—the bishops, bureaucrats, and clergy with whom western scholars, clerics and diplomats have to deal, both in international gatherings and during visits to the Soviet Union.

This paper will discuss the authenticity of the Furov Documents and their reliability as a source of insight into a fascinating period. Of all the years between the rise of Brezhnev (1964) and the beginning of the Gorbachev regime (1985), 1974 is one of the most interesting. Dmitri Dudko was preaching, Aleksander Solzhenitsyn was giving secret press conferences, Richard Nixon made his last visit and then was forced out of office, and there was constant speculation about Brezhnev's health. I am convinced that it is possible to date Furov's material with precision within this period, and this precision argues in favour of the authenticity and reliability of the data. This does not mean, of course, that all of it is true. In fact, quite the contrary is sometimes the case, as Comrade Furov seeks to communicate to the Central Committee of the CPSU the desired message.

I was Chaplain to the foreign community in the Soviet Union during the period when Furov wrote his report. Those were the detente years, and there were surprisingly many opportunities to gain access to the inner workings of the religious scene. Staff members and students at the seminaries, employees of the Department of External Church Relations on Ulitsa Ryleyeva and of the Publications Department at the Novodevichy, parish priests, and even some of the bishops were willing to speak with varying degrees of frankness. The formal statements often had to take into account the unseen listening audience.[1] There was sometimes embarrassment on both sides, as official proclamations were made. The author recalls one incident in particular, with Metropolitan Iuvenaliy, who was then head of the Department of External Church Relations of the Patriarchate—the church's 'Minister of Foreign Affairs'. In 1972, the author had to sit through a detailed recitation of the crimes of Archbishop Pavel (Golyshev).[2] A very solemn-faced Iuvenaliy trotted out a catalogue of pederasty and other unattractive vices. But having put on record the official view, he then shared a delightful anecdote. According to Iuvenaliy, Pavel was summoned to Moscow in February 1972 and presented with the ukaz, appointing him to Vologda. According to Orthodox Canon Law, the moment Pavel received the ukaz, he was no longer Archbishop of Novosibirsk. He then returned to Novosibirsk, denounced the actions of the Patriarchate in a cathedral sermon, and for good measure, ordained a flock of priests without permission before he left for Vologda. Iuvenaliy stroked his beard and muttered about how difficult it was to unscramble such canonical chaos. They had sent out Archbishop Damian (Marchuk) of Volynia and Rovno to resolve matters before the new Bishop Gideon (Dakunin) took over.[3] The only possible decision was that the ordinations were valid, if highly irregular.

Away from the formal interviews, however, there were many opportunities for frank conversation, and these grew as time went by. There was the occasional stroll in Gorky Park or VDNKh, there were the dinners at Fr. Shpiller's or at the homes of other priests, and then, of course, there was always Metropolitan Nikodim. Perhaps it is worth recording for posterity one more anecdote about that fascinating hierarch. It was a late night conversation over a bottle—the Metropolitan, a distinguished Anglican visitor, and myself. Michael Bourdeaux was mentioned. Vladyko Nikodim wagged his finger at us. 'If I have a toothache, I know I have a toothache. I don't need him to tell me I have a toothache! And if I have a toothache, I know where to go to get it fixed!'

THE DATE OF THE FUROV REPORT—A COMEDY OF ERRORS

When the Furov Report first reached the west, in 1979, there was some debate as to its date of composition. Now dating the Furov Report precisely does not prove, beyond the shadow of a doubt, that it is not a KGB exercise in disinformation, but a forgery would in all probability be either far more or far less accurate than the document which was smuggled to the west. What emerges, from a close study of the materials, is a reasonably precise date for its compilation.

Much of the discussion on the supposed date of the Furov Report revolves around three crucial lists of diocesan bishops. Furov divides them into three categories. If these categories are genuine, they reflect a crucial evaluation of the hierarchy into camps—those who co-operated with the state, those who needed watching, and those who opposed state policy. There are indeed errors and omissions in the three lists,[4] but two of the dates which have been suggested for them are demonstrably incorrect.

Professor Nikita Struve dated the Report after September 1975, and put that year on the title page of his translation.[5] This was based on a misprint in the original publication by the *Vestnik Russkogo Khristianskogo Dvizheniya*,[6] which he repeats.[7] This is pointed out by Jane Ellis.[8]

Professor Dimitry Pospielovsky dates the Report 1978. He states that: 'although the information given covers roughly the period from 1967 to September 1975 (sic), it mentions both Mstislav and Bogolep as ruling bishops of Kirov. Mstislav died in 1978, and the next incumbent was Bogolep.'[9] Ellis simply dismisses the duplication of the Kirov diocese as an error.[10] This is completely consistent with the general sloppiness of the Report. But one other factor must be noted.

If indeed, the list was compiled in 1974, and Bogolep was in Kirovograd rather than Kirov, then the rest of the hierarchs should be in their 1974 sees, rather than in their 1978 sees. This is in fact the case. If the list had been compiled in 1978, many of the bishops named would have been in new sees. For example, by 1978, Serafim of Krutitsy had retired, been replaced by Iuvenaliy from Tula, and Victorin had moved from Vienna to Tula; or, Serapion had returned from Damascus and gone to Irkutsk, Vladimir (Kotlyarov) had moved from Irkutsk to Vladimir, Nikolai had moved from Vladimir to Kaluga, and Donat had retired from Kaluga. As all of the bishops in the 1974 Furov lists are in the correct sees, except for Bogolep, it is reasonable to suppose that the telephone rang while Furov was typing his report, and he never finished typing the name—Kirov . . . ograd.

How then can the date be established? On 3 September 1974, the Holy Synod made a series of appointments.[11] All of these are reflected in Furov's lists.[12] The following are shown in their new sees: German in Vilnius, Nikolai in Perm, Khrisostom in Kursk, Mikhail in Tambov and the newly consecrated Damaskin in Vologda. Victorin is missing, as he has been removed from Perm to Vienna; and Anatoliy is missing, as he has been moved from Vilnius to Damascus. Furov's lists do not include bishops abroad, probably because the CRA was not involved in their day to day management. One can only speculate which agency would be managing overseas bishops.

Further, Furov's lists show no Bishop of Omsk, a major diocese. Mefodiy (Menzak), Archbishop of Omsk, had died on 23 October 1974.[13] On 26 December 1974, the Holy Synod decided to bring Bishop Maksim (Krokha) from Argentina to be the new Bishop of Omsk.[14]

One final datum is that Furov quotes Patriarch Pimen's letter to Kosygin, dated 5 November 1974 (not dated in the Furov Report but in the Journal of the Moscow Patriarchate).[15] This does not further limit the dating, as the letter would have been in the CRA offices for approval. The fact that Furov quotes it merely demonstrates that it was a contemporary document, that had probably passed over his desk that week.

From the date available, the author supports Jane Ellis, in dating the final version of the Furov materials to the period between 23 October and 26 December 1974, giving us a very precise window.

THE FUROV ENVIRONMENT

On 15 September 1974, just before the date of Furov's Report, a new Soviet era began. A group of Moscow artists occupied a vacant section and displayed in public a number of forbidden paintings. Trucks arrived (even a bulldozer), artists were mugged, paintings were burned, and the KGB worked-over a couple of foreign correspondents. The international outcry shocked the Soviet authorities, and a fortnight later, the first free exhibition in decades took place in Izmaylovo Park—29 September 1974 (just three and a half weeks before the date of the death of Archbishop Mefodiy of Omsk, the beginning of the two-month 'Furov' period).

Detente had meant a certain degree of relaxation—Pepsi-Cola was now available. It was supposed to be an alternative to vodka, but the children of the 'servants of the people' had discovered that vodka and Pepsi make a reasonably good mixed drink. The two-record set of 'Jesus Christ Superstar' was selling on the Arbat for 125 rubles, about the same price as the 1973 limited edition of Mandelshtam. Girls wore high plastic boots, too much make-up, and dresses carefully copied from pictures in western magazines. There was an air of unease—Nixon had fallen from power in August, there were rumours about Brezhnev's health, and arrests of dissidents were on the increase. It was a time when *apparatchiki* were still doing things according to the same old patterns, and still hoping that everything was going to work out.

You could ape the west and get away with it. Slightly longer hair was being tolerated on the young men, crosses were appearing around young necks, and there was a massive new industry in pirated cassettes of rock music. And yet, the atmosphere in government offices seemed unchanged. The ubiquitous Soviet abacus had not made way for even the adding machine, much less the calculator. Officials typed their own letters, did their own sums, and answered their own telephones. The message had not yet reached the Soviet worker that a service job could be anything but demeaning. How well the author remembers the joy of eating at the Tsentralnaya, where the waiters still remembered how to wait at table—they had not forgotten the days when the Tsentralnaya had been the Hotel Berlin.

OVIR, UPDK, Aeroflot, and even the central offices of Intourist on Manezhnaya Ploshchad, operated with handwritten ledgers. Most officials, even the relatively senior ones, seemed virtually unassisted in their actual labour, although often shielded behind many doors.

Today, the ranking Soviet bureaucrat has a secretary, trained to assist, do the menial tasks, and permit the boss to get on with his job. That was rarely the case in 1974. In those days, typing was usually poor (judging by the official Soviet letters one received), and proof-reading was virtually non-existent.

The author does not remember having met Vasiliy Grigorievich Furov, but undoubtedly he did at one or another of the numerous receptions. Two of the CRA officials stand out: first, of course, Vladimir Alexeevich Kuroyedov, a sinister little man who seemed a caricature of a Mississippi Deputy Sheriff—a cross between James Cagney and J. Edgar Hoover. The other memorable character was the official 'heavy', Pyotr Vlasovich Makartsev, who was reported to have warned the hierarchs at the 1971 Sobor, 'Whoever tries to resist the decrees on the parishes will get his leg broken'.[16] But although he was much more polished than the abrupt Kuroyedov, he seemed reptilian and calculating.

Furov is first mentioned as a Deputy Chairman of Council for Russian Orthodox Church Affairs in 1965,[17] then appears repeatedly in the articles of the *Journal of the Moscow Patriarchate*, as Deputy Chairman of CRA, throughout the period leading up to the Report.[18] He continues to appear in the same role, especially in 1978.[19] It is of particular note that he still is mentioned in the Journal on two occasions after the publication of the Furov Report in the west.[20]

One other CRA official figures prominently in the Furov materials, A. Plekhanov.[21] The author was a bit mystified, as that name had not been encountered elsewhere. But in 1984, an A. S. Plekhanov appeared in the *Journal of the Moscow Patriarchate*, as Moscow Representative of the CRA.[22] He is mentioned occasionally thereafter.[23]

Comrade Furov appears elsewhere—notably in the Chronicle of Current Events, no. 41, reporting a lecture given in May 1976 by 'visiting speaker, Furov, deputy chairman of the Council for Religious Affairs' to 'the staff members working on the Large Soviet Encyclopedia' on 'the situation of religion in the Soviet Union'.[24] The lecture was reported in samizdat after the Furov Report, but long before publication in the West.

Furov disappears from the *Journal of the Moscow Patriarchate* in 1981, until he resurfaces in 1986 as an expert on cultural and architectural monuments which are still used for public worship.[25]

WHO IS TRYING TO KID WHOM?

Societies function with mutually accepted fictions as necessary lubricants. But Soviet society, at the time of the Furov Report, abused the privilege. It was a time of bankrupt ideology, stagnant economy, apathetic labour, and disillusioned youth. The mild relaxation of detente did little to counter the societal frustration. The slogan of the day was, 'They pretend to pay us, so we pretend to work'.

Meanwhile, scattered upon the fabric of society, rather like dandruff, were slogans and more slogans. Not only did every speaker quote Lenin, but he had to pepper his speech with gems from the oratory of Leonid Il'ich Brezhnev. And the worst sycophants, it is sad to remember, were often the Bishops of the Russian Orthodox Church. Patriarch Pimen on 14 November 1982, at the Yelokhovskiy Sobor Panikhida for Brezhnev: 'The image of our beloved Leonid Il'ich Brezhnev, a man and citizen who devoted his life to the service of his people, a tireless champion of universal and just peace, will always remain in our grateful hearts. Let us, beloved, offer up our fervent prayers for the newly departed, Leonid, and may his memory be eternal.'[26]

Fifteen months later, it was more of the same for Comrade Andropov. In the words once again of His Holiness: 'We shall remember always and with heartfelt gratitude Yuriy Vladimirovich Andropov's benevolent understanding of the needs of our Church, . . . Let us, beloved, offer up our fervent prayers for the newly-departed, Yuriy, and may his memory be eternal'.[27]

Thirteen months later, there was His Holiness again, sounding like a stuck record. 'The faithful of the Russian Orthodox Church with heartfelt gratitude will always remember that Konstantin Ustinovich (Chernenko), as Head of State, satisfied the needs of our Church with benevolent understanding . . . Let us now offer, beloved brothers and sisters, our fervent prayers for the newly departed one and wish him eternal memory.'[28]

On 5 November 1974, at the time of Furov's Report, Patriarch Pimen sent a telegram to Kosygin, in which he pledged his total loyalty. 'Let me assure you, most esteemed Aleksey Nikolaevich, that the Russian Orthodox Church . . . will continue invariably to support the efforts of our country towards the consolidation of lasting peace.'[29] This telegram, proudly displayed in the Journal of the Moscow Patriarchate, is then quoted by Furov to demonstrate the total subservience of the Patriarchate to the CRA.[30] What the hierarchs say officially must conform to the pattern provided. They are not required to quote the 'Leader', but then neither does Furov, in a document meant for internal consumption.

Furov's report, as closer examination shows, is plagued by constant contradiction. He claims that religion is weak and dying; and yet, the CRA is desperate to receive greater support from the Party. He tries to show the bishops and other clergy as corrupt and stupid, but at the same time, he stresses their clever law-breaking. The CRA officials, of course, are always within the law. As the investigator tells Zotov, in Solzhenitsyn's *Krechetovka Station*, 'We never make mistakes'.[31]

The bureaucrat needs to reassure himself and his readers that the slogans really are true after all. Everybody knows to what degree confidence in the slogans has been lost, but they lie to each other, and the charade continues.

Pospielovsky quotes a fascinating illustration of attitudes towards religion in the Soviet Union during that period.[32] It is a survey among Leningrad industrial workers, covering attitudes in 1971 and 1979, years that bracket Furov's Report. In 1971, when asked about religion, 27 per cent gave 'Marxist' answers and 17 per cent made vulgar, anti-religious statements. By 1979, the Marxist answers had dropped from 27 per cent to 10 per cent, and the uncouth from 17 per cent to 4 per cent. The slogans were simply no longer being taken seriously. Contrary to the teaching of Lenin, religion was not withering away.

The truth of this Leningrad survey was observed by the author on May Day 1973. An English Canon and the author had to cross Leningrad, from the Astoria Hotel to the Theological Seminary. As the buses were not running, it meant the Metro to the end of Nevsky Prospekt, a walk around the Lavra, and entry to the Seminary from Obvodny Kanal. Two Anglican clerics in cassocks had to walk through the gathering May Day Parade. The children reacted with warmth and a certain degree of curiosity. The elderly either smiled quietly or looked embarrassed. Only occasional hostility was encountered, and then it was almost entirely from male workers, most of whom seemed to be under the influence of vodka, even at that hour in the morning.

In the early 1970s, it was becoming increasingly difficult for the anti-religious propagandists to get the people to take them seriously. Their only weapons appeared to be horror stories of the atrocities of the Spanish Inquisition, World War II photographs of priests giving

Fascist salutes, and posters of cosmonauts proclaiming 'Boga Nyet' ('There is no God'). But Furov was writing for the converted. He knew that his readers wanted to believe whatever nasty stories he could assemble about the church. As every politician knows, one of the best ways to win votes is to reassure the voters that their prejudices are acceptable after all.

THE FUROV REPORT AS A DOCUMENT

The Furov Report, as it reached the west, is a poorly assembled and somewhat disorganised collection of earlier materials, attached to a 1974 Report to the Central Committee of the CPSU. Apparently, Furov has added earlier materials to illustrate his points. He chooses extracts which demonstrate, in his eyes, the venality and deviousness of the bishops, parish clergy, and lay leaders of the Orthodox Church. I have conducted a thorough investigation of the case studies presented, and found numerous examples of corroboration—from publications of the Russian Orthodox Church and other Soviet sources. Most intriguing are the situations which are presented favourably by the *Journal of the Moscow Patriarchate*, while Furov sees them from the negative viewpoint of a Communist bureaucrat.

Detailed textual exegesis would be useful, but this paper is limited to an exploration of the reliability and authenticity of the document as a whole. I hope to publish a more critical study in the near future. In the meantime, whether the document reveals accurately the internal dynamics of state control of the church must be assessed. Should the Furov Report be cast aside as either KGB disinformation or as so full of outright falsehood as to render it utterly useless? The internal evidence suggests that it is not a forgery. And the study of Furov's version of events which can also be corroborated through church sources, itself reveals in graphic detail the gap in understanding and world view between the two.

EXTRACTS FROM THE FUROV REPORT OF 1968

Furov begins with nine pages of extracts from the 1968 Report. These have not been readily available, although they have been discussed in recent books.[33] The anecdotes, quotations from clergy, and catalogues of supposed misbehaviour illustrate the problems faced by the clergy following the new restrictions imposed by the 1961 regulations. There are some delightful contradictions, such as the complaint about a certain Father Sidyakin in Kurnary, Chuvashskaya ASSR, who lost his licence because he was a drunkard and a lecher. And what did he do? During the next year he performed 97 unregistered baptisms![34]

The primary goal of the Report appears to be justification of the state propaganda view that all clerics were 'money-grubbers'. Students of Soviet dissent will recognise this familiar accusation, as the bureaucrats use it to explain virtually any infraction of the rules.[35]

The text starts in the midst of the 1968 Report, is seemingly unedited, and is poorly typed. For example, the priest of Mordovo (Tambov Oblast), is called 'Boorodin' by Furov, when actually, he is Archpriest Aleksandr Ilyich Borodin, a prominent Tambov priest, to judge by his obituary several years later.[36] Furov appears to be using the same kind of smear tactics as the anti-religious press. Not only does the JMP article list Borodin's many honours, but tells how, during his terminal illness, Father Aleksandr was allowed to take monastic vows, and was permitted the greatest of privileges—the stricter vows of the Greater Schema, allowed in Russia only to monks in the Lesser Schema for decades. Such an honour is virtually unknown, and is a recognition of great sanctity. The strict and scholarly bishop of Tambov Mikhail (Chub) conferred this honour, and he officiated at the funeral. Here is documentary confirmation of the oft-reported CRA tactic of trying to discredit the very best of the parish clergy.

The tales are often quite peculiar—such as that of the priest Grigoriev E. G., of 'Khormany' (which turns out to be Khormaly)[37] in the Chuvashskaya ASSR. He is accused of demonstrating in church what the Report calls 'sharlatanskiye fokusy',[38] whatever that might be.

Furov accuses a Father Vitun of Lyudinovo (Kaluga Diocese) of baptismal infractions. Archpriest Nikolay Timofeyevich Vitun actually exercised a 12 year ministry in Lyudinovo, and died young (at 49).[39] He had such success that, when the village church burned down, 17 February 1976, the people rebuilt it immediately themselves. The Journal of the Moscow Patriarchate reports the events, accompanied by photographs.[40]

Although the collection may include genuine examples of unethical behaviour, a substantial number can be identified as crude attacks upon prominent and therefore threatening parish clergy, and not a single attack has been corroborated from other sources. This section may indeed provide a revealing insight into CRA tactics.

THE SPRAVKI

Attached to the Furov Report are eight brief documents, labelled as 'spravki'.[41] The first is a short undated biography of the then Metropolitan of Leningrad—Pimen (Izvekov), the present Patriarch of Moscow. Then follow seven interviews recorded by 'A. Plekhanov', a representative of the CRA. He reports on conversations with Pimen (2), Pimen and Alexiy of Tallinn (1) and Alexiy (5). Alexiy was then a young and rising Archbishop, whose later career has seen him become one of the most powerful hierarchs in the Russian Orthodox Church, as Chancellor of the Patriarchate, and later as Metropolitan of Leningrad. Five of the spravki are signed by Plekhanov (nos. 2, 3, 4, 7 and 8), and the similarities in style, typing and handwriting suggest that the other two (5 and 6) are by the same official.

The biography of Metropolitan Pimen is quite bewildering, as has been noted by other authors.[42] Its story of a double-desertion in wartime is preposterous—a first offence usually meant a firing squad. The rest of the story is even more unbelievable: that a Red Army major who had deserted and lived with false papers in time of war, then received a sentence of only 10 years, only served two years in a camp, was amnestied, and was allowed immediately to take up his priestly ministry at the Cathedral of Murom. That Pimen's prevarications are pointed out is of note, but that the matter is not pursued further can only be interpreted as a cover-up of some sort. There is possibly some truth to the rumour, current in Moscow in the early 1970s, that Pimen had been a political officer in the Red Army.[43] The author heard it from a theological student, who supposedly heard it said at the Ulitsa Ryleeva office of the Department of External Church Relations. If that indeed is the truth of the matter, then the double-desertion story is a cover-up for the acute embarrassment of the authorities that a priest could become a *politruk* major. The inclusion of this flawed and contradictory biography is the single most suspicious aspect of the entire Furov Report.

The second spravka is a Pimen-Plekhanov conversation, which took place on 31 March 1966. It tells of Pimen's dealings with two dissident priests Eshliman and Yakunin, showing Pimen in rather a better light than one might expect. Plekhanov is displeased that Pimen had lied about turning over documents to the dissidents; CRA informants on the Patriarchate staff contradicted his story.[44]

The third document, dated 21 February 1967, reveals the subservience of Pimen, and can be interpreted as further evidence from internal CRA sources of the willing loyalty to the Party, of which he has been accused over the years by Christian dissidents. He includes a personal note, mentioning his flat in Perlovka. When the author first read this, a chance remark from 1974 suddenly made sense. The author was journeying to Zargorsk for a service, and the cars stopped at the church in Babushkin, on the way. Before our group left, a parish leader remarked that the Patriarch's car had just passed. His companion replied, 'Did he turn left or go on to Zargorsk?' They laughed, and it never made sense until the mention of Pimen's flat, in this spravka. Near Babushkin, after crossing the Ring Road, is the left turn to Perlovka.

The fourth spravka is a display of synodical infighting, as both Pimen and Alexiy visit to discuss the unpleasant job of financial administration. Pimen rejects the management task, saying, in a typically Russian way: 'it's like a thief sitting on a thief, and whipping another thief!'[45]

The remaining four spravki contribute to the impression given to so many scholars and church visitors; namely, that Alexiy is an exceptionally willing servant of the Soviet authorities. It is not an attractive picture, and it is difficult to imagine the KGB wishing to forge it, much less leak it in the west. The impression given of Alexiy in the Furov Report is consistent with what many have observed about him over the following years.

There are no surprises in the seven interviews, and most merely corroborate other stories which have appeared elsewhere. The two hierarchs appear as subservient and self-serving as might be expected, from what is known of them from other sources. Some of the facts in the biography of Pimen are open to question, but it is difficult to say whether or not this is conscious disinformation by the CRA.

THE 1970 FUROV REPORT

(1) The crisis of personnel in the Russian Orthodox Church

(2) Church preaching. Attempts to modernise and revive it

(3) Monasteries

The 1970 Report has attracted less scholarly interest than the other sections. Apart from Struve's inclusion of an abridged Section 3 as an appendix, the 1970 Report is not readily available in translation.[46] The reason is obvious—it is far less interesting. The 1968 extracts provide an intriguing collection of the so-called offences of the clergy—showing us which are the particular points of CRA attack. The Spravki are crammed with juicy gossip and provide lovely ammunition for western critics of Russian Orthodox Church leadership. The 1974 Report, with its assessment of the Episcopate, the seminaries, and the publications, as well as the usual 'atrocities' of the clergy, offers far more fertile ground for commentary.

The first part of the 1970 Report deals with the natural attrition in clerical ranks resulting from the closure of five seminaries during the Khrushchev persecution (1958–64). The major topic of ecclesiastical conversation in the 1970s, after world peace (of course), was always expanded ordination training: more students at the three remaining seminaries and increased facilities, enlarged correspondence courses, and possible ordination of insufficiently trained candidates in the provinces. All three indeed did take place in the early 1980s.

The author recalls visiting an out of the way church, invited by the priest. In the sanctuary, unseen by the congregation, stood a dozen intense young men, their eyes riveted upon the priest. Nothing was said, but several days later, a member of the patriarchal staff approached the author and requested no more visits to that church. The young men had asked her to pass on the message. A visit by the chaplain of the diplomatic corps attracted simply too much attention from certain people. A saintly and courageous priest was taking a great risk, and they were protecting him. To stress the demoralisation of the clergy, Furov quotes Archpriest Pyotr Alekseevich Chel'tsov, one of the few surviving members of the 1917 Sobor,[47] and the scholarly Leningrad Archpriest, Aleksandr Vasilievich Medvedsky.[48] In the words of Chel'tsov, 'After the death of Patriarch Alexei—the end of *patriarchestvo* ("patriarchate")'.[49]

Parishes which are praised by the church also come in for criticism, such as the Church of SS Peter and Paul, in Korkino (Chelyabinsk). Furov condemns the clergy and churchwardens of Korkino for the illuminated ikons and coloured lights,[50] but their own Bishop Kliment is quoted in the *Journal of the Moscow Patriarchate* as praising them for how well they have decorated their church.[51]

The topic of the second section is preaching. Furov claims that present preaching is bad and must be kept that way. Bishops seem to be the key to ensuring that the CRA guidelines are followed, and that sermons contain pious generalities, with occasional commercials for Party foreign policy goals. This is a familiar criticism levelled against the parish clergy by dissident intellectuals, and the CRA's view is fascinating.

The only item noted elsewhere is a delightful piece of Soviet bureaucratic nonsense—the claim that there are 40 914 choir members in the Russian Orthodox Church, of whom 17 926 are paid.[52] One is reminded of the body counts at American Embassy briefings in Saigon.

The discussion of monasteries offers a brief history and some ideological comments. It is depressingly frank. For example, it openly admits that the closure of the Pecherskaya Lavra, in Kiev, was carried out under the phony excuse—*blagovidny predlog*—of a land slippage. Jane Ellis has provided an excellent and detailed discussion of this section,[53] and only one point needs to be added. As is the case elsewhere in the Furov materials, this section reveals a lack of accuracy. The sums on the chart are clearly incorrect.[54] The numbers of nuns and novices simply do not add up. As has been observed elsewhere, general sloppiness and inaccuracy are prevalent in the documents.

THE 1974 FUROV REPORT

(1) The system of episcopate in the Russian Orthodox Church and intensification of political work with it in the interest of the state

(2) The cadres of parish clergy

(3) Training of the clergy in theological schools

(4) Publication programme of the Russian Orthodox Church

(5) Executive organs, treasury, violations of the law and interference by the clergy in the management and financial affairs of religious congregations

Much has already been written about this section, ranging from the scholarly[55] to the popular,[56] and apart from the debate over the composition date of the '1974' Report, the author finds virtually no dispute with anything said by Professors Pospielovsky or Struve, Jane Ellis, or the Rev. Mr Buss. As previously noted, the errors in dating, by both Pospielovsky and Struve, stem from single errors of fact. And yet, a detailed study of the Furov materials reveals dozens of similar problems. These appear to result from careless workmanship by an uninterested bureaucrat, who knew that accuracy was unnecessary.

By way of illustration, an examination of the three lists of bishops[57] (the co-operative, the ones to be watched, and the uncooperative) will demonstrate the problems which thorough examination reveals throughout:

(1) Mstislav and Bogolep are both placed in Kirov.
(2) Meliton is called an Archbishop (he was a Bishop until 1980).
(3) Nikon is called an Archbishop (he was a Bishop until 1978).
(4) Iosif of Ivano-Frankovsk is later called Iosaf.[58]
(5) Savva of Chernovtsy is later described as at Chernigov.[59]
(6) Antoniy (Vakarik) of Chernigov is omitted, but appears later.[60]

(7) Vladimir (Sabodan) of Dmitrov is omitted.

(8) Varlaam (Ilyushchenko) of Pereyaslav-Khmel'nitskiy is omitted.

(9) Iov (Kresovich) of Ivanovo is omitted.

Had the KGB been preparing the list, it is assumed that there would be a greater degree of accuracy. The very imprecision lends an odd sort of credibility to the document. Perhaps the facts are inexact, but that does not diminish the value of the document as providing genuine insights into the inner workings of the CRA, the attitudes which motivated its bureaucrats in the early 1970s, and the value judgements they made about the church.

There was one major surprise in the three lists—the inclusion of the saintly Iosif of Alma-Ata in List I, as one of the loyal hierarchs. In fact, his supposed classification led many scholars to doubt the authenticity of the whole work. And yet, the key may lie in a simple fact—when the Sobor met in 1970 to elect a new Patriarch, Iosif's name was put forward not only by the church but by the CRA of Kazakhstan.[61] Furov may well have been merely echoing the assessment of a local CRA *upolnomochenny*.

Most scholars who have dealt with the Patriarchate of Moscow can offer anecdotes in support of the placement of one or another of the hierarchs in a particular list. In September of 1973, the author assisted the Rev. Edwin Espy, Secretary of the National Council of Churches (USA), on his visit to the Soviet Union. On 6 and 7 September, Dr Espy and his wife visited Volgograd, where their host was Bishop Pimen (Khmelevskoy).[62] On their return, their excited reactions to this remarkable Christian required a stroll in the park, and even today should not be put in print, particularly as Pimen is still Archbishop of Saratov. But suffice it to say that List III was the correct classification.

The author's work in Moscow provided opportunities to associate closely with several hierarchs. The author can corroborate personally some details of Furov's assessment of Khrizostom (Martishkin), who at the time of the 1974 Report was Bishop of Zaraysk and Deputy Chairman of the Department of External Church Relations of the Patriarchate. His excitement over his appointment to Kursk, the lack of priests, and his plans for the coming months in his new diocese were described to the author on several occasions, with simple directness and candour. It was during the visit of the National Council of Churches (USA) delegation, 26 August to 18 September

1974,[63] that the Synod appointed Khrisostom to Kursk.[64] The whole tenor of what Furov reports[65] is completely consistent with my memory of conversations with Bishop Khrizostom, down to the actual details. This portion of the Furov Report rings true.

There are several essays waiting to be written, covering the materials in the 1974 Report. The saga of Father Pivovarov, which in its own way is just as exciting as the story of Fr. Dudko, has grown in the author's notes to such an extent that it will have to constitute another paper altogether. Another topic must be the role of the Diocese of Vologda, which seemed to become almost a punishment post during that period.

The search for cross-references has been a challenge, and has, of course, revealed many more errors by Furov. There is the village near Tula, which Furov calls 'Paportniki,' which is found, on further investigation, to be the village of 'Paporotka'.[66] The CRA official in Chernigov is Comrade 'Polonsky',[67] and then he is Comrade 'Podolsky'.[68] The *Journal of the Moscow Patriarchate* settles the issue by voting for 'Podolsky'.[69] And so it goes, on and on.

The author refers the reader to his article on the problems of theological education, published during the period of the 1974 Furov Report.[70] There are quite a number of parallel statistics and similarities of information, noted by Jane Ellis, in Chapter 4 of her book.[71]

Among all the anti-clerical tales in the 1974 Furov Report one deserves the final comment—the famous fur coat of Novosibirsk.[72] As this took place during the NCCUSA visit of 1974, the author was personally involved. The American 'provocateur' in the story, according to Furov, was the Very Reverend Vladimir Berzonsky, today Rector of the Church of the Holy Trinity, Parma, Ohio, USA. In a letter to the author, Fr. Vladimir tells his side of the story:

How does one divest oneself of superfluous articles in a land of total strangers? At a reception in the home of the adorable and good man, Bishop Gideon, I thought to ask, who else, a brother priest, namely Fr. Nikolai Burdin, 'Is there someone you know who might use an extra coat I no longer have need of?' His pupils dilated, and he asked curtly: 'Do you wish to sell a coat?' 'Not at all,' I responded. 'I wish to give away my overcoat, since it would lighten my luggage considerably.' 'No, we have no need of coats here,' was his reply, and not the mock patriotic: 'We have good Russian coats,' as he self-servingly reported to his superiors. I thought nothing of it at the time, considering it perhaps to have been a simple *faux pas*, not the first in my life. When, a few years later I read it in the Furov Report my reaction was, and remains, to be infuriated by having a good intention distorted.[73]

CONCLUSION

The inner workings of the Committee for Religious Affairs are hidden behind a dingy facade on Moscow's Smolenskiy Bul'var, a five-minute walk in either direction from the Foreign Ministry or from Gor'kiy Park. It is a sad joke that, since the move of the Russian Orthodox Patriarchate of Moscow's Department of External Church Relations to the Danilovskiy Monastery, the CRA has now expanded into their former offices in Ulitsa Ryleyeva.

The Furov Report provides the only internal documentary access to the CRA, thus far available to the western scholar. The sloppiness, the insensitivity, and the mendacity revealed in the documents are highly unattractive, but it appears quite unlikely that the Furov Report is a forgery. On the contrary, it is tragically genuine. As a product of the 'mid-detente' years, it reflects all too obviously the tone of the time. As religious policy remained virtually stagnant for 21 years (from 1964 to 1985), Furov opens a very large window indeed.

But how is the credibility of the Furov Report to be judged? It comes from a world of ideological prejudice—a world where Jews have big noses, Blacks are lazy and Japanese wear thick glasses and have buck teeth. It is always easy to attack the caricatures that inhabit your own imagination. Furov's reasoning is entirely deductive, and he must find the proof texts to illustrate his sermon.

What is revealed, in most of the Furov material, is the attitudes of the CRA in a particular period. When Furov attacks a priest, some rather tedious research can sometimes unearth the other side of the story, discovering that it is often the most gifted and highly effective priests that receive the worst treatment. The statistics—numbers of priests or parishes or nuns or publications—are corroborated elsewhere, and offer only additional support for previous evaluations. Of by far the greatest interest is the picture of relationships between the CRA and the bishops, revealed particularly in the Spravki and in the 1974 Report itself. Virtually without exception, these impressions match those which outside scholars have brought back from their encounters with the Russian Orthodox hierarchs. It is sad to report that the impression is mostly negative, and Furov merely confirms and broadens our experience. It is also with some satisfaction that the outside observer sees the CRA having the most difficulty with those hierarchs who have repeatedly demonstrated the greatest integrity and openness in their dealings with the outside world.

As is so often the case with literary criticism, the material tells the critic as much about the author as about the subject. As an insight into the Russian Orthodox Church in the mid-detente years, the Furov Report is inaccurate and misleading. As an insight into the workings of the State Committee for Religious Affairs in the same period, it is invaluable.

NOTES

The author acknowledges the kind assistance of Jane Ellis. The following abbreviations are used:

Periodicals

JMPE	*Journal of the Moscow Patriarchate* (English Edition)
JMPR	*Journal of the Moscow Patriarchate* (Russian Edition)
KNS	*Keston News Service*
RCDA	*Religion in Communist-Dominated Areas*
RCL	*Religion in Communist Lands*
Vestnik	*Vestnik Russkogo Khristianskogo Dvizheniya*

Books and other Sources

Buss	*The Bear's Hug*, by Gerald Buss (London: Hodder & Stoughton, 1987).
Ellis	*The Russian Orthodox Church*, by Jane Ellis (London: Croom Helm, 1986).
KC Archive	Keston College Archive
Pospielovsky	*The Russian Church under the Soviet Regime 1917–1982*, by Dimitry Pospielovsky (Crestwood, New York: SVS Press, 1984).
Struve	*Rapport secret au Comité Central sur l'état de l'église en URSS*, by Nikita Struve (Paris: Seuil, 1980).

1. RCL, vol. 11, no. 1 (1983) pp. 109–12—the author's review of Trevor Beeson's *Discretion and Valour*, 2nd edn.
2. Ellis, pp. 240–2.
3. Vestnik, 130 (1979) p. 278.
4. Vestnik, 130 (1979) pp. 278–9.
5. Struve, p. 15.
6. Vestnik, 130 (1979) p. 287.

7. Struve, p. 36.
8. Ellis, p. 456.
9. Pospielovsky, p. 400.
10. Ellis, p. 456.
11. JMPE and JMPR, 11 (1974) p. 3.
12. Vestnik, 130 (1979) pp. 278–9.
13. JMPE, 12 (1974) pp. 15–18; JMPR, 12 (1974) pp. 12–15.
14. JMPE, 2 (1975) pp. 2–5.
15. Vestnik, 130 (1979) p. 281; JMPE, 12 (1974) p. 3.
16. Pospielovsky, p. 395.
17. JMPR, 9 (1965) p. 12.
18. JMPR, 7 (1970) p. 54; JMPR, 7 (1970) p. 56; JMPR, 3 (1971) p. 2; JMPE, 3 (1972) p. 27; JMPR, 3 (1972) p. 45; JMPR, 6 (1972) p. 1; JMPE, 6 (1972) p. 2; JMPR, 6 (1972) p. 1; JMPR, 8 (1972) p. 17; JMPE, 8 (1972) p. 18; JMPR, 2 (1973) p. 12; JMPE, 2 (1973) p. 13; JMPR, 7 (1973) p. 11; JMPE, 7 (1973) p. 12; JMPR, 9 (1973) p. 17; JMPE, 9 (1973) p. 19; JMPR, 2 (1974) p. 40; JMPE, 2 (1974) p. 38.
19. JMPE, 12 (1975) p. 7; 4 (1976) p. 4; 6 (1976) p. 9; 7 (1976) p. 26; 2 (1978) p. 10; 6 (1978) p. 11; 7 (1978) p. 39; 9 (1978) p. 15; 9 (1978) p. 64; 10 (1978) p. 3; 10 (1978) p. 6; 10 (1978) p. 10; 11 (1978) p. 19; 5 (1979) p. 17.
20. JMPE, 8 (1981) p. 16 and JMPE, 9 (1981) p. 16.
21. KC Archive. Spravki nos. 2, 3, 4, 7 and 8 are signed. Nos. 5 and 6 are in similar handwriting, although unsigned.
22. JMPE, 8 (1984) p. 38.
23. JMPE, 11 (1984) p. 17; 4 (1985) p. 6; 11 (1985) p. 44; 11 (1986) p. 8.
24. RCL, 6, 1 (1978) pp. 32–3, quoting *Khronika Tekushchikh Sobytiy*, 41 (1976) pp. 6–9.
25. *Grani Naslediya*, Sovietskaya Rossiya (Moscow: 1985) p. 35; quoted in RCL, 15, 2 (1987) pp. 206–09.
26. JMPE, 1 (1983) p. 5.
27. JMPE, 3 (1984) p. 4.
28. JMPE, 4 (1985) pp. 5–6.
29. JMPE, 12 (1974) p. 3; quoted by Furov, in Vestnik 130 (1979) p. 281.
30. Vestnik, 130 (1979) pp. 280–1.
31. *We Never Make Mistakes*, A. I. Solzhenitsyn (London: Sphere Books, 1972) p. 87.
32. Pospielovsky, p. 455.
33. Pospielovsky, p. 420 and Ellis, pp. 89–90.
34. KC Archive, '*From the Report for 1968*', p. 3.
35. KNS, 96 (1980) p. 7.
36. JMPE, 11 (1975) p. 33; 5 (1976) p. 26.
37. JMPE, 4 (1980) p. 20; 5 (1981) p. 29.
38. KC Archive, '(ib)From the Report for 1968(ie)', p. 4.
39. JMPR, 4 (1972) p. 30.
40. JMPE, 10 (1981) pp. 38–9.
41. The word 'Spravka' has no lexical equivalent in English—perhaps 'informative document'.
42. Pospielovsky, pp. 392–3; Ellis, pp. 229–32.

43. Ellis, pp. 293–4.
44. Ellis, p. 293, for a fuller discussion.
45. KC Archive, Fourth Spravka, p. 3. '. . . *sidyat zhulik na zhulikye i zhulikom pogonyayut*'
46. Struve, pp. 150–61. For the Russian text see Vestnik 131 (1980) pp. 362–72.
47. JMPR, 7 (1974) p. 17, for a complete obituary.
48. JMPE, 5 (1974) pp. 29–30, for a complete obituary.
49. KC Archive, '*From the 1970 Report*', p. 5.
50. Ibid., p. 9.
51. JMPE, 9 (1976) p. 40. See also: JMPR, 1 (1970) p. 21; JMPR, 3 (1972) p. 26; JMPR, 3 (1973) p. 30; JMPR, 5 (1973) p. 35; JMPR, 12 (1973) p. 23; JMPE, 10 (1978) p. 22; JMPE, 8 (1980) p. 21.
52. Ibid., p. 19.
53. Ellis, pp. 130–6.
54. KC Archive, '*From the 1970 Report*,' p. 26.
55. See Ellis, Pospielovsky and Struve.
56. See Buss, chapter 9.
57. Vestnik, 130 (1979) pp. 278–9.
58. Ibid., p. 300.
59. Ibid., p. 284.
60. Ibid., p. 315.
61. Pospielovsky, p. 390.
62. JMPE, 11 (1973) p. 28.
63. JMPE, 11 (1974) pp. 4–6.
64. JMPE, 11 (1974) p. 3.
65. Vestnik, 130 (1979) pp. 286–8.
66. JMPR, 5 (1972) p. 35; JMPE, 4 (1972) p. 22.
67. Vestnik, 130 (1979) p. 300.
68. Ibid., p. 309.
69. JMPE, 8 (1985) p. 45.
70. RCL, 2, 3 (1974) pp. 4–8.
71. Ellis, pp. 100–23.
72. Vestnik, 130 (1979) pp. 304–05.
73. Private letter, 19 January 1988.

18 Orthodoxy and Russian Nationalism in the USSR, 1917–88[1]

Peter J. S. Duncan

The place of Russian nationalism in the ideology of the Moscow Patriarchate has become very important. William van den Bercken, noting the preponderance of patriotic over spiritual themes in the Patriarchate's documents, has suggested that 'service to God' might have been replaced by 'service to the Fatherland'.[2] Undeniably, the Russian Orthodox Church is one of the principal centres of Russian nationalism in the Soviet Union today. In this paper, I try to examine how the church has promoted its contribution to Russian and Soviet patriotism, directed towards the Soviet State and the population; and how the state has responded.

Two terminological clarifications are in order. The Russian Orthodox Church follows the Soviet State in distinguishing between 'nationalism', which has negative connotations, and 'patriotism', which is viewed positively. The historian Academician Dmitry Likhachëv, who is himself believed to be an Orthodox Christian, has described nationalism as 'based on hate towards other peoples' and patriotism as 'based on love for one's own'.[3] Nevertheless, the 'patriotism' of both state and church has frequently contained a strong dose of Russian nationalism. The second clarification concerns the term 'Church'. In Russian Orthodoxy, the church is understood as the whole body of believers, rather than the clergy alone as is sometimes the case in the west. Nevertheless, I shall be primarily concerned here with the stance taken by the hierarchy of the Moscow Patriarchate.[4]

THE EARLY YEARS

Even before 1917, Lenin's strong antipathy to any form of religion took a particularly hostile form as far as the Russian Orthodox Church was concerned, because of the links of the latter with the

312

tsarist state. Peter the Great had abolished the Moscow Patriarchate and assured state control over the church by himself appointing the Procurator of the Holy Synod. It was not until the autumn of 1917 that the church was able to re-establish the Moscow Patriarchate. At the same time Lenin saw the adherents of the religions other than the official church as potential allies against tsarism, because of the persecution some of them had suffered. The 1918 decree on religion, separating the church from the state and the school from the church and nationalising church property, severely weakened the position of the Orthodox Church as the established faith, but had less effect on other religions. The Constitution of 1918 promised freedom of religious and anti-religious propaganda.[5]

The newly-restored Moscow Patriarchate pursued a line that was generally hostile to the atheist Bolsheviks (even in December 1917 the Sobor (Church Council) demanded that the head of the Russian State be Orthodox), although from 1919 it was formally neutral between the Reds and the Whites. The ruling Party attempted to combine frontal attacks on the Patriarchate with support for the efforts of the pro-Soviet 'Living Church' movement to take over the church from within. Under Lenin large numbers of hierarchs and priests were arrested and many believers were killed. The Patriarch of Moscow, Tikhon, was arrested in 1922. In July 1923, having been released, he published a 'confession' in which he stated that he had been involved in 'anti-Soviet activities' of which he now repented.[6] The church leaders continued to suffer arrests and exile. Since the Living Church lacked credibility with the laity, the regime sought to pressurise successive leaders of the Patriarchate to carry out its wishes. Tikhon died in 1925. In March 1927 the Patriarchal *locum tenens*, Metropolitan Sergii of Nizhny Novgorod, was released from prison. The following summer he made a declaration of loyalty to the Soviet government. He asked for the position of the church to be normalised and for a Sobor to be held to elect a Patriarch. 'We want [he said] to be Orthodox, and at the same time to recognize the Soviet Union as our civic motherland, the joys and successes of which are our joys and successes, and the failures are our failures.'[7]

Following this declaration, Sergii was allowed to take over the administration of the church and the government abandoned its support for the Living Church. The respite proved temporary; the 1929 Law on Religious Associations removed the legal right of religious propaganda, confining the churches to the role of worship. From 1929 to the mid-1930s all the religions in the Soviet Union, including the Orthodox, suffered severe persecution. This was associated with Stalin's 'left turn'; the churches were accused of backing the 'kulaks' and opposing collectivisation. Bishops and priests were sent to labour camps, and churches were destroyed, including some of great historical and architectural significance. One of the effects of this was to drive much religious activity underground; considerable sections of the Orthodox Church had already rejected Sergii's declaration of loyalty to the atheist state. As far as other churches were concerned, the Roman Catholics had been without a single bishop since 1926; and by 1939 several Protestant denominations had been destroyed. The Russian Orthodox Church itself in 1939 had 'only a few hundred clergy and open churches left, only seven bishops were still in office and all diocesan administrations, except those in Moscow and Leningrad, had had to cease their activity.'[8]

THE GREAT PATRIOTIC WAR AND STALIN'S DETENTE WITH THE CHURCH

In the late 1930s there seems to have been some slackening of the pressure on the religions, as Stalin gave priority to the struggle to develop the defence industry. On the day of the Nazi invasion, 22 June 1941, Metropolitan Sergii issued a pastoral letter urging the faithful to war to defend the fatherland. Referring to previous invasions, he spoke of the historical link between the fortunes of the Russian Orthodox Church and the nation, and of how Russian heroes had been inspired by their faith. By contrast, it was 10 days before Stalin pulled himself together and addressed the country over the radio. The church collected millions of rubles for national defence, equipping the Dmitrii Donskoi tank column and the Aleksandr Nevskii air squadron (both named after old-Russian military commanders). On 22 September 1942, after the Lithuanian Metropolitan had sent greetings to Hitler, Sergii went further towards identifying the Soviet State and Russian interests:

> . . . no Russian who does not want to betray his nation and her historical legacies and aims will go with the enemies of the Soviets, because the Soviets head our Russian national State and fight for its worldwide and international significance.[9]

Meanwhile Metropolitan Aleksii of Leningrad stayed in the city with his flock during the Nazi blockade.[10]

In September 1943 Stalin and the Foreign Minister, V. M. Molotov, received Sergii, Aleksii and Metropolitan Nikolai of Krutitsy in the Kremlin and promised to improve conditions for the church. A Sobor of hierarchs was held and elected Sergii as Patriarch of Moscow. At the same time thousands of Orthodox churches were re-opened throughout the country. Other faiths also had their position improved and regularised; the All-Union Council of Evangelical Christians and Baptists (AUCECB) was established for the Protestant groups and four Spiritual Directorates were created for the Muslims. A major factor in the change in the official attitude to religion was the experience in the western parts of the Soviet Union. Here the Nazi occupiers re-opened the churches, which were then filled with believers. This show of religious feeling must have suggested to Stalin the propaganda advantages of permitting freedom of worship. Provided that religious activity was under the control of approved bodies who would proclaim loyalty to the government, another channel of political socialisation would be created which could immediately be used to encourage the war effort.[11]

Within the context of the new religious freedom, the Orthodox Church was given a privileged position. Whereas the other faiths were administered by the Council for the Affairs of Religious Cults, the Orthodox Church was governed by the Council for the Affairs of the Russian Orthodox Church. The church was allowed to publish the monthly *Zhurnal Moskovskoi patriarkhii* (Journal of the Moscow Patriarchate), and the Patriarch's pastoral letters were published in the government paper *Izvestiia*. Following the death of Patriarch Sergii in April 1944, Aleksii, now Patriarchal *locum tenens*, wrote to Stalin, emphasising Sergii's patriotism and saying that the late Patriarch had constantly referred to Stalin as the 'God-given leader' (*Bogopostavlennyi Vozhd'*). He promised 'unchanging loyalty to the Motherland and to the Goverment headed by you'.[12] A Sobor was held in January–February 1945 to elect Aleksii as Patriarch.

A graphic example of the state's partiality to the Orthodox Church was the forced incorporation of the Ukrainian Uniate (Greek Catholic) Church into the Russian Church. This act illustrated how Soviet policy towards religion was linked with, and often subordinated to, nationality policy. The takeover was accomplished by a so-called Uniate 'Sobor' in L'vov, held in March 1946, when much of the Uniate leadership, including Metropolitan (later Cardinal) Slipyj, was in captivity. The Uniate Church, as the major denomination in the Western Ukraine, had been a bastion of Ukrainian nationalism, and with the incorporation of the Western Ukraine in the USSR Stalin sought to make the Uniates illegal. The interests of the Soviet State and the Orthodox Church coincided. The state wanted to use the Russian Church as an instrument to fight Ukrainian nationalism, and the church wished to expand its influence into territories which it considered had been unjustly torn from it centuries before. The Orthodox Church was given especially favourable conditions to proselytise among the Uniates. In practice, many Uniate priests and believers went over to Orthodoxy in appearance only, maintaining their loyalty to Slipyj.[13]

The dissident Russian Orthodox priest Gleb Iakunin wrote in 1976 a critical *samizdat* account of the activities of the Patriarchate under Stalin. He is right to see Stalin's support for Orthodoxy as part of his move to a 'nationalist-chauvinist policy', in which the church was given the role of a 'catalyst and cementing component'.[14] The Russian Orthodox Church was the traditional church of not only the Russians but also of most Ukrainians and Belorussians, covering the then three largest nationalities in the USSR (although since the revolution there had been mass support for autocephaly in the Ukraine). In return for Stalin's support, the church heaped the highest praise on him, using language normally reserved for Jesus. Stalin was 'the first man of peace', with an 'all-embracing heart which takes on itself all the pain of suffering'.[15] It was he 'whom Divine Providence chose and placed to lead our Fatherland on the path of prosperity and glory'.[16] Iakunin suggests that Aleksii expected that Stalin was about to declare the country a pan-Slav Orthodox Empire.[17]

The presentation of Stalin as 'God's chosen one' was a direct descendant of the sixteenth-century monk Filofei's portrayal of the Tsar. This concept was extended to the messianic presentation of Moscow as the 'chosen city', the 'Third Rome'. The occasion was the 800th anniversary of the founding of the city, in 1947. Archpriest N. A. Khar'iuzov, for example, combining Orthodox and Communist ideas, wrote in *Zhurnal Moskovskoi patriarkhii*:

> Now Moscow is the centre of the social life of humanity, the centre which unites all progressive and democratic elements, and in religious life Moscow is not the centre of aristocratically despotic Catholicism or of anarchic Protestantism. Moscow is the centre of true Orthodoxy, rejecting this or that extreme.

It is not only among us Russian people that the thought of

Moscow awakens the best memories of our native country, but also among the peoples of the fraternal republics, among all the Slavs, and among all the freedom-loving peoples the thought of Moscow evokes the best, bright hopes for the future . . .

Moscow is a beacon, a beacon not only for us Orthodox, but also for those seeking true, unclouded civil, national and religious freedom. Moscow is a beacon for all of toiling humanity, for all who seek religious and social truth.[18]

In November 1947 the Metropolitan of the Levant, Elie Karam, visited Patriarch Aleksii. In a speech he portrayed the Russian people as the chosen people.

I have found out a lot about the great Russian people and its Church and am now personally convinced that the Russian Orthodox Church is the *greatest* Church of Orthodoxy . . . The Lord God blesses the Russian people as He once blessed Abraham. The Russian people is like the people of the Holy Land and the Russian land can be compared with the Holy Land of Palestine.[19]

More directly, the Bulgarian Metropolitan Stefan said in 1948: 'Moscow became the Third Rome by occupying the place of the First in its confession of Christ's truth'.[20]

The last two quotations exemplify the use of the Russian Orthodox Church in promoting Soviet foreign policy. Part of the price paid by the church for its relatively privileged position in the USSR was the obligation to promote among foreign churches, and later in ecumenical church bodies, official Soviet views, as well as denying the existence of any religious persecution. The Russian Church was not successful in its attempt to take over the role of the Ecumenical Patriarch of Orthodoxy, the Patriarch of Constantinople. But, owing to the Soviet military control of Eastern Europe, it was able to establish itself as the 'elder brother' of the Orthodox churches in the Balkans, and hence promote Soviet interests through churches in Bulgaria, Romania and Yugoslavia. The Russian Orthodox Church played a major part in the World Peace Council, established in 1949 as an international front organisation to promote Soviet foreign policy.[21]

In Stalin's final years, the Patriarchate's adulation of the leader seems to have declined. The *Zhurnal Moskovskoi patriarkhii* had few references to Stalin's wise policies and in the whole of 1951 it published only one document addressed to him, on the occasion of the anniversary of the October Revolution. This expressed 'warm wishes for your health and strength for many years to [promote] the glory, flourishing and might of the Soviet Union'.[22]

THE KHRUSHCHËV OFFENSIVE

Stalin's wartime détente with the Russian Orthodox Church survived the leader by several years. But in 1959 Nikita Khrushchëv launched a campaign which seemed to be aimed at freeing the USSR from religion. The Moscow Patriarchate had already begun to propagate its historical service to the Russian and Soviet State and its import-ance for Russian culture.[23] At a Kremlin meeting on world disarma-ment on 16 February 1960, Aleksii argued that the church had unified old Russia, isolated the people from the Tartars and rallied the nation against Napoleon and then Hitler. Yet it was now under attack. (Aleksii did not specify from whom.)[24] The Patriarch's speech was indignantly interrupted from the floor.

On 18 July 1961 a Sobor of Bishops was held in Zagorsk. Here Aleksii, under intense pressure from the government, steamrollered the bishops into accepting a number of restrictions on the church. The most important was that the priest lost control over the parish. He was transformed into a hired labourer responsible to a committee which, it turned out, might be controlled by non-believers. Aleksii referred to the 'abnormal' (*nenormal' noe*) situation. No mention was made in the report of the meeting in the *Zhurnal Moskovskoi patriarkhii* of any greetings to Khrushchëv.[25] At the same time the authorities unleashed a wave of beatings, imprisonment, rape and murder against the faithful. Many churches were destroyed. All this facilitated the closure of over half the churches and the halving of the number of parish priests by the time Khrushchëv fell from power.

The church writer, Anatoly Levitin-Krasnov, claimed that the Patriarchate 'took a manifestly collaborationist position' during Khrushchëv's offensive against religion.[26] It is true that throughout that time and up to the Gorbachev period the hierarchy refused to admit that there was any religious persecution going on in the Soviet Union.

THE BREZHNEV ERA

Fathers Nikolai Eshliman and Iakunin, in a 1965 appeal to the Patriarch, accused Aleksii of allowing atheist officials to direct the activity of the Patriarchate.[27] V. Furov, the deputy head of the Council for Religious Affairs (which since 1965 has supervised all religions), submitted a report to the CPSU Central Committee in 1974. He divided the bishops into those who 'patriotically' co-operate closely with the government, those who take their religious zeal to the point of evading the law and those in between who work within the law but try to expand the influence of the church.[28]

An examination of the literature published by the Russian Orthodox Church since the fall of Khrushchëv suggests a sustained campaign by the Patriarchate (despite the low circulation of its publications) to persuade the government of its patriotism and usefulness. For most of this time the church seems to have been limited by censorship in the extent of the claims it could make for its historical role in the development of the Russian State and culture, but the thesis that the Patriarchate is devoid of freedom of action and unable to articulate any of the interests of the church is untenable. Since 1964 there have been almost no direct attacks on the Patriarchate or the Russian Orthodox Church as a whole. The theology of the Patriarchate is criticised, but its patriotism and pro-Soviet political role are acknowledged.

The Brezhnev period (1964–82) was a time when non-Russians and Russians alike were allowed (within limits) to explore their own histories and cultures. Central Asians rebuilt the monuments and mosques of Timur, and Russians rebuilt a few of their churches and monasteries. Indeed the RSFSR Ministry of Culture passed a law on the preservation of monuments the day after Khrushchëv was overthrown, and the following year the All-Russian Society for the Preservation of Historical and Cultural Monuments (VOOPIK) was established. Key figures in VOOPIK were the writer Vladimir Soloukhin and the artist Il'ia Glazunov, both of whom have explored Orthodox themes.[29] Academicians Boris Rybakov and Dmitrii Likhachëv popularised the study of old Russia. As under Leonid Brezhnev Marxism-Leninism became less attractive, interest grew in Russia's writers from the Orthodox tradition, such as Vladimir Solov'ëv, Nikolai Berdiaev and especially Fëdor Dostoevsky. A whole movement appeared in Soviet literature, known as 'village prose', which mourned the passing of the Russian village and praised the values of the peasants. A classic work of this genre was Aleksandr Solzhenitsyn's 'Matryona's House', published under Khrushchëv.[30] Solzhenitsyn's nationalist and Orthodox views went beyond the limit of what could be officially published in the Soviet Union under Brezhnev, and led ultimately to his expulsion from the country. Writers such as Fëdor Abramov, Sergei Zalygin, Viktor Astaf'ev, Vasily Belov and Valentin Rasputin continued to develop village prose through the official media, achieving great popularity among Soviet readers.

The new climate was relatively favourable for the Church to highlight its historical role. A problem for the church in explaining its role in Russian history is that as well as being the church of the Russian people it was also the church of the Russian State. In classical Marxist terms it was therefore the direct tool of the exploiting class. The Stalinist view of Russian history, rehabilitating those tsars of the Muscovite and Petersburg periods who were deemed progressive, facilitated the reception of the idea that the role of the church itself was at times progressive. The political position of the church was close to those historians and literary critics in the Brezhnev period who saw a 'single stream' in Russian history. In opposition to the Marxist concentration on the class nature of successive state formations in Russia, these saw the Soviet State as the legitimate successor to the tsarist State and eulogised them both.

One example of the hierarchy's efforts was a special issue of *Zhurnal Moskovskoi patriarkhii*, produced to commemorate the fiftieth anniversary of the establishment of the Patriarchate in 1917. It is a measure of the difficulties faced by the church and of the sensitivity of the material that this issue could not be published until 1971. The issue included a short article by K. Logachëv on the history of the church. It claimed that in old Russia 'the Russian Church exerted a huge influence on the political and civil life of the Russian people'. It strengthened the family and fought slavery.[31] The monasteries were the 'largest centres of education'. From the twelfth century, the church 'remained the only bearer of the idea of the unity of the Russian people'. The Metropolitan of Kiev and all Rus was the spiritual leader of all Russians, despite the political divisions.[32] From the fourteenth century, the church assisted the rebirth of a unified Russian State, aiding the expulsion of the Tartar and Mongol occupiers. Russian and Soviet historians attach decisive political importance in the defeat of the Tartars to the battle of Kulikovo Field of 1380. This was won by the Muscovite prince Dmitrii Donskoi after he had been advised and blessed by St Sergii of Radonezh, the founder of the Holy Trinity St Sergii Monastery (Zagorsk). Logachëv mentioned this and the role of Patriarch Germogen in defending Muscovy against the Poles and Swedes in the seventeenth century.[33] A volume published in 1980 repeated and enlarged on these themes.[34] It became routine for church statements under Brezhnev to refer to Sergii's role in World War II, and to the church's efforts since the war to promote world peace by supporting the foreign and defence policies of the Soviet State. On the other hand, the church seems to have been prevented in this period from emphasising the influence of the church over Russian culture in the eighteenth and nineteenth centuries. For example, it does not seem to have drawn attention to the fact that such writers as Nikolai Gogol', Ivan Turgenev, Dostoevsky and Lev Tolstoy all visited the monastery of Optina Pustyn in search of spiritual guidance.

Aleksii died in 1970 and, at the Local Sobor held in June 1971, Pimen was elected Patriarch of Moscow and all Rus'. In his enthronement speech on 3 June Pimen raised patriotism to the highest duty of the Christian. Quoting the words of his predecessor, he declared: 'Serving the Holy Russian Orthodox Church is inseparable from serving our Fatherland'. He added: 'Nobody can be a good Christian who is not a good and faithful son of his Motherland, ready to sacrifice everything for her glory and flourishing'.[35] Vladimir Kuroedov, head of the Council for Religious Affairs, told the Sobor of his satisfaction at the election of Pimen. He was a:

> great patriot of the Motherland, known for his active social work in defence of peace and in strengthening friendship between peoples, who has already for many years been a member of the Soviet Committee for the Defence of Peace and a member of the World Peace Council.[36]

The following day Kuroedov conveyed to Pimen the congratulations of Prime Minister Aleksei Kosygin.[37]

The year 1980 was the six-hundredth anniversary of the Kulikovo battle. It was the occasion for an outburst of Russian nationalist feeling in the Soviet media, especially the cultural journals, which was unprecedented since the Stalin era. The church took full advantage of the occasion to emphasise its patriotic role. Eight out of 12 issues of the *Zhurnal Moskovskoi patriarkhii* had material on Kulikovo. An article on the icon painter, Andrei Rublëv, linked his art to the defeat of the Tartars.[38] Archbishop Pitirim of Volokolamsk (now Metropolitan of Volokolamsk and Iuriev), the editor of the journal, claimed: 'The decisive victory, determining the cultural and historical tasks of the whole Russian people, was inspired and prepared in the Sergii-Trinity Monastery'.[39] Pimen declared at the anniversary celebration that the Kulikovo battle was very significant for Europe, which was saved from alien invasion 'at the cost of huge losses for Rus''. The church had always 'aided the State construction of Rus' and exerted a creative influence on her cultural and national development . . . the Church was for the Russian people a great inspiring force in the struggle with the enemy.' In the Great Patriotic War, the church-equipped Dmitrii Donskoi tank column 'made a major contribution to the defeat of the fascist occupiers'.[40] The church's strongest statement could not be made directly, but only through a citation from the nineteenth-century writer F. Nadezhdin.

> Russia is also greatly obliged to the Orthodox Church for her liberation from the Tartar yoke . . . Even if subsequent events had not called it to new, very great feats for the Fatherland, even if from then all its activity had been limited to its natural service to the Fatherland—to teaching, to serving God—even then we would have to recognize that it is the greatest preserving force of the Russian people against any external attack and enslavement.[41]

The Brezhnev period witnessed the development of independent Russian nationalist political activity by some of the laity and priests of the Orthodox Church and by people influenced by Orthodoxy. The 1965 appeal by Eshliman and Iakunin claimed that the 'State of Muscovy was literally nurtured by the Russian Church'.[42] The All-Russian Social-Christian Union for the Emancipation of the People (VSKhSON), a revolutionary Russian nationalist organisation, was broken up by the KGB in 1967 when it had 30 members and 30 candidates. After this most of the Russian nationalist movement came out into the open. The Moscow priest Dmitrii Dudko, with his belief in the coming religious resurrection of Russia, had a major influence on the Russian nationalist samizdat journals and Orthodox groups established in the 1970s. He affected the ideas of Vladimir Osipov, who from 1971 to 1973 published the first nine issues of *Veche*, the principal Russian nationalist journal, and in 1974 two issues of *Zemlia*, before he was arrested. *Veche* enjoyed the support of some official cultural figures such as Glazunov and possibly of some politicians, as well as the participation of former members of VSKhSON. Orthodox discussion groups, such as the Christian

Seminar organised by Aleksandr Ogorodnikov in Moscow in 1974, attracted large numbers of young people. In 1976 Iakunin and two former *Veche* contributors established the Christian Committee for the Defence of Believers' Rights in the USSR. Whereas most of the above were sympathetic to the human rights movement, Gennady Shimanov circulated his calls for loyalty to the Soviet system, which he claimed was 'pregnant with theocracy'. He predicted the transformation of the CPSU into the 'Orthodox Party of the Soviet Union'.[43]

It is difficult to determine the attitude of the Patriarchate to these groups and individuals. It did not give them any open support, either when they were formed or when the KGB moved against them in the late 1970s. As Bishop Filaret (later Metropolitan of Minsk and Belorussia) reportedly told Hierodeacon Varsonofii Khaibulin in 1971, 'Our Church is a State Church'.[44] The hierarchs may consider that actions by individuals outside the framework imposed by the state on the church weaken the position of the Patriarchate. At the same time it seems that the church leaders offered help to Iakunin and Dudko on condition that they renounce political activity.[45]

The repressions at the end of the Brezhnev period seemed to reflect a concern among the Party leadership at the spread of Orthodox ideas. After expressing his belief in a God, Soloukhin was forced in 1982 to give an assurance that he 'was and remains a convinced atheist'.[46] Under Iurii Andropov and Konstantin Chernenko there seemed to be a tightening-up directed against religion in general. In June 1983 the Central Committee held the first Plenum on ideology for over 20 years. Chernenko (then ideology Secretary) attacked 'god-seeking motifs' in literature and denounced the efforts of imperialism to inculcate a 'nationalist bias' into religious feelings.[47] But in the same year the government handed over to the Patriarchate the Monastery of St Daniil in Moscow, so that it could be restored and made the headquarters of the church in time for the Millennium. As this event approached, academic specialists debated the historical role of the church. Nikolai Gordienko denounced the church for having failed to defend the toilers against exploitation, before the revolution.[48] The basic official attitude to the Orthodox Church, however, as expressed by Kuroedov, was to emphasise its role in the Soviet period, that is, its patriotism and struggle for peace.[49]

In the early 1970s, Vladimir Osipov argued that Russian nationalism could be the bridge leading the Russian people to the Orthodox Church.

Christ and his teaching, in the final reckoning, are more important to me than nationalism. But I know the soul of the modern Russian: the national principle at this time is more alive than the religious. So patriotism, national consciousness and self-respect form the only reliable bridge to moral, cultural and biological salvation![50]

In this he followed Dostoevsky's character Father Zosima in *The Brothers Karamazov*: '. . . whoever has come to believe in God's people will also behold His sacredness, though he had not believed in it until then'.[51] The church may be following the same strategy. As well as seeking to persuade the state of its patriotism and usefulness, the hierarchs (or some of them) may be seeking to promote Russian nationalism and interest in the Russian past in the hope that this will lead members of society to the traditional faith of the Russian people.

THE CHURCH AND RUSSIAN NATIONALISM UNDER GORBACHEV

The relaxation of censorship and the development of *glasnost'* gave scope to the church to articulate more clearly its nationalist claims. Generally speaking, however, the wave that transformed the Soviet Press under Gorbachev (especially after January 1987) did not have the same effect on the *Zhurnal Moskovskoi patriarkhii*. Many old themes were simply reiterated, often in the same language. The epistle of Pimen and the Holy Synod to mark the fortieth anniversary of the Soviet victory in 1945 laid out at some length the church's record in defence of the Fatherland in the Muscovite period and the 1941–45 war (although the Petersburg period was omitted). It reiterated the patriotic duties of the Orthodox.[52]

The fortieth anniversary of the incorporation of the Uniates was marked by an article which (paradoxically) sought to justify the act by appealing to Ukrainian patriotism. Just as the 1945 victory meant that the Ukraine could be reunified in a single republic, so the L'vov Sobor allowed the Ukrainians to be reunited in a single church, the 'Mother—Russian Orthodox Church'.[53] To mark the millennium, the New Testament was to be published for the first time in Ukrainian.[54] The return to the church of part of the Kiev-Pechëry Monastery was another gesture to the Ukrainian believers at the time of the millennium. The particular role of the Russian Orthodox Church as a factor unifying Russians, Ukrainians and Belorussians was noted by Dmitry Likhachëv in March 1988. At the same time he said that Christianity was incompatible with nationalism.[55] Metropolitan Filaret of Minsk, who heads the Department of External Church Relations of the Patriarchate, referred to the significance of the millennium for 'the Russian people and their Ukrainian and Belorussian brothers, for Russia'.[56]

The ability of the Russian Orthodox Church to present itself as a force unifying the Russians, Ukrainians and Belorussians is congruent with the needs of the authorities in the present demographic situation. With the traditionally Muslim nationalities rapidly expanding their numbers and the Slavs only reproducing themselves, there has been a pronounced tendency in Moscow to see the three East Slav peoples as the ethnic and political core of the Soviet Union, and to emphasise the factors common to them. The Gorbachev leadership appears particularly sympathetic to this approach: Muslim representation has gradually disappeared from the Politburo, while Slavs have been moved into key positions in Central Asia. At present, the role of the Russian Orthodox Church as an instrument against Ukrainian separatism is revealed by the fact that over half of its open churches are in the Ukraine. This situation, for which the authorities are responsible, makes it appear more as an 'imperial' than as a Russian national church.

The rise of glasnost' (up to May 1988) did not lead the *Zhurnal Moskovskoi patriarkhii* to protest in any way about restrictions on the activity of the church. It did, however, allow it to take further its identification of Russian nationhood and culture with Orthodoxy. The March 1987 issue included a list of pre-revolutionary scholars and cultural figures who adhered to Orthodoxy, and a citation by Metropolitan Iuvenaly of Krutitsy and Kolomna of Gogol''s belief that Russia's faith had strengthened her against enemies.[57] Four months later the journal published an essay by the nineteenth-century Archbishop Dimitry of Kherson and Odessa which made a strong nationalist claim for Orthodoxy. '. . . faith created and expanded that great and indestructible Orthodox spirit, *which is not found in any other people in the way it is in the Russians* [Rossiiane]' (emphasis in original).[58] The church also began to enlarge its claim to relevance in Soviet society. An international conference on the millennium held in Moscow in May 1987 included the participation of secular Soviet academics—the first such involvement in a conference organised by the church.[59] In February 1988 was held 'the first joint meeting of religious and public figures of Moscow'. This was to discuss not only peace issues but also glasnost' and democratisation.[60] A religious conference held in Moscow in January 1988 heard a claim that democratisation in the Soviet Union was being 'accompanied by a return to cultural sources and historical memory, to the search for moral values in the spirit of classical Russian literature'. The works of Belov, Astaf'ev and Chingiz Aitmatov were not religious, but they were 'permeated with the spirit of Christian moral values'.[61]

Perhaps the most significant item was a long article by Metropolitan Filaret of Minsk. Entitled 'The Formation of Russian National Self-Consciousness in Connection with the Baptism of Rus'', it was published from July to September 1987. Having approvingly cited the views of the Slavophil Ivan Kireevsky on the Christian basis of the life of Rus', Filaret stated:

> . . . the force that really cemented the young Russian State came from the Orthodox Church . . . political unity was . . . sanctified to the Russian people by the religious idea of a united holy Rus' . . . It was the beneficent powers of the Church that saved Rus' from total catastrophe [from the Mongols and Tartars].

While Gorbachev argued for a political regeneration of Soviet society as the only means to restructure the economy, Filaret claimed:

> Only by identifying themselves—as a people—with the Church . . . did the people obtain the energy for national regeneration . . . The Russians came to see the holiness of their land as a reflection of the City of God, of Heavenly Jerusalem.[62]

Filaret went on to cite Dostoevsky's view that Russian enthusiasm for the Russo-Turkish War of 1877–78 was motivated not by pan-Slavism but by Orthodox solidarity. Russian patriotism was 'based not on narrow-minded nationalism but on the feeling of belonging to the God-man organism of the Church'. The Great Patriotic War revealed 'our national character, which blends lofty patriotism with Christian love and selflessness'. The War had led to a reassessment of the role of the church and the rediscovery of the old Russian heritage. Filaret concluded by discussing the peace activities of the Russian Orthodox Church since the war, without mentioning that these had entirely reflected the needs of Soviet propaganda. He linked Dostoevsky's view of the Russian as the 'universal person' with the church's organisation of inter-religion peace conferences in Moscow in 1977 and 1982.[63]

The church was extremely fortunate that the period leading up to its millennium coincided with the development of glasnost' in the Soviet media. (Admittedly, glasnost' also allowed the appearance of anti-Semitic Russian nationalist groups such as *Pamiat'* [Memory], which sought to use Orthodoxy for their own purposes.) From early 1987, a flood of articles appeared in the secular Press on the significance of the millennium and the position of religion in Soviet society. The Central Committee journal *Kommunist* published an article arguing that the introduction of Christianity into Kievan Rus' was important primarily because of the impact on the development of the State.[64] In March 1988 it published an unsigned editorial reassessing policy towards the churches. While reaffirming Lenin's view of the need to struggle against religion, it attacked the violations of the rights of believers in the 1930s and under Khrushchëv.[65] In his articles for *Moscow News*, Aleksandr Nezhny called for glasnost' about the treatment of the church in the Soviet past. He warned that:

> . . . many people . . . are still under the illusion that religion can be eradicated . . . It is difficult to mould society's genuinely democratic attitude towards the church and believers without first destroying the notion of the church as some hostile force, and of believers as second-class citizens.[66]

Vladimir Sorokin, rector of the Leningrad Theological Academy, complained to *Meditsinskaia gazeta* in March that the Russian Orthodox Church had been reduced to a department of the Soviet State. He called for its role to be expanded, allowing it to provide social services.[67] Metropolitan Aleksii of Leningrad and Novgorod complained to *New Times* in May about atheist literature written 'in a tone offensive to believers'.[68]

Such a change in atmosphere could develop only after signals from the top. Already, at the 1985 celebration of Hitler's defeat, Gorbachev had enquired of Patriarch Pimen as to how the preparations for the millennium were going. Among the gestures of goodwill by the state to the church were the inclusion of Metropolitan Pitirim on the Board of the USSR Cultural Fund, itself headed by Likhachëv, and the return of the Optina Pustyn and Tolga monasteries and part of the Kiev-Pechëry Monastery. In 1988 Soviet television broadcast an Orthodox Easter service for the first time. On 29 April 1988 Gorbachev received Pimen and four metropolitans in the Kremlin, to mark the millennium. The General Secretary denounced the 'tragic events' of the Stalin period (but not the persecutions under Lenin or

Khrushchëv). He made some routine comments about the role of the church in the war and in the struggle for peace. He then, however, promised a new law on freedom of conscience, in which 'the interests of religious organizations would be reflected'. Perestroika, glasnost' and democratisation concerned believers, as 'Soviet people, toilers, patriots'. The Patriarch responded by saying that perestroika had led to the opening of new monasteries and the registration of new religious communities, but there were still problems (which he did not specify).[69] Meanwhile, Metropolitan Iuvenaly suggested that '. . . we are on the brink of a new stage in the activity of the church'.[70]

The millennium was celebrated with a high level of publicity, much intended by the State for foreign consumption. A special issue of *Moscow News*, intended for distribution in Britain, proclaimed under a banner headline: '1000 years of FAITH', 'The Soviet Union is united in the celebration of a faith which, though scarred and torn with dissent, has survived since 988'.[71] The nine saints who were canonised during the Jubilee Local Sobor of the Church included Andrei Rublyov and Dmitrii Donskoi, and the model for Father Zosima, Father Amvrosii of Optina Pustyn. Iakunin and other dissidents claimed that Pimen and the senior hierarchs were too timid to take advantage of the new political climate. Indeed, it was the secular Press which was leading the fight for freedom of conscience while the Patriarchate seemed mute. It seemed that if the position of the church was to improve, it would be due less to the ability of the hierarchs to persuade the regime of the usefulness of the church as a patriotic force than to the climate of glasnost' which encouraged the believers to demand their rights.

NOTES

1. I am grateful for the assistance of Jenny Foreman of Chatham House Library, Lesley Pitman of the SSEES Library and David Grinyer of the British Library. I benefited from the comments of the conference participants, Martin Dewhirst and my mother, Lucy Duncan. I should like to emphasise, however, that all errors are entirely mine.

    I have drawn from Dimitry V. Pospielovsky, *The Russian Church under the Soviet Regime, 1917–1982*, 2 vols (Crestwood, NY: St Vladimir's Seminary Press, 1984) and *idem*, 'Russian Nationalism and the Orthodox Revival', *Religion in Communist Lands* (*RCL*) xv

(Winter 1987) no. 3, pp. 291–309; Jane Ellis, *The Russian Orthodox Church: A Contemporary History* (London: Croom Helm, 1986); John B. Dunlop, *The New Russian Revolutionaries* (Belmont, Mass.: Nordland, 1976); *idem*, *The Faces of Contemporary Russian Nationalism* (Princeton, NJ: Princeton UP, 1983); see also *idem*, 'The Russian Orthodox Church in the Millennium Year: What it Needs from the Soviet State', *RCL*, xvi (Summer 1988) no. 2, pp. 100–16; and numerous other articles in *RCL*.
A major source was *Zhurnal Moskovskoi patriarkhii* (*ZhMP*).

2. William van den Bercken, 'Holy Russia and the Soviet Fatherland', *RCL*, xv, no. 3, p. 271.

3. Dmitry S. Likhachëv, 'Zametki o russkom', *Novyi mir* (1980) no. 3, p. 38.

4. I looked at Orthodox Russian nationalism outside the hierarchy in 'The Fate of Russian Nationalism: The *Samizdat* Journal *Veche* Revisited', *RCL*, xvi (Spring 1988) no. 1, pp. 36–53.

5. This and the next three paragraphs are based mainly on: Bohdan R. Bociurkiw, 'The Shaping of Soviet Religious Policy', *Problems of Communism*, xxii (May–June 1973) no. 3, pp. 38–48; Trevor Beeson, *Discretion and Valour: Religious Conditions in Russia and Eastern Europe*, rev. edn (London: Fount, 1982) pp. 31–40, 59–71; Gleb P. Iakunin, 'Moskovskaia Patriarkhiia i "kul't lichnosti" Stalina', *Russkoe vozrozhdenie* (*RV*) (1978) no. 1, pp. 103–37 and (1978) no. 2, pp. 110–50; Pospielovsky, *Russian Church*, i, pp. 25–191.

6. Cited in Iakunin, 'Moskovskaia', *RV*, no. 1, pp. 112–14.

7. Metropolitan Sergii and the Synod of the Russian Orthodox Church, 'Deklaratsiia', 29 July 1927, as cited in Iakunin, 'Moskovskaia', *RV*, no. 1, p. 130.

8. Gerhard Simon, *Church, State and Opposition in the USSR*, trans. Kathleen Matchett (London: Hurst, 1974) p. 66.

9. *Russkaia pravoslavnaia tserkov'. Ustroistvo, polozhenie, deiatel' nost'* (Moscow: Moskovskaia Patriarkhiia, 1958) p. 214.

10. Ibid., p. 215.

11. Iakunin, 'Moskovskaia', *RV*, no. 1, pp. 134–5; Pospielovsky, *Russian Church*, i, pp. 193–209; John S. Curtiss, 'The Russian Orthodox Church during World War II', *American Review on the Soviet Union*, vii (1946) no. 4, pp. 32–44.

12. *Patriarkh Sergii i ego dukhovnoe nasledstvo* (Moscow: Izd. Mosk. Patr., 1947) pp. 135–6.

13. Bohdan R. Bociurkiw, 'The Suppression of the Ukrainian Greek Catholic Church in Postwar Soviet Union and Poland', in Dennis J. Dunn (ed.), *Religion and Nationalism in Eastern Europe and the Soviet Union* (Boulder, Colorado: Lynne Rienner, 1987) pp. 97–104; Vasyl Markus, 'Religion and Nationality: The Uniates of the Ukraine', in Bohdan R. Bociurkiw and John W. Strong (eds), *Religion and Atheism in the USSR and Eastern Europe* (London: Macmillan, 1975) pp. 104–07; Pospielovsky, *Russian Church*, ii, pp. 306–09.

14. Iakunin, 'Moskovskaia', *RV*, no. 1, pp. 103–37 (quotation, p. 135) and (1978) no. 2, pp. 110–50.

15. Metropolitan Nikolai of Krutitsy, *Konferentsiia vsekh tserkvei i religioznykh ob" edinenii v SSSR* (Moscow, 1952), as cited in Iakunin, 'Moskovskaia', *RV*, no. 2, pp. 126–7.

16. Patriarch Aleksii, *Slova i rechi*, I, p. 206, as cited in Iakunin, 'Moskovskaia', *RV*, no. 2, p. 113.

17. Iakunin, *loc. cit.*

18. Archpriest N. A. Khar'iuzov, 'Moskva', *ZhMP* (1947) no. 1, pp. 25–6.

19. Elie Karam, in Father Mikhail Zernov, 'Mitropolit Livanskii Iliia i arkhimandrit Antiokhskogo patriarkhata Vasilii v gostiakh u patriarkha Moskovskogo i vseia Rusi Aleksiia', *ZhMP* (1948) no. 1, p. 53.

20. Metropolitan Stefan of Sofia, 'Rech' proiznesennaia Blazhenneishim Mitropolitom Sofiiskim Stefanom, Ekzarkom Bolgarskim', *ZhMP* (1948) no. 8, p. 16.

21. William C. Fletcher, *Religion and Soviet Foreign Policy, 1945–1970* (London: OUP for the Royal Institute of International Affairs, 1973); Pospielovsky, *Russian Church*, II, pp. 309–17.

22. Kallistrat, Georgian Catholicos and Patriarch, and Patriarch Aleksii, 'Privetstvie Predsedateliu Soveta Ministrov Soiuza SSR I. V. Stalinu', *ZhMP* (1951) no. 11, p. 3.

23. See the 1958 publication (note 9 above), and *ZhMP* articles in 1958.

24. *ZhMP* (1960) no. 3, pp. 33–5.

25. 'Deianiia arkhiereiskogo sobora Russkoi pravoslavnoi tserkvi', *ZhMP* (1961) no. 8, pp. 3–29.

26. Anatoly E. Levitin-Krasnov, *V poiskakh Novogo grada. Vospominaniia*, part III (Tel-Aviv: Krug, 1980) p. 174.

27. Nikolai Eshliman and Gleb Iakunin, open letter to Patriarch Aleksii, 21 November 1965, in Michael Bourdeaux, *Patriarch and Prophets: Persecution of the Russian Orthodox Church Today* (London: Macmillan, 1969) pp. 194–221.

28. *Vestnik Russkogo Khristianskogo Dvizheniia* (1979) no. 130, pp. 275–344. See Oppenheim article below for further details.

29. For example, Vladimir A. Soloukhin, *Searching for Icons in Russia*, trans. P. S. Falla (London: Harvill, 1971); *I'lia Glazunov* (photo album, Moscow: Planeta, 1978).

30. Aleksandr I. Solzhenitsyn, 'Matrenin dvor', *Novyi mir* (1963) no. 1, pp. 42–63.

31. K. Logachëv, 'Kratkii obzor istorii Russkoi Tserkvi', in '50-letie vosstanovleniia Patriarshestva', special issue of *ZhMP* (1971) p. 25.

32. Ibid., pp. 31, 39.

33. Ibid., p. 51.

34. *Russkaia Pravoslavnaia Tserkov'* (Moscow: Izd. Mosk. Patr., 1980) and *The Russian Orthodox Church* (Moscow: Progress, 1982) especially chaps 1 and 3.

35. *ZhMP* (1971) no. 9, pp. 10–12.

36. Vladimir A. Kuroedov, 'Rech' Predsedatelia Soveta po delam religii', *ZhMP* (1971) no. 8, p. 5.

37. *ZhMP* (1971) no. 8, pp. 5–6.

38. V. Smirnov and A. Volgin, 'Prepodobnyi Andrei Rublëv, ikonopisets', *ZhMP* (1980) no. 7, pp. 69–79.

39. 'K 600-letiiu pobedy na Kulikovom pole', *ZhMP* (1980) no. 9, p. 68.
40. 'Slovo Sviateishego Patriarkha Pimena . . . 21 sentiabria 1980 goda', *ZhMP* (1980) no. 12, pp. 6–7.
41. A. Volgin, 'K 500-letiiu osvobozhdeniia Rusi ot mongol'sko-tatarskogo iga', *ZhMP* (1980) no. 12, pp. 72–8.
42. In Bourdeaux, *Patriarch*, p. 213.
43. For sources, see my 'Fate of Russian Nationalism'.
44. *Religious Liberty in the Soviet Union: WCC and USSR. A Post-Nairobi Documentation*, ed. Michael Bourdeaux, Hans Hebly and Eugene Voss (Keston College: 1976) p. 58.
45. Pospielovsky, *Russian Church*, II, pp. 435–41.
46. *Kommunist* (May 1982) no. 8, p. 128.
47. Konstantin U. Chernenko, 'Aktual'nye voprosy ideologicheskoi, massovo-politicheskoi raboty partii', *Pravda*, 15 June 1983.
48. Nikolai S. Gordienko, *Kreshchenie Rusi* (Leningrad: Lenizdat, c. 1985).
49. Vladimir A. Kuroedov, *Religiia i tserkov' v sovetskom obshchestve*, 2nd suppl. edn (Moscow: Politizdat, 1984) pp. 81–100, 195–237.
50. Vladimir N. Osipov, 'Pis'mo v redaktsiiu zhurnala "Vestnik RSKhD"', in *Vestnik Russkogo Studencheskogo Khriistianskogo Dvizheniia* (26 November 1972) no. 106, p. 295.
51. Fëdor M. Dostoevsky, *Polnoe sobranie sochineenii v tridtsati tomakh* XIV (Leningrad: 1972–) p. 345.
52. Patriarch Pimen and the Holy Synod, 'Poslanie . . . k 40-letiiu slavnoi Pobedy sovetskogo naroda v Velikoi Otechestvennoi voine 1941–1945 gg.', *ZhMP* (1985) no. 5, pp. 4–6.
53. V. Nikitin, 'K 40-letiiu L'vovskogo Tserkovnogo Sobora', *ZhMP* (1986) no. 3, p. 76.
54. Interview with Metropolitan Filaret of Kiev and Galicia, Exarch to the Ukraine, *New Times*, (June 1988) no. 23, p. 25.
55. 'Predvaritel'nye itogi tysiachiletnego opyta', *Ogonek* (March 1988) no. 10, pp. 9–12.
56. Metropolitan Filaret of Minsk and Belorussia, 'Millennium', *International Affairs* (Moscow: 1988) no. 6, p. 48.
57. Archimandrite Platon, 'Nravstvennoe i mirotvorcheskoe sluzhenie Russkoi Pravoslavnoi Tserkvi', *ZhMP* (1987) no. 3, pp. 65–70; Deacon Feodor Sokolov, 'Rozhdestvo Khristovo v Bogoiavlenskom patriarshem sobore', ibid., p. 10.
58. Archbishop Dimitry, 'Den pamiati sviatogo ravnoapostol'nogo kniazia Vladimira', *ZhMP* (1987) no. 7, p. 44.
59. E. Speranskaia, 'II Mezhdunarodnaia nauchnaia tserkovnaia konferentsiia v Moskve', *ZhMP* (1987) no. 11, pp. 17–21.
60. V. Sedov, 'Religioznye i obshchestvennye deiateli Moskvy za obnovlenie zhizni', *ZhMP* (1988) no. 5, p. 50.
61. E. Speranskaia, 'Novyi iazyk novogo myshleniia', ibid., pp. 46–7.
62. Metropolitan Filaret of Minsk, 'Problemy stanovleniia russkogo natsional'nogo samosoznaniia v sviazi s Kreshcheniem Rusi', *ZhMP* (1987) no. 7, pp. 72–4; no. 8, pp. 70–2 (first quotation, p. 71); no. 9, pp. 67–71 (second quotation, p. 67).

63. Ibid., no. 9, pp. 68–71.
64. Boris V. Raushenbakh, 'Skvoz' glub' vekov', *Kommunist* (August 1987) no. 12, p. 99.
65. 'Sotsializm i religiia', *Kommunist* (March 1988) no. 4, pp. 115–23.
66. Aleksandr Nezhny, 'Common History, One Homeland', *Moscow News*, 8 May 1988 (quotations), and 'The Millennium', ibid., 19 June 1988, p. 25.
67. Radio Liberty Research report for 28 March 1988, RL 139/88.
68. 'Entering the Second Millennium', *New Times* (May 1988) no. 20.
69. 'Vstrecha General'nogo sekretaria TsK KPSS M.S. Gorbacheva s Patriarkhom Moskovskim i vseia Rusi Pimenom i chlenami Sinoda Russkoi pravoslavnoi tserkvi', *Pravda*, 30 April 1988.
70. 'The Millennium of Christianity in Russia', *New Times* (May 1988) no. 22, p. 32.
71. *Moscow News*, Pergamon edn (June 1988) p. 1.

19 Religious Currents in Contemporary Soviet Literature and Film

John B. Dunlop

The Gorbachev period, with its *glasnost'* and frenetic liberalisations, has witnessed a more open airing of religious themes than had been possible under previous Soviet leaderships. As shall be seen, however, no Soviet writer or filmmaker can openly admit to being religious, and there remain religious subjects—for example, the figure of Jesus Christ—which can be discussed only with considerable caution. This paper examines the spheres of literature and film over the first three and a half years of the Gorbachev 'thaw' and seeks to determine what changes have occurred in how these two media have been treating religious themes.

More than any other art form, literature has served as the battle-ground on which the question of the appropriate limits of the airing of religious themes in Soviet culture has been fought out. As will be shown, this has been primarily due to the appearance, in 1986, of a controversial, 'best-selling' Soviet novel, which, among other surprises, introduced the figures of Jesus Christ and Pontius Pilate as two of its central characters.

In July, 1986, a noted Soviet specialist in religion, doctor of philosophical sciences Iosif Kryvelev, launched a severe attack on three leading Soviet writers, Kirgiz novelist Chingiz Aitmatov, Siberian author Viktor Astaf'ev, and Belorussian writer Vasil' Bykov. Entitled 'Flirtation with Dear Little God' [*Koketnichaia s bozhen'koi*], Kryvelev's article, which was published in the newspaper *Komsomol'skaia pravda*, was clearly intended to alert readers to the dangerous inroads being made by 'God-seeking' [*bogoiskatel'stvo*] in the ranks of Soviet writers.[1]

As most Soviet readers would have been aware, the title of Kryvelev's polemic referred to a well-known anti-religious epithet of Vladimir Lenin, while the term 'God-seeking' was used by Lenin as a weapon against such opponents as Nikolai Berdiaev and Sergei

333

Bulgakov in the first decade of this century.[2] In underlining Lenin's militant atheism, Kryvelev sought to portray himself as an erudite and devoted defender of the official Soviet ideology, Marxism-Leninism. 'To renounce a principled, consistent atheism', Kryvelev warned, 'is to renounce the very foundations of the scientific and materialistic world-view'.

Belorussian writer Vasil' Bykov was criticized by Kryvelev for a statement made in *Knizhnoe obozrenie* to the effect that the Ten Commandments remain a code of morality by which men may continue to live in the present day. It was Bykov's linking of religion and morality which particularly exercised Kryvelev. As for Viktor Astaf'ev, he too was indicted by Kryvelev for allegedly seeing a connection between religion and moral behaviour and for appearing to call, on the pages of the journal *Nash sovremennik*, for retribution against 'the defilers of churches' and 'blasphemers'.

The event which seems to have precipitated Kryvelev's article was, however, the publication of the first part of Chingiz Aitmatov's novel *Plakha* (*The Executioner's Block*) in the 1986, no. 6 issue of *Novyi mir*.[3] The 'God-seeking' sentiments discernible in this initial section of Aitmatov's novel seem to have so alarmed Kryvelev that he decided to act immediately, without waiting for the subsequent two parts of the novel to be published.

Kryvelev's attack on three leading Soviet writers was an important political event of the early Gorbachev period. His article represented an attempt by the official Soviet atheist establishment to intimidate a cultural intelligentsia emboldened by the new policies associated with glasnost'. It was hardly accidental that the three writers singled out by Kryvelev were major ones. Two of them, in fact,—Aitmatov and Bykov—had been elected the previous month, at the Eighth Congress of Soviet Writers, to membership on the eight-man Bureau of the Secretariat of the USSR Writers' Union. As for Astaf'ev, he had long been one of the most popular Soviet writers, and his short novel, *The Sad Detective*, which appeared in the 1986, no. 1 issue of *Oktiabr'*, had been a cultural milestone of the Gorbachev thaw. By exposing the errors of such influential writers, Kryvelev was attempting to reassert the primacy of ideology in Soviet cultural life and in society in general.

In reading Kryvelev's indictment, Soviet readers would have recalled a similar attack on village prosewriter Vladimir Soloukhin in 1982 on the pages of *Kommunist* for 'religious and mystical ideas and moods' contained in his work 'Pebbles in the Palm' published in the journal *Nash sovremennik*.[4] The excoriation of Soloukhin, which coincided with Andropov's gradual assumption of the ideological portfolio following Mikhail Suslov's death in early 1982, brought about a recantation and apology from Soloukhin and from the editor of *Nash sovremennik*, Sergei Vikulov, on the pages of *Kommunist*.[5] Soloukhin informed the party committee of the Moscow Writers' Organisation that he 'had been and remained a convinced atheist', and that he had never engaged in 'God-building'. Both Soloukhin and the journal *Nash sovremennik*, however, remained under a cloud until Andropov's death in early 1984. In raising the issue of 'flirtation with dear little god', Kryvelev was presumably hoping to precipitate a similar crackdown on the offending three writers.

Of the three authors singled out by Kryvelev, it was his attack on Aitmatov which was to have the greatest repercussions. While the offending passages from Bykov and Astaf'ev were contained in fairly marginal pieces, Aitmatov's alleged 'God-seeking' occurred on the pages of a major novel, one which has become a top 'best-seller' of the Gorbachev period. Under the policy of glasnost', print runs have been brought into conformity with readership demand. According to the literary weekly, *Knizhnoe obozrenie*, *Plakha* had the second largest print run (3 080 000 copies) of any book published in the USSR in 1987.[6]

An uneven, sprawling work, *Plakha* succeeded in capturing much of the political, social and ideational ferment of the early Gorbachev period. Belorussian writer and critic Ales' Adamovich has aptly compared it to the red-hot lava cast up by an active volcano.[7] *Plakha* deals boldly with such controversial issues as the Soviet drug trade, the dangerous growth of militarism, the destruction of the natural environment, and agricultural reform, but its most controversial theme was what Kryvelev called its 'God-seeking'.

The first two parts of the novel focus upon the ordeal of the son of a Russian Orthodox deacon from Pskov region, Avdii Kallistratov, who has been expelled from seminary for preaching 'heresy'. Avdii is seeking a new religion, a 'God of tomorrow', equidistant from the perceived extremes of traditional Orthodoxy and scientific material-ism. While he is a religious freethinker, Avdii is also a deeply spiritual individual who seeks to turn his fellow men from their evil ways.

In the Soviet context, Aitmatov had chosen an unusual hero for his novel. As one critic, S. Lominadze, commented: 'The figure (of Avdii) is new and unexpected for the reader. He is from the ecclesiastical milieu, which has never, it would seem, been represented in Soviet literature in the main heroes of well-known authors . . .'[8]

During the course of the novel, Avdii is required literally to ascend the cross as a result of his attempts, which recall those of Dostoevskii's Prince Myshkin, to convert hardened drug dealers and criminals to a religion of 'love'. He is thrown off a fast-moving train by the drug dealers and suspended on a tree, where he eventually dies in agony.

When he is thrown off the train by the drug dealers, Avdii, in a kind of time warp, merges temporarily with the historical figure of Jesus Christ. An obvious literary model employed by Aitmatov was Mikhail Bulgakov's well-known novel, *Master and Margarita*, which features both Christ and Pontius Pilate. Aitmatov's Jesus Christ dismisses the doctrines of resurrection and second coming as inventions of Judas Iscariot, and predicts that the end of the world 'from human enmity' is approaching.

One curious element of Aitmatov's novel is its erratic capitalisation of the word God. Before the advent of the Gorbachev thaw, Soviet censorship conventions required that the word God be written in the lower case. One wonders whether this erratic capitalisation in the novel is the result of poor proof-reading or of a tug-of-war between Aitmatov and the censors.

In August, 1986, one month after Kryvelev's attack, Aitmatov gave an interview to *Literaturnaia gazeta* in which he addressed the charge of 'God-seeking'.[9] Asked by the interviewer why he, a man of Muslim background, chose to make his hero a Christian, Aitmatov replied:

> The Christian religion sends a very strong message through the figure of Jesus Christ. The Islamic religion, in which I am included by my origin, does not have such a figure. Mohammed is not a martyr. He experienced difficult, painful days, but he was not crucified for an idea, nor did he forgive people eternally . . . Jesus Christ offers me an occasion to say something vital to contemporary man. For this reason, I, an atheist, encountered him on my creative path.

In response to Kryvelev's accusations, Aitmatov thus unequivocally declared himself to be an atheist. Some Western specialists are prepared to take such statements at face value, but it should be understood that if Aitmatov had termed himself a religious believer, his career would automatically have been over in the Soviet Union.

This is especially true for members of the Communist Party, and Aitmatov has been a party member since 1959. Based on the evidence offered by a close reading of *Plakha*, I would hazard a guess that Aitmatov is, in some sense, a religious believer. It is perhaps significant that the title of his next novel, announced for publication in *Novyi mir* in 1988, is *Mother of God in the Snows* (*Bogomater' v snegakh*).[10]

The response in Soviet cultural circles to Kryvelev's attack on Aitmatov, Astaf'ev and Bykov soon demonstrated that the year 1986 was going to be different from 1982, when Vladimir Soloukhin had been brought to his knees by the journal *Kommunist*. Feliks Kuznetsov, the powerful first secretary of the Moscow Writers' Organisation (and presently the head of the Gor'kii Institute of World Literature) has revealed that he wrote a rebuttal to Kryvelev's article, but that *Komsomol'skaia pravda* refused to publish it.[11] In December, 1986, however, the newspaper did publish a letter from poet Evgenii Evtushenko, which it accompanied with an essay by doctor of philosophical sciences S. Kaltakhchian.[12]

Evtushenko, who has been one of the most active cultural figures throughout the Gorbachev thaw, treated Kryvelev's atheistic 'dogmatism' with unconcealed contempt. Lenin's formulation 'flirting with dear little god' was, he declared, said under specific historical circumstances which do not apply to the three writers criticised on the pages of *Komsomol'skaia pravda*. Kryvelev's view of the role of atheism in Soviet society is, quite simply, outdated: 'Our socialist state is a union of communists and non-party members, of believers and atheists. Atheism is a voluntary phenomenon, not something coercively thrust upon people'.

Soviet atheism, Evtushenko complained, is often clumsy and inept. An example of this would be its broadcasting of 'entertainment shows' on Easter eve in an attempt to lure young people away from attending church.

Concerning the Bible, which Kryvelev had attacked as an immoral book, Evtushenko wrote that it represented 'a great cultural monument'. Without a knowledge of the Bible, he maintained, Soviet youth cannot understand much that is in the writings of the nineteenth-century classics, of Pushkin, Gogol', Dostoevskii and Tolstoi. The Soviet government should publish the Bible, just as it has published the Koran.

Kryvelev's view that atheism is a guarantor of morality was derisively rejected by Evtushenko. 'If only it were so! But unfortunately many so-called atheists are thieves . . . bureaucrats, toadies, and chameleons, and are in no way better than those priests who rob simple believers.' The source of morality, Evtushenko affirmed, is not atheism but culture. In contrast to Kryvelev's watchful, suspicious 'dogmatic Marxism', Evtushenko advocated a relaxed, tolerant 'true Marxism' unafraid of religion.

The same issue of *Komsomol'skaia pravda* which published Evtushenko's letter carried a rebuttal of his views by doctor of philosophical sciences S. Kaltakhchian. In contesting Evtushenko's ideas, Kaltakhchian rolled out the heavy Marxist artillery. The Twenty-seventh Party congress, he recalled, had scorned 'reactionary and religious survivals which contradict our ideology, the socialist way of life, and the scientific world-view'. Lenin's opinion on the danger represented by religion must be heeded by all communists. The term 'flirting with dear little god' is entirely appropriate for the three writers attacked by Kryvelev. Such writers can exert considerable influence on the reading masses, and their errors have to be pointed out. Lenin, Kaltakhchian noted, openly exposed the 'God-building' heresies of his political allies Anatolii Lunacharskii and Maksim Gor'kii.

Like Kryvelev, Kaltakhchian wrapped himself in the mantle of Lenin's infallibility and took a stand on the sacredness of Marxist-Leninist dogma. Significantly, however, their views failed to carry the day. In fact, it was their *'prorabotka'* (working over) of Aitmatov, Astaf'ev, Bykov and Evtushenko which was explicitly rejected by most subsequent Soviet commentators. Evtushenko's views, not those of the 'dogmatists', prevailed.

This becomes clear, for example, if one examines the three 'round-table' discussions of Aitmatov's *Plakha* which have been published in the Soviet press. The first discussion appeared on the pages of *Literaturnaia gazeta* in October 1986.[13] While many of the participants addressed the issue of 'God-seeking' in Aitmatov's novel, none of them appeared to share Kryvelev's ideological reservations. One speaker, Ch. Guseinov, attempted to play down the religious dimension of the novel, seeing it as merely a 'cover' [*obolochka*] for social criticism. Another, the distinguished Soviet philologist S. Averintsev, criticised the novel for its 'neo-Renan' orientation. The novel, he said, lacks 'spiritual sobriety' and should have adhered more closely in the Jesus and Pilate scenes to its model, the New Testament.

The lengthy round-table discussion of *Plakha* which appeared in

Voprosy literatury in early 1987 also devoted considerable attention to the treatment of religion in the novel.[14] Significantly, even the most doctrinaire speaker, D. Urnov, felt obliged to distance himself from the opinions of Kryvelev and Kaltakhchian. 'I share the alarm', he said, 'of those critics who have written about "flirting with dear little god", but I cannot accept their approach and their tone, which indeed remind one of the *prorabotka* of evil memory'. Urnov concentrated his criticism on Aitmatov's intimation in the novel that the truth was halfway between the positions of traditional Orthodox Christianity and scientific materialism.

Another speaker, E. Sidorov, dismissed Urnov's comments as being 'in the spirit of Marat'. 'It would have been better', he said, 'for I. Kryvelev to have contemplated and tried to explain to the readers of a Komsomol paper why an interest in religion has been growing in the USSR among all ages and social strata of the population . . .' In Sidorov's opinion, the reason for the marked spread of religion was 'a spiritual vacuum, a crisis of faith' in the traditional social and human values of the Soviet Union. In effect, Sidorov was pointing to the fact that Marxism-Leninism has become a 'dead' ideology with little or no resonance among the Soviet populace.

Another speaker, the critic V. Oskotskii, attacked I. Kryvelev with considerable vehemence, comparing him to the fanatic Mao Tse-tung and his 'idea of the universal victory of socialism after the destruction of half of humanity in a third world war'. Oskotskii cited Gorbachev's name frequently in his comments and appeared to want to be seen as a disciple of the general secretary.

The critic S. Lominadze insisted in his comments that Aitmatov was not preaching religious 'heresy' but rather 'atheism'. The novel's hero, Avdii Kallistratov, he said, is aware that 'materialistic science' will eventually triumph.

To summarise, while the *Voprosy literatury* commentators did not agree on the meaning of the religious dimensions of *Plakha*, none of them adopted a position similar to that of Kryvelev and Kaltakhchian.

A third round-table discussion of the novel was sponsored by the anti-religious monthly, *Nauka i religiia*, and published during the fall of 1987.[15] The harshest accuser of Aitmatov and his novel among the commentators was doctor of philosophical sciences A. Kochetov, like Kryvelev and Kaltakhchian a specialist in religion. For Kochetov, a principal reason behind the 'broad readers' interest' in *Plakha* lay 'in the very fact of its turning to Christianity'. It was an error, he said, for

Aitmatov to have attempted 'to propagandise the basic ideas of Christianity'.

Unlike the great majority of Soviet commentators, Kochetov believed that a form of Christian orthodoxy underpins the novel: 'In *Plakha* I see a retelling of the Christian teaching that sinfulness is the result of men's departure from their "divine essence", of their forgetting the saving mission of Jesus Christ, the Son of God . . .' There is also, Kochetov said, a worrisome tendency in the novel to equate lack of spirituality and indifference to social problems with atheism. Finally, the novel preaches 'a cult of sacrifice' which is 'foreign to our [Soviet] historic optimism'. The novel, he maintained, criticises materialistic science for mocking such Christian virtues as mercy and self-giving.

Kochetov's views were not accepted by the other round-table discussants. A. Romanov, an editor of *Nauka i religiia*, claimed, in contradistinction to Kochetov, that *Plakha* arouses *anti-religious* rather than religious sentiments. Avdii Kallistratov's failure in the novel, he said, is 'the failure of the Christian idea of redemption through sacrifice'.

Another critic, I. Zolotusskii, emphasised that Aitmatov's Jesus 'is not the Son of God, not a God-man'. The figures of Jesus and Pontius Pilate are introduced into the novel in order to broach the theme of 'earthly power'. The use of religious symbolism 'is not a sign of the author's religiosity'.

Like the two previous round-table discussions, the *Nauka i religiia* colloquy did not come to any agreed conclusions. It is noteworthy that the Kryvelev view, which was more or less represented by A. Kochetov, did not carry the day, even on the pages of an anti-religious monthly.

An important attempt to summarise the controversy which had been initiated by Kryvelev's article was Andrei Nuikin's, 'The New God-Seeking and Old Dogmas', which appeared in the 1987, no. 4 issue of *Novyi mir*.[16] Nuikin began by noting that the 'violent arguments' elicited by the appearance in print of the novel's first part were continuing almost a year later. He saw the articles by Kryvelev and Kaltakhchian as being of considerable political significance: 'They are two "alarm signals" concerning trouble on the literary front; concerning the discovery of suspicious deviations on the part of the whole series of writers, and not just any writers, but the leading and most authoritative ones'.

While terming himself 'a convinced atheist', Nuikin firmly distanced himself from what he called the 'dogmatic atheism' of I. Kryvelev and S. Kaltakhchian. He wrote that though he was unable to share the religious views expressed in the writings of Aitmatov, Astaf'ev, and Bykov, 'even less do I share the position of I. Kryvelev'. Rather than assailing 'our most important artists', Kryvelev should have criticised such disturbing phenomena as, for example, the growth of devil worship in the Soviet Union.

From Nuikin's perspective, the articles of Kryvelev and Kaltakhchian represented the dead hand of the past. Dogmatic atheism, he predicted, has no future in the USSR, because, quite simply, there is no longer a market for it. To bolster his point, Nuikin quoted passages from a letter written by a young Soviet teacher who dismissed the writings of Kryvelev and Kaltakhchian as 'heavy' and 'boring'. 'Dogmas, dogmas all about, and stereotypes', she complained.

Atheism, Nuikin stressed, must be the fruit of an authentic philosophical quest. There is no place in the contemporary Soviet Union for fanaticism, intolerance and the replacement of dialogue by a monologue. What is needed are educated atheists and not 'religiously indifferent' *bezbozhniki* (godless). Nuikin's position is thus close to that espoused by Evgenii Evtushenko in his letter to *Komsomol'skaia pravda*.

To sum up, the controversy sparked by Iosif Kryvelev's July 1986 article in *Komsomol'skaia pravda* shows that important changes have been occurring in the cultural sphere in the Soviet Union. In a showdown between a learned atheist spokesman and three leading Soviet writers, the atheist suffered a clear-cut and significant defeat. To be sure, religious belief was not vindicated, but 'dogmatic atheism' was deemed by most commentators to be a worse offence than 'God-seeking'. This strikes one as a noteworthy development.

Soviet film, as opposed to literature, has not served during the Gorbachev period as a battleground over the appropriate limits to be placed on the airing of religious themes. One reason for this has been that most of the significant films which have appeared to date were actually made during the Brezhnev, Andropov, and Chernenko years and then 'shelved', due to the perceived harmfulness of their subject matter. Since a rigorous censorship was in place during this period, treatments of religious subjects had to be elliptical and often quasi-Aesopian in nature. A number of Soviet filmmakers *seemed* to have an interest in religious subjects: for example, the late Vasilii Shukshin

(d. 1974); the late Larisa Shepit'ko (d. 1979); Elem Klimov, elected in May 1986 as first secretary of the Union of Soviet Filmmakers; and Rolan Bykov, director of the acclaimed *Scarecrow* (1984). However, since these filmmakers did not have an opportunity to reside in the West, the extent of their religious commitment, if any, must remain problematic. It remains politically impossible, even under the Gorbachev leadership, for a Soviet director openly to admit to being religious. Directors who are members of the Communist Party are further inhibited, as one of their obligations as communists is to carry out a decisive struggle with religion.

The film *Repentance* (1984), directed by the distinguished Georgian cinematographer, Tengiz Abuladze, was made for Georgian television under the protection of the then first secretary of the Georgian Communist Party, Eduard Shevardnadze.[17] Released in early 1987, the film soon became one of the beacons of the Gorbachev cultural thaw. The film garnered the runner-up prize at the 1987 Cannes International Film Festival and helped Abuladze to earn a prestigious Lenin Prize in 1988. *Repentance* has been 'adopted' by followers of Mikhail Gorbachev due to its strong de-Stalinising tendency. The central character of the film, the mayor Varlam Aravidze, is a composite tyrant, who is given Hitler's moustache, Beriia's spectacles, Mussolini's operatic manner, and Stalin's political modus operandi.

Less attention has been paid by both Soviet and Western commentators to the fact that *Repentance* treats a number of religious themes and makes use of traditional Christian symbols. Varlam's pivotal conflict with the painter and intellectual, Sandro Barateli, for example, comes about because the authorities have turned a sixth-century Georgian Orthodox Church into a laboratory. Powerful transformers shake the church, causing its walls to crack and damaging its ancient frescos.

Sandro, who bears a strong physical similarity to iconographic representations of Christ, is eventually arrested and 'crucified' in a basement for his opposition to Varlam. His death by crucifixion coincides with the dynamiting of the sixth-century church which he fought to save.

Sandro's daughter, Keti, who is the film's heroine, is also linked to religious themes. At the film's beginning and conclusion, we see her engaged in making wedding cakes which are adorned with Orthodox churches. The film concludes with an old woman coming up to Keti's shop and asking, 'Tell me is this the road that leads to the church [*khram*]?' 'No', Keti replies. 'This is Varlam Aravidze Street, and it is not the street that leads to the church.'

Toward the beginning of the film, we see Keti as a child playing with Varlam's young son Avel' in the children's room of her parents' home. On the wall is a small crucifix. 'Why did they torture Christ?' Avel' asks. Keti tells him that Christ was tortured for 'truth'. 'Don't be afraid', she then comforts him, 'Christ didn't die; he resurrected and flew up like a bird to heaven. Only good people are there. An evil person can't get in'. Avel' then attempts to steal the cross, which is supposed to have miracle-working properties, in order to bring his late mother back to life.

Later in the picture there is a disturbing scene in which Avel' descends into a basement bearing a candlestick. He sees the crucifix which he had tried to steal as a boy and feels an inexplicable urge to make religious confession. In the basement, he encounters a strange monk-like figure eating a fish with great relish. The monk mocks Avel's desire to confess and informs him that he is incapable of distinguishing between good and evil. 'I preach atheism but myself bear a cross', Avel' complains. Once he sees the skeleton of the fish (the fish, of course, is an ancient symbol for Christ), Avel' recognises the 'sated face' of his late father. In the words of Soviet critic Neia Zorkaia, Varlam is shown to be a 'Christ-seller and Christ eater'.[18]

After his son, Tornike, has committed suicide out of shame for the deeds of his grandfather and father, Avel' digs up his father's body—as Keti had done earlier—and feeds it to the crows.

The film is replete with religious symbolism. (Abuladze, incidentally, has admitted the influence on his picture of Anna Akhmatova's great cycle of religious poems, 'Requiem'.) To mention just one example, the victims of Varlam's terror are depicted as martyrs in white robes.

Like Chingiz Aitmatov's novel, *The Executioner's Block*, *Repentance* is focused upon religious themes. However, Abuladze, like Aitmatov, is a member of the Communist Party and is therefore required by the party rules to oppose all manifestations of religion. When asked directly by a French interviewer whether he was a religious man, Abduladze replied: 'I am not a believer in the religious sense of the word, but I believe in art as I have defined it—the search for beauty, truth, and goodness'.[19] It was the most that he could have said if he were religious.

The filmmakers Andrei Tarkovskii and Andrei Konchalovskii obtained permission in the early 1980s to go to the West to work on films, and, once there, decided to remain—Tarkovskii as a political defector; Konchalovskii as a *de facto* émigré (while continuing to hold a Soviet passport). Once these decisions became known, both became 'non-persons' in the Soviet Union; their names, for example, are missing from a comprehensive and authoritative volume on Soviet film, entitled *Soviet Cinema of the 1970s*, which appeared in late 1984.[20]

The reason that these gifted directors decided to stay in the West was the tribulation that they had undergone in attempting to make quality films during the Brezhnev period. Tarkovskii's noted film, *Andrei Rublev* (1966), was shelved for five and a half years before being released in 1971, and he was required to appeal to the presidiums of two party congresses to make his last two Soviet films, *The Mirror* (1974) and *Stalker* (1979). Konchalovskii's second full-length film, *The Story of Asia Kliachina, who Loved but did not Marry* (1967), was put on the shelf for 20 years, and his adaptation of Turgenev's novel *Nest of Gentlefolk* (1969) was assailed in the Soviet press for its alleged 'neo-Slavophilism'.

Once in the West, both Tarkovskii and Konchalovskii were able to make their religious beliefs explicit. In a number of public statements, Tarkovskii confirmed that he had been a religious man from the beginning of his career. Konchalovskii was more circumspect—he continued to hold a Soviet passport and made periodic visits to the Soviet Union—but in private conversation he emphasised his Russian Orthodox convictions. Actress Shirley Maclaine, with whom Konchalovskii entered into an eighteen-month relationship while living in Los Angeles, has left an intriguing account of Konchalovskii (whom she refers to under a transparent pseudonym) in her book, *Dancing in the Light*.[21] A non-Christian spiritualist, Maclaine devotes considerable space to outlining Konchalovskii's religious views. While her book must be used with caution, it serves as an important source for those interested in Konchalovskii's thought.

Tarkovskii's last film, *Sacrifice* (1986), which won four awards at the 1986 Cannes Film Festival, deals openly with religious themes. Set in a remote area of Sweden, the film features a retired man of the theatre, Alexander, his ex-actress wife, two children and a small circle of friends. The film is darkened by the shadow of imminent nuclear war. Appalled at this prospect, Alexander makes a fervent vow to God:

> Lord, deliver us in this terrible hour. Do not let my children die, my friends, my wife . . . I will give You all I possess. I will leave the

family I love. I shall destroy my home, give up my son. I shall be silent . . . I shall give up everything that binds me to life, if you will only let everything be as it was before . . .[22]

The next morning, seeing that nuclear war has been averted, Alexander proceeds to burn down his house and, after a chase, is taken away by men in white suits. His 'sacrifice', even of his freedom, is complete.

Like Abuladze's *Repentance*, Tarkovskii's *Sacrifice* is permeated with religious themes and symbols. The film opens with a slow examination of Leonardo da Vinci's unfinished painting 'The Adoration of the Magi', which depicts naked innocence in the midst of worldly wealth. As one critic has noted, 'it is through the sacrifice of Christ that the world is redeemed, which is precisely Alexander's ambition in the film'.[23]

The tree which is featured in Leonardo's painting launches the symbol of the tree in the film. Alexander tells his young son, Little Man, the tale of an elderly Orthodox monk who once planted a tree on a mountain and then instructed a novice to water it every day until eventually the tree blossomed. At the film's conclusion, we see Little Man watering a withered tree which his father, now in a madhouse, has planted.

Like Tarkovskii, with whom he collaborated on the script of *Andrei Rublev*, Andrei Konchalovskii has been absorbed with religious questions from the beginning of his directing career. Upon moving to the West, he succeeded, after some initial failures, in landing a contract with the Cannon group to bring out four films in English. He completed this assignment in rapid-fire order, finishing *Maria's Lovers* in 1984, *Runaway Train* in 1985, *Duet for One* in 1986, and *Shy People* in 1987.

Konchalovskii's film, *Runaway Train* is adapted from a script by the great Japanese director Akira Kurosawa, himself an admirer of nineteenth-century Russian classical literature and, especially, of Dostoevskii. It recounts the escape of two rough and often violent convicts, Manny and Buck, from a high security Alaskan prison. They flee into the Alaskan wilderness, pursued by an avenging warden who has vowed to take Manny's life. They are eventually able to board a modern, computerised, high-speed train (non-passenger), which soon becomes a 'runaway' when the engineer experiences a heart attack and jumps off the train, and when the brakes burn off. The racing train (a metaphor for the modern world) carries the two convicts through a violent snowstorm (a metaphor for life).

Improbably, the convicts discover a young woman, Sara, on the train, and she turns out to be deeply religious.

The railway authorities, surrounded by their high-tech computers (and, at one point, watching the lift-off of an Apollo rocket on television), reverse their decision to derail the train when they learn that there are people on board. They then conceive a plan to divert it onto a side rail which, they hope, will preserve the lives of those on the train.

The drama in the control room is paralleled by high drama in the train. Manny prevents Buck from raping Sara. But Manny is quite willing to risk Buck's life when he orders him to attempt to reach the engine in order to stop the train. Manny and Buck quarrel and fight. Sara, who values other lives as much as her own, keeps Manny from leaping off the train to certain death. The warden appears on a rope ladder suspended from a helicopter and boards the train, where he is taken captive by Manny. At the film's end, Manny de-couples the car carrying Buck and Sara—thereby saving their lives—while he and the handcuffed warden plunge on through the snowstorm to their inevitable death.

In an interview with Dan Yakir of the *Boston Globe*, Konchalovskii explained that *Runaway Train*:

> . . . is a film about what it means to win and lose and what it means to be moral, in short what it means to be human. The two characters [Manny and Buck] find freedom by escaping from prison, but are once again imprisoned aboard this uncontrollable, monstrous creature, the train. The film asks the questions: Is being human a burden or a curse? What price evil? Man can sometimes be worse than a beast—reach the heights of cruelty in order to survive, but he can also be good. He has a choice.[24]

Referring to the character of Manny, Konchalovskii added:

> . . . in most films of this sort, they'd make the protagonist the good guy fighting evil. Here, he is fighting good and evil inside himself. This is a dominant principle in all my films—this exploration of the struggle of human nature.

Manny is anti-religious, relies on himself and on his own strong will. But he is capable of feeling pity, as well as rage and cruelty. In his fluctuations, he contrasts with the young woman, Sara, who is consistently spiritual.

On several occasions, the film investigates the dynamics and mechanism of prayer. After escaping from prison by plunging through an icy river, Buck, his feet freezing, prays for a pair of boots; he finds a pair at the station before they board the train.

Sara prays that the door to the train's engine will open, permitting them to stop the train. The door stays closed. But the train inexplicably slows down before hurtling over a bridge; if it had gone over at full speed, it would have caused the bridge to collapse. Similarly, Sara decides to sound the train whistle just before an elderly switchman is about to derail the train, not knowing there are people on board. The film examines the subtle way in which providence interacts with human lives.

As has been mentioned, both Konchalovskii and Andrei Tarkovskii became 'non-persons' once they made a decision to remain in the West. Both, however, have recently been rehabilitated as part of the Gorbachev cultural thaw—Tarkovskii in mid-1986, and Konchalovskii in December 1987. Following the pivotal May 1986 Congress of Soviet Filmmakers, at which Elem Klimov was elected first secretary of the union and a new reform-minded secretariat was voted in, Tarkovskii's name began once again to appear in the Soviet press.[25] Overtures were even made to him to return to the homeland. Dying of cancer in Paris, Tarkovskii spurned these overtures and said that he hoped that his children would have the fortitude not to return to Russia. At present Tarkovskii's films are being widely shown in the Soviet Union, and both his 1984 film, *Nostalghia*, made in Italy, and his 1986 film, *Sacrifice*, made in Sweden, have been released there.

In late 1987, Konchalovskii's *The Story of Asia . . .* was previewed in Moscow after 20 years on the shelf. The following month, the important weekly, *Literaturnaia gazeta*, carried a lengthy interview with the filmmaker.[26] In the course of the interview, Konchalovskii noted that he plans to make a joint American-Soviet film devoted to the life of the composer Rakhmaninov.

To sum up, the Gorbachev period has witnessed an expansion of what is permissible in the airing of religious themes. Novels are being published and films released which could not have cleared the censorship under previous leaderships. There remain, however, important restrictions on the expression of religious attitudes, and, as in the past, no Soviet artist living in the Soviet Union can openly admit to being religious. Progress has been made, but there remains an uncertain and difficult path ahead.

NOTES

1. I. Kryvelev, 'Koketnichaia s bozhen'koi', *Komsomol'skaia pravda*, 30 July 1986, p. 4.
2. For an excellent discussion of Lenin's views on religion, see Bohdan R. Bociurkiw, 'Lenin and Religion' in Leonard Schapiro and Peter Reddaway (eds), *Lenin: The Man, the Theorist, the Leader, a Reappraisal* (New York: 1967) pp. 107–34.
3. Chingiz Aitmatov, 'Plakha, Roman' in *Novyi mir* (1986) no. 6, pp. 7–69; (1986) no. 8, pp. 90–148; and (1986) no. 9, pp. 6–64. See also Katerina Clark, '*The Executioner's Block:* A Novel of the Thaw', *Times Literary Supplement*, 26 June 1987, p. 696.
4. See 'Pochta zhurnala', *Kommunist* (1982) no. 2, pp. 127–8.
5. 'Pochta zhurnala', *Kommunist* (1982) no. 8, p. 128.
6. See *Knizhnoe obozrenie* (29 April 1988) no. 18, pp. 8–9.
7. See Ales' Adamovich, 'Urok pravdy', *Literaturnaia gazeta*, 17 March 1986, p. 5; and 'Protiv pravil', *Literaturnaia gazeta*, 1 January 1987, p. 4.
8. S. Lominadze in *Voprosy literatury* (1987) no. 3, p. 35.
9. 'Tsenam-zhizn'', *Literaturnaia gazeta*, 13 August 1986, p. 4.
10. See the interview with Sergei Zalygin, editor-in-chief of *Novyi mir*, in *Literaturnaia gazeta*, 26 August 1987, p. 7.
11. See Kuznetsov's comments in *Literaturnaia gazeta*, 6 May 1987, p. 2.
12. Evgenii Evtushenko, 'Istochnik nravstvennosti—kul'tura'; and S. Kaltakhchian, 'Ne vera, a znaniia' in *Komsomol'skaia pravda*, 10 December 1986, p. 2.
13. 'Paradoksy romana, ili paradoksy vospriiatiia', *Literaturnaia gazeta*, 15 October 1986, p. 4.
14. 'Obsuzhdaem roman Chingiza Aitmatova "Plakha"', *Voprosy literatury* (1987) no. 3, pp. 3–82.
15. 'Poka nebo ne pogaslo', *Nauka i religiia* (1987) no. 9, pp. 21–6.
16. Andrei Nuikin, 'Novoe bogoiskatel'stvo i starye dogmy', *Novyi mir* (1987) no. 4, pp. 245–59.
17. The scenario of *Repentance* has been published in Russian translation from the Georgian original in *Kinotsenarii* (1987) no. 2, pp. 3–18.
18. N. Zorkaia, 'Dorogoi, kotoraia vedet k Khramu', *Iskusstvo kino* (1987) no. 5, p. 48.
19. 'Entretien avec Tenguiz Abouladze', *Cinema*, 21–7 October 1987, p. 6.
20. *Sovetskoe kino 70-e gody* (Moscow: 1984).
21. Shirley Maclaine, *Dancing in the Light* (New York: 1985).
22. Cited from an excellent review of the film by Peter Green, 'Apocalypse and Sacrifice', *Sight and Sound* (Spring 1987) p. 112.
23. Ibid., p. 113.
24. Dan Yakir, 'From Russia to Hollywood', *Boston Globe*, 11 January 1986.
25. On this congress, see John B. Dunlop, 'Soviet Cultural Politics', *Problems of Communism* (November–December 1987) pp. 36–8.
26. 'A. Mikhalkov-Konchalovskii: Ostaius' samim soboi', *Literaturnaia gazeta*, 20 January 1988, p. 8.

Index

The method of alphabetisation used is letter by letter.
Principal entries on a particular subject are given in bold type.